Frederick Law Olmsted, c. 1885.

A CLEARING
IN THE DISTANCE

Frederick Law Olmsted and America
in the Nineteenth Century

WITOLD RYBCZYNSKI

SCRIBNER

SCRIBNER
1230 Avenue of the Americas
New York, NY 10020

SCRIBNER and design are trademarks of Jossey-Bass, Inc.,
used under license by Simon & Schuster, the publisher of this work.

DESIGNED BY ERICH HOBBING

Set in Caslon

Manufactured in the United States of America

1   3   5   7   9   10   8   6   4   2

Library of Congress Cataloging-in-Publication Data
Rybczynski, Witold.
A clearing in the distance : Frederick Law Olmsted and
America in the nineteenth century / Witold Rybczynski.
p.   cm.
Includes bibliographical references and (p.   ) index.
1. Olmsted, Frederick Law, 1822–1903. 2. Landscape
architects—United States—Biography. 3. Landscape
architecture—United States—History—19th century.
4. United States—Civilization. I. Title.
SB470.O5R93   1999
712'.092—dc21   99-18094
[B]
CIP

ISBN 0-684-82463-9

In memoriam
Witold Kazimierz Rybczynski
(1908–1996)

CONTENTS

HITTING HEADS

A MAGNIFICENT OPENING

Contents · 11

Standing First

Olmsted's Distant Effects

FOREWORD

THE ISLAND OF MONTREAL in the St. Lawrence River is more or less flat, except for a pronounced hill roughly in the center. The French explorers christened it Mont Réal—Mount Royal. Its dark bulk is the city of Montreal's most distinctive feature, visible from afar, and looming over the streets and buildings that surround its steep flanks. Actually, what is most distinctive about the mountain is that most of it is a public park. Not that anyone ever referred to it as a park, it was always just the "Mountain."

I spent a year in a college dorm located high up one slope of Mount Royal; later, from the upper floor of my first apartment you could see the illuminated cross on top of the mountain. My last home in Montreal was a flat on a street called Esplanade, directly facing the east slope. All in all, I've lived about twenty years in Montreal, always within walking distance of the Mountain. It was where we ran our dogs, went on picnics in the summer, tobogganed in the winter. A long, winding gravel road zigzagged up the forested slope until it reached a grassy bowl overlooking a small lake. Only one city street went through the park. It was not really a shortcut, but when I was not in a hurry, I often took this route; it was like taking a drive in the country. At one point the road went through a defile. At the far end, a breathtaking vista of the whole city stretched out to the river. On a clear day you could see all the way to the Green Mountains of Vermont.

Being on the Mountain was always a surprise. One minute you were walking on a busy city street, the next you were in a landscape of dense trees and rugged outcroppings. At first, the sound of traffic was audible, but soon it was replaced by the stillness of a primeval forest.

I remember as a college student being told that the Mountain was the work of someone called Frederick Law Olmsted, the same man who designed Central Park. I was impressed that he had come all the way from New York City, but what the work consisted of I couldn't imagine. Like most people, I took the landscape of the Mountain for granted; I thought that it was simply a nature preserve. Here was the most significant man-made object in Montreal—arguably the city's most important cultural artifact—and I thought of it as "natural." How wrong I was.

Chestnut Hill, Philadelphia

November 1995–November 1998

I have all my life been considering distant effects and always sacrificing immediate success and applause to that of the future.

—FREDERICK LAW OLMSTED

Le génie n'est qu'une plus grande aptitude à la patience. (Genius is no more than a greater aptitude for patience.)

—GEORGE LOUIS LECLERC, Comte de Buffon

SCHEMES

New Haven, 1846. (*from left to right*) Charles Trask, Charles
Loring Brace, Frederick J. Kingsbury, Frederick Law Olmsted,
and John Hull Olmsted.

They never get disheartened. I think Fred will be one of that sort. Many of his favorite schemes will go to naught—but he'll throw it aside and try another and spoil that and forget them both while you or I might have been blubbering over the ruins of the first.

—Frederick J. Kingsbury to John Hull Olmsted (1847)

CHAPTER ONE

"Tough as Nails"

WITH HIS HIGH FOREHEAD, wide-set blue eyes, and unruly hair, the young Frederick Olmsted made a strong impression. A boyhood friend described him as "a vigorous, manly fellow, of medium height, solidly built with rather broad shoulders and a large well formed head. If athletics had been in fashion he would have been high up in foot-ball and base-ball." In midlife he suffered a carriage accident that left him with a pronounced limp, but he remained a skilled small-boat sailor and an experienced horseman. He was a seasoned outdoorsman who hunted and fished, though not for sport. Later photographs usually show him pensive. He rarely looks directly at the camera, which gives him an air of self-containment, almost detachment. "His face is generally very placid," wrote his colleague Katharine Wormeley, "with all the expressive delicacy of a woman's, and would be beautiful were it not for an expression which I cannot fathom,—something which is, perhaps, a little too severe about it." But she added, "I think his mouth and smile and the expression of his eyes at times very beautiful . . . there is a deep, calm thoughtfulness about him which is always attractive and sometimes—provoking."

An odd choice of word—"provoking." Olmsted's close friend Charles Eliot Norton likewise discerned this quality. "All the lines of his face imply refinement and sensibility to such a degree that it is not till one has looked through them to what is underneath, that the force of his will and the reserved power of his character become evident." When I asked the landscape architect Laurie Olin how he would characterize Olmsted, his immediate answer was "Tough as nails." Olin is right, of course. Although the modern image of Frederick Law Olmsted is of a benevolent environmentalist, a sort of Johnny Appleseed scattering beautiful city parks across the nation, he had indomitable energy and iron determination. As a mine manager in California, he once faced down a crowd of striking miners. (They were understandably upset because he had reduced their wages.) "They tried a mob but made nothing of it," he laconically wrote to his father, "and I have lost no property only time. I shall hold out till they come to my terms and dismiss all who have been prominent in the strike." He did just that. His obstinacy often got him in trouble. Many times he chose to resign positions rather than continue on a course of action he disapproved. His most famous resignations—there were several—occurred during the long and often frustrating construction of Central Park. But there were others. Leland Stanford, the railroad magnate, engaged him to lay out the grounds of what would become Stanford University. Olmsted prepared the plans on the understanding that, as was his practice, he would also hire his own staff to supervise the work. When Stanford, who had been governor of California and was used to getting his own way, reneged on the agreement, Olmsted walked away from the job. The university was completed without him.

Another battle of wills occurred during his tenure with the United States Sanitary Commission. The Commission, a precursor to the Red Cross, was a private organization established after the outbreak of the Civil War to administer volunteer relief efforts to the Union troops. Olmsted spent two years as its first general secretary, in charge of day-to-day operations. As fund-raising efforts intensified, hundreds of thousands of dollars flowed to the Commission, whose board felt the need to exert more direct supervision over the activities of its chief executive officer. He characteristically bridled at any attempt to curtail his freedom, and a sometimes bitter struggle ensued. One of those with whom he had run-ins was the treasurer of the Commission, George Templeton Strong. Strong, best known as the author of an exceptional set of diaries, was a prominent Wall Street lawyer and civic leader. He knew Olmsted well: both men were involved in the Union League Club and in the establishment of *The Nation* magazine. Some six months before Olmsted's resignation, Strong noted in his journal: "He is an extraordinary fellow, decidedly the most remarkable specimen of human nature with whom I have been brought into close relations." Then, in obvious exasperation, he added: "Prominent defects, a monomania for system and organization on paper (elaborate, laboriously thought out, and generally impracticable), and appetite for power. He is a lay-Hildebrand."

The last strikes me as a shrewd characterization. Hildebrand, or Gregory VII, was an eleventh-century pope who is remembered for his lifelong attempt to establish the supremacy of the papacy within the Church—and the authority of the Church over the state. Olmsted, too, was trying to establish an ascendancy. He was doing it with what sometimes seemed to others religious zeal, but he did not seek personal aggrandizement. Strong commented on his colleague's "absolute purity and disinterestedness"; he recognized that Olmsted wasn't empire-building. The supremacy that Olmsted was trying to establish was that of the technician—the organizer; the authority was that of The Plan. But he was ahead of his time. His obsession with organization and planning on paper may sometimes have been clumsy, and it was certainly laborious—this was before telephones and typewriters, let alone computers and fax machines. But it was not, as Strong thought, ineffective. Olmsted successfully coordinated the operations of the Sanitary Commission, with its thousands of contributing private aid societies, and its scores of nurses and doctors. He deployed convalescent shelters, field hospitals, and hospital ships and distributed food and medical supplies over a battlefront that extended for hundreds of miles. Strong had also forgotten that it was precisely "monomania" that had enabled Olmsted to organize the labors of several thousand workers in what was then the largest public works project in the nation: Central Park.

Olmsted was one of the first people to recognize the necessity for planning in a large, industrializing country—whether in peace or war. This recognition was not yet widely shared, which is why he was often misunderstood. "He looks far ahead, & his plans & methods are sometimes mysterious," wrote Rev. Henry Whitney Bellows, founder and president of the Sanitary Commission, of his willful protégé. "[His critics] think him impracticable, expensive, slow—when he is only long-headed, with broader, deeper notions of economy than themselves, & with no disposition to hurry what, if done satisfactorily, must be thoroughly." *Long-headed* is good. It was the future that concerned him, and he had the rare patience to successfully project his plans years ahead. I think that was one of the things that finally attracted him to landscape architecture. It is a field where a long time—sometimes generations—is required for the full realization of the designer's goal.

A small incident illustrates his foresight. Once, five years after the end of the Civil War, when he was already an established landscape architect in New York, he received a letter from the quartermaster general of the U.S. Army, Montgomery Meigs. Meigs had a high regard for Olmsted, with whom he had worked during the war. The general wrote to ask advice on the landscaping of national cemeteries, for which purpose Congress had just appropriated funds. Olmsted was preoccupied with the construction of Prospect Park in Brooklyn; nevertheless it took him less than a week to draft a careful and detailed reply. As to the general design, he wrote, "the main object should be to establish permanent dignity and tranquillity." He warned Meigs that any attempts at elaborate gardening should be avoided. "Looking forward several generations, the greater part of all that is artificial at present in the cemeteries must be expected to have either wholly disappeared or to have become inconspicuous and unimportant in the general landscape." Olmsted recommended doing only two things: building a simple enclosing wall, and planting trees. The effect would be of a "sacred grove" for the war dead. What a beautiful idea!

Olmsted's artistry was always underpinned by sensible considerations, and this was no exception. Since the war cemeteries would be built in different parts of the country, he advocated using trees indigenous to each region. He also warned against the temptation to plant fast-growing species (they would be short-lived) and listed those to be avoided. Instead of buying expensive large trees, he suggested establishing nurseries next to the cemeteries where seedlings could be cultivated and transplanted after ten years or so. What if land for a nursery was unavailable? His novel suggestion: "nursery rows could be planted between the tiers of graves. They would be harmless for the time being and would disappear after a few years" as the trees matured and were relocated.

CHAPTER TWO

Frederick Goes to School

OLMSTED WAS AN ORGANIZER when organization was considered a symptom of "monomania," and a long-range planner in a period that thought of planning as "mysterious." He was a landscape architect before that profession was founded, designed the first large suburban community in the United States, foresaw the need for national parks, and devised one of the country's first regional plans. Above all, he was an artist who chose to work in a medium that then—even more than now—lacked public recognition. He was an innovator and a pioneer largely by chance. But, as Louis Pasteur, an exact contemporary of Olmsted, once observed, "Chance favors only the mind that is prepared." Olmsted's preparation was not based on formal training or education. What laid the groundwork for his later achievements was an amalgam of sensibility and temperament, coupled with an unusual set of formative experiences.

He was born in Hartford, Connecticut, on April 26, 1822. His family circumstances were comfortable. His father, John Olmsted, a local dry-goods merchant, and his mother, Charlotte Hull, a farmer's daughter, had married the year before. John was thirty-one, she was twenty-two. They christened their first child Frederick, in memory of John's older brother who had died a few years earlier. Following the new fashion among genteel Americans in the early nineteenth century, the infant was given a middle name—Law—after Jonathan Law, who was married to Charlotte's older sister, Stella.

Three years later, Charlotte bore a second son, named John Hull. The Olmsteds lived in a rented house on College Street, not the best part of town, but conveniently close to the store. The household help consisted of a cook, a handyman, and two maids. The little family seemed well on its way, but fate—which was to play a big role in Olmsted's life—had it otherwise. "When I was three years old I chanced to stray into a room at the crisis of a tragedy therein occurring," Olmsted later recalled, "and turned and fled from it screaming in a manner adding to the horror of the household. It was long before I could be soothed and those nearby said to one another that I would never forget what I had seen." Even as an adult, he could not bring himself to specify the nature of the tragedy he had witnessed. When Frederick was three, Charlotte accidentally took an overdose of laudanum while suffering from a toothache and died. It would be hard to pick a worse age to lose one's mother. One can only imagine the feelings that roiled in the boy's head: loss, pain, fear, guilt, anxiety. It was the pivotal event of his childhood.

John Olmsted grieved, but with his business to attend to and two young children to rear, he needed a spouse. Fourteen months later he married Mary Ann Bull, the daughter of a prominent Hartford druggist, and a close friend of Charlotte's. The union turned out to be solid, lasting forty-seven years until John's death. They would have six children together. Many years later, reminiscing about his father, Olmsted recalled a loving parent but a reserved and even taciturn man. "He was at bottom a rarely meek, modest, affectionate and amiable man. He had also a strong sense of justice. He was very nervous, impulsive and in a way ambitious but was crippled by . . . a very meager & unsuitable education, and mainly by excessive shyness." Frederick's tall, broad-shouldered father was a self-made man without formal education, which probably contributed to his closemouthedness. But one thing was certain: he had a good head for business. He was one of seven children, raised on a farm in East Hartford—his father had been a ship's captain. At sixteen he was apprenticed to a relative who was a merchant in Hartford. After only eight years with H. B. Olmsted & Company, he opened his own store. The prominent location on Main Street was opposite the State House and near the Congregational church and Hartford's old burying ground. The store carried a wide variety of dry goods: woolens, cottons, silks, so-called fancy goods, and carpeting. (Dry-goods stores were the immediate ancestors of the large "departmentalized" stores that opened in the 1860s.) Despite formidable competition (in 1825 Hartford had more than twenty dry-goods emporia) he prospered.

To call John Olmsted a successful storekeeper gives only a partial description of his position in Hartford society. His roots were deep. A modern commemorative pylon in the old burying ground on Main Street lists the town founders, among them three Olmsteds. These Puritans arrived in New England from Essex in 1632. The seven generations that followed were farmers, merchants, traders, shipowners—and patriots. John Olmsted's father, Benjamin, took part in Benedict Arnold's grueling march on Quebec City; one of John's uncles served under George Washington during the 1775 siege of Boston; another, Gideon, was a naval hero who commanded several privateers during the Revolutionary War. John Olmsted served in the Hartford militia, was a director of the Hartford Retreat for the Insane and the Hartford Female Seminary, and became a trustee of the local athenaeum. Like Jonathan Law, who was a lawyer and the town's postmaster, he was a local eminence in an age when local eminence mattered. During the early nineteenth century, status and influence in the United States were not yet concentrated among the wealthy few. Nor had the metropolis gained ascendancy. This was still chiefly a nation of towns, and of local, rather than national, institutions. Men of John Olmsted's class—lawyers, clergymen, merchants—were pillars of these small communities.

Naturally, such an individual would want to ensure that his sons received a good education. To that end, John Hull was sent to the Hartford Grammar School. Frederick's education took a different turn. Two months after his mother's death he was sent to a "dame's school" in Hartford; he was shifted around and would attend three in all. When he was seven years old, he boarded with Zolva Whitmore, a Congregational minister who lived in the hamlet of North Guilford, thirty-five miles away. From this kindly country parson he received religious instruction, attending the local one-room school with twelve other pupils. He was a good-hearted boy. Once after the death of a little girl, when her family was still grieving at the parsonage, Frederick went to the fresh grave and "prayed to God for Christ's sake to raise the girl, intending to lead her over to our house that she might be sent home to her mother." Nothing happened. "My attention was probably called off by a whippoorwill, and by night-hawks and fireflies.... I seldom hear the swoop of a night-hawk without thinking of it."

By his own later account the boy ran wild in the rustic surroundings, which must have been reflected in his letters home, for less than a year later he was returned to Hartford and was enrolled at a nearby grammar school. Six months passed and he was sent off again, this time to a boarding school run by a clergyman in the village of Ellington. He attended what was still a relatively newfangled institution: a high school (the first high school in the United States had been started in Boston only ten years earlier). This lasted only half a year—his father took him out of the school after the boy was cruelly punished by a teacher. From there he was sent to Newington, five miles from Hartford, to board with Rev. Joab Brace, who took in a small number of boys whom he personally tutored. Young Frederick would spend the next five and a half years with him. He was finally sent home after contracting a severe case of sumac poisoning. The following summer he studied with an Episcopalian clergyman in the village of Saybrook, on Long Island Sound. His schooling ended with Mr. Perkins's academy in East Hartford.

Here, then, is a second remarkable biographical note: between the ages of seven and fifteen, Olmsted spent only two extended periods at home, other than vacations. His stepmother was probably responsible for banishing the boy from her household: Olmsted's first extended absence from home—the spring and summer of 1828—occurred only a year after his father's remarriage. The six-year-old was sent to stay with an uncle in upstate New York for four months. Nine months after the birth of his half sister Charlotte, he was sent away to North Guilford. Having the youngster out of the house undoubtedly made it easier for Mary Ann to look after little John Hull, who was not a healthy child, and to take care of baby Charlotte, who was also sickly and would not live beyond infancy. After that, there were babies in the house for several years—Mary Ann would bear three more children while Frederick was in school. Deeply devout, she was probably the one who suggested that Frederick be sent to board with the Reverend Mr. Brace, who was reputed to be particularly effective in fostering religious conversions in young boys.

One biographer has suggested that John Olmsted's own lack of education made him especially eager to find the perfect tutor for his son. But the merchant's practical nature would surely have alerted him to the drawbacks of such haphazard schooling. Nor was John Olmsted heartless. He was careful and shrewd in business, and upright in his public dealings, but with his family—and especially the sons of his first marriage—he was exceptionally loving and indulgent. He frequently took his children on extended trips, for example. He generously and uncomplainingly supported both sons financially for many years.

Children of prosperous families were often sent away from home to further their educations. The sixteen-year-old John Hull, for example, boarded with Joab Brace for two terms and was later dispatched to Paris with a tutor for six months to improve his French. But he received almost his entire formal schooling in Hartford; his elder brother did not. He had already started dame's school in Hartford when he was sent to upstate New York. On his return, he was reenrolled in Miss Rockwell's school before being sent away to North Guilford. A year later he was back home attending Hartford Grammar School for six months before being sent to the Reverend Mr. Brace. One more period at home follows his recuperative summer in Saybrook. He returned to Hartford to the Hopkins Grammar School, which his brother was also attending, but after only four months he was moved again. This time it was only across the Connecticut River to East Hartford, where he attended a local academy and lived with his grandmother.

Some of the boy's perambulating may be explained by simple mischance—the cruel teacher, the sumac poisoning. But I see a pattern. It is of a difficult child whose parents have trouble dealing with him, and who is sent away, as such children often are, "for his own good." First one school is tried, and then another. It is no coincidence that the school in Ellington was known for its strong discipline. So was the Reverend Mr. Brace. Olmsted himself would write of his childhood: "I was active, imaginative, impulsive, enterprising, trustful and heedless. This made me what is generally called a troublesome and mischievous boy." That was hardly surprising. Olmsted had lost his mother at an impressionable age and, instead of being provided with maternal love, had been sent away, first to his uncle, then to a series of rural boarding schools. The sense of abandonment and guilt—his brother, after all, was allowed to stay home—manifested themselves as intransigence. His unsympathetic stepmother was more interested in her own family than in this unruly lad. His father was loving, but did not know what to do—except to commit him to the care of distant clergymen. Frederick's childhood was one of leaving home and being left with strangers. It was not an auspicious start.

CHAPTER THREE

Hartford

"Soap and education are not as sudden as a massacre," observed Mark Twain, who left school at the age of twelve, "but they are more deadly in the long run." Still, I find it difficult to judge the deadliness of Olmsted's education.* Its religious objective was not realized. Not only did he not experience a conversion, he developed what would eventually harden into an aversion for all organized religion. The disciplinary results were equally unimpressive. His high spirits remained unaffected, and he continued to be, as we will see, an energetic and intemperate enthusiast. Yet the years away from home did not sour him or spoil his relations with his father—he remained a loving and dutiful son his entire life. His haphazard education did leave him with a lingering sense of inadequacy. Many years later, in a letter to his friend and early sweetheart Elizabeth Baldwin Whitney, he admitted ruefully, "I was strangely uneducated,—miseducated . . . when at school, mostly as a private pupil in families of country parsons of small, poor parishes, it seems to me that I was chiefly taught how not to study,—how not to think for myself."

Like most people, Olmsted shaded his adult memories of childhood. In fact, he did learn to think for himself, as his various later intellectual pursuits would show. The Reverend Zolva Whitmore, with whom he spent his first year away from home, was not a demanding teacher, but the committed abolitionist planted the seeds of what were his student's later antislavery views. He also passed on his love of flowers and gardening. Olmsted, who recalled Whitmore with affection, looked back less

---

*One should certainly not judge it by modern standards. Formal education was neither commonplace nor a prerequisite for future accomplishments. Abraham Lincoln, born thirteen years earlier than Olmsted (in much poorer circumstances), learned to read and write at home and attended school less than a year. Nevertheless, he was able to study law on his own and obtain a license.

fondly on his five years with Brace. But to call that clergyman a country parson was misleading. He was a learned man, a Yale graduate who knew Latin, Greek, and Hebrew, and who later received a doctor of divinity degree from Williams College—hardly an unqualified tutor.

Nineteenth-century education consisted chiefly of book learning. One thing that Olmsted did receive during his early schooling was an exposure to books. His father's diary noted that when his son attended Miss Rockwell's school at the age of six, he read the Testament, Noah Webster's *Spelling Book,* a primer called *Juvenile Instructor,* and *Peter Parley's Tales.* The habit of reading is rarely the result of the classroom alone—it is usually nurtured in the home. Frederick Olmsted grew up surrounded by books; his father's obituary would describe him as "a cultivated gentleman, of large and varied reading." The young Olmsted read voraciously and widely. He found a copy of *On Solitude,* by the Swiss doctor Johann Georg ritter von Zimmerman, in his grandmother's garret. He read fiction, too: Oliver Goldsmith's *The Vicar of Wakefield* and Laurence Sterne's *A Sentimental Journey.*

The public library provided other opportunities. It was there, he recalled, that he had his first introduction to the art of landscape gardening in the Reverend William Gilpin's *Remarks on Forest Scenery* and Sir Uvedale Price's *Essay on the Picturesque.* Both British authors were important figures in the evolution of the cult of the scenic and picturesque landscape that developed during the eighteenth century and continued to flourish during the early nineteenth century. In later life, Olmsted considered *Essay on the Picturesque* one of the most important books in the history of landscape architecture. That the boy read these relatively specialized books so early attests to both his intellectual curiosity and to the excellence of the Hartford Public Library.

In fact, the casual supervision afforded by the "country parsons" stimulated his curiosity, as well as his sense of independence. Not everyone finds his own way in an atmosphere of freedom—Olmsted did. Always the "new boy" at school, he spent much time alone, usually out-of-doors. His solitary rambles gave him a lifelong love of the countryside and of outdoor activities. Years later, in a letter to his close friend Frederick Newman Knapp, who was principal of Eagleswood Military Academy in New Jersey, where Olmsted's stepsons were both enrolled, he wrote: "I see certain advantages which I enjoyed that your boys do not. These latter came to me chiefly not by systematic arrangement or deliberate and intelligent forethought on the part of my educational superintendents but through opportunities incidentally or accidentally presented to me & which I used with good will." Olmsted was on Knapp's advisory board, and his letter characteristically listed in great detail a variety of nonacademic skills that he felt young boys should acquire. Among them were bridling a horse, handling a boat, shooting, and woodcraft—all skills that he had learned early. He also stressed the importance of physical exercise. Not organized sports and gymnastics, however, but daily outdoor hikes. "A boy . . . who would not in any weather & under all ordinary circumstances, rather take a walk of ten to twelve miles some time in the course of every day than stay quietly about a house all day, must be suffering from disease or a defective education" was his slightly pompous advice to Knapp.*

When he was boarding at village schools, Olmsted hiked in the fields and forests of rural Connecticut; when he was home, he walked about Hartford. Hartford, midway between New York and Boston, had grown into a manufacturing and commercial center during the eighteenth century. The town continued to prosper during the early nineteenth century, but it remained compact enough so that everything was within easy walking distance. One of Hartford's attractions to a boy was its busy port. The Connecticut River accommodated oceangoing vessels, and international maritime trade had always been an aspect of Hartford commerce (it had occupied several of Olmsted's shipowning forebears). The variety of goods that the *Connecticut Courant* recorded as arriving in Hartford's harbor is impressive: hides from Buenos Aires, India-rubber overshoes, almonds from the south of France and nuts from Brazil, and bales of wool from Bilbao. In the Hartford *Times,* under the rubric "New And Rich Goods," are listed German and English woolens, Parisian embroidery, and Italian cravats—all available from John Olmsted, who invited "the attention of his friends and customers to his Stock of Dry Goods. now opening. being the best assortment of GOOD goods he has ever offered."

There is an advertisement in the Hartford *Times* for a "Writing School," which was conducted in Union Hall by a Mr. Strong. It must have been popular, for Strong was announcing a second term, "his present classes being full." These classes were for adults, not children. They

---

*Evidently Olmsted did not look back on his extended absences from home with bad feelings since he sent his own boys to a boarding school.

were intended to improve the penmanship of aspiring ladies and gentlemen, elegant handwriting then being considered a requirement for the
genteel correspondent. Olmsted's childhood coincided with the beginning of the second phase of what one historian has called the "refinement
of America." During the nineteenth century gentility spread from the
upper to the middle class. Gentility meant self-improvement. People
collected books. They formed scientific societies. They attended reading
clubs, literary circles, and musical evenings. They hired dancing masters,
fencing instructors, and French tutors for their children. They built more
elaborate houses, new civic buildings, and beautiful churches. They
established libraries, teaching academies, and athenaeums. "They" meant
the families of the prosperous merchants and professionals. In the case of
Hartford, this burgeoning elite, to which John Olmsted belonged, was
exceptionally active and influential. As a result, the city, whose population in 1820 was less than seven thousand, was no provincial backwater
but a place of some intellectual consequence.

There were three daily newspapers: not only the *Connecticut Courant*
and the *Times,* but also the *Connecticut Mirror.* There were two religious
periodicals: the *Congregationalist* and the *Churchman.* The *Bouquet* was a
literary journal with the charming masthead "Flowers of Polite Literature." While many of the stories, essays, and poems in the *Bouquet* were
reprinted from elsewhere, there was also original work by local writers. An
early issue contained an endorsement from one of the most popular and
prolific authors of her day, Lydia Hunt Sigourney, who was a Hartford resident. So was Noah Webster, whose first dictionary was published here.
Another local literary figure was the bookseller and publisher Samuel
Goodrich, author of the phenomenally successful Peter Parley series of
schoolbooks. Hartford society was enriched by prominent public figures
such as Catharine E. Beecher, educational reformer and principal of the
Hartford Female Seminary, the Reverend Thomas Hopkins Gallaudet,
founder of the American Asylum for the Deaf and Dumb, the country's
first free public school of this kind, as well as Horace Bushnell, theologian
and celebrated divine.* The town's literary tradition was an old one. During the late eighteenth century, Hartford had been the home of a group of
Federalist poets who came to be widely known as the Hartford Wits.

---

*Bushnell was the Olmsteds' next-door neighbor. He was considered radical, however, and
the Olmsted family did not attend his church.

Of course, Hartford was not Boston or New York. By 1830, Boston had a population of more than one hundred thousand, and New York twice that. Urbanization was a mixed blessing. Cities were dangerously unhealthy, with no effective trash removal. New York was notorious for the pigs that freely wandered the streets in search of slops. A lack of clean water and poor sanitation brought on regular outbreaks of yellow fever. The first American case of cholera was reported in New York in June 1832, and the disease quickly assumed epidemic proportions, ravaging the country as far south as New Orleans. Even Hartford was affected. There were advantages to being small, however. By September, although people were still dying in New York, Baltimore, and Washington, the *Connecticut Courant* was proud to report, "It is highly gratifying to be able to state that no case of cholera has occurred here during the past week, the city is now as healthy as usual at this session of the year." Large cities were also less peaceable. They were often the sites of civil disturbances, usually centered on slavery and abolition. In October of 1834, for example, proslavery riots swept Philadelphia; the following year a Boston mob almost lynched the abolitionist editor William Lloyd Garrison. There was no police to enforce order.*

Today Hartford is not a beautiful city. The interstate highway separates the city from the river, and although the state capitol is handsome, the downtown is an ill-assorted collection of undistinguished modern office buildings. But in the midnineteenth century, Hartford was widely recognized as an attractive town. It was surrounded by rolling countryside and preserved many of the charms of the New England village it had once been. "The town is beautifully situated in a basin of green hills . . . it is a lovely place," observed Charles Dickens, who spent three days there during his 1842 tour of the United States. People lived in neat, white-painted wooden houses with gardens surrounded by picket fences. Main Street was a broad, unpaved thoroughfare, lined by wooden sidewalks and three- and four-story brick buildings with stores below and offices and rented rooms above. Like all the streets, it was shaded by large trees. The leafy canopy spread over the town like a green blanket, pierced at regular intervals by the steeples of devout Hartford's many churches. "Of

---

*In 1829, Sir Robert Peel organized the first regular police force in London. Philadelphia followed suit five years later, but most American cities lacked regular policing until the 1840s.

all the beautiful towns it has been my fortune to see, this is the chief," wrote Mark Twain upon his first visit in 1868. "Everywhere the eye turns it is blessed with visions of refreshing green. You do not know what beauty is if you have not been here." Twain liked Hartford so much he moved there shortly after.

Olmsted's rambles took him to one or another of his scores of uncles and cousins, as well as to his grandmother Content Olmsted, whose husband, Benjamin, had died when Frederick was ten. Benjamin Olmsted had been a strong influence on the boy and had left him with a valuable memory. One day the normally closemouthed old man noticed that his grandson had climbed a tall elm that grew near the house. He told Frederick that as a boy he had planted this very tree, some seventy years earlier. "It came to me after a time as he went on talking about it," Olmsted recalled, "that there had been nothing in all his long life of which he was so frankly proud and in which he took such complete pleasure as the planting and the beautiful growth of this tree."

Olmsted's favorite relation seems to have been his namesake, Uncle Law, whom he singled out as having had "a notable influence in my education." Jonathan Law, a friend of the poet John Greenleaf Whittier, was a scholarly man, whom Olmsted recalled as reciting Latin poetry (Frederick evidently had a good grasp of Latin thanks, probably, to Brace's teaching). Charlotte Olmsted had grown up with her older sister, Stella, and Jonathan Law, so they had particularly warm feelings for their nephew. Moreover, they had no children of their own. Olmsted visited the Laws during his summer holidays. The couple encouraged his interest in plants, and he was given his own garden beds to cultivate. He also frequented the house of his bachelor first cousin Charles Hyde Olmsted, whose shipowner father had left him with a modest fortune. Charles, then about thirty years old, was a Yale graduate, but had been "brought up to no regular calling," in Olmsted's words. Charles shared his interest in nature with the boy, whom he later introduced into the Hartford Natural History Society. Like Jonathan Law, Charles was a retiring, bookish man, and he allowed his young cousin the run of his "notable library." His relations with the Laws and with his cousin underline an attractive trait of Olmsted's character, here described by a boyhood friend. "He was very fond of society, not only of young people both boys and girls but of elderly people of whom there was anything to learn—and there were few from whom he could not learn something." It was kindly elderly people such as the Laws and Charles Hyde Olmsted who helped the boy through his sometimes difficult childhood.

The landscape of Connecticut consists chiefly of gently undulating hills. The main feature is the valley of the Connecticut River, but there are many smaller rivers, and thousands of ponds and lakes. The relatively temperate climate lacks the extremes of neighboring states. The mild winters and humid summers allow the cultivation of a wide variety of trees and shrubs. This was, and is, a countryside of undramatic but exceptional beauty. Olmsted took his surroundings for granted, but they undoubtedly had an important influence on his sensibilities. The landscape of Connecticut is unusual in another way. It is, by North American standards, modestly scaled. There are no great lakes, vast prairies, thundering rivers, or craggy mountains. Even the shoreline, protected by Long Island Sound, has a benign air. Settled early, it has a tamed look that would have been apparent even in the nineteenth century, perhaps even more so then since the state was more rural, and more agricultural, than it is today. Of all New England, it is this picturesque countryside that most closely recalls that of old England. No wonder that the writing of the British landscape gardeners immediately appealed to the young Olmsted. The countryside they described was not exotic—it was familiar.

Living away from home, being moved from one school to another, gave Frederick the opportunity to experience the variety of the Connecticut landscape. But it also limited his circle of friends. Though he was warm and outgoing, not until later did he make friends—often life-long friends—easily. During his childhood, his closest companion was his younger brother, John. As the size of the Olmsted household increased through the arrival of new half sisters and half brothers, Frederick and John, separated by only three years, naturally became fast friends. The bond was strengthened by the two terms that the boys spent together in Newington under the sober eye of the Reverend Mr. Brace.

Years later, Olmsted recalled a hike with his brother to his aunt's house in Cheshire. "I was but nine when I once walked sixteen miles over a strange country with my brother who was but six, to reach it. We were two days on the road, spent the night at a rural inn which I saw still standing a few years ago, and were so tired when we arrived that, after sitting before that great fireplace and being feasted, we found that our legs would not support us and were carried off to bed. It was a beautiful region of rocky glens and trout brooks."* I imagine their adventure. It is a sunny day. The dusty road outside Hartford winds its way through rolling meadows. Olmsted is in the lead, probably talking, pointing out birds and trees in the hedgerows along the verge. He is excited about the prospect of adventure. He holds his younger brother by the hand. John is less sure about the outing. He is thinking that perhaps they should go home before it gets too late. But he goes along, trusting that Frederick will find the way, as he always seems to do.

*It does not say much for Mary Ann Olmsted's mothering that she allowed the two young boys to make such an excursion alone.

CHAPTER FOUR

"I Have No Objection"

NOVEMBER 1837 FOUND the fifteen-year-old Olmsted on the road again, but not for pleasure. He was traveling to Andover, Massachusetts, to board and study with Frederick A. Barton. Unlike the boy's other tutors, Barton was not a clergyman, at least not yet—he was studying for the ministry at Andover Theological Seminary. He taught mathematics at Phillips Academy. But Olmsted was not to attend classes at Phillips, nor to study mathematics. Barton was by profession a surveyor, and although Olmsted later referred to himself as having been "the pupil of a topographical engineer," the reality was more mundane. He was to learn a trade.

There was no dishonor in that. No less a man than George Washington terminated his formal schooling at fifteen to be apprenticed to a surveyor. Although Washington's contemporaries Madison, Jefferson, and Hamilton were college graduates, higher education was a rarity, and it remained so in Olmsted's day. A college diploma may have been required to be a doctor or a clergyman, but most professions were still learned through apprenticeship. Still, Olmsted might have been expected to go to college. His mentors, Jonathan Law and Charles Hyde Olmsted, were both college men, Yale was nearby, and John Olmsted could afford to send his son to college. There was even a relation on the Yale faculty, Olmsted's second cousin Dennison. He was a professor of mathematics and natural history and would certainly have facilitated the boy's acceptance.*

Olmsted himself explained his lack of a college education this way: "When fourteen I was laid up by an extremely virulent sumach poisoning, making me for some time partially blind, after which, and possibly as

---

*Five years later, when John Hull went to Yale, he boarded with Dennison Olmsted, roughly the same time as one of Dennison's sons, Lucius, came to Hartford to work in John Olmsted's store as an apprentice.

a result, I was troubled for several years with a disorder of the eyes and the oculists advised that I should be kept from studying." In a letter to Elizabeth Baldwin he wrote: "Because of an accident putting my eyes in some peril, I was at the most important age left to 'run wild.' . . . While my mates were fitting for college, I was allowed to indulge my strong natural propensity for roaming afield and day dreaming under a tree." The sumac story sounds far-fetched. Contact with the resin of poison sumac, as with poison ivy and poison oak, can cause inflammation of the skin, but is not known to cause ocular disorders. Olmsted's eyesight problem may have been some form of conjunctivitis. It is unclear exactly when Olmsted first experienced problems with his eyes, but it seems to have occurred in the spring when he was either fourteen or fifteen. One form of conjunctivitis—vernal keratoconjunctivitis—occurs *precisely* in the spring and is a disease of late childhood or early adulthood.

Medicine in 1836 was, of course, primitive. Whatever the cause of the eye affliction, there was not much a doctor could do. The typical physician's bag contained a syringe for enemas, and a lancet, a scarificator, and a cupping glass, for bleeding the patient. There was a pitifully small number of drugs: laudanum for pain, calomel for purging, sarsaparilla to induce sweating, and various compounds containing alcohol that were given as tonics to combat fever. Other than that, doctors could only prescribe rest and fresh air. In the early 1800s, there was a fad for hydrotherapy, and the treatment that was recommended for Olmsted's malady was seawater bathing (hence, presumably, his summers in Saybrook). Since modern remedies for conjunctivitis include washing the eyes with a weak saline solution, this may, in fact, have helped reduce the inflammation.

Conjunctivitis can be acute or chronic. It may last for several months, disappear entirely, and then reappear. The following year—again, in the spring—Olmsted suffered a recurrence of his eye disorder. His father took him to New York, to consult a Dr. Wallace, who recommended continuing the sea bathing. The doctor also made another prescription: "Advised to give up college on account of eyes." This statement appears in an excerpt from John Olmsted's journal that was included in a compilation of Frederick Law Olmsted's writings, published in 1922. The excerpt supposedly was based on a summary of John Olmsted's journal; however, it does not appear in the original journal. John Olmsted noted only that on June 14, 1837, he "went to NYK with Fred[k] by river returned Monday 19th via New Haven" and that Dr. Wallace charged four dollars to examine the boy's eyes. The 1922 compilation also includes a comment that when Frederick was with the Reverend Mr. Brace, he was "fitting for college," and quotes John Olmsted as noting that after going to school in East Hartford, the boy was "now ready to enter college." Neither statement appears in the original journal.

Someone altered the historical record to support Olmsted's contention that he would have gone to college had it not been for his poor eyesight. That does not make the contention untrue, but it does cast doubt on it. There are other questions. Would a boy with faulty vision really have been sent to learn surveying? Sighting through transits, recording columns of figures, and preparing detailed maps requires excellent eyesight. If he was headed for college, why not wait a year or two before aborting such an important decision? Finally, if only weak eyesight prevented him from entering college, why didn't he apply when the disorder cleared up?

None of Olmsted's correspondence from the period of his apprenticeship to Barton has survived, but the Olmsted collection at the Library of Congress does contain several letters written to him at the time by his father. In one letter, dated less than a year after his son arrived in Andover, John Olmsted advised him: "If you will not go back in your surveying by giving it up this term & pursuing other studies . . . I have *no objection.*" But he quickly added, "I am sorry however to have your mind unsettled on the subject of your studies." He then counseled him, "Be desirous of pursuing such studies as will most tend to your intellectual and moral improvement & to fit you for the usefulness & employment when you take your place in the great theatre of life & throw everything from you that tends to distract from this pursuit." He also reminded his son not to study in the evenings, unless he felt that his eyes were up to it.

This reference to evening study makes it clear that weak eyesight was still a concern. On the other hand, the disorder was evidently not serious enough to have been considered a major impediment to the boy's present—or future—studies. Equally revealing is the use of the term "your surveying." It suggests that the decision to become a surveyor was not the father's but the son's. Indeed, at the end of the letter, John Olmsted makes it clear that he would be happy if his son chose a different course of study, something that would lead to greater "intellectual and moral improvement."

What really discouraged Olmsted from attending college was probably his irregular schooling and the amount of cramming he would have had to do to prepare himself. He had had enough of book learning—he was never, in fact, a strong student. In any case, surveying would have appealed to his love of the outdoors. It is not difficult to imagine the impetuous boy announcing one day, "I'm going to be a surveyor." He was certainly stubborn enough to defy his father. The choice seems impulsive because not so long after arriving at Barton's, Olmsted was ready to throw in the towel.

Although his father's letter was characteristically uncoercive and left the door open for him to abandon his surveying should he so decide, the boy resolved otherwise. He would stick it out. That was a part of his stubbornness, too. Only two weeks later (father and son corresponded frequently), his father wrote to him: "I am very pleased with the account of your studies . . . & very glad to learn that you are now getting so much interested in them—I thought it could not be otherwise—At 16 or 17, if ever, we begin to feel that the time is come for us to throw off boyish notions & habits."

Olmsted would spend more than two years learning to be a surveyor. After twelve months, the now Reverend Mr. Barton moved to Collinsville, Connecticut, some fifteen miles from Hartford, to his first parish. Olmsted accompanied his tutor, despite his father's hope that his son might remain in Andover and follow a more intellectual course of study. Olmsted was intent on continuing his surveying training. He later downplayed his apprenticeship with Barton and described it as a "decently restrained vagabond life, generally pursued under the guise of an angler, a fowler or a dabbler on the shallowest shores of the deep sea of the natural sciences." Olmsted certainly would have spent a lot of time out-of-doors, for surveying is literally learned in the field. The student is assigned practice runs across difficult terrain and required to establish the distance between predetermined points and the elevation of different landmarks, and to prepare the contour plans based on these measurements. It is not demanding work. I once spent several weeks in a summer surveying course as part of my architectural training. I remember not unpleasant days spent outdoors in the Quebec countryside, and long, boring evenings when we were obliged to document the day's observations and make the detailed calculations that never quite—in my case—added up. I can imagine Olmsted enjoyed the paperwork, and he could certainly indulge his love of nature and natural scenery as he trudged across the fields, carrying his transit from one station point to another.

Since Barton had his classes at Phillips Academy, and later his parish work, to attend to, Olmsted did spend much of his time unsupervised. Hence his characterization of this as a vagabond life. At the same time, he couldn't have helped acquiring at least some of the skills that would later prove useful: how to calculate "cut and fill" (the addition and subtraction of earth when land is reshaped), how to lay out roads and house lots, as well as an understanding of how to read—and prepare—topographic maps, subdivision plans, and other survey documents. That he learned to draw is attested to by an entry in his father's diary, recording a payment of eleven dollars—a significant sum—to Wyeth & Ackerman in Andover for "Fredrk tuition drawing etc."

The apprenticeship was interrupted by summer holidays. In August 1838 he accompanied his parents and his brother, John, on a two-and-a-half-week trip through the White Mountains of New Hampshire. This was the longest vacation that Olmsted had taken with his parents since he was six and they had visited his uncle Owen in upstate New York. That journey had been by steamboat and stagecoach. This time they traveled in their own carriage, up the valley of the Connecticut River and east through Franconia Notch, where they could marvel at that curious rock formation known as the Old Man of the Mountains. They continued south to Lake Winnipesaukee and visited the coastal town of Portsmouth before returning home via Boston. Olmsted's father recorded the itinerary in his diary and also mentioned that they passed through Andover, so probably his son was dropped off with Barton.

On April 6, 1840, three weeks short of his eighteenth birthday, Olmsted returned home, his apprenticeship complete. At that age, Washington had already been working as a public surveyor for a year. Olmsted, on the other hand, seemed in no hurry to get a job. He spent most of that summer in Hartford, living in his parents' house, helping relatives on their farms, seeing family, and sailing on the Connecticut River. Unfortunately, his dear brother wasn't there to keep him company—that was the summer John had been sent to Paris. They wrote to each other frequently. "Please send us some French Periodicals & remember I am a curiosity hunter," he reminded John.

Olmsted was certainly a curiosity hunter. He was bright. But his intellect was undisciplined and expressed itself in energetic but disordered enthusiasms heightened, no doubt, by the traumatic loss of his mother. His brother was the steady one, who excelled in his studies and seemed bound for a distinguished professional career. Olmsted wasn't lazy, but his curiosity was great and his attention span lamentably short. He was also easygoing, and not too proud to bank on his father's generosity and forbearance. As for his patient father, he was starting to realize that launching this mercurial son into "the great theatre of life" was not going to be easy.

CHAPTER FIVE

New York

THE MODERN CULT of prolonged adolescence did not exist in mid-nineteenth-century America. An eighteen-year-old youth was not a "teenager" but a young adult. He was expected to begin thinking of starting a family and establishing himself in the community, and unless he was one of the small number who attended college, he was expected to earn a living. This posed a problem for Olmsted. He had lost interest in surveying. Although his vision problems appear to have cleared up, he showed no more enthusiasm for studying than earlier.

In August 1840, Olmsted left Hartford for New York to work as an apprentice clerk with the house of Benkard and Hutton, an importer of French silks and dry goods. Benkard and Hutton supplied John Olmsted's store, and he arranged the position. Poor Frederick! An outdoorsman forced into a counting house—the errant son disciplined by the exasperated father. That, at least, is the impression given by most of Olmsted's biographers. It is based, chiefly, on Mariana Van Rensselaer's biographical essay, which appeared in the October 1893 issue of *Century Illustrated Monthly Magazine*. "Placed at sixteen [*sic*] in a large importing-house in New York, he could not compel himself to commercial life," she wrote. Rensselaer's account has been widely accepted since it was based on conversations she had with Olmsted himself.

But I'm not so sure that is the way it happened. One of Olmsted's friends recalled that "perhaps being tired of routine, he [Olmsted] persuaded his father to prepare him for a business life." *Persuaded his father*—that puts a different face on it. That John Olmsted had no intention of pushing his son into a business career is confirmed by a letter that he sent to Frederick while he was studying surveying. He wrote: "I have no recollection of ever saying I wishd you to go into a store." The idea that it was Olmsted's own decision to enter the world of commerce is not

42

far-fetched. The offspring of successful businessmen often inherit some of their fathers' talents. John Olmsted had four sons, one of whom—Owen—died as an infant. Of the other three—Frederick, John, and their half brother, Albert—John showed no particular business bent, but the other two did. Albert followed in his father's footsteps and eventually became a partner in a Hartford mercantile firm; and Frederick himself was drawn to undertake commercial activities at various times in his life. His father's comment doesn't suggest that Olmsted was interested in going into the dry-goods business. But at Benkard and Hutton he was going to work in international trade, a career that promised travel to exotic places and appealed to his adventurous spirit.

He also experienced New York. The city had suffered a serious decline following the British occupation during the Revolutionary War, but by 1840 it had grown to about three hundred thousand, outstripping Philadelphia and Boston as the metropolitan center of the Northeast. It must have been a revelation to someone raised in tiny Hartford. Not that New York was an elegant place. The results—as with most boomtowns—were mixed. "Bizarre and not very agreeable," Alexis de Tocqueville had called it during his visit nine years earlier. The French aristocrat looked in vain for public architecture and found instead an individualistic, free-wheeling city characterized by "commercial habits and money-conscious spirit." There had been improvements since then—horse-drawn trolley cars were introduced on lower Fourth Avenue in 1832, and the grand buildings of New York University were completed three years later. But the city preserved its mercantile air and showed little interest in civic beautification. The chief expression of this pragmatism was the Commissioners' Plan for platting the entire island of Manhattan as a repetitive grid of crisscrossing streets and avenues. The plan was adopted in 1811, but by the time that Olmsted arrived, it was still largely unrealized. Only about thirty-four-thousand people lived north of Fourteenth Street, and many of them were farmers. The area around City Hall, which included the luxurious Astor House hotel, was the focus of city life; the business district was still concentrated at the lower end of the island.

The house of Benkard and Hutton was located in the First Ward, on Beaver Street. Although this was the oldest part of the city, there were many new buildings. The new Custom House, an impressive Greek Revival temple of white marble, was nearing completion. So was the palatial Merchants Exchange. At the head of Wall Street, work was about to begin on a replacement for the old Trinity Church. Only five years before, New York had been devastated by the biggest fire that any American city had ever experienced. Estimates of losses ranged from fifteen to twenty-six million dollars; more than six hundred buildings were totally destroyed.

The new buildings were impressive, but they could not relieve the hemmed-in atmosphere in the bustling, narrow streets of lower Manhattan. The only relief was the view of the water from the wharves that girdled the tip of the island. Olmsted knew the harbor well since part of his job was to go aboard cargo vessels to prepare inventories of new shipments of silks. As in most American cities, the waterfront was dedicated to commerce. The one exception was the Battery, at ten acres the largest park in the city. Its tree-shaded walks along the seawall made it a popular promenade, although like City Hall Park to the north, it was poorly maintained and had a neglected air. Other attempts at creating civic open space—Tompkins Square or the Washington Parade Ground (now Washington Square)—were similarly untended. There were attractive parks such as Gramercy Park and St. John's Park (no longer existing—near what is now the exit to the Holland Tunnel), but these were private and gated.

Olmsted didn't live in the city. He commuted to work by ferry across the East River from Brooklyn. Brooklyn had benefited from the growth of New York. While it was larger than Hartford, it still had some of the atmosphere of a small town. Perhaps that's why John Olmsted, who had accompanied his son to New York to make sure he was well installed, chose it. Or maybe he just wanted to make sure that the lures of Manhattan lowlife were kept at a distance. Olmsted lived in Mrs. Howard's boarding house on Henry Street in Brooklyn Heights. This part of Brooklyn would soon become a fashionable district favored by successful businessmen, but when Olmsted lived there, its character was still largely rural, with fields, trees, and individual houses. The city, whose dramatic vista across the river was visible from the Heights, was a world away.

The idea of working in one place and living in another hardly strikes us as exceptional, but in 1840 it was unusual. Brooklyn's position as one of the country's first suburbs was relatively recent, dating from the inauguration of Robert Fulton's steam ferry service in 1814. The contrast between the brick and stone city and leafy Brooklyn Heights could not have been lost on Olmsted. This introduction to suburban life is important. Suburbs would grow immensely in popularity during the second half of the nineteenth century, and Olmsted would play an important role in the process.

Brooklyn was the site of another novelty: Greenwood Cemetery. Greenwood was a so-called rural cemetery. That is, it was a cemetery for city people in a rural setting. The first rural cemetery was Boston's Mount Auburn, situated in Cambridge and consecrated in 1831. Five years later, Philadelphia followed with Laurel Hill. Greenwood was established in 1838. At two hundred acres it was the largest of the three, and its site on Gowanus Heights overlooking New York harbor (not far from Henry Street) was undoubtedly the most dramatic. These were public cemeteries (as opposed to churchyards or rural family plots), but they were more than burial places. Mount Auburn had set the pattern. Planned with the assistance of the Massachusetts Horticultural Society, it incorporated curvilinear roads, hillocks, ponds, and plantings in the natural and picturesque manner of British landscape gardening. Mount Auburn and the other rural cemeteries became popular destinations for Sunday outings and picnics. The combination of recreation and death may seem odd, but this incongruity was less intensely felt than today. Death was no stranger to nineteenth-century families; at eighteen, Olmsted had already lost not only his mother and his half sister Charlotte, but also his two-year-old half brother, Owen.

Rural cemeteries provided fresh air and greenery—and the illusion of beautiful countryside. Olmsted would have preferred the real thing. About a year after arriving in New York, he wrote to his stepmother:

> Oh, how I long to be where I was a year ago: midst two lofty mountains, pursuing the uneven course of the purling brook, gliding among the fair granite rocks, & lisping over the pebbles; meandering through the lowly valley, under the sweeping willows, & the waving elms, where nought is heard save the indistinct clank of anvils & the distant roaring of water as it passes gracefully over the half natural dam of the beautiful Farmington when the declining Phoebus gilds the snow capt hills & enlivens the venerable tower of Montevideo, then & there to be—"up to knees in mud & sand" chasing mush-squash! (Ahem!—I say; I did that, I did. That was I, & nobody else. It's mine "par brevet de invention." Entered according to the act of congress, &c.)

This short arcadian passage is intended to be satirical, as the final lines make clear. But it thinly masks a genuine sentiment: he misses the countryside. And—surprise—he can write. Not many high school graduates today know Phoebus, the Greek Apollo, god of the sun, or use words like *purling, lisping,* and *meandering.* Evidently, despite his miseducation— and thanks to his wide reading—he has developed a reasonable command of the English language as well as a strong visual sense. He just doesn't yet know quite what to do with these talents.

The rest of the letter deals with family affairs. He thanks his mother for some nut cakes, inquires about his two half sisters, Mary and Bertha (to whom he has written separately), and asks to be sent a pair of suspenders and gloves. The writer sounds cheerful. There is mention neither of his work nor of his life in the city. That is likely because he had little free time to play the tourist. This was no casual apprenticeship, as had been the case with Barton; Benkard and Hutton expected its clerks to work hard and long. The typical working day was ten to twelve hours; only Sundays were free. "The business is such that I am engaged from morning to night without ceasing," Olmsted wrote his brother shortly after arriving in New York. For someone who had never even held a summer job, it must have been a rude awakening.

Olmsted performed his work satisfactorily, for he was put in charge of handling the petty cash, an early recognition of one of his lifelong traits—scrupulous honesty. His clerical apprenticeship taught him skills that would eventually prove valuable: bookkeeping, accounting, and office organization. Because Benkard and Hutton's business was so intimately connected with France, French was spoken in the office, and Olmsted learned the language, which would be useful to him later. But that was in the future. Right now he wasn't satisfied. The routine of office work did not appeal to Olmsted; nor did its discipline. As an apprentice he was at everyone's beck and call, and at eighteen, he was rather old to be an office boy. In March 1842 he decided that the business life was not for him and returned to Hartford.

Olmsted spent the spring and the following summer doing all those things he had missed in New York. He went riding, fishing, and shooting. He also socialized, going to parties and developing an interest in young women. He took music and dancing lessons. He went boating. In July he and his brother sailed down the Connecticut River to the sea in a new sailboat that their father had bought them (their previous boat had been stolen). In September John Hull began his studies at Yale. That fall, the Natural History Society, to which Cousin Charles had introduced

Olmsted, had a visit from John James Audubon, who was setting out on a journey to Yellowstone and the Rocky Mountains. "Might I be there to see [them]," mused a wistful Olmsted. In October he did make a trip, but only as far as New Haven, to visit John. His brother's roommate was an affable young man named Charles Loring Brace (no relation to Rev. Joab Brace). Brace, from Hartford, was already known to Olmsted and would, in time, become one of his closest friends.

Fall turned to winter. Olmsted seemed content with his life of leisure. John Olmsted seems to have felt that he should allow his feckless son to find his own way. It was turning out, however, to be an ineffective child-rearing strategy. More than twenty years later, Olmsted's younger, half brother Albert found himself in a similar situation: he was working in his father's dry-goods store, but he was unhappy with the prospect of a life in business and wanted a change. He was considering whether he should study civil engineering, learn to be a watchmaker, or join the diplomatic service (he had been offered a post in Bordeaux). He turned to his older, half brother Frederick, who strongly advised him to stay put. In a touching and revealing letter to his father, Olmsted described Albert's condition in a way that clearly echoed his own, earlier predicament:

Ally has the difficulty which seems to me to belong to all your descendants—of an unusual slowness or feebleness in the development of his natural propensities & faculties. He does not know his own mind, and grows irregularly. He needs a mental and moral tonic, and to be freed from whatever is weakening to manly sedateness or steady vigor of character. He should on this account not allow himself to associate with persons younger than himself, but make himself the companion if possible, and if not the companion, then the apprentice or attendant of men older than himself—older in habits, as well as years. I don't mean that he should not play, of course, for all men of every age should, but that he should look upward & not backward in the associations of his amusements as well as his work. It is better for him now, to be a confidential servant of men, than a leader of boys. I should not say this to most boys at his age [Albert was twenty-two!], but I know the family weakness at his age.

CHAPTER SIX

A Year Before the Mast

OLMSTED WAS IDLE but not unoccupied. He was concocting a plan. He would go to sea. The idea was not as outlandish as it sounds. His cousin Francis had just returned from a South Seas voyage on a whaling ship. A Hartford friend, Oliver Ellsworth, was planning a trip to the Orient. "Ol will go to China *any*how," he informed his brother, John, "even if he has to go before the mast." The last phrase referred to Richard Henry Dana's *Two Years Before the Mast,* recently published to great acclaim. Olmsted had read this personal narrative of a young man's introduction to seafaring. It struck a chord. Dana was a New Englander; he had a problem with his eyes, which caused him to withdraw from Harvard. The sea voyage was to improve his health. The nineteen-year-old Dana signed on as an ordinary seaman and sailed from Boston around the Horn to San Francisco and back. *Two Years Before the Mast* was not an ordinary travel book—it was a cri de coeur, calculated to appeal to a young man's idealism. "We must come down from our heights and leave our straight paths," Dana wrote, "for the byways and low places of life, if we would learn truths by strong contrasts; and in hovels, in forecastles, and among our own outcasts in foreign lands, see what has been wrought upon our fellow-creatures by accident, hardship, or vice." It is possible that Olmsted thought his own voyage might also provide material for a book. After all, Cousin Francis was writing a travel book—*Incidents of a Whaling Trip* would be published the following year. So why not him?

His goal was to sail to the Orient—a natural choice. From his mentor, Cousin Charles, he heard how his great-uncle Aaron Olmsted had made his fortune in the China trade. As a young boy, he had listened to the yarns of another mariner, his grandfather Benjamin Olmsted, a colorful character who wore his hair in a pigtail and carried a silver-headed malacca cane. Benjamin made a strong impression on the young boy.

(Olmsted later inherited the cane and kept it with him the rest of his life.) Though Benjamin died when Olmsted was ten, his great-uncle Gideon, the naval hero, was a living reminder of the family's seagoing tradition.

Olmsted was lured by thoughts of adventure and the promise of seeing far-off places, but he had another incentive. He was aware that his uncomplaining parents were worried about his future. Perhaps he was even beginning to be a little ashamed of his indolence—it was almost a year since he had returned from New York. Although he definitely didn't want to be a businessman or a surveyor, he was unable to decide which occupation to follow. Going to sea at least gave the appearance of pursuing a career, and he was half-serious. This was not a pleasure cruise. He had no intention of going as a gentleman "with his gloves on," as Dana put it—he would sail "before the mast," as a common seaman. Or, at least, an apprentice seaman. Merchant ships regularly took on two or three "green boys," in addition to their regular complement. Olmsted was no longer a boy (he was almost twenty-one), but he was certainly green in seafaring.

He made up his mind before Christmas, encouraged by a chance encounter with a childhood friend, James Goodwin. Goodwin lived in New York, but he had grown up in Hartford and was visiting. Goodwin had already been to sea, and he suggested that they look for a berth together. The pair had no luck in Hartford, and at the end of March, they traveled to New York. They turned up nothing the first week. As he would so often later in life, Olmsted enlisted the help of friends and acquaintances. He turned to George and Sam Howard, whom he had met while boarding in their mother's house in Brooklyn Heights. They introduced him to Peter Morton, a wealthy Manhattan businessman who also lived in Brooklyn. Morton, in turn, suggested that Olmsted talk to George Talbot, a partner in the tea-importing firm of Gordon & Talbot. At first Talbot was concerned that the young man might be a miscreant whose family simply wanted to get rid of him. Olmsted assured Talbot that this was not the case—although he later privately admitted that "it might almost be true in one sense"—and he provided solid references. Gordon & Talbot did have a China-bound vessel that might be willing to take a green hand. He went on board the ship, which was refitting in a dry dock on the East River. The *Ronaldson* was a square-rigged bark, similar to the ship that Dana had sailed on. At 320 tons she was relatively small and carried a crew of less than twenty. Olmsted thought she had "pretty good form, but nothing clipper." He met the captain, an affable man named Warren Fox. The following day, Captain Fox informed him that he was accepted. Regular seamen were paid about twelve dollars a month; as a green hand, Olmsted would receive considerably less. But it was adventure, not money, he was after. He would be embarking for Canton in two weeks.

The *Ronaldson* left New York harbor on April 23, 1843. Olmsted's father and brother had come to New York to see Frederick off. As the ship put out and the two figures standing on the Pike Street wharf grew smaller in the distance, I imagine that the affectionate Olmsted felt sad. But he must have been excited, too. After the months of inactivity, he was finally on his way. Also, he was among friends. Goodwin had been taken on as a regular hand. Jacob Braisted, a young sailor whom Olmsted had met two weeks before by chance on the Hartford ferry, was also on board. Braisted and Olmsted had taken to each other, quickly becoming "thick as pickpockets." This was Braisted's second China voyage with Captain Fox.

Olmsted wrote home regularly, entrusting the letters to westward-bound American or English ships that the *Ronaldson* encountered on its way. In a letter to his parents sent from his first landfall, Sumatra, he wrote: "It grieves me very much to tell you [the voyage] has likewise been in many respects a disagreeable & unpleasant one."

That was putting it mildly. He had experience sailing on the Connecticut River, and he had taken steamboats down Long Island Sound to New York, but he had never been on the open sea. Like many novices, Olmsted was seasick. At first he tried to work, but eventually he was unable to leave his bunk. The four "green boys" were housed in a foul-smelling small space in steerage, deep belowdecks. He managed to get moved to the forecastle, where most of the crew lived, and shared a bunk with Goodwin, who took care of him. (Later, when Goodwin came down with dysentery, Olmsted was able to return the good deed.) It was weeks before he could eat solid food, and a full month before he recovered. But he was so weakened that he could not do his regular duties and was put to cleaning the rust from the cutlasses and pistols in the armory. This light work did not last long. Olmsted was an apprentice sailor, not a cabin boy. He was expected to perform the same tasks as the other men. These included the morning washing of the decks, as well as regular rounds of scrubbing, scraping, and painting. Bilgewater had to be pumped out daily. The rigging had to be regularly tarred. He took his turn at watch and learned to go aloft to set sails. He was soon scrambling up the ratlines, as much as a hundred feet above the deck. Here, where the swaying motion of the ship was exaggerated manyfold, he would join his mates in gingerly edging out on the yards to furl or unfurl the huge flapping canvas sails. The exhausting work made for blistered hands, cracked knuckles, and aching joints.

Olmsted was starting to settle down to the routine when they reached the Cape of Good Hope. The southern tip of Africa is always dangerous to shipping, and this time was no exception. The *Ronaldson* encountered terrible seas, rains, finally a snowstorm. A squall blew away the main topsail. Going aloft and handling the wet, icy lines became more dangerous than ever. He suffered a bad fall, although not as bad as Braisted, who survived a drop from the fore-topgallant yard, a distance of fifty feet or more. At one point the wind was so strong that the captain was obliged to furl all sails and drift for two days. Since the ship was overloaded with cargo, she lumbered awkwardly in the heavy sea. Everything—and everyone—was wet. One morning Olmsted awoke to find that he couldn't move his right arm. He had another month of light duties until the paralysis wore off and he regained his strength. He was discovering the truth of Dana's observation that "a sailor's life is at best but a mixture of a little good with much evil, and a little pleasure with much pain."

Sickness, accidents, debilitating work, and bad weather were coupled with cramped and uncomfortable living conditions. The food was monotonous: salt beef and biscuits daily, interrupted on Sundays by duff, a clammy pudding of boiled flour and molasses. As a special treat the cook would make lobscouse, a stew of crushed biscuits, potatoes, and codfish or more of the salt beef. Dana had described all this in *Two Years Before the Mast*, but it still must have come as a shock.

Twenty weeks after leaving New York, the *Ronaldson* finally anchored in Whampoa Reach, the port of Canton. Olmsted expected that once they got to their destination he would have a more interesting time. He had been looking forward to visiting China, an exotic foreign land, but it didn't turn out as he'd planned. Seamen worked a six-day week, and shore liberty was a rare privilege. Earlier, the captain had discovered that Olmsted could draw, and he had him copying sea charts. After that, capitalizing on the youth's commercial experience, he appointed him clerk and put him to work preparing invoices and writing circulars to promote the sale of trade goods. Much of the *Ronaldson*'s cargo was sold retail, and the ship was, in effect, turned into a floating dry-goods store. (This could hardly have thrilled Olmsted.) The trading goods were soon disposed of, but the shipment of tea that was to be loaded was delayed, and the months dragged on. The Whampoa anchorage was particularly unhealthy, and like many of the crew, Olmsted contracted typhoid. Malaria, too, was rampant.

It was more than a month before he set foot on land. He did see the city of Canton—on an abbreviated visit. He had with him a letter of introduction from the Reverend Mr. Gallaudet to Dr. Parker, an American missionary, but was able to make only a brief call. Olmsted had promised his friends at the Natural History Society to bring back information and specimens of Chinese flora and fauna, but there was no time for outings into the countryside. It was a great disappointment.

He made only three visits ashore. The second time he accompanied one of the passengers, Dr. John Green, who had befriended Olmsted when he was seasick. They stopped at Boston Jack's—a local ship's chandler who sold provisions to the *Ronaldson*. Olmsted was still recuperating from his bout with typhoid.

> After resting myself some time I took a short walk with the Doctor & Chinese attendants, in the streets of Whampoa, occasionally entering the shops & stores, & seeing the Chinese in their every day life. Old *gentlemen* of fortune with rich dresses & robes reaching to their feet, their long tails richly interwove with silk cord, little black satin skull caps with bright turk's heads or topknots on the *unshaved* part of the crowns. These "old knobs" we often saluted, which they gravely returned, each repeating "*chin chin*," which like a great many of their phrases means many things.

He soon got tired again. Looking for a place to sit down and rest, he heard the sound of classroom recitation through an open door. He stepped inside.

> It was a long room, not very light. The pupils generally were standing up, though there were a few desks, with books on them. I suspect they study at home mostly, as I met some boys afterwards in different places with books, who I think were going to recite. The boys all stared and

generally laughed as I came in, and some young rascals [said] in a low tone "Fanqui!" [foreign devil] I suppose the master half rose & bowed to me, but coming in from the open street, I did not perceive him at first.

At any rate, the little fellow before him never once looked up or altered his tone as he followed the letters on his book (with his young nails some half inch long). He read with a kind of singsong—first high & then low—about two pages; closed his hornbook; about face, & was trotting off without taking the least notice of me, when I took the liberty of stopping him by catching hold of his tail (about eighteen inches long). He whipped round and laughed in my face! However, I gave him a bit of Mandarin cake (which I had bought for Jack [Braisted] on board) (composed, they say, of rice flour, sugar & dry lard—very delicate & nice they are, too) for saying his lesson so perfectly. He chin chin'd me & went about his business.

Olmsted described this incident in a letter to his aunt Maria. Here is a new Olmsted: a budding journalist. He was a natural—inquisitive, sociable, observant, and skeptical. He provided his correspondents with thumbnail sketches of people, dress, architecture, and local customs that are detailed, vivid, and insightful. He was also sympathetic to his surroundings. One day, he followed a group of sailors into a temple. Instinctively, he took off his hat, for which he was jeered by his rough companions. While they fooled around, he met an elderly attendant and got a guided tour of the place.

On his last visit ashore, less than a week before the ship was to weigh anchor, he did some shopping, bringing back the usual souvenirs: a mandarin cap, a sword, a pair of chopsticks. It was a modest reminder of what had turned out to be a pitifully brief encounter with the Orient. But by now he was looking forward to seeing his family again. "Home! home! The thought of seeing you once more—Oh my, I can't sit still, to think of it," he wrote to his father as the ship was preparing to leave.

The voyage home was, if anything, more harrowing. The provisions were as bad as ever. Many of the men had contracted dysentery; others, including Olmsted, came down with scurvy. While he was lying ill in his bunk, he overheard some sailors laying odds on how many days it would be before they threw him overboard. The captain worked his short-handed crew harder than ever. Carrying a full load of tea, he was in a hurry to return—tea fetched a higher price the earlier it went on the market. Ninety days was considered respectable for a fast clipper ship to sail from Canton to New York. The *Ronaldson* made it in only 104 days and docked in New York harbor on April 16, 1844, just a week short of one year since her departure. John Olmsted was waiting on the dock. He was shocked by his son's appearance. The jaunty youth with the brand-new sailor clothes—checked flannel shirt and bell-bottom duck trousers—had been replaced by a wretched, emaciated figure: scrawny, gaunt, and ill-nourished.

Though Olmsted did not see much of China and discovered that he was not cut out for seafaring, his time aboard the *Ronaldson* was instructive. Like Dana, Olmsted had led a sheltered existence. In Hartford, and even during his sojourn in New York, he had been chiefly among people of his own social class. On board the *Ronaldson* he came in close contact with ordinary workingmen. His initial impression of his less advantaged fellow citizens was not propitious. He was sorely disappointed by the behavior of the crew, chagrined at their malingering, and scandalized by their coarse language, their drinking, and their crude behavior. "A more discontented, grumbling, growling set of mortals than our men are, you can not imagine," he wrote his parents.

His natural inclination was to side with the captain and the officers. These were men with whom he shared a common background. Moreover, Captain Fox, who had welcomed him so warmly, treated the "boys"—one of whom was his own son—decently. (Fox's solicitous treatment of Olmsted was undoubtedly colored by his awareness of the young man's personal acquaintance with the ship's owners.) As the voyage continued, however, Olmsted started to have doubts. The custom in most merchant ships was "four hours on and four hours off," which meant a twelve-hour working day. However, to take advantage of a two-week stretch of good weather, the impatient Fox required his men to work seventeen-hour days. He believed that his crew should practice what was known as the Philadelphia Catechism: "Six days shalt thou labor and do all thou art able, And on the seventh—holystone the decks and scrape the cable." To carry more cargo, the captain reduced provisions, and only a month out of New York, potatoes and fruit ran out. To save time, he refused to put in and take on fresh water, with the result that drinking water had to be rationed. To save money, he carried rotted food left over from his earlier voyage. The bread was wormy and the cornmeal was sour.

At Whampoa, Olmsted had seen how other ships were run. He concluded that the men of the *Ronaldson* had "much more cause for complaint than the crews of other vessels here . . . we are worked much longer, if not harder, & have many less privileges than are customarily allowed." "It's perfectly *ridiculous* how mistaken I was in my estimation of the character of my shipmates," he wrote to his brother, John.

It is doubtful that Captain Fox was unusually cruel. Jacob Braisted had sailed with Fox before and would have warned Olmsted if that had been the case. But the captain was single-minded in his handling of the ship. Early-nineteenth-century merchant captains were under intense pressure to shorten sailing times. The *Ronaldson* was no clipper, and making good time meant driving the men hard. The constant threat of mutiny also had to be considered. Harsh, preemptive discipline was customary. Olmsted, like Dana, witnessed at least one brutal flogging. The victim was a young boy whose offense was swearing. He was given more than twenty lashes. As Olmsted later described it, the incident drove the crew to the edge of mutiny.*

His year before the mast had been no lark. He had had a rough time. He had worked hard. He had been exposed to real dangers and real travails. Like Dana, he found out that going to sea was anything but good for your health. The poor diet, the overcrowded conditions, and the tropical diseases had taken their toll. This had left him with no great desire to pursue a maritime career, but he had nothing to be ashamed of. He had proven himself a competent seaman and made a valuable discovery. He had inner resources that matched his unpredictable ambitions.

---

*Flogging was common—in the U. S. Navy it was not abolished until 1850. Captain Fox went too far, however. The father of the boy he flogged so excessively sued. Some of the crew, including Olmsted, testified at the trial, and the court ordered Fox to pay damages of no less than one thousand dollars.

CHAPTER SEVEN

Friends

It took Olmsted most of the following summer to recuperate from his seafaring. Nothing came of his idea of writing a book about his maritime experiences. Once he recovered his health, he resumed his leisurely country life. He attended parties and other social events—many of them. He liked the company of women and thought of marriage, but there were no imminent prospects—or rather, there were too many. Maria Monds, the beautiful daughter of one of the members of the Natural History Society, had also been on a sea voyage, and she and Olmsted "had a few yarns to spin," as he put it. Nothing further came of it. He liked Abby Clark, a student at the Hartford Female Seminary, but addressed her decorously as "Miss Abby." He became close to Emma Brace, Charles's sister, but theirs was a friendship rather than a romantic attachment. He did fall in love with Frances Condit, the pretty, youngest daughter of a Hartford neighbor. He'd fantasized about her while he was at sea: "She's an angel." But she paid him no mind. "I wonder if I really shall be an old bach," he wrote in a letter to Charles Brace. He quickly added, "What a shivering idea—oh my! I tell you it's haunted me like a nightmare since this last scrape [with Frances Condit]. No! No! Sooner would I take up with one of those country girls—six of whom kissed me—oh—before I went to sea." That was Olmsted being melodramatic. In fact, young men did not usually marry until they were in their mid to late twenties, and he was twenty-two.

His father continued to be indulgent, due not only to his patience and kindness but also to his son's temperament. It was difficult to get angry with Frederick Olmsted. He did not mope around the house, getting underfoot; he was helpful, invariably good-natured and cheerful. In short, he had become a pleasure to have around. He was also carefree. He headed one of his letters to Brace: *Hartford. "I keep no note of time."*

He appeared completely unworried by the apparent lack of a settled future.

And now, I feel myself becoming impatient with Olmsted. Why can't he just get on with it? We expect the lives of people—especially people who achieve great things—to neatly follow a grand design. I think of Michelangelo or Mozart or Cézanne. Their lives resemble a game of building blocks. The blocks at the bottom are arranged first and not haphazardly, since they will support the upper levels. As the construction progresses, and more blocks are added, the structure gets taller and taller. It is carefully assembled so as not to topple. Following Olmsted's life is more like putting together a picture puzzle. All sorts of odd-shaped pieces are lying on the table. Two or three form a bit of sky, others a fragment of foliage. Here is something that might—or might not—be water. It's not yet clear how these fragments come together. Some pieces don't seem to fit anywhere. Yet all the pieces of the jigsaw are necessary. Only when the last piece is in place—when the puzzle is complete—does the design make itself evident.

I should be able to sympathize with Olmsted's situation. When I was his age—twenty-two—I had just graduated from college with a degree in architecture. Some of my friends were planning to go to graduate school, some were getting married, most were intent on starting their careers. After working briefly in an architect's office, I went to Europe. I didn't seek out a famous architect or visit celebrated buildings or settle down in one of the two centers of great architecture, Paris or Rome. Instead, I spent an entire spring on one of the Spanish Balearic Islands, where I sketched, wrote poems, fell in and out of love, and taught myself sculpture. I remember it as a short, happy chapter of my life.

While Olmsted was resting in Hartford, his brother, John, was back at Yale, repeating his sophomore year because a persistent respiratory ailment had forced him to skip classes the previous fall. That winter, his father had sent John on a three-month trip to the warm West Indies; he returned to Hartford two weeks after the *Ronaldson* berthed. Olmsted scolded his brother about studying too hard and not allowing himself more time for relaxation: "It's no wonder you got Consumption. Lord bless—'twould give a *cat 'fits'* to be mewed up in the style you propose." Olmsted went on to parody his brother's pedantic schedule: "After breakfast study and read (your selection'l do) ten or fifteen minutes, or from that to a couple of hours. Then make your calls—till twelve. Take an observation, square the yards, & write up your log. Bear a hand with it, so as to have time to write a few pages (of postscript) to Fred. Then go to soup—('Soup's ready sir!' Steward) with a clear conscience."

Olmsted's letters to his brother and his friends were larded with nautical language. It's obvious that he relished his romantic and adventurous seafaring image, and he was dining out on his year before the mast. But playing at being a retired sailor was hardly an occupation. He still didn't know what he was going to do with himself. Here is a self-portrait of the period—characteristically disparaging, but also characteristically unsentimental.

In study I am wonderfully lazy or weak and very soon get tired out. I am romantic—fanciful—jump at conclusions and yet always find headaches or convenient excuses when I want them. I have a smattering education—a little sum, from most everything useful to such a man as I—learned as I took a fancy to it. Of Arithmetic, I cypher slow and without accuracy. Grammar I know nothing of—nor the rules of Rhetoric or writing. Geography I know where I have been. History, nothing but of my own country—except what I have got incidently [sic]. I can't even spell such a word as that right.

He wasn't cut out to be a scholar, that seemed clear. He didn't like taking orders and he valued his independence. Working under others, whether in a trading house or aboard ship, didn't appeal to him. He did like the outdoors and he was not averse to manual work. But what, exactly, was he suited for?

His next career choice was less dramatic than going to sea, and less ambitious than making his way in the hurly-burly of New York. He thought he might try farming. This time, he proceeded cautiously. Was he really wiser, or was he encouraged to be prudent? I can imagine his father advising him: "I'll help you, Frederick, but this time don't rush into it. Spend a few months on a farm. See how you like it. Then decide." There was no shortage of relatives who were farmers. His mother's sister Linda had married David Brooks, whose farm, in nearby Cheshire, Frederick and John had walked to as children. He decided to start by working on his uncle's farm.

He spent the fall and winter of 1844—almost five months—in Cheshire. Once the harvest was in, he had plenty of free time and resumed his social life. Undoubtedly, the Cheshire girls were even more susceptible to the charms of the young "sailor." There was gossip—unfounded, he assured his father—of an engagement to one of Judge Basset's daughters. I'm not sure how seriously Olmsted took his apprenticeship. Probably not very seriously. "I like Cheshire pretty well," he wrote Abby Clark, but he made no mention of his farming activities. Instead, he recounted local news—an upcoming Valentine's Day tea party—and maudlin gossip. The letter comes alive in one beautiful descriptive passage.

> The effect of the ice on the evergreens is peculiarly rich. There are half a dozen young hemlocks, which I set out by the window here in the fall, and they do appear magnificent. Two of them (as I address you) have bowed their beautiful heads crown'd with fleecy light to the very ground. But where they stretch up out of the shade of the house, how splendidly their dark green feathery spray, waving and trembling with its load of twinkling brilliants, shivers and glistens in the clear bright moonlight— like the green tresses of a mermaid toss'd in the foam of a breaking wave.

This is the earliest writing I have come across in which Olmsted describes not merely a landscape, but a landscape that he has had a hand in creating.

In March he was back in Hartford. Apparently, he didn't feel that there was much more to learn from his uncle, though he was still interested in farming. Frederick Kingsbury, a classmate of John's, had a suggestion. One of his father's neighbors, Joseph Welton, was a young farmer of whom Kingsbury thought highly. Why didn't Frederick spend a few months with the Weltons? Olmsted agreed—he liked Kingsbury and valued his opinion.

Olmsted spent only three months on the Welton farm. Though not a long time, it convinced him that this was indeed the life for him. Farmwork agreed with him. He felt fit. He found he could keep up with "the boss," working all day hoeing potatoes. (He was not a hired hand; John Olmsted paid for his son's apprenticeships.) He boasted to his brother of regularly boxing with one of Welton's men. It was a cheerful household. Joseph and his wife, Mary, were good people, active in community affairs, happy in their marriage. Olmsted confessed to his brother that he would put off his own marriage for another two or three years, until he had a farm of his own. He thought it would be a good idea to be engaged sooner, however, since once he was settled down he would have "no good opportunity of selection." In any event, he hoped to be married before he was twenty-eight. This was a new side of Frederick Olmsted: enthusiasm tempered by planning.

His time on the Welton farm exposed him to a different approach to agriculture. He discovered that there was more to farming than merely outdoor work. Joseph Welton was an educated man—he had taught school before becoming a farmer. Running his farm and nursery business according to the latest principles, many of which he read about in the monthly magazine *The Cultivator,* he was, in the language of the times, a "scientific farmer."

According to the 1840 census, almost 90 percent of Americans lived in rural areas. The majority of these people were farmers. But between 1810 and 1840 agriculture in the northeast United States underwent a major change. As cities and towns provided new markets for foodstuffs, subsistence farming was being replaced by commercial agriculture. At the same time, the traditional farms of the Northeast faced new competition from the more productive farms of the Midwest. Midwestern farmers could ship their grains and livestock to Eastern cities by railroad and canal. Perishable products, however, could not be shipped such distances. So, farmers in New York and New England began to specialize in milk, butter, cheese, vegetables, and fruits, establishing dairy herds and planting orchards. Commercialization and specialization required new knowledge of fertilizers, plant nutrition, and field drainage, a knowledge based not on traditional practice but on science. Scientific farming was pioneered in Britain, but thanks to horticultural societies—and to magazines like *The Cultivator*—it spread rapidly in the United States. This type of farming, based on learning and investment capital, required a different kind of farmer: part businessman, part applied scientist.

Olmsted understood business, and applied science suited him to a tee. He became an avid reader of *The Cultivator.* Although he didn't see himself as a scholar, in fact his active intellect demanded to be engaged. Scientific farming provided the right blend of theory and practice. He confessed to Charles Brace:

> For myself, I have every reason to be satisfied with my prospects. I grow more contented—or more fond of my business every day. Really, for a man that has any inclination for Agriculture the occupation is very interesting. And if you look closely, you will be surprised to see how much honorable attention and investigation is being connected with it.

If he wanted to be a scientific farmer, he would need some formal training. In the fall of 1845 he left Welton's farm and, after a brief sojourn in Hartford, traveled to New Haven. He intended to sit in on classes at Yale, although since he was not a regular student there is no record of which lectures he attended. Yale offered a chance to spend some time with his brother and his circle of friends. The latter included, in particular, Charles Loring Brace, Frederick Kingsbury, and Charles Trask. In a contemporary studio photograph of the whole group, Brace, a rawboned youth, stares intently at the camera. Trask and Kingsbury have noncommittal looks. John Olmsted leans on Kingsbury, with his arm cocked on his hip and a coy half-smile on his face. He is strikingly handsome, with dark hair and large eyes. Frederick sits next to Brace, with his hand around his shoulder and his head turned away from the camera as he looks toward his friend. Unaccountably, Frederick alone is wearing leather gloves. Like the others, his hair is fashionably long. The photographer has placed an open book and a newspaper in the foreground. The five are dressed alike, in dark suits. But their patterned vests and floppy cravats give them a romantic air.

"A most uncommon set of common friends," Brace called them. Their similar costumes masked different backgrounds, and different futures. Trask, whose father was a sea captain, was intending to be a minister. Brace, four years younger than Olmsted, was a formidable athlete. His father was a teacher who became head of the Hartford Female Seminary and later edited the *Courant*. His aunt was married to Lyman Beecher, a well-known clergyman. Brace's family was poorer than that of the Olmsted brothers, but his intellectual background was more sophisticated. He was intensely religious and would eventually go on to Yale Divinity School and Union Theological Seminary. Kingsbury was more easygoing. Like Olmsted, he had received little formal education, but he made up for it with his quick and lively intelligence. He eventually became a local politician and a banker. If Brace was an idealist, Kingsbury was a pragmatist. It is easy to see how both would become Olmsted's close friends—they reflected his own dual propensities.

New Haven provided a more stimulating social atmosphere than Hartford. There were literary soirées, for example, to which Yale students were sometimes invited. At one of these evenings, at the home of the governor of Connecticut, Olmsted met Elizabeth Baldwin, the governor's daughter. He was impressed by her social graces, and by her prettiness. She was better educated than most young women of his acquaintance, and that, too, attracted him. They saw each other several times, but he was unable to pursue their friendship. That fall, he suffered a series of fainting spells. His father, with John Hull's ill health already weighing heavily on his mind, was concerned. Finally, in January, he ordered his son home.

CHAPTER EIGHT

Farming

OLMSTED FOLLOWED A REGIMEN of cold baths and physical exercise—chiefly horseback riding—to build up his strength. One day, outside his father's store on Main Street, Olmsted met Lizzie Baldwin, who was in Hartford visiting friends. Olmsted offered to accompany her. "I walked down in earnest & close conversation with her, westside Broadway time, twelve meridian, all white kid-dom creaking in their new boots," he excitedly wrote Brace. "Governor's daughter. Excellent princess. She's a dove. Whew! I shall fill up my letter with her." They saw each other several more times. At the end of the week, she left word that she was returning to New Haven and hoped to see him before departing. Emboldened, he asked her to go for a carriage ride. She agreed. They drove to West Hartford. "Had a good time, but no sentiment or confidential stuff at least—but a few sentences. Concert that night, fine." He was smitten. But the dearth of "confidential stuff" did not bode well. It seemed that he had misinterpreted her interest, for when he wrote to her to ask if she would correspond with him, he was rebuffed. He soon had a chance to press his suit in person. During the spring of 1846, the young people of Connecticut were in the throes of a religious revival. When Mary Ann Olmsted, who herself had been "awakened" twenty years earlier, learned that John Hull, together with Brace and Kingsbury, was actively engaged in the revival, she urged her stepson Frederick to join him in New Haven. He didn't need much persuading.

He saw Lizzie often during two subsequent visits to New Haven. She gave him a book for Christmas but was reluctant to move beyond friendship. Of course, without prospects or position, Olmsted was hardly a prize. But Lizzie was no snob. Later, she would turn down an eminently eligible suitor—a rich Boston businessman—and, ignoring her parents' wishes, marry a graduate student five years her junior. She was as strong-willed as Olmsted, which surely was part of what brought them together. But she did not fall in love with him. He was "right smack & square on dead in love with her—beached & broken backed," he confessed to his brother. At this time, he was falling in and out of love at the drop of a hat. In the same letter he also declared himself half in love with a dancing partner, Sarah Cook, and sang the praises of Olivia Day, the daughter of the president of Yale College. Still, Elizabeth Baldwin was more than a youthful infatuation. Years later he reminded her: "You lifted me a good deal out of my constitutional shyness and helped more than you can think to rouse a sort of scatter-brained pride and to make me realize that my secluded life, country breeding, and miseducation were not such bars to an 'intellectual life' as I was in the habit of supposing."

His ardor cooled. He was deeply involved in the religious revival. The essence of Congregationalist revivals was the rite of personal conversion. This intense process, which could take weeks, subjected the individual to the prayers and exhortations of his friends and ultimately produced what was described as the acute experience of God's grace, the awakening. Despite his childhood experiences with clergymen, Olmsted was earnestly interested in religion. In long conversations with Lizzie, she urged him on. But he remained indecisive. When Brace assured him that he, too, had doubts, Olmsted responded with a maritime metaphor: "Why, bless you, I'm in a real old bank fog and becalmed without steering way, at that, almost. But the sun does shine through occasionally." Both Brace and Kingsbury succumbed to Elizabeth Baldwin's fervor and were converted; so was John Hull, the least religious of the group. Eventually, Olmsted, too, proclaimed himself saved. It's not easy to judge the authenticity of his awakening. It must have been a confused moment, what with the emotional encouragement of his close friends, his desire to please his parents, and his feelings for Lizzie. In any case, his conversion—if conversion it was—was incomplete. After making a public profession of faith, converts were expected to formally join a particular church. Olmsted never did.

He remained preoccupied with farming. He was looking for a large farm where he could continue his apprenticeship and learn more of scientific agriculture. He had corresponded with George Geddes, whose three-hundred-acre farm, Fairmount, had just been awarded first prize by the

New York State Agricultural Society. Olmsted wanted to meet Geddes, who lived in Camillus, New York—near Syracuse—before he finally made up his mind. In April he traveled to New York, where he could catch a steamer up the Hudson River to Newburgh, Albany, and then on to Camillus. In New York, he dropped in to see his old friends at Benkard and Hutton. James Benkard volunteered a letter of introduction to his father-in-law, who owned a farm in Newburgh. Olmsted stopped at the Sailor's Home for news of old shipmates. He played tourist, visiting the new Trinity Church and browsing in bookstores. He treated himself to a breakfast at the Astor House, a fancy haircut, and a new plaid summer cap. In the evening, the dapper gentleman-farmer-to-be boarded a steamboat, the *Santa Claus*, for the first leg of his journey.

The editorial offices of *The Cultivator* were in Newburgh, and Olmsted had an appointment to meet its publisher, Luther Tucker, from whom he hoped to get advice about model farms. By coincidence, Olmsted arrived as Tucker was conversing with an intense young man he had recently hired to edit a new magazine, to be called *The Horticulturist*. That man was Andrew Jackson Downing, remembered today chiefly by historians, but in the 1840s a celebrated figure. His role as a prominent arbiter of public taste can be likened to that of Terence Conran in Britain, or Martha Stewart in the United States. In 1841, when Downing was only twenty-six, he published *A Treatise on the Theory and Practice of Landscape Gardening, Adapted to North America*. It was the first American book on landscape gardening that combined philosophy with practicality—both the why and the how. It also introduced its middle-class readers to the picturesque British approach to gardening. Downing was an articulate writer, and his *Treatise*, reprinted numerous times, was a great popular success. Although he was trained as a horticulturist—his family ran a nursery in Newburgh—his second book, *Cottage Residences*, was a collection of house plans designed by himself and others. He stressed an informal approach to architecture. The practical and attractive house plans were widely imitated, and in no small part thanks to Downing, Carpenter Gothic and the Hudson River Bracketed Style became staples of many Victorian private and commercial builders. Downing's celebrity attracted many commissions for private gardens and estates. At thirty-one he was considered the national authority on gardening and domestic architecture.

Olmsted was excited to meet the famous man, although landscape gardening was not uppermost on his mind. The chief subject of conversation must have been scientific farming—Downing had just published his encyclopedic *Fruits and Fruit Trees of America*. Olmsted's knowledge of agriculture evidently made a good impression. Downing asked him to keep in touch—*The Horticulturist* would be the first to publish Olmsted's writing and encourage the young farmer's literary endeavors. Tucker confirmed that Fairmount was indeed a leading example of scientific farming and provided a personal letter to George Geddes.

Olmsted spent only six months at Fairmount, but it was an important part of his education. Geddes's interests were as broad as Olmsted's; he enjoyed conversation and debate. He was relatively young—thirty-seven. His father had been a prominent engineer who had surveyed the course of the Erie Canal. Although George had studied law, he, too, had been engaged in civil engineering: railroad construction, coal mining, and land drainage. Olmsted had never met anyone like him. David Brooks and Joseph Welton had been accomplished farmers, but Geddes was a true gentleman farmer. That is, he combined scientific farming with a gentlemanly way of life. The latter involved maintaining genteel standards at home—tea was served each afternoon, and "*silver forks every day,*" Olmsted boasted to his father. Being a gentleman also meant a responsibility to the common good. While Olmsted was with him, Geddes was overseeing the construction of the first plank road (a wooden precursor of paving) in the United States. He was active in the local agricultural society and was also a prominent lay leader in the local Methodist church.

George Geddes became another in a long line of older men who befriended Olmsted. He was his mentor—and a model. Olmsted undertook an irrigation project for the farm's vegetable garden. He accompanied Geddes to local fairs and wrote a report for the agricultural society on farming utensils. He taught a Sunday-school class at two different neighborhood churches and assembled a library for one of them. "I think my taste for study and reading has rather increased," he wrote Brace. He read many farm journals and, of course, Downing's *Horticulturist*. An abolitionist, a pacifist, and an advocate of world peace, Geddes introduced Olmsted to the peace-reform journal *Christian Citizen* and the antislavery newspaper *True American*.

"This has been a good place for me. I have looked on and talked more than I've worked, but I've considerable faith that I shall make a good farmer," Olmsted informed Brace. His conversations with Geddes had reinforced his confidence in his choice of a career. Being away from Hartford and New Haven also gave him some perspective. He still cast wistful glances in the direction of Lizzie Baldwin. "Does Miss (you know) feel any way delicate about me?" he inquired of Kingsbury. There was some talk of her visiting Camillus, but nothing came of it. By then he was distracted by Sarah Porter, the pretty eighteen-year-old niece of Geddes's wife, Maria. "You ask who Sara [sic] Porter is," he wrote his father. "She's a plaguy fine girl I calculate. And my business over there is probably to fall in love with her." Nothing came of that, either.

Although he corresponded regularly with all his friends at Yale, the relative isolation of Camillus allowed him to develop more independent religious views. He found Geddes's Methodism too narrow. He did come close to formally joining the Presbyterian congregation where he taught Sunday school, but changed his mind at the last minute. He thought he might became an Episcopalian because that faith appeared to him less doctrinaire. He was attracted by Unitarianism. Finally, he confessed to Fred Kingsbury, it was unlikely that he would join any church. He went on to make this rather priggish affirmation of his beliefs.

> I will think and act right, I will find Truth and be governed by it, so far as I can, with the light God is pleased to give me. I will be accountable to none but God for my opinions and actions. Trusting in Him for light I will not fear for nor care for what man thinks of, or does towards me. I am liable to mistake myself—but so far as I *do* judge myself, this is my paramount governing principle. I hope so anyway, and except from the consciousness of yielding to temptation, and thinking and acting contrary to my own more solemn, more rational, and better intentions—as I often do most wickedly—what can I be sorry for?

Olmsted's skepticism about the value of religion was influenced by the author he had been reading that summer—Thomas Carlyle. The great writer had come to the public's attention in 1837 with his history of the French Revolution, and at the time that Olmsted read him he had just established his literary reputation with the publication of the *Life and Letters of Oliver Cromwell*. Olmsted chose to read an earlier work, *Sartor Resartus*. Perhaps only someone with an educational background as irregular as Olmsted's could be drawn to this strangely complex book. Combining philosophy, thinly veiled autobiography, and romance, *Sartor Resartus* ("The Tailor Re-Tailored") defies classification. It purports to be Carlyle's abridgment of a much longer book, *Clothes, their Origin and Influence,* the life's work of Professor Diogenes Teufelsdröckh of the University of Weissnichtwo. "So have we endeavored, from the enormous, amorphous Plum-pudding, more like a Scottish Haggis, which Herr Teufelsdröckh had kneaded for his fellow mortals, to pick-out the choicest Plums, and present them separately on a cover of our own," explained Carlyle. To complicate matters still further, *Sartor Resartus* contained additional biographical material and "interviews" with the elusive Teufelsdröckh himself. A haggis, indeed.

The German professor was an obvious fabrication—*Teufelsdröckh* is "devil's dung"; Weissnichtwo is "nobody-knows-where." But *Sartor Resartus,* despite its sometimes harsh humor, was not intended to be a parody. Carlyle described the material world as clothing, covering the invisible spiritual world that lay beneath. The material world was shabby and worn and needed to be replaced. This, according to Carlyle, accounted for the pessimism and confusion of his time. The answer was for the individual to rediscover his ethical and moral center through a transcendent experience, something akin to religious conversion. This would occur not by subscribing to religious dogma, however, but through simple, everyday work. "Produce! Produce!" Teufelsdröckh/Carlyle railed in characteristic pulpit-thumping style. "Were it but the pitifullest infinitesimal fraction of a Product, produce it, in God's name! T'is the utmost thou hast in thee; out with it, then. Up, up! Whatsoever thy hand findeth to do, do it with thy whole might. Work while it is called Today; for the Night cometh, wherein no man can work."

Sartor Resartus had been neither a critical nor a popular success. It first appeared as a series of magazine articles, and when Carlyle finally found someone to publish the book, it was received with "unqualified dissatisfaction." The British public didn't know what to make of the author's alternating comic and solemn tone, nor of his idiosyncratic, mannered prose. The book did better in America. It certainly appealed to Olmsted, who described Carlyle as "the greatest genius in the world. . . . I perfectly wonder and stand awe-struck as I would at a Hurricane."

Carlyle presents a view of the world that is romantic and idealistic—such books have always appealed to the young. I remember reading Herman Hesse's *Magister Ludi* and J. D. Salinger's *Catcher in the Rye* when I was in my twenties and thinking them extraordinarily profound. I suspect I would not find them so today. Still, such books do mark us. This was the case with Olmsted. *Sartor Resartus* dealt with questions that he was asking himself. (Curiously, Teufelsdröckh even suffered a rebuff from a highborn lady, just as Olmsted had from Lizzie Baldwin.) The hardheaded Scottish Puritanism at the core of Carlyle's thinking would have been familiar to a New Englander. So would the notion of personal conversion. The critique of organized religion mirrored Olmsted's own thinking and provided a way out of his religious dilemma. He embraced the idea that work and obligation to others could lead to redemption, a philosophy that would guide him for the rest of his life.*

Olmsted's summer at Camillus was interrupted by a two-week vacation trip that he took with his father and brother to Niagara Falls, Montreal, Quebec City, and Lake Champlain. He returned to Fairmount for one more month while considering whether to work on another farm or to start out on his own. Geddes encouraged him to establish himself nearby, but Olmsted wanted to return to Connecticut. He had his eye on a farm that had come up for sale on the shore of Long Island Sound, at Sachem's Head, about ten miles east of New Haven. The seaside location undoubtedly attracted him, as did the proximity to New Haven and Hartford. Sachem's Head, only a few miles from the village of North Guilford, was familiar territory, the site of family summer holidays and in an area that he knew well from boyhood rambles while he had boarded with the kindly Reverend Mr. Whitmore.

His father gave him the money to buy the farm. In March 1847 he moved from Hartford to Sachem's Head. His brother, John, spiritedly described the scene:

> Fred went off in great style yesterday. He had loaded a horse-cart with tools and 'fixins' and bought a big New-found-land dog, which was chained to the cart drawn by the pony (a wee bit of a Canadian animal)—a yoke of big oxen tied behind and Pepper, the white terrier, seeing to everything and taking an interest generally. I overhauled him at Wetherfield on Jerry, and, adding him behind the cart and driving the cart while Fred gave his undivided attention to hurrying up the cattle— "Whoa, gee up, get along, stock." Didn't people look—and stop and ask—"been buying?" Neptune, the dog, got into the cart at Middletown

---

*Two years later, Olmsted jokingly referred to his farm on Staten Island as Entepfuhl. Entepfuhl ("duck pond") was the name Carlyle gave to Teufelsdröckh's childhood village.

and we were followed by a regular crowd who thought it was a bear show. I saw him safely through Middletown, and left him at 3 o'clock, going towards Guilford at 2 miles the hour.

Fred is quite excited about farming and is going into it like a trooper—a retired trooper, I mean.

Author's note: I have not taken liberties with Olmsted's biography; his words are his own, his opinions are those that he expressed to others, usually in letters. Yet I also want to see the world through his eyes. The vignette that follows— and there will be others—is based on material evidence; Olmsted was writing a letter on that night and it was stormy. His thoughts and feelings are, of course, imagined.

Great Point, Sachem's Head, Connecticut

Tuesday, October 12, 1847

It is late at night. The wind is howling. A storm blows from the south, across the Sound, and slams into the Connecticut coast. Near the shore stands a lone farmhouse. There is no moon, and the building would be barely discernible in the darkness were it not for the faint glow visible of a ground-floor window. Inside, Olmsted sits at a table, alone, writing a letter. There is a temporary lull, and it's suddenly quiet enough so that he can hear the scratching of his pen and the restless movements of Neptune. Minna, the cat, and her kittens are asleep in a box in the corner. The wind resumes. A great gust rattles the windows and dislodges pieces of mortar that fall down the chimney. The house creaks and groans. Surely it can't be blown over, he thinks.

He dislikes this house. It is more than eighty years old and in disrepair. Worse, it's downright forlorn. The man who built it was a disgraced Guilford Congregational minister, driven out of the village by a charge of "grossly licentious & scandalous conduct." His poverty—and despair—are evident in the house. It has none of the picturesque qualities described in Downing's books. Never mind. He has been sketching a new house. It's part of his plan to make this into a model farm. In his mind's eye he sees the land remade. In front of the house there's a large lawn sloping down to the water's edge. Its green expanse is broken up by clumps of trees. A line of low, thick shrubbery curves from the house toward the shore. There's also a new barn and an orchard. Next week he intends to go buy fruit trees from Downing's nursery in Newburgh. Perhaps Downing will be able to recommend an architect who can look over his house sketches. But first he has to get the farm in working order. The previous owner has let things go, but all that's needed is a little work. Actually, it's more than a little. Since moving here in March, he and his hired man have spent the entire spring hauling up seaweed from the beach and fertilizing the fields. They have pruned the gnarled old apple trees and planted corn, wheat, barley, and potatoes. He hopes they will fetch a good price in New York.

He goes back to his letter. He is writing to Brace, who is back in New Haven. Charley graduated, taught in country schools for a year, and is now at the Yale Divinity School. As for Kingsbury, he, too, has continued at Yale—ever the more practical of the two, Fred has chosen the law. He wonders what they're doing tonight. Probably studying. He remembers his months at Yale. He was never good at studying, but he did enjoy the conversations and debates. There hasn't been much of that in his life recently. He wryly recalls last year asking Fred, "Do you think I shall be contented on a farm—fifteen miles from New Haven, and three miles from neighbors? I mean civilized ones, gentlemen, doctors, lawyers, and ministers." Actually, about a dozen houses stand on Sachem's Head, enough families to support the small schoolhouse. But as he guessed, his immediate neighbors are sturdy, simple farmers. He knows that they find his beautification efforts foolish. "Setting out bushes," one calls it, and he can hear the barely hidden scorn in their voices. Nor has he met any civilized gentlemen in the village. He has introduced himself to the Congregational minister—he attends the church on the town green every Sunday—but the pastor has not turned out to be a kindred spirit. On the whole he is disappointed in Guilford. It lacks the kind of social and intellectual life to which he has become accustomed.

Thank goodness he has been able to find entertaining company elsewhere. His social life centers on nearby Sachem's Head House. The two-hundred-and-fifty-room hotel is the largest summer resort on the Connecticut coast. He remembers staying here with his family as a boy. It is a favorite of proper people from Hartford, who come down by stagecoach on the new turnpike; visitors from New York and New Haven arrive by steamboat. He often runs into friends and acquaintances. What a time he had there last summer. He'd met his old Hartford neighbor, the Reverend Horace Bushnell, and taken him out sailing for two hours. It had been a chance to talk theology with the eminent *clergyman. Later, the two had played ninepins against George Geddes, also staying at the hotel, and Judge Bronson, the impressive chief justice of the New York State Supreme Court. Olmsted and Bushnell trounced the distinguished pair. Geddes, who scored lowest, was quite put out by Bushnell's victory.*

The Head House is a short walk from his farm. He goes there frequently, especially on those evenings when there is dancing. His main partner all summer has been eighteen-year-old Ellen Day of Hartford. People were even starting to talk about them as a possible couple. He likes Ellen well enough, but it is really her older sister Mary who has his heart. He has known Mary for some years but fell in love with her only the year before, after Lizzie Baldwin had turned him down.

His father, too, came down to Sachem's Head House, in July, bringing all his children with him. They were accompanied by his cousin Fanny and Uncle Owen, with whom he had stayed in upstate New York as a six-year-old. It had been fun to see them all, especially his brother. John was happy to be in the hotel. He had visited earlier and stayed at the farm, but didn't seem to like it much. Well, John was hardly in the best of spirits, what with his recent eye problems, but it was a pity that he couldn't be more enthusiastic about his brother's plans for the farm.

His father is likewise unimpressed with his agricultural efforts. His father seems to be skeptical that the cost of the improvements, not to mention the additional expense of building a new house, can ever be recovered. The amount of productive land is simply too small, he points out, and the cost of shipping produce to New York cuts into profits. It is true that most of the promontory that makes up Great Point is granite, making less than forty of his seventy-five acres arable. This is a lot smaller than the other farms he and his father visited. But Sachem's Head could be such a beautiful farm! George Geddes thought so when he came to inspect it prior to the sale last year; so did everyone else whom he had asked for advice. Now his father—who, after all, is paying for everything—is having second thoughts. He's even hinting that rather than throw good money after bad, it might be a better idea to buy a larger, more productive farm.

Sometimes he thinks his father may be right. Perhaps he did make a mistake moving here. It's not the farm—he is still sure he can make a go of it. He's not afraid of the work. Nor of the weather. He is willing to put up with occasional storms in return for the pleasure of sailing, swimming, and the views of the sea. But he's lonely. Since the end of August the hotel has been closed. No more evening dances, no more teas, no more conversation. His everyday life has become cramped and narrow. He works, eats, and sleeps. The hired man,

Henry Davis, is a nice enough sort, but not someone he can talk with about anything other than farm business. The field hand and the maidservant, who live on the second floor, are even less loquacious. Alas, Davis's wife is not a good cook. The couple have the room next door. He can hear their baby crying.

A gust of wind rattles the shutters and drives the rain hard against the windowpanes. He goes outside, partly to check on the barn, and partly just to enjoy the blustery weather. He looks back to the rocky promontory, west of the house. He shudders to remember that this is said to be the site of the oak tree where a Pequot sachem's severed head had once been exposed to serve as a warning to his fellow tribesmen with whom the English settlers were battling. Probably just a story, and two hundred years old now, although he has found a weathered old oak stump on the bluff. He walks toward the shore. Across the water he can see the dark hulk of the hotel. He can also see the white foam of the surf. There is a low booming sound, far away. The locals say it is the roar of the breakers on the exposed Atlantic shore of Long Island. The storm reminds him of his time at sea. God have mercy on sailors on a night like this, he thinks. He goes back inside, turns down the lamp, and goes to bed. Nep snores contentedly.

CHAPTER NINE

More Farming

DURING THE SUMMER that John Olmsted and his children stayed at Sachem's Head House, one of the other guests was Samuel Bowne of New York, whose wife had inherited a farm on the death of her father, Dr. Samuel Akerly. The Akerly farm was on the so-called South Side of Staten Island, in the vicinity of Eltingville. John Olmsted already knew about the farm, which had been on the market for two years. He expressed an interest to Bowne, who had extended an invitation to visit the farm, although nothing further was decided at that point.

Meanwhile, Frederick Olmsted the was busy improving his farm. In August *The Horticulturist* printed his letter (his first formally published writing) that asked about growing fruit trees in exposed, coastal locations. "I intend to set an orchard, next autumn," he explained. Downing's printed response advised liberal manuring and cultivation and recommended several apple varieties particularly suited to the seashore. That fall Olmsted harvested his potatoes. "Shall have a better crop than my neighbors," he informed Fred Kingsbury. "I shall send a parcel of them to New York at 37½ cents." In October he traveled to Newburgh and purchased seventy-five apple trees and sixty quinces from Downing's nursery. On the way back, he stopped in New York. He met the well-known architect Alexander Jackson Davis, to discuss plans for a new house.* Davis did not think much of Olmsted's sketches, but presumably as a favor to his friend Downing, he agreed to prepare a design. By early November, Olmsted had planted the fruit trees. As part of his beautification efforts, he also put in a dozen ornamental trees near the shore. They

---

*Davis, Downing's friend and frequent collaborator, had contributed to the *Treatise*. He was a prolific residential architect and one of the earliest champions of the early Gothic Revival.

"make quite a pretty show," he proudly wrote his brother, although he worried that he might lose many of them on such an exposed site.

Just after settling in at Sachem's Head, Olmsted had written to his brother: "The farm generally pleases me well. There is a good deal more beautiful and valuable wood on it than I had supposed. But then—again—there's more rocks, and there are not so many apple-trees, and the barn and house are in worse condition than I had thought them to be." It is a realistic assessment; he did not underestimate what needed to be done. Olmsted was a novice, but knowledgeable about farming and not unprepared. George Geddes, a sound judge of both character and agriculture, recognized Olmsted's abilities and treated him as a protégé. Luther Tucker, the publisher of *The Cultivator*, took him seriously, as did Andrew Jackson Downing. It is possible—although improbable—that Olmsted would have made such a serious error of judgment as to establish himself on a farm that was commercially unproductive.* But George Geddes, a sober individual and a seasoned farmer, was unlikely to have encouraged his young friend in any rash course. Nevertheless, the rocky point was hardly an ideal or easy site. As his brother sardonically put it, "There had been some vague doubt whether Fred could ever make out to live off the Sachem's Head farm, suggested perhaps by the fact that some $1000. had been expended on it to enable the total crops to be worth $200."

When I visited Sachem's Head, I understood why Olmsted had fallen in love with the place. The farms—of which there were several—are long gone. But the irregular, boulder-lined shore, the tidal creeks and salt-water marshes, and the gentle hillocks are all still there. It is not merely pretty, it is heart-stoppingly beautiful. I tried to find Olmsted's house. Unfortunately, about seven years ago it was so extensively altered that, for all practical purposes, it has disappeared. The view from what would have been Olmsted's porch looks across a sheltered cove to another peninsula, Long Point. On the high ground between the two stood Sachem's Head House (it burned down in 1865). The promontory of Great Point is gone, too, quarried level for its granite, which proved to be the most profitable product of this land. By the 1880s, though, the same beautiful scenery that had drawn the young Olmsted here had helped to turn Sachem's Head into a successful summer colony, complete with its own yacht club.

---

*The farm was certainly productive when Olmsted bought it. The deed specifically reserves from sale "all the Rye now standing on Sd. land."

Today it is a community of understated but obviously expensive year-round houses, scattered picturesquely across the landscape.

The scenic qualities of the farm did not impress Olmsted's father. He thought that the cost of improvements, such as a new house or more attractive landscaping, would have little effect on the financial value of the farm. He had occasionally invested in land, and as a businessman he expected his investments to be productive. For example, after he bought a ten-acre woodlot for his two sons, he had Frederick, who was apprenticing on the Brooks farm in nearby Cheshire, spend a week there cutting trees. The trees were to be sold, and he expected—and received—a detailed accounting. So, too, with the Sachem's Head farm. It belonged to Frederick, but on the unspoken condition that he manage it to his father's satisfaction. In this case, parental largess came with strings attached.

John Olmsted was interested in scientific farming—he subscribed to several agricultural journals—but he did not have confidence in his son's abilities to turn Sachem's Head into a model farm. When Olmsted described his plans for the future, his father remembered the enthusiastic youth who had wanted to be a surveyor one year and a merchant the next. It is not uncommon for parents—especially loving parents—to fail to realize that their adult children are children no longer, and to treat them accordingly. For most of us, receiving unsolicited critiques of our driving—or of our housekeeping—is a temporary inconvenience, nothing more. But when we are financially dependent on our parents, as Olmsted was, the inconvenience may have graver implications.

In mid-December 1847 Olmsted dutifully accompanied his brother to Staten Island to look over the Akerly farm. They returned to Hartford on Christmas Eve. A few days after the holiday, Olmsted and his father returned to New York and finalized the purchase. Three weeks later, Olmsted signed over the Sachem's Head farm to his father, "for the consideration of four thousand dollars," which was the price he had originally paid.* It is unclear why Olmsted sold the farm to his father. One possible explanation is that to encourage his son to move, John Olmsted may have agreed to buy the Sachem's Head farm, thus providing his son with funds to purchase the Akerly farm. But the new farm was larger—125 acres—and more expensive, $13,000 (almost $400,000 in modern

---

*Six years after buying the farm from his son, John Olmsted sold it to Dan L. Benton Jr., a local farmer, for $4,000, the same amount it had cost to buy.

dollars). Where did the rest of the money come from? "Father bought it," was how John Hull described it to Kingsbury. That makes it sound like an outright gift; in fact, there was a mortgage. A decade later, in a letter to his father, Olmsted would mention leasing the farm to a tenant, "for the interest on mortgage & taxes and ¼ fruit." Another letter makes it clear that the mortgage was held by John Olmsted himself. That would explain his son's regular and detailed reports of his farming activities over the years.

The Akerly farm was also by the sea, which appealed to Olmsted, and Staten Island was less remote than Sachem's Head. With New York so close there was the promise of a more active social life. In March Olmsted boarded a sloop from the Sachem's Head dock. He took what he could—tools, furniture, the remaining potato crop, and, of course, Nep and Minna—with him.

He settled down to a more comfortable life on Tosomock Farm, as he eventually called it.* The Davises were not invited to accompany him. Instead, his favorite aunt, Maria (a spinster), moved in to act as house-keeper and to oversee the servants: two maids and a boy. In addition, there were six regular field hands and occasionally one or two harvest hands. The large house was two stories high, with an attic where the help slept. There was a kitchen wing and a veranda on two sides. The lower floor, of thick stone walls, dated back two hundred years to the original Huguenot settlers; the upper stories, of wood, had been added later.

The nine bedrooms were put to good use. John Olmsted and his entire family came for most of the first summer, as they would do regularly for the next seven years. Olmsted's father, fifty-seven, intended to retire soon; using the Staten Island farm as a summer retreat must have figured in his decision to encourage his son to buy the farm. Olmsted's brother, who moved to New York in the fall and began studying at the College of Physicians and Surgeons, came on Sundays and holidays. He was often accompanied by Charles Brace, who was in New York completing his theological studies and teaching part-time at Rutger's Institute. Charles Trask, also studying theology, was a visitor, too. A less frequent guest was

---

*I have been unable to identify the source of Tosomock. Perhaps it is a combination of "toss" and "amock," which would mean "flinging oneself headlong," a good characterization of Olmsted's frame of mind.

Fred Kingsbury, who had moved to Waterbury, Connecticut, to care for his ailing mother. Brace (in a letter to Kingsbury) has left a description of those happy summer visits.

> Just wear your feet out, Fred, in tramping over the hot pavements of New York, for a day, and become thoroughly stunned by the unceasing din; then let a kind hobgoblin transplant you to a cool piazza into a comfortable armchair and slippers, with a quiet country scene before you of meadows and cattle and grain-fields, and beyond, the blue waves and the white sails, and, "some more peaches in that basket yet, Charley," and you will get a faint idea of my feelings.

Olmsted found life more convivial, and not only because his house was large enough to accommodate visiting family and friends. Staten Island was beginning to attract permanent as well as summer residents from Manhattan, particularly after the outbreaks of yellow fever and cholera in 1832, and the Great Fire of 1835. Most of the development on Staten Island was on the north and east shore. The so-called South Side, where Olmsted lived, consisted chiefly of farms, many of them belonging to wealthy New Yorkers. His neighbors included William Henry Vanderbilt, the wealthy eldest son of the famous "Commodore"; the prominent civic leader and poet William Cullen Bryant, who was also owner and editor of the *Evening Post;* the book publisher George Palmer Putnam; and Judge William Emerson, brother of the famous writer. Olmsted was at home with these people, who represented the kind of society he was used to in Hartford and New Haven. They, in turn, recognized him as one of their own.

Another of his nearby neighbors was Dr. Cyrus Perkins, a prosperous retired New York surgeon whom Olmsted met soon after arriving on Staten Island. Perkins's household at Holly Hill Farm consisted of his wife and an orphaned granddaughter with whom Olmsted became friendly. "Just the thing for a rainy day" is how he described her to Kingsbury. "Not to fall in love with, but to talk to. A real earnest thinker and only 19." Actually she was barely eighteen, but Mary Cleveland Bryant Perkins was exceptionally bright. She had grown up in celebrated literary company: Daniel Webster was a relative, William Cullen Bryant's wife was her godmother. Orphaned at the age of eight, she had grown up with her well-to-do grandparents, whose household had provided her with a grounding in both art and culture. Pretty, petite, and lively, she soon became an intimate of the Olmsted family, so much so that she was invited to spend that Christmas in Hartford. She has left us with this sketch of Olmsted at Tosomock Farm:

> Frederick was at this time 26 years of age full of life and fun. He threw himself into farming with enthusiasm, introduced system and order to his men, expecting for one thing that at knocking off time every tool used should be returned to its appointed place and that every "chore" should be done at the hour fixed, the foreman to report progress before going in to supper. He engaged in planting and dealing in fruit-trees, pears principally, which he imported from France. All was done in a simple inexpensive way, using the old buildings on the place and practicing rigid economy.

There was much to do, for the land was in a poor state. The house, on a slight rise, overlooked Raritan Bay. The fields in front of the house sloped down about a quarter of a mile to the water's edge. Across the bay one could see the lighthouse of Sandy Hook, and the Navesink Hills of New Jersey. The farm stretched about a mile from the shore to the Main Road (now called Amboy Road). The back part of the farm, near the road, was heavily wooded. Olmsted created some scenic effects. He moved the barns and outbuildings away from the house to a more discreet location behind a knoll and rerouted the approach road to the house so that it followed a graceful curve. He sodded the area around a utilitarian barnyard pond at the rear of the house and added water plants to further enhance the scenic effect. "Thus, with a few strokes and at a small expense he transformed the place from a very dirty, disagreeable farmyard to a gentleman's house," wrote Kingsbury.

Tosomock Farm is long gone. It was productive until the 1880s, although no longer owned by Olmsted. Then, since Staten Island had grown popular with vacationing New Yorkers, the farm was turned into a summer resort known as the Woods of Arden. The grounds had facilities for picnicking, boating, swimming; the farmhouse was converted into an inn. Twenty years later, the land was subdivided into residential lots and developed as Seaside Estates. I wanted to see the place where Olmsted would spend—on and off—more than seven years of his life. I parked my car on Hylan Boulevard, a road that did not exist in Olmsted's time and now runs across what would have been the front of the property. Despite its name it is really a mundane commercial strip, densely lined with suburban bungalows, garages, and drive-in restaurants. The street number that I was looking for was indicated on a faded sign. A grass-covered track led into a dense forest, presumably what has survived of the Arden woods. I walked up the track with a growing sense of anticipation, for I could see the outline of a white building among the dense trees. It was a house. The porch had long since rotted away, and the roof had been altered at one end, but I had no doubt that this was the Olmsted farmhouse, a sketch of which has survived. A large, old cedar of Lebanon grew in front of the house, most likely one of a number that Olmsted had imported from France and planted in the winter of 1850 as part of his early landscaping improvements. That the building exterior was almost intact and had not been self-consciously preserved or restored made seeing it all the more moving.

The changes at Tosomock Farm must have impressed his neighbors. Olmsted was consulted by several of them, including William Vanderbilt, about landscaping improvements to their properties. Friendly, literate, energetic, the young bachelor farmer made himself useful in the South Side community. He championed a plank road for the island; drawing on his experience with Geddes, he wrote about the subject for the local newspaper, the *Staten Isler*. He became a trustee of the local school board and a founding member of the county agricultural society. In his capacity as the society's corresponding secretary, he penned an "Appeal to the Citizens of Staten Island," encouraging them to support the society. It concluded:

> We believe [the society] will increase the profit of our labor—enhance the value of our lands—throw a garment of beauty around our homes, and above all, and before all, materially promote Moral and Intellectual Improvement—instructing us in the language of Nature, from whose preaching, while we pursue our grateful labors, we shall learn to receive her Fruits as the bounty, and her Beauty as the manifestation of her Creator.

Ostensibly about farming, the statement is representative of the broad, encompassing vision that Olmsted is beginning to develop. It reflects his reading of Carlyle, Emerson, Ruskin, and Downing. He is trying to combine economics, aesthetics, landscaping, nature, moral and intellectual improvement, and salvation. It is a bewildering mix of ideas, but he is persevering. He is making his own way.

CHAPTER TEN

A Walking Tour
in the Old Country

FOR THE NEXT TWO YEARS Olmsted devoted himself to farming. He is sometimes described as a gentleman farmer. He was certainly a gentleman and his landscaping improvements did have a purely aesthetic purpose, but Tosomock was hardly a hobby farm. He grew corn, hay, cabbages, turnips, and potatoes. After one season he concluded that he could not make a living growing ordinary crops. It cost him more to improve the fields than he could earn from selling the produce. He calculated that fruit trees, on the other hand, would pay for themselves in four years. He decided on pears. He also intended to establish a nursery business. This was a shrewd plan. Olmsted, who thus far had relied on his father's continued generosity to make ends meet, intended to make his farm profitable. But he understood the risks involved in simple farming. Although proximity to New York solved the problem of transportation, without effective means for long-term storage, perishables such as pears had to be sold immediately to avoid spoilage. Competition was fierce and prices were low. Moreover, urban markets had their own peculiar problems. Summer outbreaks of cholera in New York interrupted demand, leaving farmers in the lurch. A nursery business, on the other hand, was less susceptible to market and price fluctuations—trees could stay in the ground and could be shipped easily over longer distances, increasing the potential number of customers. It was a good moment to embark on a nursery business. Thanks to the publications of Downing and others, it had become fashionable to beautify the surroundings of houses, especially in places like Staten Island and the environs of New York where suburban and summer residences were proliferating. So-called landscape gardeners provided this service; they required nurseries that could supply them with ornamental and shade trees.

Olmsted ordered a number of saplings—dwarf pears—from Flushing, while an English neighbor and fellow member of the agricultural society suggested importing trees from Europe. Olmsted investigated shipping costs and calculated that he could make a profit of up to 100 percent. He was enthusiastic about the prospects. "In five years I shall expect to be in receipt of some hundred or two dollars from them . . . and thereafter it will be continually increasing," he wrote Kingsbury. He felt himself well qualified to be a nurseryman; he understood landscape gardening, and he had experience in trade, especially international trade, which he hoped would give him an advantage. He also had sufficient business acumen. Cultivating trees on a commercial scale both appealed to his interest in scientific farming and satisfied his sense of planning and organization.

Only one thing was still missing in Olmsted's life. "He is in the direct want of a wife," his brother observed, "and would marry almost any body that would let him." That was an exaggeration. Olmsted was a romantic. "I want somebody that I can much love and respect," he confessed to Kingsbury, "whose tastes and feelings I shall be tender and regardful of. Don't I. How in this world am I ever going to find her?" Mary and Ellen Day had proved to be brief romances; he had gotten over Lizzie Baldwin. He liked his neighbor's granddaughter Mary Perkins, but no romantic attachment developed. In any case, she seemed more interested in his brother, John, who was a frequent visitor at the farm. Olmsted was not without prospects. "Fred is reading Macaulay loud to Emily Perkins & 'Modern Painters' to Miss Stevens—and is somewhat intoxicated between the two," observed his brother. Emily Perkins (no relation to Mary Perkins) was a pretty Hartford girl of twenty-three whose family Olmsted had known since childhood. Sophia Stevens was a Vermonter who had come to Hartford two years earlier to teach in the high school. She boarded with the Olmsteds and had become a family friend. Her literary tastes were inherited from her father, an innkeeper and mill owner who was also a book collector and antiquarian. Sophia was an art lover, and she introduced Olmsted to John Ruskin's *Modern Painters*. "The Modern Painters improves on acquaintance and Miss Stevens forms an amalgam with it in my heart. She is just the thing to read it or have it read to one by. She is very sensitive to beauty—thoughtful, penetrating, enthusiastic," rhapsodized Olmsted. Sophia was twenty-three, and a serious, independent young woman. She was also a beauty, judging from a later portrait. Perhaps he found this combination intimidating, for he was drawn to

Emily. "I have got very intimate with her and gallantry and joking aside, really think her a very fine girl," he wrote his brother.

There is a photograph of Olmsted in 1850. He cuts quite a dashing figure. He is elegantly attired in a high-buttoned jacket made out of what looks like serge; a white shirt-collar protrudes above the stock that is wound about his neck. Locks of hair fall over his broad brow. The self-confident pose, with the head slightly tilted and the lips pursed, is thoughtful—neither happy nor sad. The unlined, open countenance belies his twenty-eight years. The severity that Katharine Wormeley saw in his face a decade later is only hinted at, although the expressive delicacy she commented on is evident. Altogether he is a most presentable young gentleman.

He accompanied Miss Perkins and Miss Stevens to literary evenings and book clubs during his regular visits to Hartford. (The "reading loud" that his brother commented on was a form of courtship, like going to the movies today.) Olmsted's love of books was genuine. He started to build a library at Tosomock Farm, going to bookshops on his trips to New York, and buying books at auction. "There are a lot of books that are essential to even a common library—or a country tavern parlor—that I have not got," he wrote his brother. "Such buy if you can, without fail." He read on a wide variety of subjects: everything he could find on scientific farming, horticulture, and the cultivation of pear trees; books on landscape scenery such as William Marshall's *Planting and Rural Ornament;* Thomas Babington Macaulay's *History of England;* philosophical and religious tracts, including Bushnell's *God in Christ;* a translation of Schiller's *William Tell.*

He also read travel books. One of his favorites was Benjamin Silliman's *A Journal of Travels in England, Holland and Scotland,* which he had first read as a boy, and which had particular meaning for him ever since he attended Silliman's classes (in geology) at Yale. Travel was much on his mind. Charles Brace and Olmsted's brother, John, had decided to take a trip together to Europe. Brace, who was in mourning for his dear sister Emma, who had died of tuberculosis during the winter of 1850, wanted to get away. He had completed his theological training in New York and would travel and study. John, whose respiratory problems had worsened, was going for his health as much as anything else.

It had been all of six years since Olmsted's return from China, during which time he had stayed put and diligently applied himself to farming.

Not surprisingly, he developed a powerful urge to accompany his brother and best friend on this adventurous undertaking. The problem was that he didn't have sufficient funds, so he found himself, once more, asking his father for money. But it was not just a question of money. Olmsted was aware that in abandoning Tosomock for six months he risked being accused of irresponsibility and of a reversion to the instability that had marked his earlier attempts at finding himself. Although he was twenty-eight, he really wanted parental permission.

He wrote his father a long, impassioned letter that would be almost comical were it not also touching. He starts by confessing, "I exceedingly fear my dangerous liability to enthusiasm," sternly adding, "and I mean to guard against it with all my mind in the future." In fact, the letter is one long burst of untrammeled enthusiasm. Olmsted offers his father argument upon argument, pleading, cajoling, excusing, and rationalizing by turns. Anticipating the criticism that he is absenting himself from the farm, he reasons that he will be away only during the summer, after the planting, which will be early, since he has had the foresight to plow and manure the fields already. He promises to return for the harvest. In any case, he adds, there is no cause for concern since "I have found that my men are all ambitious to do their best when I am absent." He admits that someone will have to be hired to take care of the newly planted trees, but that will only cost ten dollars, and that man will undoubtedly do a better job of it than Frederick himself. He presents his planned tour in an educational light. Think of how much he will learn from English farmers that he can apply to the farm—why, that alone will be worth the cost of the trip! For good measure, he throws in some technical information on English drainage systems. He points out that he has already in hand numerous letters of reference to British nurserymen and farmers. He has thought of practical matters: how much cheaper for him to visit England now, he points out sagely, than when he will be married and with a family. He claims that he is better than John at managing money matters, and he is sure that he can keep his expenses down to less than $140 or $160 (in fact, he would spend about $300). The trip is to be mainly an inexpensive walking tour since Brace's family has little money, and Olmsted reminds his father that he has had much more practice in roughing it than either of the other two. "In case of his [John's] sickness, I have experience among hardships, and boldness and confidence that he has not to obtain assistance and comfort." Which is all true, as his father knows. Olmsted adds that a sea voyage and hiking will also be good for his own health—he has had recurring bouts of dyspepsia all summer. Wouldn't it be a good idea, in any case, to be away from Staten Island during the New York summer cholera season? Having marshaled every single argument he can think of, he closes the letter on a note of filial obedience.

> I did not mean to argue the matter much, but I hope you won't consider my opinions as if they were those of a mere child, nor my desires as senseless romantic impulses *only*. I acknowledge so *much*, that if you can give my position candid and earnest consideration, you are in a position to judge more correctly than I, and I will make myself contented.

It is an irresistible plea, and John Olmsted does not resist. On April 30, 1850, Frederick, John, and Charley sailed from New York on the *Henry Clay*, bound for England.

The trio landed in Liverpool. They spent the next month traveling to Portsmouth on the English Channel and back to London, a journey of about 350 miles. They traveled largely on foot, occasionally taking trains and twice steamboats. They visited Bath, Tintern Abbey, and Salisbury Cathedral. Along the way they experienced some of the most beautiful rural scenery in England, working their way down the valley of the Wye and walking across the Salisbury Plain. After three weeks in London, they went to Paris, where Olmsted was to visit nurseries. They spent another month hiking in France, Belgium, Holland, and Germany. Returning to London, the three friends continued their English tour, visiting (now Northern) Ireland for a week, returning to Edinburgh, and ending in Glasgow.* There they parted company. Brace took a steamer to Hamburg, for he was planning to stay on in Germany and study for at least another year. Frederick and John boarded a ship bound for New York. They arrived on October 24—exactly six months since their departure.

Six months is not a long time, in the usual course of events, but for Olmsted the trip was an important experience. Nothing enriches travel as much as conversation, and he was in the company of John and

---

*The trip from Liverpool to London is extensively documented. However, since only two of Olmsted's letters from that period have survived, little is known about his travels in Europe and the second portion of his British tour.

Charley—who he called "two of the very greatest and best men in the world." Moreover, it was a kind of pilgrimage; he was not visiting an exotic country like China but Britain, his ancestral home.* It was also the land of his heroes, Carlyle and Macaulay, as well as the birthplace of scientific farming. True to his word, Olmsted visited many farms, often letting his two companions continue ahead while he pursued his research into the mysteries of fertilizers and orchard management. Armed with his letters of reference, he met agriculturists and nurserymen, including the engineer Josiah Parkes, inventor of a tile system for draining soils. Olmsted was seeking Parkes's advice regarding a novel drainage-tile-making machine that he was purchasing on behalf of the county agricultural society. Since Brace was interested in social reform, they also visited jails, debtors' prisons, almshouses, and village schools.

Now Olmsted could see for himself the landscapes that he had read about in the books of William Gilpin and Uvedale Price. He was overwhelmed. His first encounter with the English countryside occurred three days after arriving in Liverpool. The three companions left the city by train and, after a few miles, got off at a small station, strapped on their knapsacks, and set off.

> There we were right in the midst of it! The country—and such a country!—green, dripping, glistening, gorgeous! We stood dumb-stricken by its loveliness, as, from the bleak April and bare boughs we had left at home, broke upon us that English May—sunny, leafy, blooming May—in an English lane; with hedges, English hedges, hawthorn hedges, all in blossom; homely old farm-houses, quaint stables, and hay-stacks; the old church spire over the distant trees; the mild sun beaming through the watery atmosphere, and all so quiet—the only sounds the hum of bees, and the crisp grass-tearing of a silken-skinned, real (unimported) Hereford cow, over the hedge.

For any American the first experience of the English countryside is a revelation. It *is* greener. The light, thanks to the "watery atmosphere"—a beautiful phrase—is different. The temperate climate lacks the scorching

---

*Olmsted sought out and visited Olmsted Hall, near Cambridge, which had been the home of the de Olmstede family until the early fifteenth century. That the Hall was really a large farmhouse appealed to him "quite as much as to have found the arms of some murdering Baron over a dungeon door."

summers and freezing winters that annually batter the American landscape. The land is not only gentler, it appears more tended. English woods and meadows are the result of millennia of cultivation. American fields and forests, even in a relatively long-settled region such as Connecticut, are rude and unkempt by comparison. When neglected, they quickly revert to wilderness. In England, the wilderness disappeared a long time ago—much of the country is a garden.

England became the touchstone for Olmsted's ideas about rural scenery. He swallowed the English countryside whole, but he did more than merely succumb to its visual delights. His own modest efforts at landscaping Tosomock Farm had evidently awakened in him a desire to understand exactly how natural elements could be manipulated to create an effect of picturesqueness or sublimity. Here is what he wrote after a visit to the park of Eaton Hall, a large estate in Cheshire:

> A gentle undulating surface of close-cropped pasture land, reaching way off illimitably; very old, but not very large trees scattered singly and in groups—so far apart as to throw long unbroken shadows across broad openings of light, and leave the view in several directions unobstructed for a long distance. Herds of fallow-deer, fawns, cattle, sheep and lambs quietly feeding near us, and moving slowly in masses at a distance; a warm atmosphere, descending sun, and sublime shadows from fleecy clouds transiently darkening in succession, sunny surface, cool woodside, flocks and herds, and foliage.

The passage is striking for being as much an analysis as a description. It is as if he were compiling a checklist for future reference.

JOSTLING
AND BEING JOSTLED

Frederick Law Olmsted, c. 1860.

No man lives without jostling and being jostled; in all ways he has to elbow himself through the world . . .

—THOMAS CARLYLE

CHAPTER ELEVEN

Mr. Downing's Magazine

LEWIS MUMFORD CALLED Olmsted's combination of travel, shrewd observation, and intelligent reading "American education at its best." He suggested that Olmsted could be considered representative of a mid-nineteenth-century American type: the self-invented man. Mumford compared Olmsted to Walt Whitman, Herman Melville, and the economist Henry George, whose *Progress and Poverty* was one of the best-selling economic books of that time. Mumford could have added Mark Twain and Thomas Edison. All these men came to their calling circuitously. All had little formal schooling and a youth marked by a succession of careers, usually unrelated to their later vocations. Nevertheless, the originality of their ideas was due in no small part to the unconventional course of their early lives.

Olmsted, too, had left school early. Like Melville and George, he had been to sea; like Melville, he had been a clerk and a farmhand; and like Whitman, he was a great reader. But Olmsted differed from his contemporaries in one important respect. He was not forced out into the world by strained family circumstances. Many avenues were open to him. He could have gone into the family business like his half brother Albert. He was a valued employee at Benkard and Hutton and could easily have stayed on. He could have pursued surveying. Despite his later disclaimers, he could have attended Yale. Instead he subjected himself to a variety of experiences. There was nothing planned about it. He simply wasn't satisfied with the hand that he had been dealt—comfortable though it was. It was as if he had decided to reshuffle the cards—more than once.

A self-invented life need not be without a certain measure of stability, however. Twain, for example, spent about eight years working on Mississippi steamboats. By the time Olmsted was twenty-eight, he had devoted seven years, fully a quarter of his life, to farming. After his return from

England in October 1850, he appeared to settle down to his agricultural pursuits. He continued to enlarge his reference library. He wrote to Brace, who was still in Germany, to ask him to send books and pamphlets on corn, soils, and drainage. He was gaining expertise; at the end of the year his produce won several prizes at the County Agricultural Fair. He was involved with the agricultural society and setting up the newly arrived English drainage-tile-making machine, one of the earliest applications in the United States of this technology. He corresponded with Downing and knowledgeably discussed pear cultivation. He was immersed in his burgeoning nursery business and was awaiting the delivery of five thousand pear trees from France. Olmsted took farming seriously, and many years later, looking back on this period, he wrote: "I began life as a farmer, and although for forty years I have had no time to give to agricultural affairs, I still feel myself to belong to the farming community, and that all else that I am has grown from the agricultural trunk."

But the man who returned from Europe was not the same young farmer who had left. The purpose of the trip had been—as he had proposed to his father—education, not recreation. In that regard the experience turned out to be, if anything, too successful. Travel extended his horizons. Life on Tosomock Farm now appeared tame and inconsequential. "Everybody at home seems to be superficial, frivolous, absorbed in a tide of foam, gas and bubbles," he wrote to Brace in Germany. "Stay where you are as long as you can." Travel also awakened in Olmsted a new appreciation of his abilities. Not that he had ever lacked confidence. But he had come to think of himself chiefly as a farmer and nurseryman. Now that was no longer enough. "I am disappointed in the increased power I have over others, as yet," he confessed to Brace in another letter. "The mere fact of having been to Europe is worth nothing. To me, in looking at another, it always was an expectation of an increased value to the man—rightly so. But I have now this impression that here people do not *respect* anyone sincerely. Representative only it seems to me they bow to—as clergymen of religion, &c." Respect, a place in the world, influence over others, even power—this is a new Olmsted!

Politics beckoned. He was invited to stand as the Whig candidate for town clerk and justice of the peace. Olmsted sympathized with the Whig party and its policies of economic nationalism and a strong Union, but he declined the invitation. He had a new avocation: writing. Downing had asked him to write an article for *The Horticulturist* about his impressions of rural Germany. Olmsted considered himself unqualified for the task; he had not spent long enough in the country, and in any case, he did not speak the language. Instead, he wrote an article about a place he knew well—England—and a subject close to his heart—landscape. Or, more accurately, landscape design, for his subject was a recently built public park in Birkenhead, a suburb of Liverpool.

Birkenhead Park had been laid out in June 1844 by Joseph Paxton.* The park covered 120 acres. It was bisected by a gently curving city street and circled by a carriageway. There were no formal vistas, no straight lines at all. The picturesque ponds, random clumps of trees, rolling meadows, overgrown hillocks, and meandering footpaths reminded Olmsted of the English countryside, "very simple, and apparently rather overlooked by the gardener." What impressed Olmsted the most was that the romantic pastoral scenery was wholly man-made—the site had originally been "a flat, sterile, clay farm." In his article, which appeared in May 1851, he described how a system of underground drains fed water to the ponds, and how earth from the excavations was used to create hills. He included technical details about the construction of the footpaths: six inches of fine broken stone, three inches of cinders, and six inches of fine rolled gravel.

British and European parks were generally estates that had been donated to the city, or private aristocrats' gardens to which the public was allowed access. Birkenhead Park, by contrast, was designed specifically as a public park. Olmsted pointed out that the park was built and financed entirely by the town. He explained that part of the cost had been recovered by selling lots for private villas around the edges of the park. That citizens might build a park for themselves struck him as admirable. So did the fact that the park was open to all.

> I was glad to observe that the privileges of the garden were enjoyed about equally by all classes. There were some who even were attended by servants, and sent at once for their carriages, but a large proportion were of the common ranks, and a few women with children, or suffering from ill health, were evidently the wives of very humble laborers.

Olmsted pointed out the irony that in democratic America there was nothing comparable to what he called the "People's Park."

---

*Paxton, a gardener and builder of conservatories, would become famous for the Crystal Palace, which he built for the 1851 International Exhibition in London.

Downing had his own reason for wanting to publish an article on Birkenhead Park. In an editorial postscript, which praised the young author's "clear and pleasing account," he regretted that New York had no such public park, "no breathing place, no grounds for the exercise and refreshment of her jaded citizens." This was Downing's hobbyhorse. A year earlier he had published an article in which he complained about the paltriness of New York's squares compared to London's vast parks. Three months after Olmsted's article appeared, Downing wrote a lead essay, "The New-York Park," which spelled out his proposal of a great park for the city. Curiously, he seems to have been unaware of Birkenhead Park before reading Olmsted's article. Although he had visited England the same year, likewise passed through Liverpool, and even met Paxton himself, the eight "Letters from England" that he published in *The Horticulturist* did not mention Birkenhead.

Olmsted had discovered Birkenhead Park by accident. Three days after arriving in Liverpool, he and his companions crossed the Mersey to Birkenhead to start their walking tour. They stopped in a bakery to buy buns and talked to the baker about the merits of American versus French flour. As he bid them farewell he mentioned a new park. They decided to visit it and left their knapsacks in the store, for the park was some distance away. When Olmsted saw Birkenhead Park, he immediately realized that "gardening had here reached a perfection that I had never before dreamed of." He excitedly sought out the head gardener and recorded the details that he would later include in his article.

Olmsted was not just writing magazine articles; he had decided to write a full-length book. While he had been in Europe, he had kept a diary, parts of which, in the form of letters, he had sent to friends and family. He now gathered these, together with his notes, into a travel book. He was probably emboldened in this attempt by reading the numerous travel letters that Brace was sending from Germany to newspapers in New York, Boston, and Philadelphia. Olmsted was also encouraged by his neighbor George Putnam. Putnam had terminated his partnership with John Wiley two years before and now published chiefly literary titles under his own name. He wanted to include Olmsted's book in a new series he was planning to launch called "Putnam's Semi-Monthly Library for Travelers and the Fireside." Olmsted's enthusiasm, as well as the vivid letters he already had in hand, had convinced Putnam. In any case, he was not taking a large risk; there was no advance, and the 10 percent royalty was to be paid only after expenses.

The article on Birkenhead Park would become a chapter of Olmsted's book. Meanwhile, he wrote another article, this time for a prestigious monthly, the *American Whig Review*. "A Voice from the Sea" is neither an agricultural essay nor an excerpt of the book. It is a spirited account of the sad lot of the working seaman. He had begun the essay while sailing to Liverpool with Charley and John. Olmsted skillfully juxtaposes episodes from that voyage, when he was a passenger, with his earlier experiences as a seaman on the *Ronaldson*. He includes a vivid description of the brutal flogging of the young boy. The tone is both authoritative and outraged. His condemnation of shipboard working conditions is powerful. He also has ideas on how to improve the situation. He proposes new laws, and paying overtime for longer hours. He suggests establishing schools for mariners that would teach practical skills, which, in turn, would make greenhorns more valuable, hence likely to be better treated. Such schools would also provide continuing education for sailors ashore.

Like Richard Henry Dana, Olmsted sympathized with the sailors. Unlike Dana, however, he was not an idealistic reformer. He admitted that sailors were seldom saints.

> Suspicious, distrustful, often dishonest and hard-hearted themselves, the captain is partly right in thinking they would not understand, could not trust, and might fail to reward a worthy, generous and manly command. Trained like brutes, they must be driven yet like brutes. The old wrong has produced the evil, and the evil excuses the present wrong; and thus here, as often elsewhere, both are perpetuated. Such are always the hardest cases for the philanthropist, where heedless, fanatical, impracticable reformers are for ever making mischief.

This underlines the complex nature of Olmsted's mind. Now twenty-nine, he had grown out of his early, easy enthusiasms. Suspicious of facile solutions to difficult problems, he was developing a rare ability to see both sides of a question, no matter how opposed or contradictory—the test, as F. Scott Fitzgerald would later point out, of a first-rate intelligence.

CHAPTER TWELVE

Olmsted Falls in Love
and Finishes His Book

DURING THE YEAR after returning from Europe, while Olmsted was busy with his book and magazine articles, he resumed his correspondence with Emily Perkins. She was the "fine girl" from Hartford with whom he had read Macaulay. It was not immediately a romantic attachment, judging from a comment that Olmsted made in a letter to Brace. "I doubt if I shall ever 'love' till I marry (or am engaged) but I shall not marry a woman that I shall not be very likely to love very dearly when I safely can. *I do not know such a one* [emphasis added]." That was written in January 1851. Several months later, after spending some more time with Emily, he changed his mind. That summer they discussed marriage, and before the autumn, they were engaged. The engagement was, at first, known only to the families, but in due course it was made public. The prospective bride customarily set the marriage date. Emily wanted to marry in the early fall but agreed to a slightly later date to allow Frederick to attend to the harvest. It was a brief engagement at a time when engagements could last years.

It appeared a promising match. They moved in the same circles. They had known each other for two years. Olmsted was acquainted with several of the immediate Perkins family, and Emily's first cousin was his old flame Lizzie Baldwin. Like Frederick, Emily belonged to Hartford's genteel class of merchants and professionals. Her family background was formidable. Her grandfather was Lyman Beecher, her uncle was another famous churchman, Henry Ward Beecher, her aunts were Catharine E. Beecher and Harriet Beecher Stowe, who would achieve international fame with *Uncle Tom's Cabin*, which was published the following year. Her father was a Hartford politician in whose law office Fred Kingsbury had studied. The attractive, dark-haired Emily Baldwin Perkins was twenty-two, seven years younger than her fiancé. She was intelligent, well-educated, urbane. She was a catch.

And then she got away. The engagement was made public in August, and before the end of the month, Emily's mother wrote to Olmsted that her daughter wished to be released. Mrs. Perkins gave no particulars, but she asked to meet Olmsted in New Haven. It must have been an awkward confrontation. We do not know what caused Emily to change her mind. Her parents did not object to the marriage. Olmsted, who did not smoke and drank in moderation, probably had no skeletons in his closet. In any case, the upright youth was well-known to the Perkins family and held in high esteem by Emily's cousin Elizabeth Baldwin.

It is not necessary to imagine that scandal was involved. Nineteenth-century engagements were terminated for many reasons. One young woman called off her engagement—to a Harvard student—simply because she felt he was too reserved and did not "upon intimate acquaintance become the more open & frank." Another asked her fiancé to release her because of her own "moments of indifference." Such accounts are a reminder that young Americans of Frederick and Emily's generation considered romantic love a prerequisite for marriage. An important function of courtship, especially for women, was to authenticate the depth of this emotional attachment. Men considered the engagement a necessary formality before they *could* marry; but women saw it as a period when they could test their own—and their fiancé's—feelings and decide if they *would* marry. At times a broken engagement could be the ultimate test—the serious supplicant was expected to prove himself by persevering and patching things up. This is unlikely to have been the case with Emily. If she had been merely testing Frederick, she would not have involved her mother (parents normally did not play a role in mid-nineteenth-century courtship). More likely, Emily simply fell out of love. Perhaps Frederick, busy on the farm, did not pay enough attention to her. Or it may have dawned on her that she wanted more out of life than growing cabbages on Staten Island. Emily did get married—only fourteen months later—to Edward Everett Hale, an ambitious young clergyman from Worcester, Massachusetts. Possibly Hale was the reason for the breakup, although the only surviving documentary evidence indicates that he met Emily two months *after* the engagement was called off.

Olmsted's broken engagement puzzled his father. Several months later, John Olmsted wrote to Sophia Stevens: "Pray tell me what it is makes Fred so happy since his disappointment, as it is call^d? He seems like a man who has thrown off a tremendous weight. Can it be that he brot [*sic*] it about purposely?" Olmsted left no written evidence of his feelings about Emily, but possibly he got cold feet and realized that he was not ready for marriage. His convenient absences on the farm would have given Emily ample reason for doubt. But I do not think that he was as unaffected by the episode as his father supposed. He may not have been miserable or openly brokenhearted, but Emily was the last of his long string of youthful infatuations. For the next eight years there would be no romantic attachments, no angels, no "plaguy fine girls." Olmsted seemed destined to become an "old bach," after all.

He must have felt left out. Sophia Stevens, the Olmsted family friend, was marrying a schoolteacher in Burlington, Vermont. Frederick Kingsbury was married in April of that year to Alathea Scovill, the daughter of a wealthy Waterbury industrialist. Charles Brace was still abroad, and still single, but he was in love with Letitia Neill, a Belfast girl he had met during their tour. Lizzie Baldwin, too, was about to become engaged. Most important of all was the betrothal of his brother and Mary Perkins. The circumstances were bittersweet. The couple had announced their engagement just before the European trip. John's health had not improved as a result of his travels, however, and by the summer of 1851 he was visibly worse. Finally, the bleeding from his lungs made it impossible to ignore what everyone feared: he had tuberculosis.* Nevertheless, Mary bravely stood by him, and they decided to marry that fall.

The first part of Olmsted's book, titled *Walks and Talks of an American Farmer in England,* appeared in February 1852; the second part followed in October. He dedicated the first volume to his mentor and friend George Geddes. That was appropriate, for this is not an ordinary travel book, but one intended especially for farmers. He devotes entire chapters to British agricultural practices: the cultivation of beets, orchard diseases, farm implements. His wide range of interests leads him to many other subjects as well. He writes about education, politics, culture, and everyday

---

*During the nineteenth century, tuberculosis was known as the "great white plague" and reached epidemic proportions in America, as it did in Europe. Yet while there was no cure, the course of the disease was uncertain: Thoreau died of tuberculosis at forty-four; Emerson at seventy-eight.

life. He describes how people dressed, behaved, and talked. He had already shown in his correspondence from China that he had an ear for dialogue, and his "talks" with English men and women of all backgrounds enliven the book and provide agreeable and often humorous interludes to the discussions of crop-raising and animal husbandry. The author's artistic side is also in evidence—the books include a dozen attractive woodcuts made by John William Orr (who had illustrated Downing's *The Architecture of Country Houses*) after Olmsted's own sketches.

He was a perceptive observer. The descriptive passages are vivid and detailed. His descriptions of landscapes are particularly successful—I have already quoted his impressions of Eaton Hall in Cheshire. Here he is in Chester, standing on the town wall with his two companions, looking down into the marketplace.

Odd-looking vehicles and oddly-dressed people are passing in the street below us: a woman with a jacket, driving two stout horses in one of those heavy farm-carts; an omnibus, with the sign of "The Green Dragon," very broad, and carrying many passengers on the top; the driver, smartly-dressed, tips his whip with a knowing nod to a pretty Welsh girl, who is carrying a tub upon her head. There are scores of such damsels, neat as possible, with dark eyes, and glossy hair half covered by white caps, and fine, plump forms, in short striped petticoats and hob-nailed shoes. There goes one, straight as a gun-barrel, with a great jar of milk upon her head. And here is a little donkey, with cans of milk slung on each side of him, and behind them, so you cannot see why he does not slip off over his tail, is a great brute, with two legs in knee-breeches and blue stockings, bent up so as to be clear of the ground, striking him with a stout stick across his long, expressive ears. A sooty-faced boy, with a Kilmarnock bonnet on his head, carrying pewter pots, coming towards us, jumps suddenly to one side, and, ha! out from under us, at a rattling pace, come a beautiful sorrel mare, with a handsome, tall, slightly-made young man in undress military uniform; close behind, and not badly mounted either, follow two others—one also in uniform, with a scarlet cap and a bright bugle swinging at his side; the other a groom in livery, neat as a pin; odd again, to American eyes, those leather breeches and bright top boots. Lord Grosvenor, going to review the Yeomanry, says the printer. His grandfather built this gate and presented it to the corporation; you can see his arms on the key-stone.

Walks and Talks is more than the account of a reporter. The author has opinions on a variety of subjects. When he is not discussing orchard blight, he is debating prison reform with British jailers, or explaining the etymological difference between English as spoken in Britain and America. He is interested in social conditions. He scathingly points out that the circumstances of English laborers are more degraded than anything he has seen elsewhere, even among Chinese coolies. He does not neglect the tourist sights. At Tintern Abbey he finds the guide so irritating he does not enjoy the experience; he much prefers Winchester Cathedral. On the whole, he favors ordinary places, farmhouses, and country inns. He never hesitates to recount what he thinks are useful lessons to his countrymen. In Hereford, for example, a visit to a public park is an opportunity to remind his readers that "not a town have we seen in England but has had a better garden-republic than any town I know of in the United States."

The first part of *Walks and Talks* was also published in England. When the second part appeared, Putnam made available a single-volume version of the work, "a splurgy, thick book," according to its proud author. There was sufficient interest that a second edition appeared in 1859. In the preface that he wrote especially for that edition, Olmsted drolly describes himself as walking on "one farmer's leg and one sailor's leg, with the help of a short, crooked, half-grown academic sapling for a walking stick." *Walks and Talks of an American Farmer in England* is hardly a literary masterpiece. But for its author's later fame it would not have survived, and even so, it is little more than a curiosity. Although it contains lively sketches of both places and people, it is too idiosyncratic in its attempt at encyclopedic breadth and in its obsessive details. Moreover, its origin in letter-writing is often transparent: the narrative does not flow smoothly. But despite its drawbacks, it is a respectable first book. And Olmsted accomplished something that is rare for a novice writer. He began to develop his own voice. It is a reasoned voice, inquisitive and good-natured. The voice is often heard in his letters, and it is surprisingly authoritative, although without the irritating touch of pedantry that so often marks the autodidact. Despite—or, rather, because of—his unconventional education and youthful experiences, he converses comfortably on a wide variety of topics. No wonder that one of the reviewers of *Walks and Talks* referred to Olmsted as "one of our original young Yankee farmers."

The first prominent review of *Walks and Talks* appeared in *The Horticulturist*. A publicist would have no trouble finding quotes, for it is a rave.

"Here is a book of travels with a smack of novelty about it," it began, and went on to praise the author: "A very pleasant bit of travel he has made of it, with no dust in his eyes—for Mr. OLMSTED is one of the new school of American farmers, without a single old prejudice, wide awake on all questions of the times, and a believer in the largest interpretation of the future of the people." The unidentified reviewer recognized the breadth of Olmsted's interests and quoted at length numerous passages, both descriptive and technical. Downing accorded the exceptionally long review a lead position in the magazine. Such tacit endorsement was important. When Olmsted's essay on Birkenhead Park had appeared in *The Horticulturist*, the forthcoming book was not mentioned and the author was identified merely as "Wayfarer"; his "A Voice from the Sea" was unsigned; an essay in the *Hartford Daily Courant* was signed only "F." But when a second excerpt of *Walks and Talks* appeared in the December 1852 issue of *The Horticulturist*, both the book and its author were clearly identified. "Fred. Law Olmsted" had become somebody whom readers might recognize.

There were other reviews. The *American Whig Review* informed its readers that Olmsted was the author of the earlier "A Voice from the Sea" and praised his "natural and unprejudiced impressions." *Cummings Evening Bulletin* of Philadelphia was brief but complimentary: "our farmer observes closely and writes spiritedly." *Harper's New Monthly Magazine* called the book "eminently popular, in the true sense of the term," and concluded that it "cannot fail to be a favorite with the great mass of readers." *The Horticulturist* ran a review of the second volume that was as fulsome in its praise as the first review: "His sketches of landscape, and of particular scenes and objects in the landscape, exhibit such glowing warmth of feeling, such a practical knowledge, as we would only expect in one exclusively devoted to the study of nature." Like the earlier review, this one quoted at length from the book.

Whether Downing himself wrote *The Horticulturist*'s review of the first volume of *Walks and Talks* is not known, but he did not write the second. Three months before the second volume of Olmsted's book appeared, Downing drowned in a tragic Hudson River steamboat accident that claimed seventy lives. He was only thirty-six, but was America's best-known professional landscape gardener. His plan for transforming the area between the Capitol and the Washington Monument into a "national park" had recently been approved by Congress. Had he lived, he would undoubtedly have been chosen to design and build New York's Central Park, a project that he had so vocally supported. Little could Olmsted imagine the effect of Downing's death on his own career. Sorrowfully—and gratefully—he dedicated the second volume of his book to the man who had both inspired and assisted him.

CHAPTER THIRTEEN

Charley Brace Intervenes

ALL THE TIME that Olmsted was becoming engaged—and unengaged—to Emily Perkins, and writing, Charles Brace was in Europe. After separating from Frederick and John in Glasgow and returning to Germany, he spent the winter in Berlin, learning German and studying. In the spring of 1851, he decided to set out for Hungary. He was supporting himself as a correspondent for several American newspapers, and Hungary, which only three years earlier had waged an unsuccessful war of independence against its Austrian occupier, was a subject of popular interest. Olmsted encouraged his friend. "If you could get to Hungary and really know the people, take an unprejudiced view of their condition and character, learn what really is their revolutionary impulse," he wrote, "it would be most interesting and valuable." Following visits to Prague and Vienna, Brace arrived in Hungary. He enjoyed a pleasant two weeks of Magyar hospitality. While he was touring Transylvania, the Austrian police suddenly placed him under arrest. He was charged with having subversive material in his possession, and with being an emissary of Hungarian patriots abroad. The charges were nominally true—he did have a revolutionary pamphlet, as well as a letter of introduction from a Hungarian exile. The United States had been the only government to formally recognize the short-lived Hungarian republic, and Americans were known to be sympathetic to the revolutionary cause.

The idea of Charley Brace as a spy seemed ludicrous to his friends at home, who assumed it was all a simple misunderstanding. "I anticipate your most interesting letters now, describing Austrian prison discipline—size of your cell, weight of your chain, etc.," joked Olmsted in a letter, trying to lift his friend's spirits. But it was no joke. Brace was imprisoned for five weeks. He was put on trial—thirteen times—and finally released from prison thanks to the intercession of the American chargé d'affaires. Returning to Vienna, he found himself under police surveillance and soon felt obliged to leave the country. He returned to America via Belfast, where he paid court to Letitia Neill.

Brace returned to New York on December 13, 1851. Given the American interest in Hungary, he gave several public lectures, denouncing "oppression and tyranny." He also wrote a book about his Transylvanian adventure. *Hungary in 1851: with an Experience of the Austrian Police* garnered favorable reviews, both in England and America. But writing was not the career he sought; nor was he interested in becoming a conventional clergyman. He turned his attention to social work among New York's poor, particularly the city's vagrant boys. In 1853 he helped to establish the Children's Aid Society, of which he was appointed the chief executive officer. At twenty-seven, Charles Loring Brace had found his life work. This upright, selfless man would successfully direct the Society in its good works for the next thirty-seven years.

Hungary in 1851 was published only two months after the first volume of *Walks and Talks*. Of the two books, Brace's was more exciting—espionage and imprisonment made for a more dramatic story than tramping the English countryside. The two thousand copies of the first edition sold quickly, more quickly than *Walks and Talks*. Brace's success was all the more striking given the speed with which he had written the book, and given his evident lack of interest in pursuing a literary career. But if Olmsted was chagrined, he did not show it. He was happy to have Brace home. Charles Brace was his dearest friend—other than his brother. Olmsted and Brace's friendship found its chief expression in conversation—they loved to talk, and not just to talk, but to argue. In a letter to Kingsbury, written in the fall of 1848, Brace described a boisterous Sunday visit to Tosomock Farm.

> A wild stormy day and we spent it at home. A sea-beach in a storm is no unfit place for worship, is it? But the amount of talking done upon that visit! One steady stream from six o'clock Saturday night till twelve, beginning next day, and going on till about twelve the next night, interrupted only by meals and some insane walks on the beach! And this not like ours together, easy, discursive, varied, but a torrent of fierce argument, mixed with divers oaths on Fred's part, and abuse on both! However I must say Fred is getting to argue with the utmost keenness,—a regular Dr. Taylor mind in its analytic power! But what is queerest, never

able to exercise that power except in discussion! He is another Taylorite in his virtue theory. I shouldn't be surprised if he turned out something rather remarkable among men.

The Dr. Taylor that Brace referred to was Nathaniel Taylor, a Yale theologian who was a famous debater. Religion was one of the subjects that Brace and Olmsted discussed. The idealistic but practical Brace had come to espouse an activist form of Christianity, rooted in good deeds rather than piety and prayer. Olmsted, by this time, had lost most of his interest in formal religion. Describing another Sunday Staten Island visit to Kingsbury, Brace wrote, "It does *not* mean, I am almost sorry to say, much going to church." But he added, "Perhaps no day in the year is more intellectual than this Sunday of ours. There is earnest talk all day long on the great problems of life and eternity; not flippant discussion, or prize matches between intellects, but, as I do believe, a serious and rational investigation." The two agreed on many things—Olmsted, too, thought that helping others was the highest calling, although his friend could not help noticing that Olmsted appeared in no hurry to pursue it.

If religion was the subject of "earnest talk," then what accounted for the "torrent of fierce argument"? It was slavery. By the mid-1800s, slavery had become the most contentious political question of the day. Shortly after the turn of the century, the African slave trade had been prohibited (although it continued illicitly), and all the Northern states had either abolished slave-owning or adopted measures to gradually eradicate it. But slavery did not die out. Because of the widespread adoption of Whitney's mechanical cotton gin (invented in 1793), cotton cultivation in the Southern states became highly profitable. Since cotton plantations depended on slave labor, the demand for slaves went up. Instead of dying a natural death, as many of the Founding Fathers had hoped, slavery revived. Between 1800 and 1850, the slave population of the United States went from less than 1 million to almost 3 million.

The population of the North was also growing, and political power in Congress shifted from rough parity between North and South to 2:1 in favor of the free Northern states. (Slaves could not vote, of course.) New free states in the North entered the Union. The South saw the expansion of slavery into new states as the only solution to redress what it perceived as a political imbalance. A series of Northern concessions resulted. In 1820, the Missouri Compromise prohibited slavery north of the 36°30' line, but admitted Missouri (which was north of the line) to the Union as a slave state. Arkansas entered as a slave state in 1836, Texas in 1845. The latter event led to war with Mexico, the outcome of which added more than a million square miles of new territory—almost half of which lay below the 1820 line—to the United States. The so-called Compromise of 1850 provided for California's admittance as a free state but, in return, did not proscribe slavery in the other new territories. The Compromise also called for stricter laws in the Northern states: the Fugitive Slave Act was to ensure the return of runaway slaves to their Southern masters.

Like most Northerners, Olmsted held contradictory ideas about slavery. On the one hand, he believed that slavery was inimical to both the Constitution and to natural law and thought that the new territories of the West should be free states. On the other hand, he was not prepared to risk the Union by calling for the wholesale abolition of slavery in the South. Like many Americans, he sometimes wished the problem would simply go away. He once expressed agreement with his father's support for the American Colonization Society, whose aim was to resettle freed slaves in Africa. This had been Jefferson's idea, too, although Olmsted, unlike Jefferson, was not wedded to this position and did accept that freed slaves could become full citizens—eventually. He supported emancipation, but he wanted only *gradual* emancipation. This attitude reflected more than mere political pragmatism. Olmsted thought that slavery had ill-prepared its victims for citizenship. Freedom was the slaves' "natural right," he wrote in *Walks and Talks,* but it required restoring to them "not the liberty first, but the capacity for the liberty." He wanted freed slaves to be given liberties when and as they showed they deserved them. He was unclear exactly how long this would take. After all, he had grown up in Connecticut, where, although slavery was prohibited, blacks were still not permitted to vote (only Maine, New Hampshire, Vermont, and Massachusetts granted suffrage to freed slaves). He found it natural that freed slaves were second-class citizens.

Of course, his contacts with freed slaves—or slaves—were minimal. This was a drawback, for Olmsted always thought clearest when his ideas grew out of personal experience. Lacking that, he sought a conciliatory, middle position in the debate: "I think both sides now very wrong," he wrote Brace. "The law of God in our hearts binds us in fidelity to the principles of the Constitution," he wrote in *Walks and Talks.* "They are not to be found in 'Abolitionism,' nor are they to be found . . . in hopeless, dawnless, unredeeming slavery." It was an awkward argument, as Olmsted himself was the first to admit.

Brace, on the other hand, was a staunch abolitionist. He saw things simply: the federal government should abolish slavery, immediately and universally. He found the Fugitive Slave Act repulsive. "Before, this slavery has rested with the South. Now, it is brought home on our free Northern shoulders," he wrote to a friend. "We become personally responsible for the slavery of a fellow-being. And I had rather see a dozen Unions broken than do such a wrong." Such extremism set Brace apart from both the Olmsted brothers and Frederick Kingsbury, who were all moderates. Brace worked hard at converting his "orthodox friends," as he referred to them. He once brought William Lloyd Garrison, the famous editor of the militant antislavery newspaper *The Liberator*, to Tosomock Farm for one of the Sunday debates; another time he invited Theodore Parker, an abolitionist preacher. "Why won't you follow your reason in the Negro Suffrage question?" he demanded of Kingsbury. When John Hull didn't share his outrage over the Fugitive Slave Act, Brace wrote in exasperation from Germany: "After reading your letter of January 15th on Slave Law, I don't understand it. I can't understand it. Does Fred [Olmsted] think so? Do all good men there think so? Is America going to the devil?"

Fred did not think so. He strongly opposed the Fugitive Slave Act. He once wrote that he would be prepared to harbor runaway slaves and "shoot a man that was likely to get them." He likewise opposed the Compromise of 1850, even though it was brokered by Daniel Webster, whom he admired. On the other hand, he continued to support the Whig party in the 1852 presidential elections. He agreed with Brace that slavery was a curse on the United States, but he was unwilling to declare slave owners immoral. It was not just a question of good versus bad, Olmsted argued. You had to look at both sides of the issue. Thus he pointed out in *Walks and Talks* that the degraded circumstances of many English farm laborers were often worse than those of American Negroes. This was partly a defensive reaction to British criticism of American slavery, but it did represent his position, that a slave society as existed in the South was not entirely bad. But how do you know that? Brace must have responded. How can you be sure? Have you been there? Have you seen it? Olmsted would have had to admit that he hadn't.

Perhaps just such a conversation gave Brace an idea. If his friend would see slavery firsthand—and write about it—he would surely change his mind. Moreover, he wanted to get Frederick Olmsted off his farm to "exercise that power" that Brace felt sure he possessed. The opportunity presented itself in mid-1852, when Brace, who moved in literary circles in New York, was talking to Henry J. Raymond, the editor of the *New-York Daily Times* (later renamed the *New-York Times*). Raymond, who had started the newspaper only the year before, was looking for a correspondent who would travel in the South and write knowledgeably about the material conditions of its everyday rural life. Slavery was obviously an important issue, but the editor, who was a moderate, did not want an abolitionist who would merely use the series as a platform—he wanted an objective observer. Brace suggested Olmsted. With his Whig views, his farming background, and his travel-writing experience, he would be perfect.

Raymond met Olmsted and offered him the job. Olmsted was thrilled and agreed immediately. As he later recalled, the whole meeting took five minutes. Brace correctly foresaw that the idea of being a "Special Correspondent" would appeal to his friend. It was a chance to combine his two loves: traveling and writing. Equally important, it was a chance to affect the course of the slavery debate. Olmsted was sure that if only he could dig out the *facts* of the matter, reason would prevail. Here was an opportunity to convince people of the middle course that he favored. Travel in the South could also provide him with valuable material for a book. As he excitedly wrote to Kingsbury, such a book would consist of "observations on Southern Agriculture & general economy as affected by Slavery; the conditions of the slaves—prospects—tendencies—& reliable understanding of the sentiments and hopes & fears of sensible planters & gentlemen that I should meet." He would leave in December, after the harvest, and travel for several months. Since he would be paid about ten dollars (three hundred dollars in modern dollars) for each article that was published, he reckoned that living cheaply he would come out a few hundred dollars ahead. His nursery business was doing well—he had orders for four hundred dollars' worth of trees—and the orchards were finally starting to produce. The farm could easily take care of itself during his winter absence, he reasoned. In any case, Brace had volunteered to attend to any pressing business that might arise. There was nothing holding him back.

CHAPTER FOURTEEN

Yeoman

The Mississippi River, North of New Orleans

Wednesday, February 23, 1853

It is late at night. A steamboat is slowly making its way against the current. Olmsted is on the deck, leaning on the railing, watching the passing water, whose waves and ripples reflect the light from the cabin windows. The sound of the rhythmic sloshing of the paddle wheels is occasionally punctuated by laughter and conversation from the lounge. It rudely interrupts his reverie. He is happy to be outside, away from the other passengers. He finds them vulgar and boorish, interested only in drinking and card-playing.

But that's been the pattern of this trip, he thinks ruefully. He has been traveling for more than two months and has met precious few people with whom he can talk. Or, at least, talk intelligently about the subjects that interest him and that he is committed to writing about. Although he carries letters of introduction to several plantation owners, it has proved more difficult than he expected to arrange these visits. In many cases, people are simply not at home. Many are evidently absentee landlords. Frequently, he has been misdirected and spent hours lost on backcountry roads. He has discovered that traveling in the South is not easy. For one thing, the distances are large; this is not England, where a short hike takes you easily from one village to the next. Nor is it Connecticut or New York, with their good roads and effective public transportation. Once south of Virginia, he has found that schedules are rarely adhered to and service is slipshod and makeshift. To his dismay—and discomfort—most of the hotels are as ill-kept and slovenly as their clientele.

He remembers the trip from Norfolk, Virginia, to Raleigh, North Carolina, about one hundred and sixty miles. That is less than the distance from New York to Boston, which have recently been joined by rail. But what would have been a simple, daylong train journey in the North, here turned out to be a series of misadventures. He arrived in Norfolk after visiting the District of Columbia and Richmond, and spending Christmas with Fred Kingsbury's uncle in Petersburg, Virginia. He also made a detour to see the Great Dismal Swamp, as a favor to Harriet Beecher Stowe, who planned to use this locale as the setting for her second antislavery novel.* In Norfolk, he found that the only good hotel had been closed down due to insufficient business, and when he did find a room, there was rainwater from a leaky roof puddling on the floor, and no fireplace. It was January, and he was so cold and damp that he was obliged to go down to the warm but smoke-filled and stinking public bar. He sat in a corner and listened to the landlord and his drunken cronies complaining loudly and obscenely about the infidel abolitionists, chief among them the author of Uncle Tom's Cabin!

The next morning, as he was about to have breakfast, he was told he would have to leave immediately or he would miss his train. He suspected he was being cheated since he had already been charged for the meal—this had happened to him once before. Nevertheless, he hurried to catch the ferry across the river to the railroad station. He and the porter carrying his luggage arrived at the dock just in time to see the stern of the departing boat. There was nothing to be done, so he bought some food from a market stall and sat down to wait. Twenty minutes later the ferry returned. His anxiety about missing the train—and having to spend another twenty-four hours in that dismal hotel—was aggravated when, halfway across the river, the paddleboat began to drift with the current because its stoker had gone to sleep. Finally, they arrived at the railroad station, a full half hour late. The train had not left; indeed, the ticket office was not even open. It was another hour before they pulled out of the station.

The tracks ran eighty miles to Weldon, North Carolina, where a stagecoach was to carry the passengers fifteen miles to the village of Gaston, another railhead. By now it was well past lunchtime; the coach driver told him he had time to eat. At the inn he wolfed down some cold sweet potatoes. Fifteen minutes later he hurried outside, only to find that the stage, with his two valises on board, had left. The landlord, who had neglected to notify him, now pleasantly suggested he should stay the night. He declined and jogged up the road, soon overtaking the lumbering coach.

The road was so muddy and rutted that progress was slow, and often pre-

---

*Olmsted wrote two letters to Stowe describing the Swamp. *Dred: A Tale of the Great Dismal Swamp* appeared three years later.

carious. At one point the coach turned over entirely on its side. It took four hours to reach their destination. Or almost to reach it. The stagecoach driver stopped abruptly and announced that it was too late in the day and this was as far as he would go. They were on the bank of the Roanoke River. Gaston was on the other side, a mile upstream, he told his now thoroughly distraught passengers. A scow across the river would come—"You just holler," he said, and drove away. No amount of hollering could convince the ferrymen to traverse the river—evidently there were too few passengers to make it worthwhile. As night fell, Olmsted volunteered to stay behind and guard the trunks and valises while the rest of the company walked up the road and crossed the railroad bridge to Gaston. One of the men soon returned with a barge and a gang of Negroes, and the baggage was soon loaded and brought up the river to the village.

The train that was to have taken them to Raleigh was long gone. When Olmsted asked one of the railroad men how often the advertised connection between the stagecoach and the railroad occurred, the answer was "Not very often, sir; it hain't been once, in the last two weeks." He and the other stranded passengers were forced to stay overnight in a dismal hotel, undoubtedly operated by the railroad company, he thought. The next afternoon, the train arrived—one and a half hours late, this time. His journey to New Orleans continued in a like fashion: missed connections, delayed trains, bad roads, misinformation, indifferent service, and swindling publicans.

Now Olmsted glances up at the barely visible, dark shore. He can see the glimmering lights of what he assumes must be plantation houses. That's where he's going now, to visit a plantation. Fashion Plantation, in St. Charles Parish, belongs to the only son of former president Zachary Taylor. He knows Dick Taylor from Yale and is looking forward to seeing him, and to learning about the detailed operation of a sugar plantation. He has already visited several plantations in Virginia and Georgia, but he is not satisfied that he really understands plantation life. It has proved more difficult than he expected to glean information from suspicious owners, closemouthed overseers, and silent Negroes. On the whole, he is discouraged with his journey so far. The vicissitudes of travel, and the few days that he spends in each place, have made it difficult to arrive at any coherent impression of Southern slavery. His writing is not going well, either. After a flurry of fourteen articles written while he was in Virginia, he has produced only four in the last six weeks.

At least he is being published. He has in his coat pocket a fresh copy of the February 16 New-York Daily Times, which he has picked up in New

Orleans. It contains his first article. He had privately admitted to his father that he thinks the first two articles are the "poorest of the lot," but still, he feels pride at seeing his own words in print—on page two, no less. Raymond has written a fulsome editorial introducing the series. Olmsted agrees with the editor's observation that most writing about slavery is from a preconceived point of view, but will his own reports really be able to "supply a defect which every unprejudiced person, at all interested in such inquiries, cannot fail to have felt"? It is an ambitious claim, perhaps too ambitious. Nor is he happy about the headline that Raymond has assigned to the series: "The South, Letters on the Productions, Industry and Resources of the Slave States." It promises more than he fears he will be able to deliver.

The ship's bell rings, as it does every time they are about to dock. The clerk comes to tell him that in ten minutes they will be at Fashion. He goes to the deck at the bow of the steamboat. As they near the shore, he can see a Negro holding a lantern. The steamboat runs straight in and he is easily able to jump onto the levee. As the steamboat starts to pull away, the clerk throws a package and a bundle of newspapers ashore and tells the Negro that they are for his master and one of his neighbors.

"Do you belong to Mr. Taylor?" Olmsted asks the Negro.

"Yes, sir. Is you going to our house, master?"

"Yes."

"I'll show you the way, then, sir."

They walk off into the darkness. Behind them, the steamboat is already in midstream, resuming its journey.

Olmsted was right about his first two articles: they are not very good. They contain little of the descriptive writing that enlivened the pages of his travel book, and precious few accounts of personal encounters and conversations, at which he excelled. Unlike his correspondence from China, the writing is flat and sounds contrived. He is trying too hard to deliver "the facts," and he overwhelms the reader with statistics. Writing of Richmond, for example, he strings together information about the cost of coal and wood, the price of imported staples, the mean summer and winter temperatures, and discusses the mortality rate—all in a single paragraph. He tends to get bogged down in trivia. Instead of describing his journey down the Potomac, he pedantically computes the speed of the steamboat (12½ miles an hour) and the cost of the journey (3.6 cents a mile) compared to the cost of railroad travel (4⅔ cents per mile). Why is this significant? He does not say. He can't resist digressing onto his favorite topic, scientific agriculture, and devotes two long paragraphs to the right way to spread guano, then follows with a detailed description of the comparative advantages of different reaping machines. He seems not to understand that what might have been appropriate for the audience of *Walks and Talks of an American Farmer* will not interest the reader of the *New-York Daily Times.*

Raymond must have been dissatisfied, too; he complained to Brace, who had assumed the role of intermediary. Actually, Olmsted hoped his friend would look over his writing and make improvements, although it appears that Brace passed the pieces to Raymond unaltered. Informed of his editor's displeasure, the novice correspondent fumed: "I can't write different sort of letters. If Raymond wanted statesmanship and generalizations he is at the wrong shop." It was not statesmanship that Raymond wanted, however, but engaging reporting. Olmsted's problem was that although he had written a book and several magazine articles and, like most of his contemporaries, was an accomplished letter writer, he had no experience as a working journalist. It is no wonder that he had so much trouble. He was not used to observing, analyzing—and writing—on the run. As he had done with farming, he learned on the job. He taught himself to compress; to focus each report on a single subject; to balance data with local background; to restrain his natural urge to describe and explain every detail; and to let the people he met speak for themselves. He gained confidence, and the articles improved. His visit with Taylor turned out to be fruitful and provided much useful material.

Although he became a skilled reporter, he was never a stylist in the literary sense. Edmund Wilson called his writing "pedestrian" and observed that his clumsy syntax often caused him difficulty in expressing himself. *Pedestrian* is too harsh, but the critique is just; Olmsted's prose does sometimes get tangled, especially when he is trying to summarize his usually complicated conclusions. However, Wilson had a high regard for Olmsted's Southern reporting. "He [Olmsted] tenaciously and patiently and lucidly made his way through the whole South, undiscouraged by churlish natives, almost impassable roads or the cold inns and uncomfortable cabins in which he spent most of his nights," observed Wilson. "He talked to everybody, and he sized up everything, and he wrote it all down."

It is the breadth of Olmsted's curiosity that makes his writing compelling. He began his third article with a description of a Negro funeral. He came upon it as he was riding in the country one Sunday afternoon; he was the only white person in attendance. His account of the graveside singing and preaching is vivid and comes to life as he successfully renders the vernacular of the mourners. (Olmsted had a real gift for mimicry.) Indeed, while he was unsympathetic to the "wild and barbarous" singing and chanting, he had to admit that "I was deeply influenced myself by the unaffected fine feeling and the simplicity, natural, rude truthfulness and absence of all attempt at formal decorum in the crowd."

He learned the journalist's knack of making his points though anecdotes. This passage recounts his brief exchange with a Virginia planter:

"I have raised hay, potatoes, and cabbages, on my farm in New York, that found a market in Richmond," I say to a planter, "but here you have a capital soil for such crops; how is it you don't supply your own market?" "Well, I should be laughed at if I bothered with such little crops," he replied. So it is—they leave such little crops to the niggers and Yankees, and then grumble because all the profits of their business go to build "Fifth-avenue palaces," and "down-east school houses." They will not bear it any longer, they are going straightway to do something for themselves—what? Establish a dignified State line of steamers to—Antwerp!

Without a long-winded analysis, Olmsted deftly put his finger on one of the reasons for the backwardness of the South (and a common failing of many third-world countries today): the tendency to focus on lucrative export crops such as tobacco, rice, and cotton and the inability to foster a diversified local economy.

Occasionally, Olmsted allowed himself to simply describe what he saw. Riding outside Savannah, he came upon a tree-lined drive leading to a plantation house.

On the other side, at fifty feet distant were rows of old live oak trees, their branches and twigs slightly hung with a delicate fringe of gray moss, and their dark, shining, green foliage meeting and intermingling naturally but densely overhead. The sunlight streamed through and played aslant the lustrous leaves and waving, fluttering, quivering, palpitating, pendulous moss: the arch was low and broad; the trunks were huge and gnarled, and there was a heavy groining of strong, dark, rough, knotty branches. I stopped my horse, bowed my head, and held my breath. I have never in all my life seen anything so impressively grand and beautiful.

This description is notable not so much for the language but for the light it casts on the sensibility of its author. The boyhood rambles in the Connecticut countryside had had their effect. Olmsted did not only look at his natural surroundings, he studied them and scrutinized their composition with as much attention as another might examine a great painting or listen to a work of music.

In his editorial introducing the series, Raymond had described his special correspondent as an "intelligent gentleman, of decided ability, large experience, practical habits of action and of speculation, known already to the world by his published works." What exactly these published works were was left to the reader's imagination, however, for Olmsted's name was never used. This was common practice. Authors of regular columns were often identified by pen names. Olmsted signed his letters "Yeoman." Discretion was necessary, since the series began being published while he was still traveling in the South, and feelings against perceived abolitionists sometimes ran high. Except when formal introductions were necessary, Olmsted did not identify himself as a reporter; indeed, he often affected a Southern accent and was frequently not recognized as a Northerner. He took great pains to mask the identity of the people he interviewed. His sense of journalistic responsibility—so different from today—required him even to disguise the exact location of a plantation when he felt that the owner might be embarrassed by his own remarks, or by Olmsted's observations.

One day, Olmsted was traveling on a train to Richmond, Virginia. At a station, a white lady accompanied by her young daughter and a mulatto girl and a black nanny boarded the carriage. He politely offered his seat so that the group could sit together. The two young girls laughed and talked together and appeared to him to be friends. He noticed that the mulatto girl—"bright and very pretty"—was dressed just as expensively and behaved with equal aplomb and propriety as her white companion. Later, the four travelers shared a snack from the same wrapper. "Many people at the North would have been indignant or 'disgusted' with such proceedings," he wrote, "but they excited no attention here." In fact,

Southern railroads required all blacks to travel in second class, although this rule was not closely followed and so-called house servants regularly accompanied their owners in first class. As Olmsted observed, these blacks were frequently well-dressed and well-mannered and appeared to be somewhat intimate with their masters. This in no way mitigated their oppression in Olmsted's eyes, but he could not resist pointing out to his Northern readers that at least some slaves were accorded more humane treatment in the South than freed Negroes would have received under the same circumstances from people in the North who considered themselves more tolerant.

Raymond underlined Yeoman's neutrality in the slave debate: "Although he probably has opinions of his own upon the general subject of Slavery, he has no prejudices concerning it which will disqualify him as a dispassionate and accurate observer of facts, or detract from the weight due to the judgment he may form in regard to them," he wrote, concluding that "upon this subject his opinions remain to be formed according to the facts he may meet." Raymond was clearly trying to anticipate the charge that his reporter was merely an abolitionist mischief-maker. Olmsted, too, was sensitive to Southern sentiments and bent over backward to appear nonpartisan. Hence his inclusion of the story about the Richmond train. In the same article, he advised his readers that the real focus of his investigation would be on agriculture and on the general conditions of everyday life in the countryside. He offhandedly added, "No man can write of the South and put Slavery entirely in the background." A month later, in a subsequent article, he even went so far as to claim, "I did not intend when I commenced writing these letters to give much attention to the subject of Slavery."

He was being disingenuous. As he had pointed out to Kingsbury before leaving Staten Island, the opportunity to investigate slavery had attracted him to the undertaking. He had an ambitious goal: saving the Union. His plan was to ignore entirely the moral issues that formed the abolitionists' platform, which, in his opinion, only served to polarize the two sides. Instead, he would argue the case against slavery on economic grounds. Southerners contended that they needed slaves to support their way of life. Olmsted wanted to demonstrate that, on the contrary, slavery was a burden, not a benefit. If he could convince people of this, he hoped slavery might be abandoned voluntarily; it would also silence the strident calls of abolitionists for drastic action, which he feared would lead to conflict.

He arrived at the economic argument early. While he was still in Richmond and only twelve days into his trip, he wrote to Brace that "I shall be able to show conclusively, I think, that free labor is cheaper than slave (I have a two page letter on it now). The difficulty only consists in the want of hands (white) and the bad effect of slave faithlessness, corrupting them." He described at length in his fourth article how he had visited a farm operated by a Quaker convert who had freed his slaves and replaced them with paid white laborers. The farmer told Olmsted that he reckoned that he had saved money.

Olmsted's argument about the economic shortcomings of slavery had several strands. He emphasized that slaves had no incentive to work either hard or efficiently. Again and again he compared the superior productivity of Northern labor to the relatively feeble efforts of slave workers. Once he recounted watching a group of slaves on a construction site carrying bricks. They appeared to him to be almost immobile. The master began to admonish them to work harder, but soon gave up. "It would only make them move more slowly still when I am not looking at them, if I should hurry them now," he explained, "and what motive do they have to do better? It's no concern of theirs how long the masons wait. I am sure if I was in their place I shouldn't move as fast as they do."

Olmsted witnessed the caning of a black woman for shirking work (actually he only witnessed the beginning of the punishment—he was too shocked to stay). It was evident to him that corporal punishment, especially when it was brutal—which was often the case—was ineffective, for it also penalized the slave owner. An injured slave was likely to be even less productive than before, and he still had to be fed while he recuperated. Olmsted observed that on those plantations where beatings were commonplace, slaves often ran away and hid in the forest or swamp—not permanently, but for short stretches of time. Feigned sickness was another common technique for avoiding work; so was malingering. If his own employees at Tosomock had acted that way, Olmsted pointed out, he would simply have dismissed them. But a slave could not be fired. He might be sold, but then he would have to be replaced, and the cycle would continue.

Not only were slaves unwilling workers, they were mostly unskilled. Olmsted discovered that the great unresolved conundrum of Southern slave owners was "how, without quite destroying the capabilities of the negro for any work at all, to prevent him from learning to take care of himself." Most Southern states made it illegal to teach slaves to read and write, and Olmsted estimated that only one in five among house servants, and one in one hundred of the field hands, might be able to read haltingly. Lacking schooling, instruction, or apprenticeship, the majority were kept ignorant. This obviously affected their work habits. They mistreated farm animals, for example. He was told that the reason that mules, rather than horses, were commonly used was that they were more resistant to abuse and neglect. Generally slaves were not trusted with machinery or with good tools—which further reduced their productivity.

Traveling on a train in South Carolina, Olmsted met an elderly farmer. When the man discovered that Olmsted, too, owned a farm, he asked him:

"Do you work any niggers?"

"No."

"May be they don't have niggers—that is, slaves—to New York."

"No, we do not. It's against the law."

"Yes, I heerd 'twas, some place. How do yer get yer work done?"

"I hire white men—Irishmen, generally."

"Do they work good?"

"Yes, better than negroes, I think, and don't cost nearly as much."

"What do yer have to give 'em?"

"Eight or nine dollars a month, and board, for common hands, by the year."

"Hi, Lordy! and they work up right smart, do they? Why, yer can't get any kind of a good nigger less'n twelve dollars a month."

"And board?"

"And board 'em yes; and clothe, and blank, and shoe 'em, too."

Paradoxically, while they were untrained and unskilled, slaves were expensive. The lucrative cotton trade had driven up the price of field hands to more than a thousand dollars a head, which raised the cost of slave and nonslave labor throughout the South (slave owners often rented their slaves, hence the twelve dollars a month mentioned above). All activities that used slave labor were affected. That was why it was cheaper for Virginians to import their potatoes or cabbages from the North.

Slave owners in noncotton states often sold slaves to cotton planters. Once, in a New Orleans street, Olmsted observed a group of about twenty slaves whom a local plantation owner had recently purchased. "Louisiana or Texas, thought I, pays Virginia twenty odd thousand dollars for that lot of bone and muscle." He glanced at a nearby steamboat, full of settlers from Europe, preparing to sail up the Mississippi to the Midwest. "Yonder is a steamboat load of the same material—bone and muscle—which, at the same sort of valuation, is worth two hundred and odd thousand dollars," he mused, "and off it goes, past Texas, through Louisiana—far away yet, up the river, and Wisconsin or Iowa will get it, two hundred thousand dollars' worth, to say nothing of the thalers and silver groschen, in those strong chests—all for nothing."

The other part of Olmsted's argument was that slavery had a corrupting effect on society as a whole. As his trip progressed, he found more and more evidence to support his claim. Because manual work was done by slaves—hence was a kind of punishment—it was not highly valued; because slaves worked slowly, laggardness became customary; because slaves tended to work carelessly, carelessness was the norm. He observed that all who dealt with slaves "have their standard of excellence made lower, and become accustomed to, until they are content with slight, false, unsound workmanship. You notice in all classes, vagueness in ideas of cost and value, and injudicious and unnecessary expenditure of labor by thoughtless manner of setting about work." Much of the incompetence and inadequacy that he witnessed during his journey he attributed to this lackadaisical attitude on all sides.

Olmsted's South bore little resemblance to the mythic Old South of elegant mansions and graceful cotillion balls. This was no accident. Before the trip Olmsted had complained of the "spoony fancy pictures" that appeared in contemporary books and articles and portrayed Southern life as aristocratic and genteel. He saw that the Southern gentry represented only a tiny fraction of society, and consequently he devoted relatively little space to them. He knew that there were enlightened planters such as his friend Dick Taylor, but on the whole, he did not have a high opinion of Southern society. Although he saw some beautiful plantation houses, he found civic society in towns to be woefully undeveloped. Although this part of the United States had been settled as long as—or, in some cases, longer than—the Northern states, he was shocked to find that it was a different, backward country. Beyond Virginia, he wrote, there were few libraries, colleges, or concert halls. Local book and newspaper publishers were rare. That was hardly surprising. Literacy—among whites—was considerably lower than in the North.

Unlike Harriet Beecher Stowe, who wrote *Uncle Tom's Cabin* on the strength of a single, fleeting visit to Kentucky, Olmsted observed slavery for several months. His first impression of black slaves gave rise to some harsh judgments. "The negroes are a degraded people," he wrote in the *Times*, "degraded not merely by position, but actually immoral, low-lived; without healthy ambition, but little influenced by high moral considerations, and in regard to labor not [at] all affected by regard for duty." His view was critical—not racist. It seemed to him that slaves were kept in a perpetual—and destructive—condition of dependence. "Slavery in Virginia, up to the present time, however it has improved the general character and circumstances of the race of miserable black barbarians that several generations since were introduced here, has done nothing to prepare it, and is yet doing nothing to prepare it, for the free and enlightened exercise of individual independence and responsibility," he concluded.

The conviction that freed slaves would be unprepared to instantly assume the duties and responsibilities of free citizens was central to Olmsted's gradualism. He never changed his opinion that wholesale abolition was ill-advised. But encounters with individual slaves did cause him to temper his views regarding their personal qualities, and to recognize that their degraded condition was neither innate nor permanent. He discovered that some slaves possessed property and had savings. He learned that some free blacks owned plantations (and slaves). He met slaves who were blacksmiths and mechanics and was impressed by their abilities and intelligence.

Once, while he was being driven back to New Orleans after visiting Dick Taylor's plantation, he struck up a conversation with the driver, William, a house servant. Olmsted commented about the possibility of free slaves being sent to Liberia, an idea that he had discussed with Taylor. "Why is it, massa, when de brack people is free, dey wants to send em away out of dis country?" was the response. Olmsted was taken aback. He had assumed that blacks would be grateful for the opportunity of returning to Africa. He was also embarrassed to admit that many whites were afraid of blacks and would be happiest to see them depart. Seeking to change the subject, he asked William what he would do if he were set free.

"If I was free, massa; *if I was free*" (with great animation), "I would—well, sar, de fus thing I would do, if I was free, I would go to work for a year, and get some money for myself,—den—den—den, massa, dis is what I would do—I buy me, fus place, a little house, and little lot land, and den—no; and den—den—I would go to old Virginny, and see my mudder. Yes, sar, I would like to do dat fus thing; den, when I com back, de fus thing I'd do, I'd get me a wife; den, I'd take her to my house, and I would live with her dar; and I would raise things in my garden, and take 'em to New Orleans, and sell 'em dar, in de market. Dat's de way I would live, if I was free."

Olmsted was evidently touched by the slave's simple—and not unreasonable—version of the American pursuit of happiness.

Such conversations, and there were many throughout his journey, enabled Olmsted to write convincingly not only about the institution of slavery, but about slaves themselves. It would be too much to say that he was able to see slavery through the eyes of slaves, but he did emphasize the humanity of American blacks. "I cannot see how it can be doubted that the beings called negroes are endowed with a faculty, which distinguishes them from brutes, of perceiving the moral distinction of good and evil; of loving the good and regretting the evil which is in themselves. They are, beyond a question, I think, also possessed of independent reasoning faculties," he wrote.

As Brace had hoped, Olmsted's ideas about slaves and slavery did undergo a transformation as a result of his firsthand experience of the South. Although he strove mightily to present both sides of the slavery question in his *Times* reports, by the end of his trip, his moderate views had hardened considerably. Here is the bellicose tone with which he ended the series:

> Yet, mainly, the North must demolish the bulwarks of this stronghold of evil by demonstrating that the negro is endowed with the natural capacities to make a good use of the blessing of freedom; by letting the negro have a fair chance to prove his own case, to prove himself a man, entitled to the *inalienable rights of a man* [emphasis added]. Let all who do not think Slavery right, or who do not desire to assist in perpetuating it, whether right or wrong, demand first of their own minds, and then of their neighbors, FAIR PLAY FOR THE NEGRO.

The reference to the second sentence of the Declaration of Independence is unmistakable, as is the call for integrating freed slaves into American society. The man who once wrote his father, "Hurrah for gradual Emancipation and a brisk trade with Africa," has come a long way.

CHAPTER FIFTEEN

A Traveling Companion

AFTER LEAVING FASHION PLANTATION, Olmsted spent three more weeks in Louisiana. He was captivated by New Orleans. "There is no city in America so interesting to a traveler, or in which one can stroll with more pleasure and with so long-coming weariness," he informed his readers. Olmsted visited New Orleans only fifty years after the Louisiana Purchase. Although the city had grown rapidly under American rule, it retained much of its colonial past. Most of the original French buildings—of wood—had perished in fires; the characteristic brick and wrought-iron architecture was a product of the forty-year Spanish occupation that had ended in 1801. But traces of the French city remained in the original street layout and in the Creole patois that Olmsted found charming if not always easy to understand. He stayed at the St. Charles Hotel, ambled among the orange trees in the Place d'Armes, and sat in sidewalk cafés. He thought himself back in Paris.

He carried a letter of introduction to Thomas Bayne, a lawyer who had been a Yale classmate of Brace and John Hull's. Olmsted interviewed Bayne about Louisiana's unique legislation governing the legal status of enslaved and free blacks. The so-called Code Noir, which dated from the French colonial period, defined no less than nine major categories of mixed race such as mulatto (white and black), quadroon (white and mulatto), *sang-mêlé* (white and *quarteron*), and many more subcategories. Despite—or perhaps because of—such distinctions, Louisiana was unique in the South when it came to tolerating relations between blacks and whites. Bayne introduced Olmsted to the city's cosmopolitan quadroon society. Olmsted was fascinated by this demimonde of "free people of slight African blood," especially by the women. "They are generally very pretty," he wrote, "and often extremely beautiful. I think that the two most beautiful women I ever saw were of this class." He devoted most of one of his *Times* reports to a remarkably candid discussion of the liaisons that took place between women of mixed race and white gentlemen. He made the practical if unconventional argument that such domestic arrangements were a better choice for young unmarried men than resorting to the street prostitutes who were common in New York. It is impossible not to read a wistful, personal note into his account of these marriages of *convenance,* as he called them. It was almost a year and a half since Emily Perkins had turned him down, and no one had succeeded her. However, there is no evidence that he succumbed to the charms of these New Orleans beauties.

After leaving New Orleans, he visited several more plantations, among them that of Meredith Calhoun, one of the largest cotton growers in the South, who owned fifteen thousand acres and more than seven hundred slaves. Olmsted spent two days there, interviewing both Calhoun and his overseers. Olmsted had originally intended to proceed up the Red River to Texas, but various exasperating delays—and lost luggage—caused him to cut short his western excursion. He traveled north by Mississippi steamboat as far as Memphis. From there, by a combination of rail and stagecoach, he traversed the upcountry of Mississippi, Alabama, Georgia, the Carolinas, and Virginia, finally arriving in Washington. This last portion of his journey—more than seven hundred and fifty miles—he covered in less than two weeks. He was hurrying home for the spring planting.

He reached Tosomock Farm on April 6, 1853, almost four months to the day after his departure. Over the next summer and fall he busied himself with farming. He continued to write. The *Times* had started the series when he was halfway through his trip; eight of his articles had been published by the time he returned home. Working from his early drafts and travel notes, he continued to supply the newspaper with reports that chronicled his experiences and encounters up to and including the visit to the Calhoun plantation.

Olmsted's reporting is remarkable. He combines descriptive narrative with statistics and information in a way that has become commonplace in modern journalism but was unusual in the mid-nineteenth century. He never stoops to punditry. He does not lecture but gently steers the reader to the conclusion that the facts demand. He understood that ordinary people are worth listening to, and he lets them speak for themselves. He records exactly what they say, slang, dialect, grammatical errors, and all. It gives his articles a lively, novelistic immediacy.

The *New-York Daily Times* published forty-six articles in all (only two were rejected), an average of almost one a week. The final article appeared on Monday, February 13, 1854, in its usual position at the top of page two. In the same issue, Raymond editorialized that these were "decidedly the best reports that have ever been made, of the industrial condition and prospects of the Southern section of the Union." Not everyone agreed with Yeoman's evenhandedness. Some Southern pro-slavery advocates thought him too critical. "[The *Times*] sends a stranger among us 'to spy out the nakedness of the land,'" thundered the editor of the *Savannah Republican*. "What is its object, if it be not an evil one?" On the other side, some die-hard Northern abolitionists found the economic reports too tolerant and "designed to gloss over the evils of Slavery." Controversy did not displease Raymond. He commissioned Olmsted to return to the South. Yeoman would pick up his trip where he had left off and continue on into Texas, which had been admitted as a slave state eight years earlier.

At this time, Olmsted was not alone. His brother, John, and Mary, since married, had just returned from Europe. Thanks to the elder Olmsted's generosity, they had been living in Italy and Switzerland, hoping that a change in climate would improve John's health. Since fresh air and outdoor exercise were (mistakenly) thought to be an effective treatment for tuberculosis, John, who did not feel strong enough to establish a medical practice, decided that a farm might be the best place for him. Shortly after Olmsted returned from the South, John, Mary, and their new son, John Charles (born in Geneva), moved to Tosomock Farm. When Frederick announced that he was leaving on a second trip, his brother suggested that he should accompany him. As John later put it: "[My] motive for this journey was the hope of invigorating weakened lungs by the elastic power of a winter's saddle and tent-life." One can understand that Olmsted was not thrilled by the idea of taking an invalid along on what promised to be a strenuous outing. But he could not really object, for by then he had been enlisted in what was becoming an Olmsted family project—taking care of John.

The brothers left Staten Island on November 10, 1853. They traversed the upcountry of Kentucky and Tennessee by a combination of rail, stagecoach, and riverboat. After reaching Louisville, they continued down the Ohio River to the Mississippi, and directly south to New Orleans. Their ultimate destination was the town of Natchitoches,

Louisiana, not far from the Texas border. This was as far west as Olmsted had reached the previous spring, and there they planned to purchase horses and begin their saddle trip.

They did not dawdle on the way, except for a detour to Nashville to visit the home of Samuel Perkins Allison, a Yale classmate and friend of John's. Allison belonged to a wealthy family that was among the largest slave owners in Tennessee. He was intelligent, educated, and immersed in local politics, having recently run—unsuccessfully—for Congress. Olmsted was eager to meet him—this was just the sort of informed Southerner to whom he needed to talk. The trio engaged in two days of intense debate, since with Olmsted talk always turned in that direction. He liked Allison, but the frank conversation disabused Olmsted of any idea that the Southern gentry might be ready to compromise on slavery. Allison was unrepentant about the need for slaves. He adamantly insisted that the South "*must* have more slave territory"; he even believed that California would eventually become a slave state. Olmsted was unnerved that such views could be held by someone he considered a "good specimen of the first class gentleman of the South." He had hoped that his own moderate ideas might be shared by the Southern gentry. Instead, he complained in a letter to Brace, "they do not seem to have a fundamental sense of right. . . . Their moving power and the only motives which they can comprehend are materialistic."

Allison's hope that slavery would spread was not idle speculation. On January 23, 1854, Stephen A. Douglas would introduce the Kansas-Nebraska Act to the Senate. This legislation was enacted by Congress two months later, overturning the long-standing Missouri Compromise. Henceforth, the new territories of Kansas and Nebraska would be free to decide whether to outlaw slavery. This enraged abolitionists and raised the hopes of the pro-slavery factions.

By the time that Douglas proposed his bill, Frederick and John were in Texas. They made their way through the eastern part of the state ("an unpleasant country and a wretched people," wrote Olmsted). In January they arrived in San Antonio, then a rapidly growing little city of about six thousand. Olmsted found its picturesque mixture of peoples and building styles as interesting in its own way as New Orleans. Around the main plaza stood an old Spanish stone cathedral, buildings of adobe, and recently built hotels and stores of brick. San Antonio was the site of several missions, including the famous Alamo, which was used as an armory and still bore the scars of its 1836 siege. The main street was crowded with Mexican drovers, Plains Indians, and American soldiers. The men all carried revolvers (as did Frederick and John), and gunfights were common. The town amusements, according to Olmsted, were a troupe of Mexican acrobats who performed in the street, and a local theater company that served up "horrors and despair, long rapiers, and well oiled hair." There was also, he observed sardonically, the occasional hanging.

Frederick and John planned to go to Mexico, but were advised that it was too dangerous for solitary travelers. They were unable to find a guide, or a party to which they could attach themselves, and had to wait. Meanwhile, they made several camping trips into the surrounding region, less for journalistic purposes than as part of John's putative cure.

Winter turned to spring. They were in no hurry. They made excursions into the prairie, went up into the Guadalupe Mountains, and traveled as far as the Gulf of Mexico. Frederick rode Nack, a roan "Creole pony"; Fanny, a mare, was John's mount. They were also accompanied by Judy, a bullterrier, and Mr. Brown, the pack mule. Mr. B, as he was called, carried their supplies, which included a bag of books. When it rained, they would stay in their tent, reading. Olmsted sketched.* There were long talks around the campfire at night. They marveled at the Western landscape, the enormous sky, the vast plain, so different from the tame Connecticut countryside of their boyhood. Frederick was a month short of his thirty-second birthday, John was twenty-eight. I am tempted to say that they were playing at cowboys—except that this term did not come into popular use until at least twenty years later. The cowboys they did see—they were called drovers—were mounted on mules and were not old Texas hands but young Easterners, working their way west to the California gold fields.

Olmsted described this idyllic period in a letter to an acquaintance in New York:

> We are traveling about, without definite aim, in an original but on the whole, very pleasant fashion. The spring here is very beautiful. The prairies are not mere seas of coarse grass, but are of varied surface with

---

*His later books on his Southern travels included woodcuts prepared from his travel sketches.

thick wooded borders and many trees and shrubs, standing singly and in small islands. Having been generally burnt over or the rank grass fed closely down, they have very frequently a fine, close, lawn-like turf, making an extremely rich landscape. At this season, moreover, there are a very great variety of pretty, small, modest flowers. . . . We ride and take along with us a pack-mule which carries our tent, bedding and stores. Always in the evening we search out a pleasant spot by some water-side and take plenty of time to pitch our tent securely & make every thing comfortable about us. So we have from fifty to a hundred pleasant spots we could find in this great wilderness. It gives me an entirely new appreciation of the attachment of nomad tribes to their mode of life. I was always however much of a vagabond.

CHAPTER SIXTEEN

The Texas Settlers

OLMSTED KEPT SENDING REPORTS back to the *Times*. When he got to
Natchitoches, he immediately recorded his impressions of the town,
which was the jumping-off place for settlers "pursuing their Western
destiny," as he put it in his newspaper account. This region was less well-
known to New Yorkers, and with Raymond's encouragement, Olmsted
included more background information on "frontier scenes and incidents." He met Texas Rangers, Indians, and pony express riders. He
recounted fighting a prairie fire (started by "the Doctor") and watching a
cattle drive. He described life in a frontier fort and included an eyewit-
ness's account of a Comanche raid.

He discussed social and economic conditions—and, of course, slavery.
Texas confirmed Olmsted's earlier observations about the negative
effects of slavery. Indeed, the primitiveness he was coming to associate
with a slave-owning society was, if anything, emphasized by the rough
conditions of the frontier. But he did discover something new and unexpected. Shortly after crossing the border from Louisiana, he and his
brother were caught in a bitterly cold north wind. They sought shelter in
a log cabin that turned out to belong to German settlers, who offered
them a bed for the night. The fastidious Olmsted admired their snug
home—which compared favorably with the poor accommodations he
had experienced two days earlier at the house of an American rancher.
The next morning, they were served breakfast.

There was also *pfannekuchen*, something between a pancake and an
omelette, eaten with butter and sugar. The sugar was refined, and the
butter yellow and sweet. "How can you make such butter?" we asked, in
astonishment. "Oh, ho! it is only the American ladies are too lazy; they
not work enough their butter. They give us fifty cent a pound for our

butter in San Antone! yes, fifty cent! but we want to eat good butter, too." Such was the fact. At the house of the American herdsman, who owned probably one hundred cows, there was no milk or butter—it was too much trouble. . . . The German had a cow driven into a pen to be milked at daylight. His wife milked her herself. The American owned a number of negroes. The German was happy in the possession of freedom, undebilitated by mastership or slaveship.

Olmsted was curious about these enterprising settlers who were so different from the rough and uncouth people he had encountered on his previous Southern travels. He learned that his hosts were part of a large German immigrant community that had come to western Texas in the early 1840s. They told him about several German settlements near San Antonio. Nine days later the brothers stopped in one of these, Neu Braunfels. The town was unremarkable: small houses with verandas lining a wide main street. One of the houses had a sign hanging over the porch: "Guadalupe Hotel, J. Schmitz." Inside, the brothers found a neat public room, furnished in dark oak furniture with stenciled panels and scroll ornaments on the walls. The four men smoking at one of the tables greeted them politely as they entered. The food they were served in this Texas *Gasthaus*—on a clean, white tablecloth!—was excellent.

During the time they spent in the region of San Antonio, Olmsted and his brother revisited Neu Braunfels several times. The town and the immediate vicinity were home to about three thousand people, the majority of whom were German immigrants. Neu Braunfels must have reminded Olmsted of Hartford, for it had a full complement of stores, small tradesmen's shops, blacksmiths, wagon-makers, tailors, shoemakers, as well as doctors' and lawyers' offices. As in New England—and missing in most of the Southern settlements he had visited earlier— there were numerous signs of civic improvement: a local newspaper, free schools, and private academies. In addition, he discovered many associations: an agricultural society, a mechanics' institute, and clubs for music, dancing, gardening, and political debate.

Notably absent in Neu Braunfels was slavery. The one black slave in town belonged to an American; the Germans did not own slaves and, on the whole, were opposed to slavery. One can imagine Olmsted's excitement. Here was living proof of his hypothesis that a conscious decision not to adopt slavery provided a superior economic and social foundation for building a civilized society.

There were several German settlements: Fredericksburg, Neu Wied, and Sisterdale. San Antonio, too, had a large German community. There they met Adolf Douai. Douai, Saxon-born, had arrived in the United States two years earlier. He was well-educated—he had a doctorate in philosophy from the University of Koenigsberg—a freethinker, and a committed republican. Like many of the German immigrants, he had fled Germany after the unsuccessful revolution of 1848. He was also editor of the *San Antonio Zeitung,* a weekly newspaper. Douai, only a few years older than Olmsted, was in many ways a Saxon version of Charles Brace—energetic, high-minded, idealistic, and a committed abolitionist. He and the Olmsted brothers took to one another immediately. Douai accompanied them on a trip to Sisterdale. He introduced them to the scholars and professional men who were the leading figures of the expatriate community. "Educated, cultivated, well-bred, respectful, kind and affable" was how Olmsted described them. He felt at home among these kindred spirits.

Olmsted was enthusiastic about the German settlements and devoted several detailed *Times* articles to this subject. He never failed to underline the connection he saw between the vitality of these communities and the absence of slavery:

> In Neu-Braunfels and the surrounding German hamlets, there are five *Free Schools* for elementary education, one exclusive Roman Catholic School, a town Free School of higher grade, and a private Classical School. In *all* of these schools English is taught with German. The teacher of the higher department of the central town school is paid four hundred dollars a year; that of the primary department, (a female,) two hundred dollars. I have been several times told by Americans that the only reason that there were no negroes owned by the Germans in the town was, that none were rich enough to buy one. This may be the case, but if so, the provisions they have made for the education of their children are certainly liberal, and promise much for the future intelligence and industry of the white community. That such a community—generally industrious, active-minded, and progressively intelligent—can never exist in intimate connection with enslaved labor, I am well convinced.

In one of his articles, he predicted the eventual division of Texas into several smaller states (as was possible in the original annexation act) and considered it likely that the areas where the majority consisted of German settlers would form a free-soil state. "And such a State, self-governed by such a people, I hope to live to see there," he concluded. He actually hoped to see it *and* live there. At one point, Frederick and John seriously considered joining the German settlers. It seems to have been John's idea. He had undertaken this trip with half an eye to finding a home in a warm climate, and Frederick, with his habitual enthusiasm, agreed that they should become pioneers together. They wrote home describing their plans. They needed Mary's approval—and their father's financial aid. If both were forthcoming, they planned to spend the summer making preparations for the move.

Either Mary or John Olmsted—more likely both—refused to endorse their proposal. That was hardly surprising. From the distance of Tosomock Farm, the idea of the two brothers becoming Texas pioneers and joining a group of German political exiles must have sounded far-fetched. Finally, it seemed that way to them, too, and they gave up the notion. Being unable to find a traveling party, they also gave up the idea of a trip through Mexico. They contented themselves with a brief, four-day outing, guided by a retired Texas Ranger. (They found conditions across the border just as dangerous as they had been told.) Nor did they go to California, as Olmsted had hoped. They could have joined one of the cattle drives and wagon trains that were westward bound, but I think that their adventurous spirit was flagging. On April 24 they left San Antonio and started their journey home.

CHAPTER SEVENTEEN

Yeoman Makes a Decision

ON MAY 26, 1854, the brothers arrived at Bayou Sara, Louisiana, a little town on the Mississippi River. Here they parted company. John had decided that he could not continue the saddle trip. His health had not improved; far from it, he felt worn. He wanted to get back to Staten Island and his family as quickly as possible. He boarded a steamboat bound for New Orleans, where he could take passage to New York. Frederick decided that he would go on alone. He was no less fatigued than his brother, but he wanted to revisit the cotton-producing region that he had passed through so precipitously the year before. Taking Judy the bullterrier, and mounted on Belshazzar, a stallion that had replaced Nack, he set off with "a deep notch of sadness," as he later recollected. It took him slightly more than two months to reach Richmond, Virginia—almost a thousand miles in the saddle. There, he boarded a steamship bound for New York. He, Bel, and Judy arrived at Tosomock Farm on August 2. This time he had been away almost nine months.

This final leg of Olmsted's trip proved a valuable experience. Traveling alone was less pleasant, but it made him a more effective observer. He brought a seasoned traveler's eye to bear on his surroundings. This area, which he referred to as the backcountry, was less urbanized and less economically developed than either the Atlantic seaboard or the Deep South. There were smaller plantations, rural communities, and common farms.

For most of this part of the trip Olmsted was unencumbered by the need to write regular reports to the *Times*. "Letters from the Southwest," as his series was titled, ends abruptly with the thirteenth letter describing his excursion into Mexico. It is unclear exactly why Raymond cut the series short. He was not displeased with Olmsted's reporting, for he subsequently published two of the unused letters as unsigned editorials. The *Times* consisted of only eight pages. Since advertising and commercial notices regularly consumed two or three pages, space was at a premium. Raymond probably decided that his readers were more interested in the territories of Kansas and Nebraska, where Douglas's act had stirred up the pro- and antislavery factions, than in German settlers and Texas cattle drives.

Shortly after arriving in Staten Island, Olmsted started to write the first of three books based on his Southern travels. *A Journey in the Seaboard Slave States* describes his trip from Virginia to Louisiana. Although the forty-six newspaper articles comprised sufficient material for a book, he did not intend to write merely a compilation. He wanted to support his findings with more "facts," which involved considerable background reading: government reports, almanacs, and a prodigious number of newspapers and magazines. He made slow progress, not the least because he continued to write occasional articles for the *Times*. Prompted by a dramatic maritime collision, he wrote letters on the security of ocean steamers and the behavior and treatment of merchant seamen—his old concern. He conducted a newspaper survey on the working conditions of farm laborers and reported the results in a feature article. He reviewed a German book on American slavery. The author, Friedrich Kapp, was then living in New York. Olmsted had met his uncle in Texas, and he and Kapp began agitating for a free state in western Texas.

The latter issue had come to the fore in September, when John received a letter from Adolf Douai. Antislavery sentiment on the part of some of the progressive German settlers was running high, he wrote. A Free party had been formed and had produced a powerful reaction on the part of native-born, slaveholding Americans against the immigrants. There had even been talk of lynch law and reprisals against the *San Antonio Zeitung*, which supported the Free party. The newspaper's nervous shareholders decided to sell. Douai appealed to the two brothers to help him secure a loan of $350 to buy the newspaper. They responded by circulating an appeal among their acquaintances and friends, including Charles Brace and Henry Ward Beecher. "A Few Dollars Wanted to Help the Cause of Future Freedom in Texas," signed by Olmsted, raised more than two hundred dollars. The money was forwarded to Douai as a donation. Olmsted worked hard to support his German friends. He helped locate a supplier of newsprint. He purchased English type for the newspaper, which would henceforth be bilingual. He canvassed for new subscribers. He convinced Raymond to publish editorials in the *Times* encouraging Northern emigration to western Texas. Olmsted also promised Douai to write a fortnightly article for the *Zeitung*.

Olmsted's efforts as a journalist and political activist did not go unnoticed. He began to acquire a reputation in New York. He spent more and more time in the city. He frequently met Brace, now busy directing the Children's Aid Society. Through him he was introduced to New York's literary world. He began to understand that to be taken seriously in this world he would have to cease being a part-time farmer and devote more time to becoming a full-fledged man of letters. He consulted with his friends. He learned of a young publisher, Joshua Dix, who had just bought the well-regarded *Putnam's Monthly Magazine* from George Putnam, Olmsted's Staten Island neighbor. Dix was a friend of Brace's and knew Olmsted. They reached an agreement: Olmsted would become the third partner in Dix, Edwards & Company. He started working with them in March 1855 and wrote his father, "I should *probably* [emphasis added] take up my residence in New York."

A month later Olmsted moved from Staten Island to rented rooms on lower Broadway. It is inaccurate to say that he simply lost interest in farming. When he set out on his Southern travels, he must have had in mind his old mentor George Geddes, who combined farming with a wide variety of nonagricultural activities. But Geddes had inherited a large, productive farm and was a wealthy man. After eight years as a farmer, Olmsted still depended on his father's financial support—about $1,000 a year. The farm was not paying its way. On the other hand, he had earned a total of $720 (about $20,000 in modern dollars) from the *Times* for his two series. This was a modest income for what amounted to fourteen months of beginner's work, but it was evidence that perhaps his talents lay in that direction.

Olmsted's father, who still held a note on the farm, agreed. He had pinned his hopes on John, who—it was now clear—would remain an invalid. Frederick, on the other hand, did seem to be having some success with his writing. In his own quiet way, John Olmsted was proud of his eldest son's achievements. He advanced Frederick five thousand dollars to invest in the publishing firm and instructed him to sign over title of the farm to his brother. This Frederick was willing to do. John and Mary had been living at Tosomock for two years. They now had a second child, Charlotte. In many ways it must have seemed to Frederick that it was now more their home than his. John agreed to take over the farm. He had to live somewhere, after all, and Mary's modest inheritance of seven hundred dollars a year meant that he did not have many options. Yet he was not thrilled with the prospect of becoming a farmer. "I regret to be left in the lurch, but I suppose things will go on as they did in his absence last summer," John wrote to his half sister Bertha. His despondency is palpable. His tuberculosis was getting worse. Now he also had to deal with a farm that was showing the ill effects of two years of desultory management by his neglectful brother. It was not Olmsted's finest hour. He told his father that his absence in New York would be temporary, "for a year perhaps." Yet he knew—at least so I think—that he was leaving for good.

CHAPTER EIGHTEEN

"Much the Best Mag.
in the World"

MAGAZINE PUBLISHING, which had been a cottage industry at the beginning of the nineteenth century, had been transformed by urbanization, greater literacy, and increased leisure time into a mass-market enterprise. In 1825 there were fewer than one hundred magazines in the United States; by 1850 there were at least six hundred. Olmsted's decision to enter this dynamic field indicates his ambition. After years of depending on his father, he wanted financial success as well as intellectual prominence. He hoped that Dix, Edwards & Company would provide both.

It was not an unreasonable expectation. *Putnam's Monthly Magazine* was only two years old but it already had a reputation. Its circulation of almost twenty thousand could hardly match the one hundred thousand of its chief rival, *Harper's Monthly,* but its literary standing was higher. The success of *Harper's* was based on serializing English novels by such lionized writers as Charles Dickens and Sir Edward Bulwer-Lytton. This had the double virtue, to the publisher, of being both popular and cheap— since *Harper's* did not pay royalties to foreign authors. *Putnam's* was different. As its masthead announced, it was the "Magazine of *American* [emphasis added] Literature, Science and Art." It published Melville, who was not then well-known, as well as essays, poetry, and short stories by Thoreau, Longfellow, Hawthorne, and Fenimore Cooper.

Joshua Dix, only twenty-four, had big plans for the fledgling firm. He had purchased the American publishing rights to Charles Dickens's popular weekly periodical, *Household Words.* He was thinking of starting a magazine for children. He also intended to branch out into book publishing. He assured Olmsted that *A Journey in the Seaboard Slave States* would be one of their first titles.

The first order of business, however, was to assemble a staff to write and edit *Putnam's*. Charles Briggs, the founding editor, had stepped down. His brilliant assistant was George William Curtis. Curtis, a genial, handsome man and a popular public lecturer, was two years younger than Olmsted. He was already a well-known author and wrote a widely read column in *Harper's*. He was offered the editor's position but agreed only to read and edit manuscripts. He probably wanted to see how the magazine would fare under its new owners. Two other *Putnam's* alumni also agreed to help: Charles A. Dana, a literary critic, and Parke Godwin, whose specialty was political commentary. All three were seasoned journalists. This still left the post of editor vacant. Dix had worked for George Putnam, but as a clerk; Arthur Edwards had no background in publishing. They were businessmen. Olmsted, a published author and journalist, was the only partner equipped to deal with the literary affairs of the firm. He became the managing editor.

He loved it. He was inexperienced but had the help of Curtis, as well as Dana and Godwin. His organizational abilities came to the fore. Curtis half-jokingly referred to him as Mr. Law. A large part of Olmsted's responsibility was dealing with contributors. His outgoing nature helped. In Boston he met Longfellow and James Russell Lowell, as well as the Harvard botanist Asa Gray; in Concord he visited Emerson; he went to Andover to solicit articles from Harriet Beecher Stowe; and in New York he dined with Washington Irving and chatted with William Makepeace Thackeray, who was in the United States on a lecture tour. He acquired an essay by Thoreau and a short story by Melville. He was elected a member of the Press Club. Just as he had planned, he was becoming an active citizen in what he called the "literary republic." At this time, too, he met a friend of Curtis's, Charles Eliot Norton, a young man with literary interests who lived in Cambridge.

Olmsted was happy. The circulation of the magazine improved. The new owners had overcome the first hurdle: maintaining the high standard set by George Putnam. The *Times* referred to the new *Putnam's* as "the most original magazine published in this country." One day Curtis excitedly told his colleagues that, according to Longfellow, Thackeray had called *Putnam's* "much the best Mag. in the world." Less than two months after arriving in New York, Olmsted proudly related to his father:

> The best writers seem already to have acquired confidence that we can
> be depended upon to do our duty strongly & boldly and that the Maga-

zine is to be more than ever the leading magazine and the best outlet of thought in the country. This is more than half the battle. If we can get the writers, there is little fear but that we shall get the readers. It is generally understood that we have capital enough at command and shall pay generously & promptly, and the consequence is that we are now declining every day manuscripts that we should have accepted during the first month.

He was boasting. Dix, Edwards & Company was chronically short of capital. To succeed it needed to grow; to grow it had to spend money. It acquired several books for publication; it purchased *Schoolfellow,* a children's magazine. Abruptly, Edwards informed Olmsted that there would not be sufficient funds to advance him the printing cost for *A Journey in the Seaboard Slave States* as previously agreed. Dix, Edwards & Company would distribute the book, but Olmsted would have to find the five hundred dollars himself.* Shamefacedly, he turned to his father for the loan.

By the end of the year his book was ready for publication. Its full title was *A Journey in the Slave States, with Remarks on Their Economy.* Thanks to the profusion of these "remarks," the book had grown to almost twice the length of the original newspaper series. The book was not his only sideline. He continued to help Adolf Douai, whose newspaper was foundering. He sent him articles and personally guaranteed his printing debts in New York.† He contacted the New England Emigrant Aid Company, which had been founded for the express purpose of promoting free-soil settlement. This led to an extended correspondence with one of the Emigrant Aid Company's leading figures, the Reverend Edward Everett Hale, who lived in Boston. By a remarkable coincidence, this clergyman was the husband of his ex-fiancée, Emily Baldwin. It was not, at first, an easy relationship. After four years, Olmsted still felt the sting of Emily's rejection. In one of his letters to Hale that is otherwise all business, he closed with the following candid confession: "I can't well write a word to you without

---

*Authors generally financed their own books. Olmsted's earlier agreement was unusual and probably part of his original arrangement with Dix, Edwards & Company.
†When Douai publicly called for the creation of a new free-soil state of Western Texas, he encountered strong opposition not only from Americans but also from many in the German community. Advertisers and subscribers abandoned the paper. Despite Olmsted's help, Douai was eventually forced to close the newspaper.

much emotion even now, but I am anything but a miserable or even a dis-satisfied man & most sincerely. Your friend, Fred. Law Olmsted."

Hale and the Emigrant Aid Company were embroiled in advancing the free-soil cause in Kansas. In preparation for the day when "popular sovereignty" would decide whether the territory would be a free or a slave state, pro-slavery squatters from Missouri had started to post claims to border lands. The Emigrant Aid Company countered by sending anti-slavery people from New England to Kansas. They settled in border towns such as Topeka and founded Lawrence, named in honor of one of the prominent supporters of the Company. In March 1855, five thousand pro-slavery Missourians crossed into Kansas and stuffed ballot boxes to elect a pro-slavery legislature. The antislavery settlers elected their own government. The situation grew dangerous. There was violence. The free-soilers in Lawrence felt threatened. The Emigrant Aid Company sent them a shipment of two hundred rifles disguised as schoolbooks. The weapons were mordantly referred to as "Beecher's Bibles," after Henry Ward Beecher, who was a vocal supporter of the antislavery settlers.

Like Beecher, Olmsted regarded the situation in Kansas as critical. He was a moderate on abolition, but he was not a pacifist. "I suppose that you will be helping them to *arm* in Kansas," he wrote Hale, "which is a better thing & I don't want to divert anything from it." Through Hale, he met a leader of the Lawrence militia and became his official representative in New York. Olmsted organized a public appeal that raised more than four hundred dollars. It was his responsibility to purchase the weapons, and he energetically immersed himself in arms dealing. He sought out a British veteran of guerrilla warfare and with his advice determined that instead of more rifles the besieged settlers would be better served by heavier defensive weapons. He went on a shopping spree at the New York State Arsenal and purchased a mountain howitzer together with fifty rounds of canister and shell and, for good measure, added five hand grenades, fifty rockets, and six swords. He told the private sellers that the shipment was intended for "landing in boats on some foreign coast." The helpful Olmsted also forwarded the free-soilers a copy of *Manual of the Patriotic Volunteer, on Active Service, in Regular and Irregular War*, the relevant sections underscored in ink.

A Journey in the Seaboard Slave States was published in January 1856. Olmsted had earlier showed it in galley form to George Ripley, the founder of

Brook Farm, who was now *Harper's* literary editor. Ripley, whom Olmsted considered the best critic in the country, advised that it would be an undoubted literary success but tactfully warned that the book's commercial appeal might be limited. That was a well-considered judgment. It took three months to sell the first run of two thousand copies. A second printing of one thousand was ordered. That took a further two months to sell. The third printing, two thousand copies, remained largely unsold. Olmsted was disappointed. "There can be little doubt that the book will pay eventually 20 per cent. on cost of publication," he had assured his father. Instead, he would be lucky to break even.

The feeble commercial success of *Seaboard Slave States* had several causes. It was a daunting tome—more than seven hundred densely packed pages.* The freshness of Olmsted's original reporting was dampened by the reams of documentary research that he had included. Two years before, when Yeoman had written about the South, there was comparatively little antislavery literature; now the market was flooded. As the violence escalated in Kansas, the public believed less and less in compromise. Olmsted's moderate position now appeared too tame. This was apparent the following year, when Hinton Rowan Helper published *The Impending Crisis of the South: How to Meet It*. Helper, a South Carolinian turncoat, made the same argument about slavery's negative effects on the economy of the South as Olmsted had, and he likewise anchored his book in copious statistics. But Helper's writing, unlike that of the gentlemanly Olmsted, made no pretense at evenhandedness. It was extreme, intemperate, and vituperative. The manuscript was so inflammatory that no respectable publisher would accept it. Helper had to have it printed by a New York book agent who required extra payment as a guarantee against financial loss. To everyone's surprise, the book became a cause célèbre. It was banned and burned in the South; in the North, it sold hundreds of thousands of copies and was the subject of acrimonious debate. Helper is largely forgotten today, but his book was second only to *Uncle Tom's Cabin* in its impact on popular antislavery sentiment.†

Olmsted tried hard to be fair. But the general public—then as now—was attracted by easy answers. Easy answers were something he refused

---

*To avoid the expense of two volumes, the typesetter used small, compressed type for the long quotations that Olmsted scattered liberally throughout the text.
†The irony was that Helper was an embittered crank who despised blacks.

to provide. His conservative instincts required careful—and lengthy—exposition. He knew that his book was too long. "I am much worried by its bulk," he wrote his father. "This ponderosity becomes a goblin of botheration to me." Ponderosity, indeed. He could have shortened it, but he didn't. That was his stubbornness. He would follow the course he had set himself, whatever the results.

The book was not a commercial success, but it was critically well-received. Ripley had been right about that, too. It was lauded by the *Liberator* and the *Christian Examiner* in Boston, by the *National Era* in Washington, and, of course, by *Putnam's*. Hale, writing in the *North American Review*, called the book "singularly fair," but primly added, "It cannot, of course, be wholly free from travelers' mistakes, but we have not detected any." This was ungrateful considering that Olmsted was advancing Hale's literary career by publishing him in *Putnam's*. Harriet Beecher Stowe was more generous. In a long article on antislavery literature in the *Independent*, she gave *Seaboard Slave States* pride of place—"the most complete and thorough work of this kind," she called it. "The book is very thorough and accurate in its details, and is written in a style so lively and with so much dramatic incident as to hold the attention like a work of fiction." Welcome praise coming from that celebrated writer.

Seaboard Slave States soon appeared in Britain, where its critical reception was, if anything, even warmer. A firsthand account of life in the American South was a novelty, and Olmsted's reasoned position on slavery appealed to the British. A favorable review first appeared in the *Athenaeum* and was quickly followed by a two-installment review in London's *Daily News*, and long, laudatory reviews in the *Examiner*, the *Times*, and the *Saturday Review*. "Mr. Olmsted observes with accuracy and reflects with care . . . although he is not prepared with a remedy for American Slavery, he is a careful and temperate pathologist of the disease," wrote the reviewer of *Household Words*. Both *Fraser's Magazine* and the *Edinburgh Review* used *Seaboard Slave States* as the basis for feature articles: "What Are the United States Coming To?" and "Political Crisis in the United States." *Fraser's Magazine* was in the forefront of Victorian periodicals. The *Edinburgh Review* was the most influential quarterly of the day—among its regular contributors were Olmsted's boyhood heroes Carlyle and Macaulay. In a way he was now in their company.

CHAPTER NINETEEN

Abroad

By the end of 1855, Dix, Edwards & Company had published only seven books. The slim list included a short biographical sketch by Emerson and an essay by George Curtis. There were two crowd-pleasers: *The History of Tom Thumb,* by the prolific British novelist Charlotte Mary Yonge, and *The Holly-Tree Inn,* Charles Dickens's latest Christmas story. British writers such as Yonge and Dickens were popular with American readers, and if the firm was to expand, it needed more such work. Both Dix and Olmsted felt it was shortsighted—not to say dishonorable—to pirate foreign books as *Harper's* was doing. They decided that the best course of action was to establish formal relationships with British publishing houses by becoming their official agent in the United States. This would give the firm a jump on the competition, who were mostly importers. Dix had already engaged a London representative, but it was decided that this ambitious undertaking required one of the partners to go to England in person. Olmsted was the obvious choice. The magazine seemed to be running smoothly, so he could relinquish his editorial duties. The prospect of travel always excited him. He wasted no time. Accompanied by his half sister Mary, he made the frigid transatlantic crossing in mid-February of 1856.

After spending three weeks in London, they traveled to Paris. There they met Bertha, his other half sister, who had been sent to France to study. She was staying with an Olmsted family friend, Sophia Stevens, now Sophia Hitchcock and recently widowed. Sophia was now living in Paris, thanks in part to John Olmsted's apparently boundless generosity. Frederick had courted her six years earlier, before becoming engaged to Emily Perkins. He and Sophia corresponded regularly and had remained friends.

The foursome set out on a two-month Continental tour. They visited the French Riviera, then hardly known to tourists, and continued into Italy, following the usual itinerary of Americans abroad. Springtime on the Arno, the crumbling monuments of Rome, the ruins of Pompeii, the Grand Canal. What a change this was from Olmsted's earlier journeys! Not a walking tour or a backwoods saddle trip, but traveling in style, escorting three attractive young women to boot. After a hard year of working on his book and the magazine, he had earned a vacation.

They took a turn through central Europe and visited Vienna and Prague. In Dresden, Olmsted left them and went to London. He remained there most of that summer, attending to business. He negotiated an agreement with the publisher of *Fraser's Magazine;* he traveled to Scotland to meet with the editors of the *Edinburgh Review.* His aim was not merely to acquire literary properties. As he explained to Dix:

> What I chiefly hope to do in the next year is to unobtrusively obtain the friendship and confidence of the publishing *body* for our house. To convert the present confidence of those who consign to us into a really active friendship, to make them desirous to serve us, and if we are to be (I hope not) considered here as the rivals of Bangs [a New York book dealer], to make them our partisans, to make them do our advertising, blow our trumpets, sound our praises, vindicate our character & advantages.

I find this an impressive statement coming from someone who would, until then, have been better described as impetuous rather than far-sighted. This is the first real evidence of his long-headedness. Of course, he was now older—thirty-four—but this suggests that a new side of him was emerging: the planner. It is also evidence that Olmsted, far from being a poor businessman, had sound commercial instincts.

He found the time to do some writing of his own and started on an introduction to his new book on the saddle trip through Texas. He also resurrected "Yeoman." Learning that a Southern congressman had caned an antislavery senator into insensibility on the floor of the Senate chamber, he wrote an article for the *New-York Times:* "How Ruffianism in Washington and Kansas is Regarded in Europe."

The first glowing British reviews of *Seaboard Slave States* appeared during this period. This was no coincidence. He was promoting his book to English reviewers, even as he was discussing publishing business. As the author of a serious and well-received book on American slavery, and an editor of the esteemed *Putnam's,* he was treated as a man of letters, not as a commercial representative. Thackeray invited him to one of his annual dinners for *Punch* contributors. Olmsted, who had already acquired several books from the publishers of *Punch*, recommended to his partners in New York that they consider distributing the humor magazine but cautioned: "I would not like to have you risk any financial embarrassment for it."

He was astute enough to recognize that British humor might have a limited appeal in the United States, but there was another reason for his prudence. He was concerned about *Putnam's*. His suspicions had been raised by an unpleasant incident arising from his acquisition of a set of woodcuts and electrotypes that he thought would make interesting illustrations in the magazines. His partners disagreed. They brusquely informed him that "there should be no more purchases on our account without our consent." They pointedly added, "We can use our money to better advantage here." Olmsted was always prickly when his judgment was called into question; moreover, "our money" was also his money. An acrimonious exchange of letters followed. He learned from his brother that the magazine's circulation was declining. John also informed him that he and their father had been approached by Dix with a request to invest in the firm. (Neither had accepted.) All this suggested that Dix, Edwards & Company was not financially sound.

For the moment there was little Olmsted could do. His father, stepmother, and half brother Albert were arriving in England at the end of July. John Olmsted had sold his interest in the dry-goods store five years earlier. He had retired—he was only sixty—not on account of his health but of his principles; "one of the partners did something he did not approve of," according to his daughter-in-law. He was financially comfortable and decided to spend a year traveling abroad with his family. It was his first visit to Europe. Frederick met them in Liverpool and, retracing the route of his walking tour, brought them to London. After a week in the city, they journeyed together through the Low Countries and Germany. This was like the family outings of his youth, except that now he was leading the party, playing tour guide, showing off his accumulated Continental lore. They eventually made their way to Dresden, where Bertha and Mary were waiting.

Olmsted returned to London. His plan was to spend another year consolidating his relationships with British publishers. However, there was more disturbing news from New York, this time concerning Arthur

Edwards. Olmsted liked Dix, but his relations with Edwards, who had opposed his participation in the firm, had been cool from the start. They had had a serious row about the advisability of paying British authors. Olmsted, who was fastidious in financial matters, had been shocked to learn that Edwards believed in commercial expediency. So when Dix wrote that their partner had made serious bookkeeping "errors," Olmsted was ready to believe the worst. Reading between the lines, and already concerned that he was being shut out of his own business, he worried that the firm was heading for insolvency. He reluctantly concluded that he was wasting his time in London.

When he returned to New York in October 1856, he had a letter of resignation ready. He had lost confidence in Dix and suspected Edwards of downright dishonesty. But George Curtis, whom he greatly admired and who had become a fast friend, allayed his fears. Curtis had overcome his reticence and was now editor of the magazine and a full partner in the firm. He brought not only probity and experience to the venture, but additional funds. Mollified by Curtis, and persuaded by Dix that the financial irregularities were only a misunderstanding, Olmsted agreed to stay, though he chose not to play any further role in the day-to-day affairs of the firm. It appeared that he had added publishing to his growing list of failed careers, but this would be an unfair judgment. Whatever problems plagued the firm were not his doing. His editorial work on *Putnam's* was a success; his representation on behalf of the firm in London was likewise fruitful. He was good at his job, but once it appeared that his long-range plans had little chance of being brought to fruition, he lost interest. Moreover, with Curtis now firmly—and publicly—in charge of the magazine, he could only play a secondary role. This did not attract him. He was not a good subordinate.

As was often the case, his loss of interest in one activity was accompanied by his intense involvement in another. *A Journey Through Texas*, as his next book was titled, was almost ready for publication. He had not dashed it off during his European travels. As usual, the Olmsted family were a team. The father helped his sons; Frederick took in John Hull and his family when they returned from Europe; now it was John who returned the favor. The preface explained: "Owing to the pressure of other occupations, the preparation of the volume from the author's journal has been committed, with free scope of expression and personality, to his brother, Dr. J. H. Olmsted, his companion upon the trip." It is hard to know how much the book owes to John, since Olmsted's original travel journal has been lost. When the book is compared to his reports in the *Times,* the differences are small. It is likely that John was judicious in his use of the "free scope of expression and personality." He did not insist on having his name included on the title page.

A Journey Through Texas is a considerably shorter book than its predecessor. The journey itself is described in about four hundred pages. John thought that the earlier book was much too long and did not add background research; he avoided ponderous blocks of statistics and long newspaper extracts. He could not stop his brother from including some supporting documentation, but since the book was complete by the time Frederick returned, this was simply added to the main body of the text as a final chapter, "Regional Characteristics," and a lengthy "Statistical Appendix." The rest of *A Journey Through Texas* is a straightforward, readable narrative. Olmsted called it "my best book . . . because edited by my brother."

At least one part of the book was entirely Olmsted's—the long introduction, which he had written in London, titled "A Letter to a Southern Friend." The "friend" is unidentified; he may have been apocryphal, or someone like Samuel Perkins Allison, with whom he and John had argued about slavery in Nashville. The literary device is ingenious, underlining Olmsted's sympathy for Southerners. But this time his evenhandedness did not lead him to mince words. Here, for example, he describes the two chief reasons for the continued survival of an institution that he considers not merely immoral but irrational:

> First: Slavery educates, or draws out, and strengthens, by example and exercise, to an inordinate degree, the natural lust of authority, common as an element of character in all mankind. To a degree, that is, which makes its satisfaction inconvenient and costly—costly of other means of comfort, not only to the individual, but to the community.
>
> Thus, a man educated under the system will be disposed no longer than he is forced, by law or otherwise, to employ servants or laborers who may make demands upon him, and if those demands are refused, may in their turn legally refuse to obey him. He will prefer to accept much smaller profits, much greater inconveniences, than would a man otherwise educated, rather than submit to what he considers to be the

insolence of a laborer, who maintains a greater self-respect, and demands a greater consideration for his personal dignity, than it is possible for a slave to do.

Secondly: The power of exercising authority in this way is naturally overmuch coveted among you. It gives position and status in your society more than other wealth—(wealth being equivalent to power). It is fashionable with you to own slaves, as it is with the English to own land, with the Arabs, horses; and as beads and vermilion have a value among the Indians which seems to us absurd, so, among you, has the power of commanding the service of slaves. Consequently you are willing to pay a price for it which, to one not educated as you have been, seems absurdly high. Nor are you more likely to dispense with slaves, when you have it in your power to possess them, than the Chinese with their fashion of the queue, Turks with their turban, or Englishmen with their hats.

We need no restrictions upon fashions like these, which are oppressive only to those who obey them. Such is not the case with the fashion of slavery.

The purpose of the introduction was to make an explicit connection between his experiences in Texas and the current debate about the expansion of slavery into the new Western territories. He leaves no doubt about where he stands. He makes the strongest possible case against the spread of slavery beyond the South. Finally, he comes down on the side of vigorous—and, by implication, violent—opposition. "Any further extension or annexation of slavery, under whatever pretense or covering it is attempted," he writes, "will only be effected in contemptuous defiance of the people of the Free States." Yeoman, like the rest of the country, is feeling obliged to take sides.

Dix, Edwards & Company sold out the first printing of twenty-five hundred copies in only a month. The brothers, who had decided to split the proceeds—John to get two-thirds—soon began to receive royalty payments. Or, rather, Frederick received the payments, for John was no longer in the United States. His health had deteriorated once more, and he had had enough of Tosomock Farm. In January 1857, shortly before the book appeared, he and his family left for the warmer climate of Cuba. From there, they planned to travel to southern Europe.

Laudatory reviews of *A Journey Through Texas* appeared in all the major newspapers. The description of the German settlements in Texas, which had not appeared in the earlier *Times* reports, made a strong impression. The critic of the *North American Review* voiced a common sentiment: "The German colonies of Texas, which [Olmsted] describes with minute fidelity, are a living refutation of the assertion that white men cannot work under a Southern sun, and that the culture of cotton requires the forced labor of black men." The extensive coverage in the British press also focused on the German settlers. Indeed, a translation of the book appeared in Germany the following year.

The next phase of the free-soil fight between the pro- and antislavery forces could well take place in western Texas. Seeing a chance to advance his book at the same time as his principles, Olmsted sent pages of *A Journey Through Texas,* bound into pamphlets, to the New England Emigrant Aid Company. Through Hale he distributed copies of the book to various influential figures. This produced several supportive editorials in the *Times.* He also wrote to the Cotton Supply Association in Liverpool, urging them to send British settlers to western Texas. The response was less than enthusiastic; still, Olmsted planned a visit to England at the end of the year on behalf of the Emigrant Aid Company.

Olmsted convinced Dix, Edwards & Company to publish Thomas Gladstone's *The Englishman in Kansas: or, Squatter Life and Border Warfare.* The author, a relative of the great politician, was a correspondent for the London *Times* who had reported to his paper on events in the disputed territory. Olmsted contributed a tough-minded introduction to the book, as well as a supplement that brought the reader up-to-date with recent events. He wrote with a sense of urgency. A pro-slavery legislature had been installed in "Bleeding Kansas," where hundreds were being killed in the fighting. The Supreme Court's Dred Scott decision had effectively annulled the Missouri Compromise. Chief Justice Roger Taney himself had declared that blacks—free or enslaved—were not American citizens. The doors to compromise were rapidly closing. "It is the crime of a coward and not the wisdom of a good citizen to shut his eyes to the fact, that this Union is bound straight to disastrous shipwreck," Olmsted warned in the introduction, "if the man at the helm maintains his present course." "The man at the helm" was a veiled reference to President James Buchanan, a pro-slavery Democrat whose policies Olmsted found reprehensible. He ended on a distinctly militant note with a stirring quotation from Thomas Jefferson: "The time to guard against corruption and tyranny is before they shall have gotten hold on us. It is better to keep the wolf out of the fold, than to trust to drawing his teeth and talons, after he shall have entered."

April had seen big changes at Dix, Edwards & Company. The financially troubled firm had finally been called to task. "The creditors exonerated Curtis and me and distinctly reproved D. and E. whom they obliged to withdraw, giving us all their interest and liabilities," Olmsted wrote Kingsbury, reminding him to "throw jobs in our way." Curtis asked Olmsted to stay on as a partner with him and J. W. Miller, a printer who was carrying the bulk of the company's debt. Olmsted agreed, at least for the moment. Three months later he officially withdrew from the firm. He was not leaving a sinking ship. Miller and Curtis had secured a loan of ten thousand dollars from Curtis's wealthy father-in-law, Francis George Shaw. *Putnam's* circulation had not risen, but the magazine was turning a profit. The book publishing venture had expanded to include more than forty titles, including a uniform edition of Curtis's own popular works, Melville's *The Confidence Man*, Thoreau's *Cape Cod*, and a reissue of *Walks and Talks of an American Farmer in England*.

It was an amicable parting. Curtis agreed that Olmsted could return to work part-time at the end of the summer. This arrangement would allow him to pursue his own writing as well as his free-soil activities. For the moment, however, he wanted to complete his current book, *A Journey in the Back Country*, the third volume of his Southern anthology.

Morris Cove, Connecticut

Sunday, August 9, 1857

It is a lazy, late-summer afternoon. Facing New Haven Bay, four miles from the city, is a small seaside inn. It is the kind of place that attracts New Yorkers who want to escape the oppressive heat of the city. Olmsted is one of the guests.

He has been here for more than two weeks. He would have preferred to go to Tosomock Farm, now occupied by a tenant. The inn is convenient. This is not a vacation. He has been working on his book as well as preparing the extracts that are currently appearing weekly in the New York Daily Tribune. *It was good of Greeley to agree to run the series, which is called "The Southerners At Home." Too bad he isn't identified as the author. He wishes he could have signed it "Yeoman," but Raymond would have had a fit.*

He is sitting at a desk. Papers and travel notebooks are spread out untidily in front of him. He is not writing, however. He is leaning back in the armchair, reading a letter. It is from George Curtis, postmarked New York, three days ago. He has reread it many times, and he is still stunned by the words: "We failed today! It was unavoidable."

The firm of Miller & Curtis has declared bankruptcy. The creditors just wouldn't wait any longer. There is something in the air: bankers are getting edgy. People are starting to talk about a crash.* Poor Curtis has lost his own money and also has to answer to his father-in-law. Olmsted himself is well to be out of it, although he may still be dragged into the bankruptcy proceedings. He may be found liable for some of the company's losses. He wishes he could ask his father or John for advice, but they are both still in Europe. He'd better talk to Judge Emerson, his old Staten Island neighbor. He'll know what to do.

The bad news has thrown his own plans into question. He was hoping to support himself by working with Miller & Curtis. That prospect is gone. What's worse, when he quit the firm, he left his father's investment as a loan, so now he owes him five thousand dollars. Where is the money to come from? The Texas book is doing well, but not well enough to cover his debts. In any case, sales will be stopped until the creditors finish disposing of the assets of the firm. And how long will that take? What a depressing business this all is.

He decides to go downstairs. It is teatime and the lounge is starting to fill up. He takes his usual table. He can see the sparkling waters of the harbor through the windows. A lady with a parasol accompanied by a little boy in a sailor suit comes through the door. The boy is carrying a kite. They must have been on the beach. Seaside, summer vacations, childhood: he could be back in Sachem's Head.

"May I sit down?"

Olmsted looks up and recognizes Charles Wyllys Elliott. Elliott, who owns an ironworks, is a leader in the New York business community. Olmsted has come to know him well since Charley Brace introduced them five years ago. The forty-year-old Elliott had been something of a mentor: he helped Brace to found the Children's Aid Society, and he lent his support to Olmsted's efforts to

---

*Two weeks later, the failure of an insurance company and a burst speculative bubble led to the so-called Panic of 1857. Several banks collapsed. Among the more than five thousand businesses that failed were the popular Philadelphia magazine *Graham's;* John P. Jewett & Company, the publisher of *Uncle Tom's Cabin;* and Miller & Curtis's chief competitor, the New York book dealer Bangs Brothers & Company.

arm the Kansas settlers. Like Olmsted, he is an ardent free-soiler, but they share other interests. Elliott has worked as a landscape gardener and horticulturist and once studied under no less than Andrew Jackson Downing. He also is a literary man. He has written a biography of Toussaint-Louverture, a book on rural architecture, another on witchcraft, and has just published a two-volume history of New England. In other words, his mind is as eager and undisciplined as Olmsted's own.

They briefly discuss Miller & Curtis's failure—Elliott was a frequent contributor to Putnam's *magazine. Since April he has been a member of the newly created Board of Commissioners of the Central Park. He is a political progressive and the vice president of the city's Republican party, but his presence on the board is also a reflection of his experience in landscape gardening.*

The idea of a large park for the city, which Downing had proposed six years earlier, is becoming a reality, Elliott tells him. Olmsted is well aware of this. Ever since the city acquired the eight-hundred-odd acres of land, the Democratic mayor and the infant Republican party (which dominates the state legislature) have been in intense political struggle as to who will control this enormous public works project. The Republicans have prevailed. This state-appointed commission is the result.

As a former Whig and now a Republican, Olmsted is interested to hear an account of the feuding inside the commission. The current issue, Elliott tells him, is the appointment of a superintendent, who will be in charge of the workforce and of organizing a park police. It is a delicate business, and they still haven't found the right man. Since the chief engineer overseeing the project is a mayoral appointee, the Republican members of the commission, who are in a majority, want a Republican. At the same time, to ensure the cooperation of the reform Democrats, the new superintendent cannot be perceived to be a "practical" man, that is, a party hack. He must be someone able to manage the park independently of politics.

"I am delighted to hear it," says Olmsted. He heartily disapproves of the patronage and corruption that mark New York municipal affairs. "There's no limit to the good influence a park rightly managed would have in New York, and that seems to be the first necessity of good management."

"I wish we had you on the commission, but as we have not, why not take the superintendency yourself?" says Elliott. "Come now."

"I take it? I'm not sure that I would not if it were offered me," he answers, good-naturedly playing along with Elliott's jest. "Nothing interested me in London like the parks, and yet I thought a great deal more might be made of

them." He is embroidering a little—he hasn't given much thought to parks since he wrote that article for Downing, which was more than six years ago.

"Well, it will not be offered you; that's not the way we do business. But if you'll go to work, I believe you may get it." Eliott adds forcefully, "I wish that you would!"

"You are serious?" It dawns on Olmsted that his friend is not just making conversation. He really means it.

"Yes; but there's no time to lose."

"What is to be done?" Olmsted leans forward. He has to think some more about this, but it may be the solution to his financial problems.

"Go to New York and file an application; see the commissioners and get your friends to back you."

"I'll take the boat tonight and think it out as I go. If no serious objection occurs to me before morning, I'll do it."

HITTING HEADS

John Olmsted, c. 1860.

Mary Cleveland Olmsted, undated.

"Wherever you see a head, hit it" is my style of work, &
I have not yet sowed my wild oats altogether.
—FREDERICK LAW OLMSTED TO JOHN OLMSTED (1862)

CHAPTER TWENTY

A Change in Fortune

AFTER SPEAKING WITH CHARLES ELLIOTT, Olmsted hurried back that very evening to New York. The next day he consulted James Hamilton, an influential New York politician and the son of Alexander Hamilton. James Hamilton, who had helped Olmsted with his free-soil campaign, urged him to apply for the position and offered his assistance. Emboldened, Olmsted called on John Gray, the vice president of the commission (the president was away), with a letter of introduction from Elliott. Gray, a Republican, was impressed by Elliott's strong endorsement, but he told Olmsted that he would need the support of the board's treasurer, Andrew Haswell Green, a reform Democrat who often sided with the Republicans. Gray also suggested that Olmsted meet the chief engineer, Egbert Viele. Green was supportive, Viele less so, but Olmsted was sufficiently encouraged that he immediately wrote a letter to the commission. He presented himself in the best possible light without altogether distorting the truth:

> For the past sixteen years my chief interest and occupation has been with those subjects, familiarity with which is most needed in this office. Economy in the application of agricultural labor has especially engaged my attention, and my observations on this subject have been extensively published and discussed in this country and reprinted in Europe. For ten years I have practically engaged in the direction and superintendence of agricultural laborers and gardeners in the vicinity of New York.
>
> I have visited and examined as a student most of the large parks of Europe—British, French, Italian and German; and while thus engaged have given special attention to police details and the employment of labor in them.

It was true that he had supervised workmen, though only five or six, nowhere close to the five or six hundred who were already employed on the park. His Southern reporting could be described as dealing with "economy in the application of agricultural labor," though his real "chief interest" for the last four years had been journalism and publishing.

Hamilton had advised him to seek letters of support from prominent New Yorkers, and Olmsted canvassed his friends and acquaintances. Parke Godwin, with whom he had worked on *Putnam's*, wrote warmly that the candidate was "a practical farmer, a man of exquisite tastes, most delightful habits and decided character." Asa Gray, the eminent Harvard botanist, was also fulsome: "I desire very simply and sincerely to say that I know Mr. Olmsted well, and that I regard him as eminently fitted for that position. I do not know another person so well fitted for it in all respects, both on practical and general scientific grounds; and I have no doubt that if the choice falls upon him, he will do great honor to the situation and to his already high and honorable reputation."

Hamilton wrote the text of a separate petition:

> The subscribers earnestly recommend Mr. F. Law Olmsted for the office of superintendent of The Central Park New York—From this Gentleman's practical training as an agriculturist, His horticultural writings— His talents and character we believe him eminently qualified for the duties of that office—and that from his perseverance and industry he will perform them with usefulness to the Public; and credit to himself— September 1857

This document was signed by seven New York notables, including Hamilton, David Dudley Field, a prominent lawyer, and the wealthy philanthropist Peter Cooper. The most impressive signatory was Washington Irving, the grand old man of New York letters. There were several applicants. A building contractor and a surveyor had the qualifications but were considered too politically partisan. John Woodhouse Audubon, the son of the famous naturalist, was a skilled draftsman but did not impress the board. The two strongest candidates to emerge were Joel Benedict Nott, a chemistry professor at Union College in Schenectady, and Frederick Law Olmsted.

One of the commissioners later maintained that it was Washington Irving's support that swung the final vote. Olmsted claimed not to be sure exactly why he was chosen. That was false modesty: he was an attractive candidate. He was young—Nott was sixty years old—and obviously energetic. His professional credentials were hardly more meager than those of a professor of chemistry. Olmsted had made a name for himself as a result of his *Times* articles, his books, and his work on *Putnam's*. His own petition contained almost two hundred signatures—two hundred!—including that of William Cullen Bryant, the editor of the *New York Evening Post*. Bryant's endorsement was important, for in 1844 he had been the very first (even before Downing) to call for the creation of a New York park. Since the idea of a large public park was a novelty, Olmsted's firsthand knowledge of European parks (he had, after all, written about Birkenhead in *The Horticulturist*) was an asset. So were his politics. His efforts on behalf of the free-soilers made him welcome to the Republicans. His complete lack of involvement in municipal politics—and his reputation for scrupulous honesty—reassured the Democrats, especially Green, who, together with Elliott, championed Olmsted's appointment. Finally, his cultural and social background and his deep Yankee roots were like those of the majority of the commissioners. He was one of their own. The final vote was eight for and one against.

Only in hindsight can this moment be described as the auspicious beginning of a new career. Olmsted obviously worked hard to get the job. Yet it was not more than that—a job. This was after all quite a comedown: from editing "much the best Mag. in the world" and hobnobbing with Longfellow and Thackeray, to being a sort of glorified foreman. He saw himself as a man of letters, so what impelled him to seek this practical position? The annual salary was to be three thousand dollars when Olmsted applied, but arguments among the commissioners reduced it by half. At that point he almost withdrew his name from contention, but "having had time to reflect, 'what else can I do for a living?,' & also considering that the salary will probably be increased, if I prove the importance & responsibility of the office, I let it alone." When he did get the position, he ruefully admitted in a letter to his brother that "on the whole, as the times are, I shall think myself fortunate if I can earn $1500."

His eyes were open. He had put on the best possible front for the commissioners. He understood that chiefly his literary contacts had got him the job. He knew that these carried little weight with Egbert Viele, a hard-boiled West Point graduate and army veteran. Olmsted expected political intrigues. "I shall try the frank, conscientious & industrious plan," he wrote his brother, John, laconically adding, "and if it fails, I shall have learned something more & be no worse off."

The Colonel Meets His Match

OLMSTED'S FIRST DAY on the job was inauspicious. He showed up at Viele's office and, after being kept waiting, was peremptorily sent off with an underling on a tour of the site. His guide purposely led him through the worst terrain. Olmsted's street clothes were soon covered in mud, and he thought himself the butt of a crude joke. The workmen he encountered likewise treated him casually. The young gentleman was obviously an interloper. They knew that he had no real power—he could not hire or fire. They owed their jobs—and their political allegiance—to the Democratic party and its representative, the chief engineer.

Colonel Egbert Ludovicus Viele—he insisted on the military title— was not someone to be trifled with. A small man with a heavy mustache, he affected a rough, intimidating manner that hid his genteel, Knicker- bocker background. His father, a judge and a regent of the University of the State of New York, was a state senator; his Dutch forebears had set- tled in upstate New York in the early seventeenth century. The thirty- two-year-old Viele had spent six years in the military, serving in the Mexican War, and fighting Indians on the Southwestern frontier. After resigning his commission he had come to New York, where he set himself up as a civil engineer. He had no training in this field—he had been in the infantry, not in the prestigious Corps of Engineers. Nevertheless, intelli- gent and enterprising, he knew how to organize men and get things done, and he persevered. He was employed by the State of New Jersey to con- duct a topographical survey. Subsequently Fernando Wood, the mayor of New York, appointed him chief engineer of the projected Central Park.

Viele's first task was to prepare a topographical survey. Although he had no background in landscape gardening, he proposed a design for the park. His straightforward, functional plan had the practical advantage of being adapted to the terrain and exploiting the existing natural features. A winding drive made a circuit of the park, to be traversed by four streets. There was a cricket ground and a botanical garden; he accorded pride of place to a fifty-acre parade ground. The Viele plan was officially accepted by Mayor Wood; however, when state legislators stripped the discredited mayor of many of his powers, this changed. The new park commissioners retained Viele to complete the survey, but set aside his plan. Ostensibly the reason was aesthetic—the design was held to be unimaginative. There was also reluctance to vest total control over the park in a Democratic appointee. On top of this disappointment, Viele was now saddled with Olmsted, this literary gent who, he suspected, didn't know the first thing about the practical world.

Viele seriously misjudged Olmsted—and his abilities. The man who had ridden through Louisiana bayous and across the Texas plains was tougher than Viele imagined, and smarter. Within only a few weeks of his arrival, Olmsted made his presence felt. Some of the commissioners, including Elliott and Green, were disaffected with their arrogant chief engineer. In a deliberate snub, the board asked Olmsted to prepare a comprehensive report on draining the low and swampy land. Subterranean drainage was precisely one novel subject with which Olmsted was intimately familiar. It took him less than two weeks to submit a report. Unlike his literary writing, which was sometimes convoluted, Olmsted's technical prose was a model of clarity. He described details, prices, and schedules. Drawing on his Staten Island experience, he included a long discussion of the benefits of manufacturing the drainage tiles on the spot. He quoted from current British technical journals. He reminded the commissioners that he had met Josiah Parkes, the world authority on underground drainage, and had inspected several installations in England and Ireland. He mentioned diplomatically that the chief engineer had to be consulted, while he left no doubt of his own expertise. A week later he submitted an equally authoritative report on tree planting, estimating the number, species, and cost of the trees required. Thus he defined the full range of his landscape-gardening knowledge. Round one to the literary gent.

The commissioners' faith in their enterprising superintendent grew. In October they gave him full authority to hire up to one thousand laborers, and to dismiss those who were ineffective or malingerers. This was crucial, since many of the jobs were political sinecures. Soon Olmsted wrote proudly to his father: "I have got the park into a capital discipline, a perfect system, working like a machine." In January the commissioners increased his salary to two thousand dollars, which was what Viele was being paid.

In less than four months Olmsted had won the confidence of the board. He had taken firm control of his responsibilities, outmaneuvered Viele, and been given a raise—all as he had planned. But now he was overwhelmed by a singular personal tragedy. On November 13, 1857, his brother, John, wrote that his health had taken a considerable turn for the worse. He was in Nice, bedridden, and heavily sedated with opium. He was failing fast. "It appears we are not to see one another any more—I have not many days, the Dr says." Eleven days later he was dead. He died attended by Mary and his three children, as well as by his father, stepmother, and half sisters, who had hurried from their European tour to his side. He was buried in the Protestant cemetery overlooking the Mediterranean. He was thirty-two.

Nothing prepares one for a death in the family. Olmsted felt the loss all the more, as he and his brother had recently spent so much time together: on the farm, roughing it in the Southwest, editing the final manuscript of *A Journey Through Texas*. "In his death I have lost not only a son but a very dear friend," wrote his father. "You almost your only friend." That was an exaggeration—Frederick had many intimate friends, not the least of whom was his father. But the two brothers were unusually close. John's last letter included a sweet farewell: "I have never known a better friendship than ours has been & there can't be a greater happiness than to think of that—how dear we have been & how long have held such tenderness."

Frederick Law Olmsted's father owned a dry-goods store in Hartford, Connecticut. The small-town Main Street, shown here in 1863, had not changed much since Olmsted's youth, except for the streetcar lines. The store was halfway down the street, on the right side of the photograph.

Bustling South Street in New York, where as a young clerk in 1855, Olmsted went on board sailing ships to tally cargo for the importing house of Benkard & Hutton.

The twenty-one-year-old Olmsted sailed to China as an ordinary seaman on a merchant ship. He reached Whampoa, the port of Canton, but only managed to go ashore three times.

Olmsted witnessed more than one slave-whipping while traveling in the South as a correspondent for the *New-York Daily Times*. His book, *A Journey in the Seaboard Slave States*, in which this illustration appears, was published in 1856.

This engraving from the 1857 edition of Olmsted's *A Journey Through Texas* is based on one of his sketches. It shows him and his brother, John, camping in west Texas. They named the bull terrier Judy; the pack mule, Mr. Brown.

During the Civil War, Olmsted was secretary general of the United States Sanitary Commission which operated field hospitals, dispensaries, and hospital ships and employed scores of surgeons, nurses, and health inspectors. Of his women volunteers, Olmsted said: "They beat the doctors all to pieces."

Oso House, in Bear Valley, on the California frontier, astride the Mother Lode. Olmsted spent two years here managing the vast Mariposa Estate, a gold-mining operation. The stagecoach carried people and mail to the closest large town, eighty miles away.

John C. Olmsted took this family photograph in July, 1885. Olmsted, wearing a pith helmet, is flanked by his two children, Marion and Rick; his wife, Mary, is leaning against the tree. The two women on the right are unidentified guests.

Frederick Law Olmsted, circa 1890.
"What a good ancient philosopher you look like!"
exclaimed his friend Charles Eliot Norton.

Shy and diffident, Olmsted's step son, John C. Olmsted,
became a partner in F. L. & J. C. Olmsted, Landscape Architects.
He played a major role in the design of the Emerald Necklace,
Boston's extensive park system.

Visitors to Chicago's World's Columbian Exposition of 1893, looking down from the roof of the Manufactures and Liberal Arts building at the basin that was the focus of the Court of Honor. Olmsted picked the site beside Lake Michigan and planned the fair grounds.

The builders of Biltmore.
On the left, behind Olmsted, is the architect, Richard Morris Hunt;
on the right, the young client, George W. Vanderbilt.

Frederick and Mary Olmsted at Biltmore Estate in the early 1890s, not long before he
withdrew from active practice. Olmsted not only designed the gardens and parkland
surrounding the house, but also established an extensive, scientifically-managed forest.

Fairstead, Olmsted's home and office in Brookline, Massachusetts.
"Less wildness and disorder I object to," he once said of his garden.

It was in McLean Asylum, in Waverly, Massachusetts,
whose grounds he had earlier designed, that Olmsted spent his final years.

Mr. Vaux

THE OLMSTED FAMILY returned from Europe in mid-January 1858. In a welcoming letter Olmsted brought his father up-to-date. *A Journey in the Back Country* was now substantially complete, save for a chapter on Southern politics. Olmsted was trying—without success—to find a publisher who would reprint *A Journey in the Seaboard Slave States* and *A Journey Through Texas*, which had gone out of circulation with the demise of Miller & Curtis. At the end of his letter, Olmsted added that he was "living with my partner Mr. Vaux, & up at the park every other day."

Calvert Vaux, two years younger than Olmsted, had been born in London. At nineteen he became an apprentice to a London architect who specialized in restoring Gothic churches. For unexplained reasons, Vaux left before completing his apprenticeship and spent the next four years knocking about the London architectural scene. A talented draftsman, he supported himself by doing illustrations for printers. In August 1850 he was introduced to a visiting American, Andrew Jackson Downing. Downing was in England looking for an architectural assistant. As a result of his house-pattern books and his flourishing landscaping practice, he was being approached by clients who wanted him to design houses. He needed an architect. He and Vaux—an intense, small man (only four feet ten inches) with a full beard and an artistic demeanor—hit it off. A week later, Vaux sailed with his new employer to New York.

Working under Downing's direction, Vaux designed a dozen or so residences, ranging from country estates in the Hudson Valley to a large seaside villa in Newport, Rhode Island. After Downing's tragic death, Vaux continued to practice in Newburgh with some success, eventually forming a partnership with Frederick Withers, another English architect who had worked for Downing. Vaux was ambitious and saw himself as Downing's heir; to consolidate that position, he published a Downingesque house-pattern book, *Villas and Cottages*. When he got a large commission in New York for a bank building, he concluded that his future lay in the city, and after four years he and Withers split up. Vaux, now an American citizen and married with two children, moved to New York.

He was soon caught up in the debate over Viele's Central Park proposal. "Being thoroughly disgusted with the manifest defects of Viele's published plan I pointed out, whenever I had a chance, that it would be a disgrace to the City and to the memory of Mr. Downing (who had first proposed the location of a large park in New York) to have this plan carried out," he recalled. Viele's pragmatic plan was not really that bad. In fact, his naturalistic layout largely followed Downing's precepts, but it was the work of an engineer and lacked that elusive quality, "good taste," that Vaux prized. He was acquainted with two of the park commissioners: Charles Elliott, who had been a friend of Downing's, and John Gray, the bank vice president, for whom Vaux & Withers had recently designed a residence as well as an office building. They arranged for Vaux to speak to the board. His impassioned testimony undoubtedly did much to convince the commissioners to set aside the chief engineer's plan. In August 1857 the board announced a public competition for the design of Central Park.

Vaux intended to enter the competition. Six years earlier he had been introduced to Frederick Law Olmsted at Downing's Newburgh nursery. Vaux now approached Olmsted and asked him if he would consider entering the Central Park competition with him. Vaux was no novice in landscape design. He had assisted Downing on many large projects, such as the plan of a farm near Poughkeepsie for Matthew Vassar, the wealthy brewer and future founder of Vassar College. He had also helped Downing with a major park commission: a 150-acre public garden between the Capitol and the Washington Monument, in Washington, D.C. Why did he approach Olmsted? He later maintained that he was attracted by Olmsted's writings and by his familiarity with the site, and that Olmsted's position as superintendent was not a consideration. This strikes me as disingenuous. Vaux was shrewd enough to appreciate that politics would play a role in the competition. He knew that Olmsted was currently the favorite of the board, hence someone with whom it would be advantageous to be associated.

Olmsted found Vaux's proposal attractive. He was still brokenhearted at his brother's death and ashamed of the commercial failure of his publishing venture. "I was just in mind to volunteer for a forlorn hope," he later recalled to his biographer, the architectural critic Mariana Van Rensselaer. He then added mysteriously: "There was something else of which I have told you nothing, and I shall tell you nothing which made absorption in the work of the moment the more necessary for me." Not surprisingly, he was reluctant to reveal that several thousand dollars of personal debt had drawn him into his life's work. He owed money not only to his father but also to his friends, his landlord, even to his stableman. He might even be held responsible for the indebtedness of Curtis's bankrupt publishing firm, whose legal affairs were in the courts. Debt made it "the more necessary" for him to enter the competition. "If successful, I should not only get my share of $2,000 offered for the best, but no doubt the whole control of the matter would be given me & my salary increased to $2,500," he wrote his father.

Olmsted first cleared the matter with Viele. The chief engineer, who was himself preparing an entry, said that he had no objection to Olmsted's participation, as several other park employees were competing. Olmsted and Vaux started working on the plans sometime in the fall of 1857. They met nightly and on Sundays in Vaux's house on Eighteenth Street. The deadline, originally set as March 1, was extended to April 1. Even so, they were a day late. Their project, titled "Greensward," was the last to be submitted.

The thirty-three entries included eleven designs by people who were—or had been—associated with the park, not only the chief engineer and the superintendent, but also gardeners, engineers, surveyors, and clerks. The competition attracted only two entrants from outside the United States. Notably absent were some of the better-known American landscape gardeners: Eugene Baumann, who had been responsible for landscaping the New Jersey suburb of Llewellyn Park; Adolph Strauch, the expert Prussian-born landscape gardener who was in charge of Spring Grove cemetery in Cincinnati; and the celebrated Horace Cleveland, who was then laying out Sleepy Hollow cemetery in Concord, Massachusetts. Cleveland's partner, Robert Morris Copeland, did enter. So did Howard Daniels, who was responsible for planning cemeteries in Columbus, Cleveland, and Poughkeepsie. No prominent landscape gardeners were on the jury. There had been a proposal to invite the superintendent of Liverpool's Birkenhead Park, as well as Jean-Charles-Adolphe Alphand, the French engineer who had supervised the transformation of the Bois de Boulogne into a public park, but neither was present.

The jury consisted solely of the commissioners. They deliberated four weeks. Three projects were disqualified, including the French entry, which required razing the old reservoir to make room for a *Champ de Mars.* There were nine rounds of voting. The entry that treated the park as an allegorical map of the continents, with ponds serving as oceans, did not receive much support, nor did the entries that turned the park into a kind of amusement ground. The jury was looking for something more dignified. Susan Delafield Parish, the sole female entrant, did not get any votes. Copeland, who was probably the most experienced landscape gardener competing, was not a finalist; neither was Viele, to his everlasting chagrin. The jury appears to have been divided politically between two different contemporary fashions in park design: Democrats favored the formal European approach while Republicans opted for the picturesque English style. The entrants were supposed to have been anonymous, but it appears likely that their identities were known since three of the four prizes went to park employees, and voting was along party lines. Fourth prize was accorded to Howard Daniels for an accomplished design that, on the whole, followed the European tradition of a monumental civic space, complete with replicas of ancient temples; French, English, Dutch, and Italian gardens; and a formal avenue running up the center of the park.* The third prize went to two park commission clerks whose chief qualification appears to have been a family tie with one of the commissioners. Second prize was awarded to the superintendent of gardeners, Samuel Gustin. The *Times* later dryly commented on the mediocrity of the second- and third-place finishers: "We do not find in them the decided merit discovered by the Board." Gustin, a Democratic appointee, had the solid support of the three Democrats. The vote for first place was unequivocal. The six Republicans, together with the reform Democrat Andrew Green, all cast their votes for the same project: Greensward. Vaux and Olmsted had won.

---

*The descriptions of the entries are from the written reports; only three of the submitted plans have survived.

A Brilliant Solution

THE COMMISSIONERS WERE no doubt influenced by politics, but they picked a remarkable design nonetheless. It is worth examining Vaux and Olmsted's plan in some detail. Like all the competitors, they were required to incorporate a large number of specified features: three large playing fields, a parade ground, a winter skating pond, a major fountain, a flower garden, a lookout tower, and a music hall or exhibition building. Scattering these about the site would create a piecemeal impression—an overall organizing principle was required. Vaux and Olmsted looked to Downing. He had described his vision of the New York park only in general terms: "broad reaches of park and pleasure-grounds, with a real feeling of the breadth and beauty of green fields, the perfume and freshness of nature . . . lovely lakes of limpid water, covering many acres, and heightening the charm of the sylvan accessories by the finest natural contrast . . . the substantial delights of country roads and country scenery." That was not much help. Winning a competition requires standing out from the crowd. Vaux and Olmsted knew that many of the entrants would follow Downing's naturalistic teaching (in fact, two-thirds of them did). They needed something more.

Downing had one insight that provided an inspiration. "Pedestrians would find quiet and secluded walks when they wished to be solitary," he wrote, "and broad alleys filled with thousands of happy faces when they would be gay." The "broad alley" that was Vaux and Olmsted's starting point in planning Greensward was a quarter of a mile long, a pedestrian boulevard flanked by double rows of American elms. They called it the Promenade, although it was almost immediately renamed the Mall. It led to a large formal terrace and a fountain on the shore of the skating pond. Emerging from the canopy of elms, one would have a vista across the water to a rocky bluff. The bluff was a tangled, natural landscape of rhododendrons, black oak, and azaleas, many of which were already growing. On the top of the bluff, which was the chief geological feature of this part of the park and was known as Vista Rock, they proposed a martello tower, "but by no means a large one, or the whole scale of the view will be destroyed." The ensemble—Mall, terrace, lake, bluff, tower—became the central feature of the southern half of the park.

It was a brilliant solution. The city had been able to acquire the rocky and swampy land for the park in part because it was unsuitable for normal real estate development. Vaux and Olmsted turned this liability to an advantage by exploiting the craggy outcrops and turning the lowlands into lakes. The Mall was a nod (but only a nod) to the European tradition of formal landscape gardening favored by many of the commissioners. It was large enough to provide a commensurate sense of scale, but not so large that it overwhelmed the rest of the park, which was intended to appear natural. Although the Mall was formal, it was informally placed on one side and at a slight angle to the edges of the park. This left plenty of room for the parade ground (now called the Sheep Meadow) and a ten-acre playground (the Ball Ground). These were side by side and gave the impression of a single large rolling meadow.

Illusion lay at the heart of Greensward. It was all very well to talk of green fields, limpid water, and sylvan accessories, but aside from the rock outcroppings that Vaux and Olmsted incorporated into their design, the site was not rich in attractive natural features. Worse, it was disfigured by an old reservoir that stood awkwardly in the very center, on the site of the present-day Great Lawn. A new reservoir was being built immediately to the north, but this large body of water, bounded by embankments, could not function as a landscape attraction. (Vaux and Olmsted surrounded it with a bridle path.) The chief shortcoming of the Central Park site was its shape. Although it was almost eight hundred acres and stretched nearly two and a half miles from 59th to 106th Street, it was only half a mile wide.* To maintain a sense of a natural landscape, Vaux and Olmsted took great pains to create diagonal views that directed attention away from the intruding views of the buildings that would be built along Fifth and Eighth Avenues.

Perhaps their most successful illusion—certainly the most original—

---

*In 1863 the park was extended north to 110th Street, its present boundary.

was the way that they dealt with the competition program's difficult requirement that four or more public streets traverse the park. City traffic would have been a noisy and dangerous intrusion and would have destroyed the effect of country scenery. Vaux and Olmsted placed the streets in large excavated trenches, eight feet below ground. Like the British ha-ha, or sunk fence, the sunken streets dealt with a functional necessity in such a way that the visual continuity of the landscape remained undisturbed; pedestrian ways, carriage roads, and bridle paths simply bridged the streets. This also had the advantage of allowing the park to be closed at night without interrupting traffic. No other entry included this feature.

"The great charm in the forms of natural landscape lies in its well-balanced irregularity," Vaux had written in *Villas and Cottages*. He dedicated this book to Mrs. Downing and to the memory of her husband, just as Olmsted had dedicated the second volume of *Walks and Talks of an American Farmer in England* to Downing. Not surprisingly, Downing's influence was strongly felt in Greensward. What *is* surprising is the extent to which Olmsted and Vaux diverged from Downing's teachings. He had imagined the park as a site for "winter gardens of glass, like the Great Crystal Palace, where the whole people could luxuriate in groves of the palms and spice trees of the tropics." He described zoological gardens, horticultural and industrial shows, and "great expositions of the arts." Downing's vision combined recreation with instruction. Many of the contestants took his advice to heart and provided museums, zoological and botanical gardens, and large exhibition halls. In several entries, a glass structure on the lines of the Crystal Palace was made the focal point of the park; one included an Italianate concert hall, complete with fountains and terraces; three entries provided a track for horse racing.

Vaux and Olmsted did none of these things; in fact, they minimized the number of architectural structures. Greensward included two ornamental towers and a military gate to the parade ground, but the other buildings were small and utilitarian: a changing room for cricket players, a small stables, a police station, and a house for the superintendent. They underlined this in their report:

> Buildings are scarcely a necessary part of a park; neither are flower-gardens, architectural terraces or fountains. They should, therefore, be constructed after dry walks and drives, greensward and shade, with

other essentials, have been secured, and the expenditure for them should be made with entire reference to the surplus funds at the disposal of the commission after the park is constructed . . . in our plan the music hall, Italian terrace, conservatory, flower garden and fountains, are but accessories of a composition in which the triple promenade avenue [the Mall] is the central and only important point.

Nor did Greensward owe much to Downing's only public park. Downing had designed the Washington, D.C., park as six distinct areas, each developed according to a different theme: a perfect circle of elms in front of the executive mansion, a meadowlike garden surrounding the Washington Monument, a formal evergreen garden, and so on. It was a somewhat clumsy attempt to apply the principles of residential gardening on a larger scale. One must look elsewhere for Greensward's precedents. They are found among the picturesque rural cemeteries. Brooklyn's Greenwood and Philadelphia's Laurel Hill introduced landscaping features such as winding paths, naturalistic ponds, and secluded groves. The other precedent was Paxton's Birkenhead Park, with its carefully contrived vistas, its contrast of meadows and copses, its subordination of artifice to the scenic effects of vegetation and water, and above all, its being a single, unified design.

The *New-York Daily Times* article that announced the results of the Central Park competition noted "the established character for good

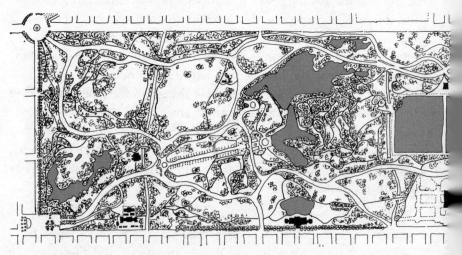

Central Park, New York (c. 1880).

sense and liberality of Mr. OLMSTED, the actual Superintendent of the Park," and "Mr. VAUX . . . creditably known from his connection with the lamented Mr. A. J. Downing." The reporter referred to Messrs. Vaux and Olmsted, then Olmsted and Vaux, then Vaux and Olmsted, in an unconscious attempt to fairly apportion credit for the design. Olmsted and Vaux themselves always maintained that the design of Central Park was a collaborative effort. But who did what?

It is fairly easy to surmise the division of labor with regard to the competition documents: Vaux, the accomplished draftsman, would have had the leading role in preparing the "before and after" sketches that were an effective part of their submission; Olmsted probably oversaw the writing of the report and the preparation of the budget estimates. He also compiled the planting lists, which, like his earlier report to the board, were explicit and detailed. Both men probably collaborated on the site plan; Vaux's son later recalled that family and friends were enlisted in drawing the thousands of trees and dotting the grass pattern on the ten-foot-long drawing. One of Vaux's British friends, a mercurial architect named Jacob Wrey Mould, who would play a major role in Central Park, also helped. So did Vaux's brother-in-law, Jervis McEntee, a Hudson River School painter, who contributed a small painting of the view of the existing park from the proposed Terrace.

It has been suggested that Vaux, as an experienced architect, should be

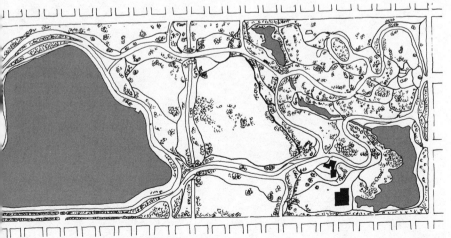

accorded a disproportionate share of the credit for the creative aspects of the plan. Had the park been a purely Downingesque design, that might be a plausible claim. Yet many of the key ideas in the plan have no precedent in either Vaux's or Downing's work. Olmsted's keen analytical mind was an important asset. So was his experience in surveying, his drawing ability, his intimate knowledge of Birkenhead, not to mention his familiarity with the Central Park site, over which he spent most of his days ranging on horseback. Nevertheless, while Vaux might have entered the competition alone, the opposite is not true. Rather, as Mariana Van Rensselaer recounted: "Together they had all the knowledge and ability required; but alone, Mr. Olmsted is always anxious to explain, he could at that time have done nothing to good purpose."

cA Promotion

A FEW DAYS AFTER the competition results were announced, the winners met in Vaux's architecture office. It was a sweet moment: after the months of hard work and the weeks of anxious waiting for the jury to decide, success. As they were dividing the prize money, Vaux said how much he had enjoyed their partnership. He would regret to see it come to a close. He had his architectural practice to attend to, and Olmsted would be busy as superintendent of the park. Olmsted was nonplussed. How could Vaux talk of withdrawing? Did he think that constructing what they had drawn was going to be that simple? Vaux had no idea what the park board was like. It was constantly offering suggestions, trying to cut costs, meddling. Moreover, the Democratic commissioners were going to make trouble; after all, none of them had voted for Greensward. And had Vaux forgotten the chief engineer? The Colonel was difficult to deal with under the best of circumstances; he was bound to be a sore loser. Their plan had won, but it would almost certainly require adjustment. Olmsted did not feel able to deal with all this alone—Vaux had to continue to work with him. The architect was reluctant, but finally he agreed. On May 10, 1858, the board authorized Olmsted as superintendent "to call in the services of his associate."

Only a few days later Olmsted announced that he had been offered a promotion: henceforth he was to be not only superintendent but also architect-in-chief. Five years later he acknowledged that he ought to have insisted that Vaux be given an official position that recognized his coauthorship of the plan as well as his sole responsibility for the design of such significant architectural features as the Terrace. "I was technically not an architect & it was putting me under false colors, and I wanted you to be the Architect & to have that title. . . . The Commissioners' arrangement was a bungling one," he admitted to Vaux. But that was later. At the time he accepted the "false colors" readily enough. It may have been thoughtless, but it was not—as some biographers have suggested—selfish. He thought of the new position as a direct extension of his superintendency. It was his hard-earned right.

Vaux was officially the architect-in-chief's "assistant." He had no interest in management or organization, which he considered tedious, so he was quite willing to cede the superintendency of the park to his colleague. But, as a founding member of the American Institute of Architects, which was struggling to establish its professional legitimacy, he was irritated by Olmsted assuming the title of "architect," let alone "architect-in-chief"! He thought that this slighted his own role as codesigner of Greensward. But he had to admit to himself that it was better for Olmsted to take charge than for somebody else. Had he realized the extent to which Olmsted would be thrust into the limelight, he might have voiced his disapproval. But he didn't. In his diffident way, he chose to remain silent.

Vaux's silence masked an important difference between the two men. Like most architects, Vaux considered design to be his paramount responsibility. Once a project was conceived and committed to paper, its implementation was more or less a mechanical task undertaken by others. This was reflected in his standard professional fee, two-thirds of which was for preparing drawings and one-third for supervising construction. Olmsted, perhaps because of his farming background, understood the difference between building design and landscape design. He referred to the Greensward plan as a "preliminary study" or a "sketch." He, more than Vaux, appreciated the extraordinary organizational skills that would be required to flesh out this sketch, and to orchestrate the construction of a project as colossal as Central Park. He was also interested in overseeing the administration of the park after its completion, which was the reason for the "House for the Superintendent" in the plan. He understood that a landscape designer, unlike a building designer, was setting in motion a process that would take years and ultimately decades to complete. He spelled this out in his grateful letter of acceptance to the board, paraphrasing a passage from *Walks and Talks of an American Farmer in England:* "What artist so noble as he who, with far reaching conception of beauty and designing power, sketches the outlines, arranges the colors, and directs the shadows of a picture upon which nature shall be employed for generations before the work he has prepared for her hand shall realize his intentions."

Gratitude was certainly in order. The combined positions of superintendent and architect-in-chief incorporated all the power he desired. "He shall be the chief Executive officer of this Board, by or through whom all work on the Park shall be executed, and shall have the government and supervision of all employees at the Park," declared the official minutes of the commissioners' meeting. His salary was raised to twenty-five hundred dollars a year. At the same time the board abolished the position of chief engineer and dismissed Viele.* It had all happened just as Olmsted had foreseen. The literary gent had won.

The commissioners authorized Olmsted to proceed with the Greensward plan, "subject to such modifications as may be suggested from time to time by this Board." The modifications were not long in coming. The commissioners had already proposed, as cost-saving measures, narrowing the width of the carriage drives and eliminating one carriage entrance. These suggestions Olmsted and Vaux readily accepted. Not so the proposals of Robert Dillon and August Belmont, two Democratic commissioners. They disliked the Greensward plan, partly because it was supported by the Republicans, partly because their backgrounds (Dillon's, Irish-American Catholic; Belmont's, German-Jewish) did not incline them to the English landscaping tradition. Unable to block Vaux and Olmsted's plan, they now attempted to modify it. They proposed a perfectly straight, two-mile-long promenade, called Cathedral Avenue, running almost the full length of the park. It traversed the lake on a suspension bridge, continued up to Vista Rock, and ran along the top of the old reservoir, cutting a crude swath through the natural landscape that Vaux and Olmsted's plan had so carefully created.

Dillon and Belmont's amendments—there were seventeen of them, including eliminating the sunken roads—were made public and were debated in the press. Editorialists who favored the amendments accused Olmsted of being a political appointee and an inexperienced farmer who had stolen his ideas from Viele. Dillon took out advertisements in the newspapers. He himself had proposed that Olmsted be appointed

---

*Two years later Viele sued the City of New York and received compensatory damages for unjust dismissal. However, his claim that his first plan for Central Park had been copied by half the competition entrants—including Greensward—was not upheld. Still, the embittered Viele always described himself as the true designer of Central Park.

architect-in-chief; he had expected that the young superintendent would be a pushover. Olmsted cleverly enlisted the help of his journalist colleagues, including Richard Grant White of the *Morning Courier & New-York Enquirer,* Henry Raymond of the *Times,* Charles Dana of the *Tribune,* and his friend Parke Godwin. The tide turned. In the end, the board voted down the Dillon-Belmont proposal.

Olmsted had strenuously objected to Cathedral Avenue because it would destroy the natural character that was the key element in his vision of the park. Central Park was to be an American version of the "people's park" that he had written about seven years earlier. Yet it would not just be a larger version of Birkenhead Park. One of Olmsted's periodic reports to the commissioners ended with this extraordinary prediction:

> The time will come when New York will be built up, when all the grading and filling will be done, and when the picturesquely-varied, rocky formations of the Island will have been converted into foundations for rows of monotonous straight streets, and piles of erect, angular buildings. There will be no suggestion left of its present varied surface, with the single exception of the Park. Then the priceless value of the present picturesque outlines of the ground will be more distinctly perceived, and its adaptability for its purpose more fully recognized. It therefore seems desirable to interfere with its easy, undulating outlines, and picturesque, rocky scenery as little as possible, and, on the other hand, to endeavor rapidly and by every legitimate means, to increase and judiciously develop these particularly individual and characteristic sources of landscape effects.

"Judiciously develop" was an understatement—the picturesque outlines of the park would be the result of considerable artifice. A system of underground pipes would drain the swampy flats; the lowest areas would be excavated and turned into lakes. Ridges and boulders were to be blasted out where the subterranean roads crossed the park. Barren soil needed to be fertilized and seeded for meadows. The open farmland, long since denuded of vegetation, required extensive planting—three hundred thousand trees and shrubs, by Olmsted's estimate.

On September 1, 1858, New Yorkers lining Broadway to watch the parade celebrating the first transatlantic telegraph were greeted by an odd sight. A contingent of workmen were marching in squads of four, with evergreen boughs decorating their hats. Horse-drawn wagons followed,

draped with muslin banners reading ENGINEER CORPS. These were Olmsted's men. He wanted to remind New Yorkers that the construction of
Central Park was under way. By the end of the year he would have more
than 2,300 workers at the park (the number would ultimately swell to as
many as 3,600). Many were recent immigrants; more than three-quarters
were Irish laborers. There were also Italian artisans and German gardeners. Manpower was crucial, for the millions of cubic yards of stone and earth
that were moved, and the hundreds of thousands of cubic yards of granite
that were excavated, were moved, and excavated by hand. The world's first
mechanized stone-crusher was constructed for use in Central Park, and
steam engines were used to drive stationary derricks, but a practical
steam-tractor had yet to be invented, and motive power came from either
humans or horses. Materials were transported by horse cart, and teams of
horses drew the heavy rollers that compacted the drives and walks (effective steamrollers did not become common until after the mid-1860s).

A cadre of engineers—the Engineer Corps—oversaw the work. Olmsted appointed William H. Grant superintending engineer. He was
forty-three, an experienced railroad and canal builder from upstate New
York (more experienced, in fact, than Viele). Grant, in turn, recruited a
group of young engineers. With Olmsted's support, these appointments
were made on the basis of ability and technical knowledge, rather than
social or political connections. These capable, dedicated men and their
assistants were responsible for the organization and management of the
labor force.

Vaux was in charge of all things architectural. His assistant was Jacob
Wrey Mould. Mould, an off-beat character, was already infamous for his
polychrome First Congregational Church—now destroyed—known
derisively to New Yorkers as the "Church of the Holy Zebra" due to its
striped exterior of yellow limestone and red brick. Mould's talent as an
ornamentalist played a decisive role in the design of Central Park. The
original plan called for few structures other than the Terrace, but one of
Dillon and Belmont's sensible proposals, accepted by the board, was the
need to separate pedestrian walks, bridle paths, and carriage roads. The
separation required many bridges—more than forty in all. Vaux and
Mould gave each a distinctive design and used a variety of materials:
masonry, wood, and cast iron. An iron bridge over the skating pond—
now called Bow Bridge—was their supreme creation. Over the years,
several buildings were also added to the plan: the Belvedere Castle, a

children's dairy, a boathouse, and a casino. In addition, they designed numerous arbors, rustic shelters, and landscaping elements such as benches, walls, and lampposts.

Olmsted hired two individuals previously employed by the Commission who would be intimately associated with the development of Central Park. Ignaz Anton Pilat was a young Austrian-born gardener who had studied botany at the University of Vienna and had been employed in the Imperial Botanical Gardens at Schönbrunn. He had worked for the Commission preparing a botanical survey of the site and had submitted an "unofficial" entry to the Central Park competition. Olmsted hired him to be foreman of the gardeners, but within three years the able Pilat replaced Gustin as chief gardener, a post he would occupy for the rest of his life.

The other prominent member of Olmsted's team was George Edwin Waring Jr., a remarkable man whose early career paralleled Olmsted's. The son of a Connecticut merchant, he left school at sixteen, tried several careers, and was then apprenticed on a model farm to learn scientific agriculture. He was soon writing and lecturing on the subject. Waring moved to New York, where he met Olmsted. The two became friends, and since that was when John was in Europe, Waring became a tenant at Tosomock Farm. Several months later he was hired by the Central Park Commission as an agricultural engineer. He, too, had entered the competition. His design was unremarkable, but his report on drainage was "very full and thorough . . . and will be valued by the Board," according to the *Times*. Olmsted placed Waring, who was only twenty-five, in charge of drainage.*

Without Grant's experience of large-scale public works, Vaux and Mould's architectural skills, Pilat's plantsmanship, Waring's inventiveness, and the Engineer Corps's mastery of organization and logistics, Greensward could not have been realized. It takes nothing away from Olmsted's later reputation to emphasize the abilities of the people with whom he worked on Central Park. These abilities are all the more important since the years Olmsted spent on Central Park could be considered his graduate school—these exceptional men were his teachers. He was too intelligent to delude himself about his lack of experience. He also learned something that was to stand him in good stead for the rest of

---

*Waring went on to have a distinguished career in municipal sanitation that included championing waterless toilets—earth closets—pioneering sanitary sewerage, and creating New York's first effective street-cleaning department.

his career: how to delegate authority to talented subordinates. Once, a year later, when Olmsted was away on an extended trip, Waring wrote to him: "Your successor at the helm does not know much of human nature . . . [everyone] does less work than he did under your system of placing some confidence in men's sense of honor & duty." Waring had put his finger on one of Olmsted's most valuable qualities, his capacity to engender intense loyalty in the people with whom he worked. That, too, was to be a hallmark of his professional career.

He was not at all a figurehead; he was too strong-willed and too ambitious for that. If his background did not make him an expert, it certainly equipped him to oversee all aspects of the park. He could discuss surveying with Grant, planting with Pilat, drainage with Waring, and landscaping with Vaux. He, better than any of them, understood that their common goal was neither technical nor aesthetic. It was, above all, civic and social:

> It is one great purpose of the Park to supply to the hundreds of thousands of tired workers, who have no opportunity to spend their summers in the country, a specimen of God's handiwork that shall be to them, inexpensively, what a month or two in the White Mountains or the Adirondacks is, at great cost, to those in easier circumstances.

Frederick and Mary

JOHN HULL OLMSTED'S DEATH had left Mary with the responsibility for three children—John, Charlotte, and baby Owen, born three months before his father's death. She might have lived in Hartford, where John Olmsted would have taken her under his wing, as he had the widowed Sophia Hitchcock. Instead, in the summer of 1858, Mary and the children moved to Tosomock Farm, recently vacated by George Waring. They stayed only a few months. Perhaps she sought comforting memories and found only loneliness; the prospect of spending a winter on the isolated farm could not have been appealing. She rented a house in Manhattan. Her new home was near Olmsted's office, which was in an old farmhouse on the edge of Central Park. They saw each other often. She naturally turned to her late husband's dearest friend and her closest relative for support. The children soon grew accustomed to Uncle Frederick's visits.

On Monday, June 13, 1859, Frederick and Mary were married. The quiet civil ceremony, performed by Daniel Tiemann, the mayor of New York, took place in a house that stood in Central Park, on Bogardus Hill (now called the Great Hill). No record of their courtship survives. Some biographers have speculated that a sense of duty, not romance, led him to marry. After all, John's last letter to Frederick closed with "Don't let Mary suffer while you are alive." But it is not far-fetched to presume that Frederick and Mary, drawn together by the death of a person they both cherished, fell in love. It was not a spring romance—she was twenty-nine, he was thirty-seven. They had known each other for almost eleven years. Childbearing had removed the bloom of Mary's early youth, but she was still as "comfortably pretty" as he had found her when they first met. He was an attractive man—he now cut a dashing figure, with a handlebar mustache and long, wavy hair.

Olmsted knew that he was assuming responsibility for a family; she understood that she was marrying someone with a demanding position. After years of solitary life he sought domesticity; she offered it. Like all marriages it was a contract, and it proved remarkably durable. They weathered some difficult times. They had four children together, and they successfully raised their combined families. Frequently apart, they corresponded regularly on a variety of subjects. Tiny Mary (she was less than five feet), with her bright mind and lively disposition, was more than a match for Olmsted's energetic intelligence. He shared with her not only the family life he craved but also his professional concerns. It was a fortunate union.

There was no time for a honeymoon. Olmsted, who had been working all-out for the last year, could not get away. The board demanded visible evidence of progress. The skating pond was completed in only six months, in time for the winter of 1858; the Ramble was finished by the following summer. To maintain public order, Olmsted organized a force of twenty-four park keepers—one of the first uniformed and well-disciplined police forces in the nation. He devised a panoply of regulations: commercial vehicles were prohibited from using the drives, for example; speed limits discouraged racing; animals were forbidden to graze in the meadows; gambling and prostitution were energetically excluded; the park was closed after nightfall.

Opening parts of the park to the public was politically expedient, but quickening construction raised costs. So did the changes to the original plan, such as the many new bridges. Much of his time was spent explaining and justifying these rising costs to the commissioners. The two years that he had spent working on the park since becoming superintendent, adding to the sudden duties of parenthood, proved too much even for the indefatigable Olmsted. His energies flagged. He and Mary went to Saratoga Springs for a few days, but the waters failed to work a cure. "I feel just thoroughly worn-out, used up, fatigued beyond recovery, an older man than you," he wrote his father. In September the board voted him a six-week leave of absence. He was to go on a tour of European parks. To facilitate matters, the grateful commissioners also voted him the princely sum of five hundred dollars for his expenses. On September 28, 1859, three months after his wedding, he sailed from New York; Mary and the children did not accompany him.

*   *   *

Olmsted wasted no time. The very day that he landed in Liverpool he revisited Birkenhead Park and obtained "full particulars of its construction, maintenance, and management." Two days later he was in Birmingham looking at the sewage works. He met the mayor and interviewed him about Aston Park, the newly opened city park. He dropped in at Chatsworth, hoping to meet Paxton, but the famous gardener was not at home. He visited the Derby Arboretum, designed by the Scottish horticulturist John Claudius Loudon.

And so it went. He toured country estates and the great parks of London. He was taken around the Royal Botanical Gardens of Kew by their superintendent, the famous botanist Sir William Jackson Hooker. In Paris he met Jean-Charles-Adolphe Alphand, the chief aide of Baron Haussmann, who was then rebuilding Paris for Emperor Napoleon III. Alphand, an engineer, was responsible for the Bois de Boulogne, a vast two-thousand-acre public park in the suburbs of Paris. Olmsted also found time to tour parks in Brussels and Lille. He talked to engineers, gardeners, administrators, and police commissioners. The personal contacts he made would prove invaluable. The firsthand information he gathered was likewise priceless: he collected books, plans, and technical information, and hired a photographer to document some of the parks. He purchased trees and shrubs to be sent back to New York.

He brought a critical eye to these visits. He was not impressed by the current English fashion for gardening. The taste for elaborate flower beds and specimen gardening, which he termed "botanic beauty," seemed to him misguided. Writing to Sir William Hooker, who had sent him documentation of Kew Gardens, Olmsted confessed: "I find that the simplicity without refinement of art, if indeed not without art, of Stoneleigh and Charlecourt, and the fine artistic simplicity of Trentham, give me a much greater pleasure, and that it seems to me far more worthy to be striven for than the beauty for which certainly much greater study, skill and labor has been expended." Olmsted was telling Hooker that he preferred the old to the new. The grounds of Stoneleigh Abbey had been redesigned by Humphry Repton in 1808; Charlecourt (Charlecote) Park and Trentham were older than that—they had been laid out by Repton's predecessor, the eighteenth-century gardener and architect Lancelot "Capability" Brown.

The prolific Brown built more than 170 private parks and gardens in his long career. His work is simple, large scale, and sublimely beautiful. Brown wrote no treatises or books, and he was not well-known to Olmsted. The landscape writers who had influenced the youthful Olmsted—William Gilpin and Uvedale Price—considered Brown old-fashioned. Price, who wrote in the 1790s, criticized both Brown and Repton for their lack of variety and intricacy. He argued the merits of an accidental picturesque landscape: "In hollow lanes and bye roads a thousand circumstances of detail promote the natural intricacy of the ground: the turns are sudden and unprepared; the banks sometimes broken and abrupt; sometimes smooth, and gently, but not uniformly sloping; now wildly overhung with thickets of trees and bushes; now loosely skirted with wood: no regular verge of grass, no cut edges, no distinct lines of separation." This is the precise opposite of Brown's carefully composed groups of trees, and undulating swathes of lawn sweeping down to the smooth curvature of the lakeside.

Trentham, which Olmsted visited in November, has all these ingredients: turf, trees, water. The centerpiece of the Staffordshire estate is a man-made, three-quarter-mile-long lake, complete with several islands and bordered by a large wood. Brown, who "improved" the estate for Lord Gower between 1775 and 1779, also rebuilt the house, although the building that Olmsted saw in 1859 was constructed later, as were the formal parterre and a terrace overlooking the lake. At the head of the terrace stood a bronze statue—erected by Gower's grandson—a replica of Cellini's Perseus and Medusa.

The statue is still there, its back turned to the beautiful lake, gazing across the parterre to an empty square of lawn where the grand house once stood. The estate is now a campground. It appears a rather down-at-heel operation that has, thankfully, not greatly impinged on Brown's park. The overcast September morning I was there, my only companions were several fishermen. Except for the disfigurement of a water-ski ramp, the lake was pretty much as Olmsted had seen it. The artful curve of the shoreline and the positioning of the islands create a sense of limitless expanse. The beauty of this landscape is natural, but it is not an imitation of nature. It is a work of art. As a young man Olmsted had imbibed Gilpin and Price's romantic notions of country scenery, and the Brown-designed parks that he later visited during his English walking tour—Chatsworth, Eaton Park, and Wynstay Park—made only a slight impression on him. As a practitioner, he was now in a better position to appreciate Brown's achievement. He called Trentham "the best private garden in England."

The country estates that Brown worked on were large. At three or four hundred acres Trentham is relatively modest; the park of Blenheim Palace, Brown's masterpiece, covers more than two thousand acres. A modern landscape scholar has characterized Capability Brown's method as a "standard formula of artificial water, clumps and belts of trees ... stretched over a landscape as far as funds and property would allow, and clearly at a lower cost of planting and maintenance than a formal style." That makes it all sound a little too easy, but it is true that Brown, who was responsible for building—and not simply designing—the parks, was concerned with maximizing his clients' budgets. He invariably adjusted his ideas to the "capabilities" of the topography—hence his nickname. He was an experienced plantsman, but his interest was the landscape, not the garden. He was concerned with creating a unified experience, just like Olmsted and Vaux in Greensward. Like them, he built on the natural advantages of a site but did not hesitate to radically rearrange nature. He referred to this as "place-making." Greensward was not directly influenced by Brown, but in the work of this great gardener, Olmsted—likewise a park-*builder*—discovered a precedent for the soundness of his own views.

Olmsted was broadening his tastes. He was impressed by Brown, but in France he admired the late-seventeenth-century formal gardens of Versailles and Saint-Cloud, both the work of the celebrated André Le Nôtre. He examined the great boulevards and *rond-points* that Haussmann was then building in Paris. He visited the Bois de Boulogne eight times. All in all, it was an intense journey. Olmsted's itinerary, which he later dutifully reported to the board, listed more than thirty individual parks, estates, arboretums, and zoological gardens; he also saw many "public and private grounds of lesser importance." The six-week tour stretched to three months. There was little time for rest, and the cold, damp fall weather was not ideal. Yet, on his return, Olmsted assured the board that he felt himself in "greatly improved health." As would happen again in years to come, he was invigorated by a European visit. No doubt, the absence of day-to-day responsibilities and decisions lifted a heavy burden. More than that, he was enjoying himself. Central Park was known to British and European landscape gardeners, and he was received as an equal by the small fraternity of park-builders. When he started to work with Vaux on Greensward, he had been a novice. Now he was becoming a recognized expert.

Comptroller Green

OLMSTED RETURNED a week before Christmas 1859. Work on Central Park was proceeding at an astonishing pace. Soon the portion south of Seventy-ninth Street and the old reservoir would be substantially complete. The board's strategy of garnering popular support had paid off— the park was already a great success. The first winter that the pond froze produced a mania for ice-skating in the city. The bridle paths drew upper-class horseback riders. The so-called carriage parade became fashionable. The rich had their own coaches (and sleighs for the winter); the middle class could rent a hack for one or two dollars an hour. Others came to stroll, feed the swans, or boat on the lake. Starting in July 1859, the board inaugurated free Saturday-afternoon band concerts, attracting throngs. Attendance skyrocketed; Olmsted estimated that some days as many as one hundred thousand people were in the park. A contemporary description sets the scene:

> Few landscapes present more attractive features than that of the Park on a music day. Thousands of brilliant equipages throng the drives. The waters of the Lake are studded with gaily-colored boats, appearing now and then in striking contrast with the green foliage that fringes its banks; the water-fowl float proudly over its surface; children play on the lawns; throngs of visitors from divers climes move among the trees, whose leaves, fanned with the soft lays of the music, wave silent approval; all seems full of life and enjoyment; and as some familiar strain breathes a sweet influence around, the whole appears like some enchanted scene.

If this breathless portrait sounds too good to be true, one must remember that for mid-nineteenth-century Americans, Central Park really was a magical place. Not just a pretty setting for recreation, it was an aesthetic experience. A few years later an enterprising photographer published an album titled *The Central Park,* consisting of fifty-two plates that took the reader step-by-step though the park.* The accompanying text explained each tableau in such elevating sentiments as "atmosphere," "sublimity," and "character."

Olmsted should have been basking in the satisfaction of a job well done. Yet all was not going smoothly. He was under fire from the board to cut costs. The commissioners cannot be faulted for worrying about expenses. The sum originally authorized for construction was $1.5 million. A year later, as the result of the amendments to the plan, this was increased to $2 million. In January 1860 the state legislature was asked to approve an additional $2.5 million, which raised the total cost to about three times the initial estimate. Some speculated that by the time that the park was finished, the total cost might be as much as $13 million; others put the figure even higher.

Costs were raised by the commissioners' demand to accelerate the work and to increase the size of the labor force (Central Park was the largest public works project in the country at a time of recession and high unemployment). Then, as now, large construction projects had cost overruns. Vaux and Olmsted had understandably been optimistic in their first estimates. In truth, neither they nor anyone else in the United States had experience building such a large park. The standards of the Engineer Corps were high—and hence costly. A Swiss engineer who was brought in by a state Senate committee to make a detailed evaluation of the work attested to the high quality of the construction and to the excellence of the overall organization. "Much better than any other public work in the United States," Herr Kellersberger reported.

Still, the legislators in Albany, while supporting the park, pressured the board to reduce costs. Some of the work on the northern portion of the park, such as two sunken roads, was postponed. Bridge materials were changed from expensive quarried bluestone to fieldstone and wood. The elaborate flower garden was deferred—indefinitely, as it turned out; it was eventually replaced by the Conservatory Water. Vaux convinced the commissioners to keep the Terrace as he and Mould had designed it,

---

*By coincidence, the author of the text was Frederick Perkins, the brother of Olmsted's ex-fiancée, Emily. Although Olmsted knew Perkins well, he had nothing to do with producing the book.

but plans for the music hall, the palm house, and the conservatory were shelved. Now Olmsted found his independence curtailed. The board demanded that he prepare detailed cost estimates in advance, and that he seek prior approval for expenditures.

It fell on Commissioner Green to enforce this new regime. On October 6, 1859 (while Olmsted was sailing to Europe), Green had been appointed comptroller of the park. Andrew Haswell Green has sometimes been portrayed as a penny-pinching bureaucrat. That is unfair. He was a man of substance, as his later career demonstrates: he served as comptroller of New York, rebuilding the city's finances after the disastrous reign of Boss Tweed; he initiated and led the movement to consolidate the five boroughs into greater New York; he played an important role in the formation of the New York Public Library and the Metropolitan Museum of Art; he was a trustee of the Brooklyn Bridge; and he founded the American Scenic and Historic Preservation Society.

Two years older than Olmsted, Green was a large, handsome man of energy, intelligence, and probity. He was born in Worcester, Massachusetts. Despite his lack of a formal education, he determined to follow his father into the law. At age twenty-two he came to New York and apprenticed with Samuel J. Tilden, who operated one of the most successful corporate practices in the city. Green was admitted to the bar only two years later; Tilden made him his partner—and his protégé. He was appointed to the Board of Education and in only four years was its president. Thanks to Tilden, who was then in the state legislature, Green was made a Central Park commissioner. His rise there was equally rapid. He became treasurer and served as president. When the board felt the need to assert a greater control over finances, it created the new position of comptroller specifically for Green. He was "to act as treasurer, and carry out the orders of the board, and devote his entire time to the duties of the park." The latter point was important. Green was the only commissioner who had a full-time, paid position. This effectively made him the chief executive officer of the park.

Green and Olmsted had much in common. They were old-stock New Englanders from small towns. They had little formal education. They had been farmers (as a youth Green had spent almost a year helping to run a Trinidad sugar plantation). They loved the outdoors. They believed in the primacy of efficient planning and organization. They argued strenuously that the public service should be independent of patronage and politics.

They were scrupulously honest. They were ambitious, self-made men, engrossed in their work and devoted to the success of the park.

They began as friends. Green actively supported Olmsted's candidacy as superintendent and championed Greensward. It was during Green's presidency that Olmsted had been appointed architect-in-chief. In the early days of the park the two bachelors were often in each other's company. After Olmsted married, Green, who remained single his entire life, regularly came to Sunday dinner. He visited Mary often when Olmsted was in Europe. When Green became comptroller, the friendship soured. He bombarded Olmsted with letters, demanding explanations for the slightest expenditure, questioning decisions, on occasion even countermanding his orders. Green became overbearing. This rankled Olmsted, who was never good at taking orders. The comptroller was parsimonious in public as in private life, demanding to know where every penny was going. Olmsted, who tended to be large-handed, wanted discretion to spend as he pleased. Green did not understand technical issues. He sometimes demanded foolish economies. Once he objected when Olmsted ordered some willow trees cut down. "It is quite expensive to get trees on the Park," Green complained. It took several letters from Olmsted to convince him that willows were not particularly expensive trees, and that the removal was ordered to avoid their roots clogging adjacent underground drains.

Both men were right in their own way. Green feared that if costs were not brought under control, the park might not be completed; Olmsted was concerned about posterity and wanted everything done properly, which often meant expensively. Theirs was an uneasy collaboration: both were somewhat imperious; and their management styles were at odds. Green formed his opinions carefully and stuck to them; Olmsted made long-range plans but also made last-minute changes in the field. He once explained to the board, "The best conceptions of scenery, the best plans, details of plans—intentions—the best, are not contrived by effort, but are spontaneous and instinctive." Olmsted appointed able assistants and gave them a free hand; Green liked to exercise personal control over every one of his subordinates. That included Olmsted.

Mount Saint Vincent, Central Park

Sunday, October 21, 1860

It is a brisk fall day and the trees are already starting to assume fall colors. This low hill overlooks 106th Street, the park's present northern boundary. A flat area on top of the hill is the site of a group of three-story wooden buildings surrounded by large verandas. One building, of brick, capped by a tall spire, resembles a chapel. Until four years before this was the motherhouse of the Sisters of Charity, who run St. Vincent's Hospital on Eleventh Street. Now the buildings belong to the Park Commission. Since shortly after their marriage, Frederick and Mary Olmsted have occupied several rooms in the empty convent; Vaux and his family live nearby in what had been the priest's residence. The offices of the superintendent and architect-in-chief are also here. On Sunday the offices are closed. Instead of the usual commotion, there is quiet.

Olmsted is sitting on a veranda on the south side of the building. Since the veranda is glassed-in, he is comfortably warm in the afternoon sun. Immediately adjacent to the building is an attractive garden, with grass and clumps of trees whose leaves are starting to change color. Beyond, the landscape is in disarray, a giant construction site. The trace of the old Boston Post Road cuts an ungainly diagonal between piles of excavated earth and fresh gravel. There are few trees and the ground is strewn with boulders. There is still no sign of the great meadow that he and Vaux have planned for this area. About half a mile away he can see the banks of raw earth that mark the edges of the new reservoir being built by the Croton Aqueduct Board. This area should have been planted over by now, but relations between the board and the Park Commission have not been smooth. But they are making progress.

He is in an easy chair. His extended left leg is supported by a footstool. The leg is bound in a splint and bandaged from hip to toe. A pair of crutches lie on the floor. He has been writing a letter, and as he awkwardly shifts his position, the movement causes him to wince. It is six weeks since the accident and he is mending, but slowly. Today is the first day he has been able to sit himself down without assistance. The leg still hurts.

He can't complain. His thigh is broken in three places. It was so badly shattered that the bone protruded from his torn flesh. The surgeons concluded that if the leg was not amputated, gangrene would probably set in. Gangrene was fatal—he would be dead in a week. Yet he was in such a weakened state that if the leg were cut off, he might not survive the operation. They decided to do nothing. He had less than one chance in a hundred of recovery, his doctor later told him. One chance in a hundred—and he is still alive.

It had happened this way. One Monday evening after work he had gone for a drive with Mary and their new baby, John Theodore. He wanted to try out a new horse that he was thinking of buying. As they were passing through Carmansville, near Washington Heights, the horse bolted. It was Olmsted's own fault—he was exhausted and had fallen asleep, dropping the reins. As he stood up to retrieve the reins, the runaway carriage struck a lamppost. He was flung out and landed on a large boulder. The next thing he remembered, he was lying on the ground unable to move. He looked up to see Mary clutching the baby, both of them unhurt. She quickly took charge and he was carried on a shutter to a house across the street. The oddest thing was that it belonged to his boyhood friend Charlie Trask, whom he had not seen in years.

Olmsted resumes his letter. It is addressed to his father. He has been describing his slow recovery, but he does not want to harp on his injury. He writes instead about John and Charlotte's new tutor, Miss Centayne. "It is a regular school business, with silence, order & discipline for two hours, which order & discipline is the best of it for them. They have music & dumb-bell exercise & ten runs across the court for 'recess.'" He discusses the current campaigns of Garibaldi in southern Italy. He tells him that his friend Friedrich Kapp, with whom he worked on the free-soil cause in western Texas, has just published a history of American slavery. The book is prefaced by a handsome dedication to Olmsted. He describes the recent visit of Albert Edward, the Prince of Wales, to Central Park. The prince ceremoniously planted an English oak; Green, who had appropriated the role of host, planted an American elm alongside. Olmsted and Vaux witnessed the ceremony, but were not introduced to the prince. "Only as they were leaving, some one pointed me out to the Prince & he turned & bowed to me several times until he caught my attention and I returned his salute."

Olmsted writes of everything except the one thing that is foremost in his thoughts. His son, John Theodore, is dead. He died suddenly of infant cholera, only eight days after the carriage accident. He was exactly two months old. Olmsted knows that his father, who has lost three of his children, sympathizes with him and would like to know how he and Mary are doing. He will have to read between the lines. "Mary rather worse—pretty constant sharp and sick headache. Took advice of doctor yesterday—simply ordered to be quiet & take it easy. Only wants strength." Poor Mary! It has been hardest on her. He has his work to occupy him. He is still not mobile, but his staff make their reports at his bedside, and he has himself carried about the park regularly on a litter chair. Without the activity he might have been overwhelmed.

He has stopped writing now. He is staring out at the park—his park—but his eyes are unfocused. The sheet of paper slips from his fingers and flutters to the floor. He does not notice. He sits a long time. Eventually, as the sun swings around to the west, the shaded veranda turns cool. He painfully eases himself out of the chair with the help of the crutches and limps indoors.

King Cotton

ON AUGUST 1, shortly before the accident, *A Journey in the Back Country* finally appeared in print. He had finished it three years earlier. The publisher was Mason Brothers, who also reissued *A Journey in the Seaboard Slave States*. Unlike its predecessor, *Back Country* was written from start to finish rather than compiled from newspaper articles. The successful balance between anecdotes, conversations, vivid descriptions, documentary references, and sociological data makes this by far the best of the Southern trilogy.

Olmsted's two-month horseback ride had taken him through some of the poorest, most backward, and most isolated regions in the South. *Back Country* continues the theme of his earlier books: the corrosive effects of rural slavery on economic and social life.

> I will not here conceal for a moment that I was disappointed in the actual condition of the people of the South, citizen and slave; that the more thoroughly and the longer I was acquainted with that which is ordinary and general, the greater was my disappointment. In the present aspect of affairs, it would be an affectation of moderation if I refrained from expressing my conviction that the larger part of the people of the South are in a condition which can not be too much deplored, the extension and aggravation of the causes of which can not be too firmly and persistently guarded against.

However much he deplored Southern society, Olmsted remained consistent in his opposition to abolition. The previous year, John Brown had led an unsuccessful slave uprising at Harpers Ferry. Brown was hailed as a martyr by Emerson, Longfellow, and Thoreau—but not by Olmsted. "I do not see that a mere setting free of the blacks, if it could be accomplished, would surely remedy these evils," he wrote in the preface.

He understood, as many did not, that the problem was not emancipation itself, but what would *follow* emancipation. He predicted that successful emancipation could not be accomplished at one stroke but would take several generations. He had no illusions about the depth of popular prejudice against blacks. "I do not now say that it is, or is not, right or desirable, that this should be so, but, taking men as they are, I think a happy and peaceful association of a large negro, with a large white population, can not at present be calculated on as a permanent thing." (The Jim Crow era would prove him right.) Yet he remained hopeful that change was possible. "It would be presumptuous in any man to predict when, or in what manner, slavery is to *end*," he wrote, "but, if the owners of slaves were so disposed, it appears to me that there would be no difficulty whatever, politically, financially, or socially, in *diminishing* the evil of slavery, and in preparing the way for an end to it [emphasis added]."

It was now more than seven years since his first Southern trip. With the appearance of his third book, the broad scope of his investigation became evident. Among thoughtful people, Olmsted's ambitious undertaking was received with accolades. "No more important contributions to contemporary American history have been made than in this volume and the two that preceded it," wrote James Russell Lowell, who had succeeded Longfellow at Harvard and was also the editor of *The Atlantic Monthly*. Lowell's friend Charles Eliot Norton wrote to the British poet Arthur Hugh Clough: "Olmsted's 'Journey in the Back Country' is worth reading. I regard Olmsted's three volumes of travels in the Slave States as the most important contributions to an exact acquaintance with the conditions and result of slavery in this country that have ever been published." That was high praise, coming from someone who was starting to make his mark as a critic, essayist, and author. The *North American Review* praised Olmsted's impartiality, reasonableness, and conciliatory tone, calculated to "rebuke and allay both Northern and Southern fanaticism." The London *Times* proposed that "a new edition of the whole series would be an addition to our economic science, as well as a help to a better knowledge of the difficulties of our American kinsmen." It was all very gratifying, especially when the *Westminster Review* contrasted *A Journey in the Back Country* favorably with Hinton Helper's vitriolic *The Impending Crisis of the South*.

Olmsted needed cheering up. The death of an infant son coming on top of a crippling accident was a hard blow. He survived both catastrophes, but he was not unscathed. The accident left him with one leg an inch shorter than the other and a permanent limp. Like Byron, he overcame the infirmity largely by ignoring it. "Though the lameness is decided, it is scarcely observable," wrote Katharine Wormeley, who met him the following year, "for he gives you a sense that he triumphs over it by doing as if it did not exist." John Theodore's death was more difficult to disregard. In photographs of this period, Olmsted first exhibits that pensive, detached demeanor that Wormeley described as "severe."

Nothing slowed him down. When he was not being carried around the park, he was working on a new project. In July 1860 he and Vaux were engaged by the Central Park Commission to plan the eighteen hundred acres of Manhattan Island that lay north of 155th Street (where the street grid of the Commissioners Plan of 1811 ended). Olmsted elaborated his vision from his sickbed. Tenth Avenue would be extended to the tip of the island as a commercial thoroughfare. The rest of Washington Heights would be a garden suburb. Circuitous roads lined by "villa residences" on large lots would follow the contours of the topography. His intention was to ensure the "tranquillity and seclusion—freedom from the turmoil of the streets—and means and opportunities for amusement and exercise which can not be had in a town mansion, certainly not without the liability of observation from neighbors or the public in the streets." With all the publicity attendant on Central Park, Olmsted & Vaux, as the new partnership was called, seemed likely to prosper. The consulting fee for Washington Heights was $2,500; and there already was a second commission, a large estate in New Rochelle.

Olmsted was pleased with this work, not the least because he was still financially strapped. His annual park salary was now $4,000, but in addition to his new family and his existing debts, he had assumed partial financial responsibility for the failure of Miller & Curtis. The case had finally worked its way through the courts. Through a legal technicality, Curtis's father-in-law, Francis George Shaw, had been held liable for the bankrupt firm's debts and made to pay $24,000 in claims. Curtis felt honor-bound to reimburse Shaw (it took him all of sixteen years). Although Olmsted was not legally responsible, he would not allow his friend to shoulder the entire burden. Olmsted's lawyer, William Emerson, calculated that his portion of the debt amounted to $8,000, and Olmsted undertook to repay this amount. Among other things, he signed over all the royalties from *A Journey in the Back Country* to Shaw.

*   *   *

"I hope I shall have been worth saving against odds," Olmsted had written his father after the accident. Now things were looking up. But Central Park was not going well. He found himself increasingly on the defensive in his relations with Green, who had taken over everyday management during Olmsted's convalescence. The comptroller continued to question the smallest expenses. Did the men really need rubber coats and boots? Why did the winter uniforms for the park police cost so much? Was it necessary to assign so many workers to the maintenance of the skating pond? Each request required a considered response from Olmsted. His frustration is obvious in his closing remarks in one of these letters: "I know your time is employed with more important matters, but so it is but right that some of mine should be." He also adds this postscript: "We are again, since some days, obliged to *borrow* coal to keep at work in these offices—the third time, at least, this winter." Borrowing coal! This is how petty the dispute had become.

On January 22, 1861, matters came to a head. Olmsted submitted his resignation in a brief, formal letter. The board took no action but invited him to elaborate his reasons to a meeting of the executive committee a week later. He began by modestly explaining a sense of personal failure. In preparing a report on the next year's work, he said, he had concluded that not enough remained of the last appropriation—$820,000—to complete the park. He realized that work had fallen behind schedule. In other words, more had been spent and less achieved. What was worse, he—who was responsible for organization and planning—could not explain where the money had gone.

> Have the bridges and arch ways taken more money than you voted for them? Those we built ourselves have not. The cost of those built by contract we don't yet know. Have the roads cost more than we reckoned? They have, a small percentage. Has the embankment material from outside cost more than we reckoned? It has not. What is it that has cost so much more and why? That is what I cannot tell you. That is what I want to know. That is what I have no means of knowing.

Then his tone changed. He reminded the commissioners that they themselves could not avoid some of the blame for this state of affairs. They had severely limited his authority over expenditures. "Instead of $100 being put in my hands and my being required afterwards to account for it, using it at my discretion, I find myself obliged to advance the money out of my private means. And when after three or four months I send my bill for it, I send vouchers for items of 12 ½ cents and then, Sir, I can not be reimbursed until I have undergone a cross-examination for an hour, it may be, as to the necessity under which I had been constrained to pay the said 12 ½ cents." Such a state of affairs was not only humiliating, it was inefficient.

He scolded the commissioners for denying him an adequate staff. He reminded them that there had once been talk of hiring a foreign expert—Jean-Charles-Adolphe Alphand, Sir Joseph Paxton, or Sir William Hooker—to design the park. "If either of those gentlemen had undertaken the laying out and general supervision of the park, he would undoubtedly have brought some portion of his professional staff with him—because such assistants as those gentlemen are accustomed to employ are not to be *had* here." "I know what I say, gentlemen," he added. "I have been in their offices and I *know* what sort of assistance they have." He admitted that when he had started, he was hardly to be compared with these illustrious figures. Yet this was no longer true. After two years of superintending every detail of the park, he now found his judgment called into question. This, despite the fact that no less than four investigating commissions had found no fault with his management. "Have you heard any one call me a careless, an inefficient, a lazy or neglectful officer? I believe the worst that has been said of me, Sir, is that I am a mild enthusiast." He closed by raising the one question that he knew was uppermost on everyone's mind: his relationship with Green.

It was no secret that the two men were at loggerheads. He denied that this was the real reason for his resignation. Then he artfully recounted that others—including other commissioners—had warned him that Green was conspiring against him. Of course, he didn't believe it himself. He desisted from making any personal accusations, but he made it clear that the board would have to choose between Green and himself. "With such an arrangement as you have made of the relative and associated duties of myself and Mr. Green, no two men who have much self-respect could work long together without quarreling. I have not quarreled with Mr. Green, and I am not going to quarrel with Mr. Green. But, I repeat, gentlemen, that all this shows me that you yourselves recognize something wrong in your machinery. And the mending of the machinery, gentlemen, is your business, not mine." With that statement, he ended his presentation. He had spoken for almost three hours.

A resignation by the well-known architect-in-chief coming so soon after the state Senate hearings into park finances would have caused a public scandal. This was something the commissioners wanted to avoid, as Olmsted well understood. Yet they were not ready to overrule Green. Instead, they promised that changes would be made if Olmsted withdrew his resignation. He did so. Over the next few months he continued to struggle to get a grip on the park budget. Whether he really lacked the staff and resources to prepare the paperwork—as he had told the board—or whether the vast project with its myriad public and private contractors was beginning to get away from him is not clear. What is plain is that he still had difficulty controlling park expenditures—and he continued to smart under Green's unceasing directives.

Meantime, to bolster his position, he evoked support from the press. In March an article on Central Park appeared in the *New York World* that singled out "the able superintendent." The following month, *The Atlantic Monthly* published a long article on the subject of urban parks, focusing on Central Park. The author (suggested by Olmsted) was the Reverend Henry Whitney Bellows, a prominent New York churchman and civic leader. Bellows roundly praised Olmsted's achievement and emphasized his importance. "He is precisely the man for the place,—and that is precisely the place for the man. Among final causes, it would be difficult not to assign the Central Park as the reason of his existence."

Despite this campaign, the board did nothing. Perhaps Olmsted did not pursue his case as energetically as he would have under different circumstances—he was still in a weakened state after his accident and could get around only on crutches. He was also distracted. Olmsted & Vaux had two more commissions: landscaping the grounds of the Bloomingdale Insane Asylum on the Upper West Side and planning a rural cemetery in Middletown, New York. He was also busy with a new book project. In January the London publishing house of Sampson, Low, Son & Company had sent him several favorable reviews of *A Journey in the Back Country* and a proposal. They were interested in publishing an abridged version of his Southern trilogy. Olmsted agreed. Unable to edit and update the vast amount of material alone, he hired Daniel R. Goodloe, a newspaper editor, to assist him. It took them three months to pare down more than six hundred thousand words to less than half that amount.

The British publisher hoped to capitalize on British interest in the American slavery question. Britain was the chief market for Southern cotton, more than a million tons a year. Many in the Southern states believed that British dependence on Southern cotton was so great that if hostilities were to break out, Britain would side with the South. Just the threat of British intervention, they hoped, would be enough to constrain the North. "No! you dare not make war upon cotton; no power on earth dares to make war on it," boasted Governor James H. Hammond of South Carolina, ". . . cotton is king." Thus Hammond unwittingly provided Olmsted with his book's title: *The Cotton Kingdom: A Traveler's Observations on Cotton and Slavery in the American Slave States.*

Olmsted hoped to influence British public opinion. He recognized that the Southern states' total dependence on exporting cotton was also their chief weakness. Without British markets, the Southern economy would collapse. He pointedly dedicated his book to the great English philosopher and economist John Stuart Mill, "as an indication of the honour in which your services in the cause of moral and political freedom are held in America." Mill, in turn, wrote an antislavery article on the American crisis the following year in *Fraser's Magazine.* He acknowledged the writings of "the calm and dispassionate Mr. Olmsted." Olmsted was also cited by the Irish economist John Elliot Cairns in his influential critique, *The Slave Power. The Cotton Kingdom* was widely reviewed in the British press and sold quickly enough that it was reprinted two years later. It undoubtedly had a small role in hardening some British attitudes against the Confederacy, which was never formally recognized by Great Britain.

In this condensed form of *The Cotton Kingdom,* Olmsted's Southern writing has survived to the present day as a minor classic. Arthur M. Schlesinger Sr., who edited the 1953 edition, described it as "the nearest thing posterity has to an exact transcription of a civilization which time has tinted with hues of romantic legend." He praised Olmsted's account as "an indispensable work in the process of recapturing the American past." Yet at the time, it must have appeared to its author as only a partial success. Whatever hopes Olmsted had of influencing his countrymen were thwarted by the rapid unfolding of events. The previous year Abraham Lincoln, a moderate who was nevertheless publicly committed to preventing the spread of slavery, had been elected president. South Carolina immediately seceded from the Union. It was soon followed by Mississippi, Florida, Alabama, Georgia, Louisiana, and Texas. By February 1861, when Olmsted and Goodloe started working together, Jefferson Davis was elected president of the Provisional Government of the Confederate

States of America. On April 12 a Confederate battery opened fire on Fort Sumter in Charleston Harbor. A few days later Virginia seceded, followed by three more states. In July Congress formally declared war on the Confederacy. By the time *The Cotton Kingdom* appeared in print—November 1861—the two sides were fully engaged. There was no going back.

Three days after the attack on Fort Sumter, George Templeton Strong wrote in his diary: "Events multiply. The President is out with a proclamation calling for 75,000 volunteers." Men flocked to recruiting barracks. Olmsted organized a home guard of a hundred Central Park employees and drilled them every Sunday. He was a patriot and wanted to take an active part in the war. He wrote to his father that he was considering volunteering for the navy. Given his infirmity, that was hardly realistic. It was more likely that he would serve in some administrative capacity. Henry Whitney Bellows invited him to become a member of the board of directors of the Woman's Central Association of Relief, an organization that was inspired by Florence Nightingale's activities during the Crimean War. Hearing that Bellows was going to Washington to seek government support, Olmsted asked him to intercede for him with the government. He was interested in becoming superintendent of "contrabands," as former slaves in the custody of the government were called. "I have, I suppose, given more thought to the special question of the proper management of negroes in a state of limbo between slavery & freedom than any one else in the country," he wrote Bellows. "I think, in fact, that I should find here my 'mission,' which is really something I am pining to find, in this war."

While Olmsted planned what he might do in the war, his position on Central Park was unaltered. In March he tried again to pressure the board to act. This time his tone was conciliatory: "I do ask . . . if it is thought impracticable to secure a very decided change in the direction that I have indicated, that I may be definitely relieved of the responsibility of the superintendence of the work of construction." The commissioners still did not act. They were divided between Olmsted and Green. They appreciated Olmsted's achievements. The southern half of the park, now largely complete, was unquestionably a success. The problem was that it was expensive—or, at least, more expensive than anyone had expected. Green promised to control costs. And costs, not aesthetics, were uppermost in their minds. Finally, in June, they decided—on Green.

Henceforth the comptroller would oversee expenses, hire and fire park employees, and have overall supervision of construction. Olmsted's three-year tenure as architect-in-chief of Central Park was at an end.

The board had called Olmsted's bluff. For bluff it was: he did not resign. He remained as superintendent, continuing to oversee "finishing, planting and maintenance."The board did agree to some of his demands. He could requisition the staff he needed from among the park employees. He was granted greater financial autonomy. He could overdraw up to five hundred dollars a week on approved expenses; he could personally authorize new expenses of up to one hundred dollars a week.

These were significant concessions. The board made its decision on June 6. On June 20 Olmsted received an unexpected offer from the Reverend Mr. Bellows. Bellows wrote that he had succeeded in convincing the federal government to officially sanction private relief efforts for the war—President Lincoln had authorized the formation of the United States Sanitary Commission. This civilian agency would monitor the health and sanitary conditions of troops and would advise the army's Medical Bureau. Bellows had been appointed president of the Commission, and he was writing on behalf of his board. Would Olmsted consider becoming resident secretary, or chief executive officer, of the new organization?* Olmsted accepted immediately and departed New York for Washington a week later.

"I have made no definite arrangement with C. P. Com.," he wrote his father. "I presume it will result in my accepting an advisory connection with the park at a reduced salary." The commissioners could hardly object to his wartime service, and they did grant him a leave of absence at half pay, on the understanding that he would maintain his connection with the park. His new salary at the Sanitary Commission was two thousand dollars a year. It was, from his point of view, a good solution. He could influence the completion of the park without the daily humiliation of working under Green's augmented authority; and he could do his part in the war. Like most Northerners, he did not expect the war to last long, a month or two at the most. This would be a short break, just when he needed it. As Mary put it, "The appointment is a great honor to Fred, and the change in employment will do him good."

---

*The other person considered for the position had been Edward Everett Hale.

A Good Big Work

THE REVEREND HENRY WHITNEY BELLOWS, a genial, handsome man, was eight years Olmsted's senior. Like Horace Bushnell and Henry Ward Beecher, he was an establishment clergyman, a gifted orator, and an energetic civic leader. A native of Boston and a graduate of Harvard Divinity School, Bellows came to New York to be the pastor of the First Congregational Church—he had commissioned Jacob Wrey Mould to design the dramatic new building. He was a founding member of the Century Association, a gentlemen's club (of which Olmsted was a member) that promoted literature and the fine arts, and he was active in New York's literary world. That was how he had encountered Olmsted, who approached him to write for *Putnam's*. Both were Republican and moderate reformists. Bellows had a high opinion of Olmsted. "Mr. F. L. Olmsted is, of all men I know, the most comprehensive, thorough & minutely particular organizer," he once wrote. "He is equally wonderful in the management of principles & of details. His mind is patient in meditation, capable & acute, his will inflexible, his devotion to his principles & methods, confident & unflinching." Bellows was a shrewd judge of character. He understood that Olmsted's talents came at a price. "I won't guarantee you peace, comfort, daily satisfaction, if you harness in . . . with O," he warned, "but I will promise you larger, better & nobler results (with whatever amount of friction in getting them) than you can secure under any other."

Bellows had great hopes for the Sanitary Commission. "Our plans have a breadth and height and depth which no similar military philanthropic undertaking ever had, since the world began," he told a friend. To achieve this end he had assembled a board of accomplished professional men. His cofounders were Elisha Harris, a young physician who was superintendent of the Staten Island quarantine hospital, and

William Van Buren, an ex–army surgeon and a professor at the University of the City of New York. Oliver Wolcott Gibbs was a physician and an eminent chemist; John S. Newberry had served as an assistant surgeon in the army; Cornelius Rea Agnew was surgeon general of the New York State militia. Not all the commissioners were doctors. George Templeton Strong, who became the treasurer, was a New York lawyer. Samuel Gridley Howe, at sixty the oldest member, was a Boston philanthropist who, as a young man, had organized the medical staff of the Greek army during the 1820s revolt against the Ottoman empire. The vice president of the Commission was Alexander Dallas Bache, a West Pointer and a professor of natural philosophy and chemistry at the University of Pennsylvania. He was also the superintendent of the United States Coastal Survey and thus represented the federal government. So did the three army officers on the board: a captain in the engineering corps, a major in the subsistence bureau, and Robert Wood, who had until recently been acting surgeon general of the army's Medical Bureau.

As soon as Olmsted arrived in Washington, he got down to work. In ten days he inspected twenty troop encampments around the city. (One of the soldiers he met was George Waring, now a major in a New York regiment.) Olmsted was appalled at what he found. The volunteer army seemed to him entirely disorganized. The soldiers were slovenly and undisciplined; the officers struck him as little better. The more he saw, the more discouraged he became. The officers of the Medical Bureau were pointedly unhelpful—they did not hide their resentment at the intrusion of a civilian in their affairs. Government officials were downright obstructive. Olmsted despaired that he was wasting his time. "I do not get on very well; do not accomplish much & shall not I fear," he informed Mary in one of his frequent letters home. He also fretted that his living allowance was not sufficient to cover the high cost of life in Washington—he was staying at the fashionable Willard's Hotel. "I am inclined to regret at present that I accepted the post," he wrote, but added: "I can hardly give it up."

Olmsted was in New York when news of the first major battle of the war reached him. The Union army invaded Virginia and on July 21, 1861, encountered the enemy near Manassas Junction. The Union troops outnumbered the Confederates. Yet at the height of the battle, the Northerners fell back. The retreat turned into a rout as the horde of soldiers swarmed all the way back to Washington, mixed with crowds of panicky

Washingtonians who had come to the battlefield expecting to witness an easy victory. The next day it rained heavily. Only the impassable roads— and the Confederates' caution—saved the capital from being overrun.

Olmsted hurried back to Washington. He described the beaten troops as a "disintegrated herd of sick monomaniacs." He meant that they were shell-shocked—although that is a term from a later war. "They start and turn pale at the breaking of a stick or the crack of a percussion cap—at the same time they are brutal savages. That is the meaning of 'demoralization.' It is a terrific disease." If demoralization was a disease, the Sanitary Commission had a responsibility to look into it, he reasoned. He immediately assembled a team of investigators. Four were physicians, including John Hancock Douglas, a young New York doctor who would become Olmsted's closest colleague on the Commission. Ezekiel Brown Elliott, an actuary, brought statistical expertise to the team. Frederick Newman Knapp, a cousin of Bellows's, was a minister. He, too, would become Olmsted's friend. Charles Brace came down from New York to assist in the inquiry. Olmsted sent them out with instructions to "elicit information as to the condition of the troop before, during, and after the engagement." To make sure that they did not miss anything, he provided them with a questionnaire of seventy-five items.

Six weeks after the battle, Olmsted presented his report to Bellows and the board. "Report on the Demoralization of the Volunteers" does not mince words:

Our army, previous to and at the time of the engagement, was suffering from want of sufficient, regularly-provided, and suitable food, from thirst, from want (in certain cases) of refreshing sleep, and from the exhausting effects of a long, hot, and rapid march, the more exhausting because of the diminution of vital force of the troops due to the causes above enumerated. They entered the field of battle with no pretense of any but the most elementary and imperfect military organization, and in respect of discipline, little better than a mob, which does not know its leaders. The majority of the officers had, three months before, known nothing more of their duties than the privates whom they should have been able to lead, instruct, and protect. Nor had they, in many cases, in the meantime, been gaining materially, for they had been generally permitted, and many had been disposed, to spend much time away from their men, in indolence or frivolous amusement, or dissipation.

In this long and detailed report, Olmsted placed the blame for the demoralization of the troops not only on the circumstances surrounding the battle but on the conditions present *before* the battle: lack of preparedness, inadequate training, incompetent leadership. Such a damning indictment of the government was too much for Bache and the army officers. They threatened to resign if the report was made public. Even George Templeton Strong, who considered it "an able paper," felt that "its publication would have done mischief—would have retarded recruiting." The report was never released. Still, Olmsted's elaborate social survey was a turning point for the Commission. It convinced Bellows that the deficiencies of the official government agencies charged with taking care of the sick and wounded were severe. It was also becoming evident to all that this would not be a short war. "It is no longer right for the Commission to proceed on the supposition that it is meeting a wholly temporary emergency," Olmsted advised. "Measures should also be taken to establish the organization of the Commission for the duties which it shall undertake for the war on a firm basis." He calculated that a working capital of fifty thousand dollars would be required, as well as a monthly revenue of not less than five thousand dollars. It was a conservative estimate.

The United States Sanitary Commission became a large organization. "It is a good big work I have in hand," Olmsted wrote his half sister Bertha, "giving me absorbing occupation and that sort of connection with the work of the nation without which I should be very uncomfortable." Olmsted personally created this effective bureaucracy from scratch, something he had been unable to do in Central Park. He established a strictly hierarchical organization with himself at the head. Immediately under him were three associate secretaries—Newberry, Douglas, and John Foster Jenkins, another New York physician. Each was responsible for a geographic region: the West (really the Midwest); the area between the Mississippi and the Alleghenies; and rest of the East.

The first function of the Commission was to monitor conditions among the troops in order to advise the army's Medical Bureau. Olmsted sent more than twenty sanitary inspectors (assisted by so-called agents) into the field. The inspectors were experienced, university-educated medical men. Olmsted's instructions to a neophyte describe the scope of their duties:

1st   The visitation of regimental camps, the object and method of which you will find indicated in a proof-sheet of instructions enclosed. These instructions are imperfect and incomplete, but your own judgment will supply their deficiency. It is only necessary to say that the main object is not to obtain a record but to facilitate and insure the giving of instruction and advice where needed.

2nd   The visitation of Hospitals:—the object of which is to stir up the surgeons and nurses by an exhibition of watchfulness and interest in their doings; to observe the wants of the patients and administer to them as far as possible. (See Resolutions 37 & 41, and 43, enclosed).

3rd   To look after troops arriving, departing, or passing through by rail: The arrangement may be more perfect at Baltimore than here, where a man is most usefully employed in and around the station, giving information and advice, setting stragglers right, conveying word to friends, and making the sick comfortable amidst the confusion, disorder, and ignorance which prevail with new comers.

The inspectors were to focus on prevention. They were given checklists (180 items!) concerning drinking water, rations, discipline, mortality, sickness, hospital accommodations, and so on. They also distributed pamphlets to army surgeons on new medical and surgical practices.

The Sanitary Commission's second task grew in scope as the war went on. It became obvious that the army was unprepared to attend to the needs of the vast volunteer force. The Sanitary Commission took it upon itself to make up for this deficiency. Olmsted established a dozen depots behind the lines from which the inspectors and agents could draw supplies. He designated local voluntary relief organizations, generally controlled by women, as subsidiary branches of the Commission. They were responsible for collecting, storing, and shipping donations to the depots. Many of the donations were in kind: blankets, bandages, clothing, baked and canned goods. Local branches in major cities raised funds used to purchase medicine, surgical supplies, foodstuffs, wine and brandy (which were invaluable stimulants), cots, tents, wagons, and horses.

Before all this could be accomplished, a hurdle had to be overcome: the army's Medical Bureau. The Bureau had actively resisted the formation of the Sanitary Commission. The Commission, in turn, considered the Bureau poorly organized and ineffectual. The Medical Bureau had been designed to serve a peacetime army of fifteen thousand men; it was unprepared to deal with the hundreds of thousands of volunteers. At the beginning of the war the army had only twenty-six surgeons, of whom fully one-third were untrained. Nevertheless, the Bureau resisted any attempt at reform. For example, the army would not permit Olmsted to launch a public appeal for blankets since this would imply that the troops were not being well taken care of by the government. (Eventually Montgomery Meigs, the practical quartermaster general, issued his own appeal.) The advice of the Commission inspectors often fell on deaf ears since army surgeons were promoted according to military seniority rather than medical skill. Olmsted put much of the blame for this situation on the surgeon general, Clement A. Finley, whom he considered a "self-satisfied, supercilious, bigoted blockhead." In October Bellows, Olmsted, and several members of the board met with President Lincoln and demanded Finley's replacement. Lincoln, who had once referred to the Sanitary Commission as a "fifth wheel to the coach," refused. So did the secretary of war, Simon Cameron, a man of dubious reputation, responsible for the notorious corruption of the War Department.

In an attempt to discredit Finley, Cornelius Agnew planted stories critical of the surgeon general in the *New York World.* Unexpectedly, other New York papers came to the surgeon general's defense, and the Commission found itself the object of criticism. Olmsted quickly organized a response—a long report for the Secretary of War that he leaked to the press. "I want that as soon as practicable after this [report] is out, there should be a grand simultaneous expression of confidence in the Commission," he instructed Bellows, "which shall completely counteract the effect which has unquestionably been mischievous of the Times' & other attacks upon us." The nastiest attacks were in the *Times,* signed "Truth." The author was a young woman with whom the editor Henry Raymond appears to have been romantically involved. Olmsted coolly made sure that Mrs. Raymond was alerted. Soon the letters from "Truth" ceased. But what turned the tide was his "Report to the Secretary of War." It was pure Olmsted: an exhaustive and candid review that synthesized the Commission's work thus far and clearly—and uncompromisingly—spelled out solutions for the future. The papers praised it. Even the *Times* admitted that the Commission represented "humanity ministering to wants and sufferings that would become horrors but for such merciful ministrations."

*   *   *

Amid the political intrigues Olmsted regularly returned to New York to work on Central Park, although with increasing apprehension that his advice was neither wanted nor welcome. In October 1861 Mary gave birth to a child. "We have a girl," he informed Charles Brace, "which though not what the country wants now is to me personally more agreeable than a man-child would have been." Little Marion was a healthy baby who pouted and made faces at her father, who had hurried back from Washington. Mrs. Lucas, the nurse, said it was just stomach cramps, but Olmsted thought it was a sign of character. "They used to call it spunk when I did it," he maintained with fatherly pride.

In November he revived Yeoman and wrote an article for the *New-York Times*. In "The Rebellion: How to Reason with the South—How to Deal with the Slavery Question," he made the original proposal to establish sanctuaries in occupied areas where runaway slaves would be offered safe haven. He had introduced a similar idea years before in *A Journey in the Seaboard Slave States*. The resulting depletion and demoralization of plantation labor, he argued, would have a serious effect on the South's war effort.

His renewed interest in slavery was spurred by a recent event. The previous month, the federal navy had seized parts of the South Carolina coast, including the harbor of Port Royal and the sea islands of Hilton Head and Edisto, which contained some of the richest plantations in the South. The plantations and the slaves were considered spoils of war (slaves were not automatically freed—the Emancipation Proclamation was still a year away). The secretary of the treasury, Salmon P. Chase, a rigid antislavery advocate, resisted leasing the plantations and their workers to private interests and instead appointed a lawyer named Edward Pierce to supervise the so-called contrabands on behalf of the government. Olmsted saw an opportunity to demonstrate that free slaves could become self-sufficient laborers. He met with Pierce, who was sympathetic. So was Secretary Chase; but he was reluctant to spend public money on a social experiment. Olmsted then drafted a bill "to provide for the occupation and cultivation of the cotton and other lands in possession of the United States" and convinced the Republican senator from Connecticut to sponsor it. The bill, introduced in February 1862, allocated funds for medical care and supervision and regulated the amount that the slaves, who were referred to as "indigents" and "vagrants," would be paid. Olmsted carefully avoided the contentious issue of emancipation, but his gradualist sentiments were plain. He lobbied hard for the bill. He prepared a petition for his father to circulate in Hartford. He solicited help from prominent members of the Commission board: Bellows, Bache, and Howe. He corresponded with influential friends: George Curtis and Charles Eliot Norton. He wrote to President Lincoln.

An editorial in the *New York World* called for a government commission on Port Royal. "Mr. Fred. Law Olmsted probably combines more qualifications for such an office than any other man in the country." This time Olmsted had nothing to do with the newspaper coverage, but the idea of becoming personally involved had occurred to him. "I shall go to Port Royal, if I can, and work out practically every solution of the Slavery question—long ago advocated in my book," he told his father. "I have talked it over with Mary and she agrees." He was not being disloyal to Bellows. At this point the future of the Sanitary Commission was far from certain. Its funds were running low, Lincoln was not supportive, and Finley appeared firmly entrenched as head of the Medical Bureau.

To break the logjam, in December 1861 Bellows and Olmsted tried a different tactic. They prevailed on the chairman of the Senate's Military Affairs Committee to introduce a bill calling for the reform of the Medical Bureau. The legislation was drawn up by William A. Hammond, an army physician whom the Commission was backing as Finley's replacement. Olmsted mobilized support for the bill. He arranged for prominent civic leaders to lobby congressmen. He enlisted the support of George Opdyke, the mayor of New York, as well as General George McClellan, the commander of the Army of the Potomac.

Olmsted was becoming versed in Washington politics. While he was pushing his two bills through Congress, he concluded that the real authority over the confiscated plantations lay not with the Treasury but with the War Department: it would be the future military governor of Port Royal who would have the real power to effect the changes that Olmsted advocated. So, when Salmon Chase wrote him that Pierce wanted to return to his law practice, and that—at Pierce's insistence—he was offering Olmsted the position of supervisor, Olmsted turned him down. Instead, he offered his services to the newly appointed secretary of war, Edwin M. Stanton.

Olmsted had several balls in the air. When he refused Chase, he did not mention the War Department, but told him that he was considering an alternative job offer. In fact, Mayor Opdyke had asked Olmsted to be the next street commissioner of New York. This influential and powerful post combined planning, constructing, and maintaining not only streets but also piers, wharves, and public buildings. Olmsted was tempted—not least by the five-thousand-dollar salary.

In April the balls fell to the ground. Olmsted's political instinct about Port Royal had been correct, and his efforts on behalf of the contrabands did bear fruit, but he misjudged his own qualifications. Stanton appointed a military man—a brigadier general—to oversee the confiscated plantations. As for Opdyke, he was unable to garner the necessary support for Olmsted's nomination—the threat of a disinterested commissioner controlling political patronage proved too great. On the other hand, at the Sanitary Commission the situation accidentally improved. Secretary Stanton, a stiff Ohioan, had an altercation with Finley over an unrelated matter—and fired him. With Finley's departure, opposition crumbled, and in April the House passed the medical reform bill. A little later, Hammond was confirmed as surgeon general. "Our success is suddenly wonderfully complete," Olmsted wrote his father.

Nevertheless, he remained undecided about his future. The reinvigorated Commission was planning a flotilla of hospital ships. Olmsted was in charge of organizing the venture but warned his father, "Yet it may all slip up, so don't talk of it." Olmsted briefly considered the post of commissioner of a soon-to-be-created Bureau of Agriculture and Statistics. He thought it respectable, comparatively quiet—and permanent. "The alternative is going in & trying to build up a landscape gardening business—an alternative that even at forty, I am not likely to follow very steadily, I fear," he wrote his father. "'Wherever you see a head, hit it' is my style of work, & I have not yet sowed my wild oats altogether," he added cheerfully. Wild oats, indeed! He was now well into middle age.

Yeoman's War

THE SECRETARY OF WAR agreed that the army would lend vessels and crews to the Commission. The Commission would outfit, staff, and operate the ships. In March 1862 the Army of the Potomac—more than one hundred thousand men—under McClellan had been transported by sea to the mouth of the James River. The plan was to move up the broad peninsula that was bounded by the York River on the east and the James on the west and attack Richmond, the capital of the Confederacy.

The first Sanitary Commission ship, the *Daniel Webster,* a side-wheel steamboat, sailed from Alexandria, Virginia, at the end of April. Olmsted—who had not joined the Bureau of Agriculture and Statistics, after all—was on board. He was taking personal command of the Hospital Transport Service, a hurriedly organized venture that he could not entrust to a subordinate. The Commission's relationship with the Medical Bureau was still strained. Someone with authority was needed to make sure that the operation ran smoothly. In any case, he was glad to get out of Washington. And he was finally in the navy. Better still, it was his own little navy.

Olmsted's first task was to convert the vessels to hospital use, which involved tearing down partitions and building wards, bunks, kitchens, and storerooms. He had canvas awnings constructed to shade the upper decks. The Hospital Transport Service eventually consisted of more than a dozen vessels. Shallow-draft boats navigated the creeks and brought casualties to the riverboats that acted as floating hospitals. The *Wilson Small,* a side-wheel paddle steamer, served as Olmsted's headquarters. A supply ship provisioned the hospital ships. Larger steamboats ferried the wounded to the military base at Yorktown or transported them north to Washington and New York. The boats were an odd assortment—cavalry transports, river steamers, tugboats, merchant vessels, and two clipper ships. The largest ship could hold as many as one thousand casualties; smaller vessels carried two or three hundred.

By mid-May, the Hospital Transport Service was headquartered at White House, twenty miles up the Pamunkey River, a tributary of the York. This railhead, about forty miles east of Richmond, was now McClellan's main supply base. His army was poised outside the city. It had taken him more than three weeks to march up the Peninsula. There had been little fighting, yet casualties poured into White House, victims of dysentery and malaria. A typhoid epidemic was a threat. Olmsted took charge. Tents were set up ashore to act as way stations. The under-nourished men were fed and nursed before being loaded aboard the hospital ships and ferried to Yorktown.

Olmsted had two sterling assistants. He brought Frederick Knapp with him from Washington. Knapp had the crucial job of provisioning the hospital ships with food, drinking water, brandy, quinine, ice, and clothing, as well as the usual medical supplies. Robert Ware, an energetic young Boston physician and a Commission inspector, was the chief surgeon. Another valuable aide was James Grymes, a Washington physician and a friend of Knapp's. The heroic Grymes was untiring in his efforts despite his own ill health—he was tubercular. The rest of Olmsted's staff consisted of surgeons, medical students, and nurses. There was also a group of volunteers, young ladies from the local aid societies that had given Bellows the original impetus to form the Sanitary Commission. Katharine Wormeley was a thirty-two-year-old unmarried woman from Newport, Rhode Island. "As far as I can judge, our duty is to be very much that of a housekeeper," she observed. "We attend to the beds, the linen, the clothing of the patients; we have a pantry and store-room, and are required to do all the cooking for the sick, and see that it is properly distributed according to the surgeons' orders; we are also to have a general superintendence over the conditions of the wards and over the nurses, who are all men." Olmsted, who was generally skeptical of the usefulness of volunteers and preferred paid workers, came to admire the women's cheerfulness and untiring dedication. "They beat the doctors all to pieces," he said. The women, in turn, were devoted to him.

The Commission workers referred to Olmsted as the "Chief." "In little things as well as in great things no one opposes his will," observed Wormeley. That was only partly true. As the head of a civilian agency in a war zone, Olmsted was at the beck and call of the military. He answered not only to the medical director of the army—an inflexible man named Tripler—but also to the quartermaster department, the camp commandant, and even to McClellan's staff. Montgomery Meigs, the quartermaster general, was usually helpful, but he did not hesitate to commandeer a hospital ship for other uses at a moment's notice. The army transports were inferior to those of the Sanitary Commission. Olmsted was frequently called on to fill in whenever an emergency arose, which further complicated his schedules. Much of his time was spent sorting out conflicting directives and dealing with overbearing army officers, many of whom had never heard of the Hospital Transport Service or the Sanitary Commission.

Still, he persevered. On May 31 the Confederates sallied out of Richmond and attacked McClellan's left flank near Fair Oaks station. The resulting battle was inconclusive but bloody, with five thousand casualties on each side. Soon boxcars full of Union wounded—also wounded Confederate prisoners—started arriving in White House. Olmsted put all the available transport ships into operation. The *Elm City*, a 760-ton steamer, ferried five hundred men at a time to Yorktown; three hundred and fifty wounded were crammed into the *Daniel Webster;* the old *Knickerbocker* was likewise crowded with wounded. As the shore hospitals filled up, Olmsted ordered the transports to farther ports such as Annapolis and Boston.

Nothing had prepared the Commission staff for the maelstrom of confusion, suffering, and death. The army treated casualties with scant attention. Trainloads of wounded were dumped on the riverbanks. Olmsted provides a graphic description of the scene:

At the time of which I am now writing, Monday afternoon [two days after the battle], wounded were arriving by every train, entirely unattended or with at most a detail of two soldiers to a train of two or three hundred of them. They were packed as closely as they could be stowed in the common freight cars, without beds, without straw, at most with a wisp of hay under their heads. They arrived, dead and alive together, in the same close box, many with awful wounds festering and alive with maggots. The stench was such as to produce vomiting with some of our strong men, habituated to the duty of attending the sick & wounded of the army.

The heat and humidity were insufferable. The hospital ships filled up with screaming wounded. Surgeons worked around the clock. Wormeley and the other women bravely tried to assuage thirst, hunger, and pain. "You *can't conceive* what it is to stem the torrent of this disorder and utter want of organization," she wrote to her mother. "To think or speak of the things we see would be fatal. No one must come here who cannot put away all feeling. Do all you can, and be a machine,—that's the way to act; the only way."

The nightmare continued for a week. There was barely time to eat or sleep. To make matters worse, everyone suffered from a mild but persistent diarrhea. The doctors worried about Olmsted's health, but it was Knapp who finally came down with malaria and had to return to New York. Another Commission member broke down and became hysterical; he, too, was shipped home. "The horror of war can never be known but on the field," Olmsted wrote Mary. "It is beyond, far beyond all imagination." Still, he felt he and his staff had made a difference. "If we had not been just where we were and just so well prepared as we were, I can not tell you what a horrible disgrace there would have been here to our country." He estimated that of the two or three thousand casualties who were brought to White House, his ships had transported seventeen hundred.

A major battle for Richmond was in the offing, but for the moment there was little to do except prepare and attend to the constant flow of sick men. There was near panic on June 13, when General Jeb Stuart's cavalry, on its famous three-day reconnoitering ride behind the Union lines, briefly occupied Tunstall's Station, less than four miles away. Stuart's men failed to stop a train that brought the news to White House. Olmsted immediately ordered the hospital ships to weigh anchor. Stuart had every intention of destroying the supply base. Only the delayed return of two marauding squadrons prevented him from doing so.

While McClellan, in his now chronically hesitant way, slowly prepared to attack Richmond, Robert E. Lee, commanding general of the Army of Northern Virginia, acted. On June 25 Lee's forces attacked. They failed to break through the Union lines, but Lee, as audacious as his opponent was timid, continued his thrust. The next day he won a decisive victory. He pressed on, hoping to encircle his enemy. The shaken McClellan pulled back to the James River, where he could use his gunboats to advantage. This meant abandoning White House. On June 27 a flotilla of ships, including the Hospital Transport Service, sailed away, just ahead of the Confederate forces. Olmsted referred to it as the "skedaddle of the Pamunkey."

The new supply base was Harrison's Landing, on the James River. The *Wilson Small* arrived there on June 30. Olmsted and the others could hear the boom of cannons at nearby Glendale. On the next day, the sound of battle was even closer. Soon McClellan's army began to arrive at Harrison's Landing. A major and a chaplain came on board the *Wilson Small*. They were eagerly questioned. "Defeat! No; we have retreated but we never turned our backs on them. We have faced and fought and beaten them for five days." That was true. But the fact remained that during what became known as the Seven Days, Lee had driven his opponent twenty miles back down the Peninsula; Richmond was no longer threatened. The Union forces regrouped and prepared to resist an attack. It never came. McClellan believed that he was vastly outnumbered. In fact, the two armies were evenly matched. Yet the Confederates, who had suffered severe casualties, were not in a position to take the offensive.

Still, about four thousand wounded were at Harrison's Landing. This time, there was little of the confusion that had followed the battle of Fair Oaks. Treatment and transport functioned smoothly. This was largely due to the appointment of a new medical director: Jonathan Letterman. Letterman, who would go on to organize the army's first effective ambulance service, was young and innovative. He believed in the value of sanitary principles and sound organization. He impressed Olmsted. "I like him at first sight better than any Surgeon U.S.A. whom I have seen," he wrote. "He asks & offers cooperation, and will have it with all my heart, so far as it is worth-while to give it."

Yet Letterman's appointment finally undermined the work of the Hospital Transport Service. With a competent medical director in charge, the efficacy of the army's own transports improved, making the Sanitary Commission's parallel service unnecessary. On July 13 Olmsted wrote Bellows recommending that all transport operations be consolidated under the Medical Bureau. Bellows agreed. The hospital ships were costing the Commission about twenty thousand dollars a month, leaving precious little for its other activities. The hospital ships and stores were turned over to the quartermaster's department. The emergency was over. After eleven weeks, Olmsted and the others prepared to return home.

An estimated eight thousand to ten thousand casualties were carried by Olmsted's ships. The death rate in the Peninsular Campaign was 165 per thousand, which was about half the rate experienced by the British army during the Crimean War. Much credit was due to the Hospital Transport Service. It is harder to assess the effect of this wartime experience on Olmsted himself. It certainly wore him out physically, as it did all his coworkers. He was neither a starry-eyed idealist nor a romantic, so the horrors that he saw did not disillusion him. If anything, the bungling and incompetence that he witnessed convinced him of the value of sound organization. Nor did his experience turn him against the war. He remained convinced that an unequivocal military victory—however long it took—was necessary to destroy slavery and reestablish a healthy Union. What must have been a great satisfaction to him, apart from the comfort that he brought to the wounded soldiers, was the exceptionally close relations that he established with his colleagues—Knapp, Ware, Grymes, Wormeley, and the others. Let us give the last word to that fine woman Katharine Wormeley.

Did I say somewhere that Mr. Olmsted was severe, or something of that kind? Well, I am glad I said it, that I may now unsay it. Nothing could be more untrue; every day I have understood and valued and trusted him more and more. This expedition, if it has done no other good, has made a body of lifelong friends. We have a period to look back upon when we worked together under the deepest feelings, and to the extent of our powers, shoulder to shoulder, helping each other to the best of our ability, no one failing or hindering another. From first to last there has been perfect accord among us; and I can never look back to these months without feeling that God has been very good to let me share in them and see human nature under such aspects. It is sad to feel that it is all over.

CHAPTER THIRTY

"Six Months More Pretty Certainly"

OLMSTED RETURNED from the Peninsula in poor health—he had contracted a serious case of jaundice. "I grew daily more yellow, until I could have passed for rather a dark mulatto; the whites of my eyes gave place to a queer glistening saffron colored substance, and my skin became flabby leather, dry and dead." In July he spent a week on Staten Island with his family—not at the farm, which was still occupied by a tenant. He traveled to Walpole, New Hampshire, where he stayed with Frederick Knapp, who was recuperating from malaria. From there he joined Mary and the children in Hartford. His health did not improve. At the end of the summer one of the commissioners took the matter in hand and took Olmsted to Saratoga Springs for ten days. There was no time for a lengthy convalescence. On September 16, 1862, Union and Confederate forces joined battle near Antietam Creek, Maryland, about sixty miles from Washington. It was the bloodiest single day of the entire war. The Sanitary Commission reacted quickly. Olmsted, fearing that the railroad would be choked with traffic, sent supplies by wagon train; they arrived on the battlefield twenty-four hours ahead of anything else.

Olmsted continued to visit New York regularly, although by this time his relationship to Central Park had changed. He was no longer a part-time superintendent. Instead, earlier that year, the commission had appointed the firm of Olmsted & Vaux "Landscape Architects to the Board." The partners shared the $4,500 annual fee; Olmsted took $2,000, but assured Vaux that he was prepared to make do with less if Vaux, who was doing the brunt of the work, needed additional funds. (A few months later Vaux became seriously ill. Olmsted reduced his own share of the fee to $1,200.)

Olmsted missed his family. In October 1862 Mary and the children moved to Washington. He rented a furnished house that cost $125 a month, more than they could really afford. "We will be as frugal as we can," he advised Mary, "& San. Com. must pay me enough for it." He added: "Well, I think I have got to be normally in Washington for six months more pretty certainly—at least six months, don't you?" Olmsted hardly expected the war to be over in six months—by then, no one did.* "Six months more" referred to his apprehension about the future of the Sanitary Commission. Its national role was being called into question by the rise of two rival voluntary-aid organizations. The first was the Christian Commission, representing Protestant ministers, the American Tract Society, and the Young Men's Christian Organization. Unlike the Sanitary Commission, which, following Olmsted's secular views, was decidedly nonsectarian, the Christian Commission put great emphasis on holding prayer meetings, and on distributing religious tracts and Bibles. It lacked official stature, but its religious mission attracted public support. The second rival was the Western Sanitary Commission, an independent organization based in St. Louis and created by the famous explorer General John C. Frémont. Frémont was violently opposed to slavery; in August 1861 he had declared martial law in Missouri and unilaterally freed all the slaves of secessionist owners. Lincoln eventually relieved Frémont of command, but the Western Sanitary Commission continued and found ready financial support among New England abolitionists.

Also critical, in Olmsted's view, was the regional factionalism that had emerged within the Sanitary Commission itself. John Newberry was the associate secretary responsible for the Western division. Contrary to Olmsted's instructions, Newberry gave local branches in cities such as Cincinnati and Indianapolis considerable autonomy. The states of the Midwest, who resented what they perceived as Eastern bias, insisted that money raised in a particular state should be used only for the relief of its own soldiers. At the same time, when the Commission received a large donation from California, the Cincinnati branch—reversing the logic—demanded its "fair share." Such provincialism was exactly what Olmsted, who believed that the Commission must be a *national* organization, wanted to avoid. His efforts to impose discipline were complicated by

---

*Lee's advance into Maryland had been stopped at Antietam, but the Union had not yet begun an offensive. Nor was a peaceful resolution possible after Lincoln issued the Emancipation Proclamation, which freed all slaves in the Confederate states.

the fact that Newberry, nominally his subordinate, was also on the board of the Commission.

The governance of the Sanitary Commission had undergone a major change. During Olmsted's absence in Virginia, John Foster Jenkins was acting general secretary. Jenkins was a loyal subordinate but, mild-mannered, he did not exercise strong leadership—he preferred to leave that to the Executive Committee. The Committee, which was founded only to deal with small matters that might come up between board meetings, took over. It consisted of Bellows, Strong, Gibbs, and two of the medical men, Agnew and Van Buren. They now met daily (in New York) and issued directives for the acting general secretary to carry out.

The Executive Committee continued its overseeing role even after Olmsted returned. He hated being second-guessed. "If Jenkins or Knapp ask me for instructions, instead of taking hold to answer them, I think, 'What have the Committee said about that?' 'How is that under the rule of the Committee?' 'What will the Committee think about it?'" The Committee questioned his decisions about hiring and firing. In December it passed a resolution limiting the general secretary's discretionary spending to one thousand dollars, except in emergencies. This drove Olmsted to consider resigning. Only the exhortation of Bache, the vice president of the board, who had become a close friend, persuaded him to stay.

It was starting to be Central Park all over again! Yet this was different. There was no dark shadow of Green; Olmsted's personal relations with the members of the Committee were good. George Templeton Strong, the treasurer, did want more financial control, yet he and Olmsted agreed on most political issues. Strong had such a high opinion of Olmsted that he thought he would make an excellent secretary of war. "I believe that Olmsted's sense, energy, and organizing faculty, earnestness, and honesty would give new life to the Administration were he in it," Strong confided to his diary. Bellows, too, admired Olmsted, as did Van Buren. Agnew was a strait-laced religious man who sometimes found Olmsted too tolerant with subordinates, but he was fond of the general secretary—it was he who had taken Olmsted to Saratoga Springs. Olmsted and Gibbs liked each other immensely. They spent a lot of time together discussing the need for a social and political loyalists' club to promote national unity. Their efforts, supported by Bellows and Strong, led to the founding of the Union League Club of New York.

Part of Olmsted's problem was of his own making: he was overdoing it. "He works like a dog all day and sits up nearly all night," Strong noted in his diary, "doesn't go home to his family (now established in Washington) for five days and nights together, works with steady, feverish intensity till four in the morning, sleeps on a sofa in his clothes, and breakfasts on *strong coffee and pickles!!!*" No wonder he was short-tempered and picked quarrels with the Executive Committee.

The Committee rejected Olmsted's advice to centralize authority. It was rattled by the popular success of the Christian and the Western Sanitary Commissions and wanted to avoid controversy. The board proposed that Olmsted and Knapp make a tour of Midwestern cities to placate Newberry and his fiercely local partisans, and perhaps even to seek cooperation with the Western Sanitary Commission in St. Louis. Olmsted agreed but he was not sanguine. "I go west for personal recreation," he told Bellows wryly, ". . . and to cultivate a friendly feeling amongst all concerned by a little white lying, and also to demonstrate the fact that we are not obstinate mules and are willing to give way to people's mistakes & to pretend that we don't think them mistakes." But of course he was not made to be a diplomat. It is likely that the commissioners were happy to get Olmsted out of their hair. George Templeton Strong later admitted in the privacy of his diary: "There will be a battle when the Commission meets, and incredible as it seems to myself, I think without horror of the possibility of our being obliged to appoint somebody else General Secretary."

Olmsted and Knapp were gone six weeks. They visited Cincinnati, Chicago, St. Louis, and Cleveland. They had amicable if inconclusive meetings with Newberry at his headquarters in Louisville. Bellows and the board wanted news of conditions in the field. Olmsted and Knapp made two visits to war zones. First they went to Murfreesboro, Tennessee, where the Union Army of the Cumberland had recently fought a battle. They were welcomed by General William Rosecrans, an outspoken supporter of the Sanitary Commission. The second visit took them to Grant's Army of Tennessee, which was camped north of Vicksburg. They inspected a Commission hospital ship and met Admiral David Porter, whose gunboats and ironclads were anchored south of Vicksburg. Porter's men were showing signs of scurvy. (Olmsted had two hundred barrels of potatoes and onions put on board the flagship.) They dined with General Ulysses S. Grant. His siege of Vicksburg had so far been a failure, and his military future seemed dim. Most people who first met the unpretentious general were unimpressed—not so Olmsted. "He is one of the most engaging men I ever saw. Small, quiet, gentle, modest—extremely, even uncomfortably, modest—frank, confiding and of an exceedingly kind disposition. He gives you the impression of a man of strong will, however, and of capacity, underlying these feminine traits." This was how many people described Olmsted himself.*

The great fortress of Vicksburg commanded the Mississippi; Grant's latest plan was to build a canal through the swamps and transport his troops to the other side of the city. The young captain in charge of the work was William Tecumseh Sherman's chief engineer, Captain William LeBaron Jenney. Olmsted was not impressed by the size of the canal (which, indeed, proved too shallow and was abandoned), but he and Jenney hit it off. The Massachusetts-born Jenney was trained as an engineer but was interested in architecture and gardening. He had studied in Paris and they talked excitedly of that city's parks and architecture. The peculiarity of the circumstances did not escape Olmsted.

> Reminiscences of Cranch and Fontainbleau [sic]; of student-life at the Politechnique [sic] and Centrale, discussions of the decorations of the Louvre, had a peculiar zest in the midst of raw upper Louisiana plantation, where nature's usual work is but half-done; looking across the River into tree-tops hung with the weird Spanish-moss, vultures floating above; shouts and turmoil of a gang of contrabands tearing down the gin-house of the plantation—Captain Janney [sic] wants the material for bridges—the drums beating and bugles sounding for evening parade behind the distant boom of Farragut's big guns on the Hartford, pitching shells at intervals into my quondam host's, Dick Taylor's, rebel batteries at Warrenton.

The last was a reference to his friend Dick Taylor, now a major general in the Confederate army. Olmsted had visited Fashion Plantation ten years earlier.

Olmsted returned to Washington on April 14. He cagily informed Bellows that he did not wish to immediately resume his duties as general secretary (Jenkins was once again serving as acting general secretary). He wanted to prepare a report on a reorganization of the Sanitary Commis-

---

*Grant and Olmsted were exact contemporaries, both born in 1822, one day apart.

sion and present it to the board at its mid-June meeting. He was resigning without resigning. Bellows could hardly refuse. He knew that to do so might push Olmsted to really step down. Olmsted himself was not hopeful. "If I should leave the Commission Sanitary, as I am liable to do at any moment," he wrote his father, "I should be obliged to call on you to tide me over to the next berth."

The reason for Olmsted's remark was an offer by his father to lend him three thousand dollars to improve Tosomock Farm, which was still unsold. Even though John Olmsted generously asked for a repayment of only two thousand dollars, Olmsted declined; he felt he was in no position to take on more debt. This led to a rare quarrel. His father thought Frederick was being ungrateful—and impractical. He accused him of not taking enough care of the farm, and he reproached him for throwing over his job on Central Park. "You have no right to demand of me invariable success in everything," Olmsted responded testily. "I act always on certain, plain, simple principles of management. Generally they carry me through. Once or twice they have failed. Where is the man whose management never does fail." The rift did not last long. A few days later, John Olmsted wrote a conciliatory note. Olmsted responded: "However wanting in sagacity I may be, I am obstinate only in honest dutifulness." Still, his father's criticism struck home. Olmsted was not confident about his financial future. Earlier, Vaux had warned him that Green and the Commission were making his life impossible—he might have to step down. Olmsted agreed. On May 12 Olmsted & Vaux resigned as landscape architects to the Board. Not only did that mean the loss of $1,200 a year, but it also closed the door on his hope of returning to the superintendency of Central Park.

As one door closed, another opened. The man who helped to open it was E. L. Godkin. Edwin Lawrence Godkin was the son of a prominent Anglo-Irish clergyman. Godkin was brilliant but mercurial. He gave up law school in London and worked for a publisher. He wrote a history of Hungary, became a journalist, and spent two years covering the Crimean War. He returned to Belfast to work on the *Northern Whig* and was offered the editorship—he was only twenty-five. Instead, he emigrated to the United States. He arrived in New York in 1856 and soon met Olmsted, who was then writing *A Journey Through Texas*. Godkin, nine years Olmsted's junior, greatly admired Olmsted's Southern reporting and used it as a model when he went South as a correspondent for the London *Daily News*. Their friendship blossomed. "I would limp ten miles to talk an hour with him," said Olmsted. A handsome, witty, charming man, Godkin presently married into a prominent New Haven family and spent the next two years in Europe. When he returned to New York, he and Olmsted saw each other often.

Shortly after Olmsted came home from his Western trip for the Sanitary Commission, Godkin wrote: "I have been thinking and talking a great deal about a first class weekly paper ever since I saw you. . . . I don't know whether you were in joke or earnest in saying you would go into such a scheme with me; but if in earnest, I need hardly say I should be very glad to make some such arrangement." Olmsted was not joking, and the two were soon making plans. Their idea was to publish a weekly newspaper that would "secure a more careful, accurate and elaborate discussion of political, economical and commercial topics, than is possible in the columns of the daily press." This was to be a paper of opinion: supportive of the war, antislavery, Federalist, and opposed to states' rights. A weekly newsmagazine was a new idea. Olmsted and Godkin hoped that "at some time in the course of every week many men can find an opportunity, and will have an inclination, to deliberately read three or four articles in which real thought and study are brought to bear upon matters of public interest."

They could not decide on a name for the newspaper. They toyed with "The Loyalist" and "The Week"; Olmsted even considered "Yeoman's Weekly." Between themselves they called it "the paper." The division of labor was clear: Godkin would be the editor; Olmsted, the publisher. On June 25 he organized a small meeting at the Union League Club of New York to test the waters. The paper, which was expected to sell for twenty cents a copy (the *New-York Times* cost three cents), was not to be a mass-market publication, but according to their prospectus it would be commercially viable in time. What was needed was working capital—forty thousand dollars—to cover the first year of operation. Olmsted's plan was to seek sponsors rather than investors. After his presentation a wealthy businessman immediately pledged a thousand dollars. Howard Potter, a lawyer, William J. Hoppin, a founding member of the Century Association, and George Templeton Strong agreed to serve as trustees. "The thing starts so favorably," Olmsted wrote Mary excitedly the next day, "I shall go into it strong, meaning to succeed."

He was in New York on July 4 when word of the battle of Gettysburg reached the city. He coordinated the Commission's relief effort, which was massive—the Union side had suffered twenty-three thousand casualties during the three days of fighting. He toured the encampment and met General Meade. Olmsted was disappointed that Lee's invading force had escaped, but was heartened by the news that Vicksburg had finally fallen to Grant, and that Rosecrans was winning in Tennessee. The tide had turned. "I think we can hold our heads up with good conscience again," he wrote Mary.

The outcome of his own battles within the Sanitary Commission was less auspicious. He had proposed a reorganization plan to the board in June. It was a sensible compromise: decentralize the supply function of the Commission by creating four geographical departments, while maintaining central control over inspection, research, and general policy. The board accepted his plan. Newberry, who disliked the proposal, threatened to resign. The Chicago branch of the Commission objected to being required to collaborate with the Western Sanitary Commission. The board, concerned over the threat of regional splintering, backed down. Newberry, allowed to go his own way, promptly printed his own fund-raising circular, *The Sanitary Reporter*. Meanwhile, the Executive Committee undermined Olmsted's efforts, making contradictory public statements and privately criticizing his methods. The careful system of organization he had put in place was unraveling. "I am really oppressed beyond endurance by my grief that the grand purposes which I have had at heart in the Commission should appear to me to be sacrificed to little personal whims and good purposes of a narrow and ambiguous kind," he protested to Bellows.

Olmsted was ready to step down. He had promised Mary "six months more," and the six months had come and gone. But the fund-raising for "the paper" was not going well. He asked Bellows to approach New York benefactors, but with few results. He sent Godkin to Cambridge with a letter of introduction to Charles Elliot Norton. Godkin and Norton became close friends, but were not successful in finding patrons. Altogether, in one month Olmsted and Godkin raised only three of the forty thousand dollars. Olmsted told himself that it was because it was summer, and many people were away in their country retreats. One hot August day in Washington, he ran into his old friend from *Putnam's*, Charles Dana, who was now serving as assistant secretary of war. Naturally, talk turned to "the paper." What did the experienced editor think of the idea? "I don't believe it will succeed," Dana responded bluntly. Then, not wanting to dishearten Olmsted, he added, "But I am not sure, and I shall be glad to have it tried."

CHAPTER THIRTY-ONE

A Letter From Dana

A PHOTOGRAPH OF OLMSTED at this time shows him sitting in a wooden armchair, reading what appears to be a newspaper. He is fashionably dressed in a well-cut jacket and high-buttoned waistcoat of matching dark cloth, and light-colored trousers. A starched white collar peeks out above a patterned cravat. He is not wearing any jewelry, except for a wedding band. He still has a mustache, and his hair, thinning on top, is long in the back. He appears lean and fit, although his serious countenance shows signs of tiredness. Or perhaps he is bored with sitting still for the photographer. Though slouched in the chair, he does not look relaxed. He appears ready to jump up at a moment's notice, as if he is waiting for something to happen.

Fate played a major role in Olmsted's career. "Yes, but is he lucky?" Napoleon Bonaparte is supposed to have asked about a general. Olmsted was lucky. Raymond's offer to write about the South, Elliott's suggestion that he might make a good Central Park superintendent, Vaux's proposal to collaborate on Greensward, Bellows's invitation to lead the Sanitary Commission—all had come to him unsolicited, and all occurred at opportune moments. And now it happened again.

The chance meeting with Charles Dana in Washington had started it. The following week, Dana was approached by a group of New York businessmen. They were looking for someone to manage a large California gold-mining property that they had recently purchased. He declined the offer. Remembering that Olmsted seemed to be casting about for a new position, Dana recommended him. One of the owners was George Opdyke, the mayor of New York, who had earlier tried to recruit Olmsted to be street commissioner. A few days later, Dana wrote to Olmsted that the manager's job was his for the asking. Olmsted was with Mary and the children at Knapp's summer house in Walpole, New Hampshire, when he received the offer. "I am rather disposed to decline it chiefly, or partly, because I think it might be too much for me," he casually mentioned to his father. Yet he immediately left Walpole for New York.

His eagerness is understandable. The gold mine in question was not just any mine, but the huge Mariposa Estate. A contemporary assayer described it as "one of the most gigantic mining operations in the world." The property covered seventy square miles and included six mines, two towns, a railroad, and a tenant population of about seven thousand. The previous owner was none other than General John C. Frémont. The Mariposa Estate was originally a Spanish land grant—Las Mariposas. Frémont, a key participant in the annexation of Upper California, had acquired the land two years before the great California gold rush. The estate was located astride the fabled Mother Lode, and Frémont became a rich man. Nevertheless, his political activities at the state and national levels—he ran unsuccessfully for president—ate up his fortune. In 1863, more than a million and a half dollars in debt, he sold the estate to Morris Ketchum, a millionaire New York banker. Ketchum founded a public company, the Mariposa Company, the group that had now approached Olmsted with the offer to manage the Estate.

Olmsted arrived in New York on Sunday, August 9; the next day he met Opdyke and some of the trustees of the Mariposa Company. They were anxious to get Olmsted; they urgently needed a manager, and with his experience of running Central Park and the Sanitary Commission, he was a strong candidate. They offered him an annual salary of ten thousand dollars and one hundred shares of company stock. They wanted an immediate decision. First, Olmsted assured himself that the new owners were "respectable, steady, careful capitalists." Morris Ketchum's reputation was unassailable. The illustrious board included Frémont himself, as well as Opdyke. Olmsted consulted Oliver Gibbs's geologist brother, who had spent a decade in California and the Northwest. Olmsted spoke to George Templeton Strong and to Howard Potter, a trustee of "the paper" and knowledgeable about California. All advised him to go. So did David Dudley Field, who was now legal counsel to the Mariposa Company. Jenkins and other friends had personal misgivings about Olmsted's departure but thought he could not afford to pass up the opportunity. John Olmsted was decidedly in favor; so was Mary.

On Wednesday Olmsted wrote to Mary: "I think that I shall make up my mind tonight, and *if the result of enquiries today* is favorable, shall decide to go." The results were favorable. He resolved to visit the Mariposa Company offices on Saturday. Then he received a letter from Bellows—an impassioned plea not to accept the position. "I don't know a half-dozen men in the whole North, whose influence in the next five years I should think more critically important to the Nation," he wrote. "I don't know how it is to come *in*—whether by means of the Newspaper (which I think can be made to go) or by means of political office—but I am sure it is to be largely felt." This was not simple flattery. Bellows understood Olmsted. He knew that Olmsted shared his own concern for public service, and he thought that Olmsted was destined for greater things than overseeing a gold mine.

> *The country can not spare you at such a juncture.* I think *you* must *feel this in your bones.* I don't think you can make up your mind to become the agent of a set of money-makers on the Pacific Coast—let them offer you a fortune or no, while Providence is holding out the splendid opportunity of usefulness in the Nation and to Humanity—at the most critical and serious lustre of its history! You are not the man to throw away your duty and your reward at once, into the Mariposa claim.

Their professional disagreements had not affected their friendship. Olmsted valued Bellows's opinion and was stung by the imputation that he was shirking his civic duty. So instead of going to the Mariposa office he wrote Bellows a letter. He emphasized that he had to think of his family. He described his dissatisfaction with the situation at the Commission. He did concede that if the newspaper project were on a more solid footing, he might stay, even if it meant making a financial sacrifice. Finally, he promised that he would wait until the following week before making a final decision.

Olmsted spent the next day—Sunday—at the Sanitary Commission's office mulling things over. He wrote a second letter to Bellows. In it he reiterated—at great length—the points he had made the previous day. He said that he appreciated Bellows's opinion of his prospects, but judged it extravagant. He made it clear that he was disappointed with the Executive Committee. "If the Sanitary Commission had trusted me as it originally proposed to do, it would have accomplished more than it has done." In part, he blamed himself: "I see what ought to be done but I can't get other men to see it." On one thing, he had clearly already made up his mind. "Whether I go to California or not, I shall expect some instructions for winding up my official affairs," he wrote. "My interest in the Sanitary Commission has ceased."

Bellows's answer contained a hard remark: "I think the faith of many, already pinned unconsciously to you, would fail and grow cold, if you should quit the field under what would seem to be a pecuniary temptation." Strong was more understanding. "Olmsted has not a mercenary nerve in his moral organization," he noted in his diary, "but he has a wife & children to provide for—and he wants the luxury of paying certain debts of the old Putnam's Magazine concern with which he was connected, for which he was never legally liable nor morally liable, so far as I can make out." Yet Olmsted did consider himself morally liable. He still owed George Curtis's father-in-law $7,500; in addition, he had further debts of $4,500. "If I should die, my wife & children would be in absolute poverty." The thought weighed heavily on him. He was not in the best of health. This was a time without life insurance, Medicare, or Social Security. Were he to die, his family's welfare would depend completely on whatever he could leave them. At the moment, that was less than nothing.

California represented an opportunity to clear his debts and—finally—to accumulate some savings. Attractive, too, was the idea of returning East as a rich man—for Olmsted had no intention of spending more than five years in California. "A poor man is considered a failure," he reminded Bellows, "and can not command deep confidence in his undertakings for public ends." This was not a rationalization. Most of the men in public life did come from wealthy families. If he, too, had money, he would be taken more seriously and would be freer to assume the sort of civic responsibilities that Bellows alluded to.

Like many Easterners, Olmsted considered the Western frontier to be savage and uncivilized. Nothing he had seen in Texas had changed his mind. He expected the Mariposa Estate, which was two hundred miles inland, to be "dreary." Nor did he have any illusions that running the mines would be easy. The owners had been frank with him about past mismanagement; there was a lot to do. But he was confident he could succeed. "If they will really put the management in my hands as they propose, for two or three years, I know (humanely speaking) that I can astonish them."

Bellows's response to Olmsted's letters contained a final plea: "My ambition for you, has been to see you in some independent position, the Head of a Bureau, a department, the editor of a Great Newspaper." By then it was too late. Olmsted had made up his mind and officially accepted the position of manager of the Mariposa Estate. Sometime the following week, he attended a meeting of the Executive Committee to announce his resignation. "Olmsted has completed his arrangement with the Mariposa people and is to busy himself for five years in a mountain gorge of California," George Templeton Strong sardonically wrote in his diary. But ever the honest observer, he added, "We can ill spare him."

On September 1, 1863, Olmsted officially resigned from the Sanitary Commission. Two weeks later he was on board the steamship *Champion*, bound for San Francisco. That morning, the *New-York Times* contained an editorial titled "Departure of Mr. F. L. Olmsted for California." Written by E. L. Godkin, it was a fulsome tribute that recounted Olmsted's activities of the last decade: the writing on the South, Central Park, the Sanitary Commission. Godkin lamented the loss of Olmsted to public service. He concluded:

> We can only console ourselves by the reflection that few leave behind them so many delightful reminders, not only of his taste and talent, but of his hearty love of liberty and justice, and of his unwavering faith in their ultimate triumph; and that none carry with them more fervent wishes for their happiness and success.

A generous and heartfelt accolade; to Olmsted it may have sounded like an obituary.

Never Happier

Bear Valley, California

Friday, January 1, 1864

A plastered stone building houses the company store of the Mariposa Estate. Above the store is a suite of rooms that serves as the manager's office. Today part of the space has been converted into a dining room. Desks have been moved aside and a long table stands in the center of the room. It is covered with the remnants of a New Year's Day dinner.

The guests have all left. Olmsted is reclining on a sofa. The dinner went well, he thinks. A little bit of civilization in this barbarous place. They were sixteen in all: twelve gentlemen and four ladies. He had invited all the mine superintendents. He is slowly getting to know them; they strike him as capable men. The guest of honor was Judge Lewis Jones, accompanied by his wife and sister. He likes Jones. He was a superintendent of the Estate and is now a county judge. Jones is a Unionist, but most of the superintendents are Southerners and avowed Secessionists. Olmsted managed to steer the conversation away from politics. It helped that Pieper and Martin were there, he thinks. He has known them a long time. They both came out with him from New York on the Champion. *John Pieper, assistant superintending engineer on Central Park, is now his chief engineer. His wife and baby appear to be settling in well. Howard Martin is a bachelor. He was chief clerk of Central Park and followed Olmsted to the Sanitary Commission. Now he is chief accountant of the Mariposa Estate.*

Charles Wauters, his French valet, comes in to clear the last of the dishes. Charles takes them back to the nearby hotel, Oso House, where the food was prepared. Olmsted's indigestion is bothering him—he shouldn't have eaten so much. Maybe he should get up and walk around. He gets up and crosses into the room where he normally works. A partially emptied crate of books is on the floor. It is from Mason Brothers, the New York publisher and bookseller. He picks up one of the leather-bound volumes and leafs through it. The crate contains a full set of Sir Walter Scott: twenty-seven novels and six short stories. It is a parting gift from the Washington staff of the Sanitary Commission. Just the thing, especially now that his eyes ache and his head throbs every time he sets pen to paper; reading, for some reason, doesn't distress him. He will have to see a doctor soon. But not that sawbones in Mariposa—he will find a good physician the next time he is in San Francisco.

Knapp must have thought of the books. Dear Knapp! He remembers reading his last letter: "Ever since you left the whole house has had a sort of lonely look to me—as after the death of some dear friend on whom we had leaned and as if we had lost a something which we were never to get back. Every day and night I feel it." It had made him cry, that letter. Before Olmsted left, they had privately discussed the possibility of Knapp coming to join him in California, at least once the war started to wind down. He made the same suggestion to Godkin; if he doesn't make progress with the paper, he might consider it. Olmsted has also written to Jenkins that there is need for a good doctor on the Estate.

It is three and a half months since he left New York and he misses his friends. In spite of his headaches, he devotes a lot of time to answering letters. He writes about his everyday life to Mary, about the scenery to his father, about his loneliness to Knapp, about politics to Godkin and Brace, and about his plans to improve Bear Valley to Ketchum. A month ago he sent a long letter to Vaux. Vaux still frets about not receiving recognition for his work on Central Park. Lately, he has written that he feels slighted by Godkin's farewell editorial in the Times, *which he thinks overstates Olmsted's contribution to Greensward. In fact, the editorial mentioned Vaux by name, and if he is unhappy, he should complain to Godkin, Olmsted thinks. He has enjoyed working with Vaux, but the little Englishman can be trying sometimes.*

Olmsted has also heard from Bellows. The board of the Sanitary Commission has finally accepted Olmsted's resignation officially—with "profound regret"—but has requested that he continue to serve as a board member. Olmsted agrees. He has already contacted the Commission's California branch in San Francisco on Bellows's behalf. He is glad that Bellows and he have remained friends. Before Olmsted left New York, Bellows asked him to take his young nephew, Henry, with him to California. Henry is now working as a clerk in the company store at the Princeton mine. He is a likable fellow, but as

Olmsted has just written his uncle, he needs a wife—or a sister as a companion—to steady him lest he run wild in this uncivilized place.

Olmsted's habit is to go for a walk at sunset. He puts on a coat—it is a cool evening—and goes downstairs. The street is almost empty. A woman in a large straw hat and black pantaloons hurries by. She is Chinese; more than half the miners on the Estate come from China. Olmsted admires the Chinese; they are more industrious—and cheaper to employ—than his other workers. The Italians, too, are hardworking. They also grow most of the produce. As for the rest of the miners, they are a rough lot, interested mainly in gambling and drinking. The Estate has let wages run up higher than at other mines, and Olmsted knows that, sooner or later, he is going to have to reduce their pay.

He walks up the street of Bear Valley, or Campo del Oso as the Spaniards called it. This remote site in the foothills of the Sierra Nevada was where Frémont established the headquarters of his mining empire. He named the large mountain that dominates the valley Mount Bullion. The auspicious name really refers to his father-in-law, Senator Thomas Hart Benton, popularly known as Old Bullion because of his opposition to paper currency. Millions of dollars of gold bullion have been shipped from Bear Valley. Yet after more than fifteen years the settlement remains little more than a makeshift mining camp. It has a population of two or three hundred people. A score of buildings line the single, dusty street. In addition to the miners' shanties and tents, there are three saloons, two livery stables, a billiard parlor, a bakery, and a bathhouse—no church, no school. The most substantial structure is Oso House, a large stone structure surrounded by a shaded veranda. Originally built by Frémont for his own use, it is now a hotel and shares space with the Wells Fargo office. Mail is dropped off every other day; it takes more than a month for a letter to arrive from the East. Stockton, where there is a telegraph station—and a steamer connection to San Francisco—is eighty miles away, more than a day's ride. Mariposa, the county seat, is about twelve miles in the other direction.

Olmsted walks away from the village. His limp is more visible as his stride lengthens. He climbs a large knoll in the middle of the valley. From the top, he admires the view. At the south end of the valley five miles away he can see Mt. Ophir, the site of another of his mines. The light from the setting sun is an odd violet-gray. The bare mountainsides are dotted with thorny chaparral and young pine. It reminds him of the heathery hills of Scotland. When he first arrived, he was repelled by this harsh landscape, so different from the lush, green hills of New England. It is beginning to grow on him.

A plume of smoke indicates the nearby Indian camp. The natives have a bad reputation among the miners, who scornfully call them Diggers because of their habit of grubbing for roots. The village of Bear Valley looks pitifully small below. He wonders if anything can ever be made of this place. He has written to Ketchum that his strategy is to devote the next six months to studying how the Estate can be put on a solid economic footing. To that end, he has engaged a mining consultant, William Ashburner. Ashburner, a former member of the California Geological Survey, is a New Englander and a graduate of Harvard and the École des Mines in Paris. He is considered the authority on mining on the Pacific coast. He and Olmsted have a lot in common and are becoming fast friends. Ashburner has proposed sinking an exploratory mine shaft, and building a large, modern stamp mill. Olmsted wants to diversify the income of the Estate. Thousands of acres of potentially valuable farmland only need water. He has asked Pieper to study the feasibility of constructing an irrigation canal. The canal could also be used to float logs down to the Estate for use as construction material and fuel.

When he and Pieper were exploring a possible route for the canal, they came across a remarkable sight: a grove of enormous ancient trees. Olmsted has never seen anything quite as grand as the 250-foot-tall giant sequoias. "Strangers from another world" is how he described them to Mary. It is one of the places that he wants to show her. He longs to see his family. They will be here soon; in fact, they may be aboard the steamer that is scheduled to leave New York two days hence on the long journey to Panama, whence they will journey by rail across the isthmus and catch another ship that will bring them to California. He still has not heard definite news of their departure date. When he does, he will know when to go to San Francisco to meet them.

Twilight does not last long in these mountains. He retraces his steps down the hill. He does not hurry. The distractions of Oso House, where he is living, are few. He may stop in the office and do some work—he likes to work at night and get up late in the morning. There are letters to answer, and reports to read. Barring that, there is always Sir Walter Scott.

Not until February 11, 1864, did Godkin telegraph Olmsted that Mary and the children were departing. The entire voyage would take a full month. Olmsted made plans to meet them in San Francisco. He had just completed a report for the Mariposa board describing the Estate's finances. The detailed investigation confirmed his fears. Only two weeks after arriving in Bear Valley he wrote to Mary: "Things are worse here than I dare say to anybody but you—and to you with a caution. There is not a mine on the Estate that is honestly paying expenses." He and Martin pored over the books and discovered that the previous management had deferred repairs and maintenance in order to show an increase in profits. The richest deposits were rumored to have been held in reserve until just before the sale in order to inflate the price. The prospectus prepared by Frémont included an assayer's optimistic prediction—"It is my conviction that the amount of gold-bearing quartz that could be extracted is beyond all calculation"—and maintained that "the property is now producing from $60,000 to $100,000 per month, half of which, at least is profit." When Olmsted arrived, he found that production had fallen precipitously to $25,000 per month. Moreover, his own careful inventory of the Estate's physical assets was 40 percent lower than the original owners' estimate.

He assumed that inefficiency accounted for these discrepancies. After all, the previous manager of Mariposa, Trenor Park, was now an officer of the new company, as was Frémont himself. Olmsted might have been less sanguine had he known that shortly after his departure from New York, the company issued a leather-bound monograph that reiterated the exaggerated production claims and predicted that annual net earnings of the Estate would eventually exceed $2 million. "The Board do not feel justified in promising immediately the handsome returns indicated," the report primly warned, ". . . but the Board feel that the question of time involved is of small importance compared with a thorough and reliable system of driving the mines." The person responsible for devising this system would be the new manager, Fred. Law Olmsted, who was praised for "his acknowledged and widely extended reputation for integrity, ability, and remarkable administrative faculty." The last statement, at least, was true.

The board of directors approved the proposed irrigation canal but withheld the necessary funds until the Estate's income improved. Olmsted undertook to increase production. He sent Pieper to the Nevada Territory to learn about a new process of milling ore; he ordered work to start on the exploratory shaft and the stamp mill. Martin reformed the bookkeeping procedures. To decrease costs, Olmsted ordered that single men be compelled to live in the company boardinghouses, which were currently underutilized. As an encouragement, he reduced the rates for room and board from one dollar to eighty-five cents a day and declared that henceforth the boardinghouses would be run at cost. This last was a conciliatory gesture, for he also put into effect another policy. He did what any conscientious manager of a troubled enterprise must also do: he trimmed labor costs.

The miners found their daily wages suddenly reduced from $3.50 to $3.15. They went on strike. They were emboldened by the success of a walkout the previous summer that had compelled Olmsted's predecessor to retract a disciplinary measure. Olmsted had not expected a strike, since the reduction was slight and the new wage was competitive with that of other California mines. Yet he was not prepared to back down. "I don't want the men to think that they can ever expect to gain anything from me by striking,—and the sooner they learn this the better in every respect shall we be situated," he wrote the president of the Mariposa Company. He hired substitutes. The striking miners tried to disrupt work. Olmsted posted men at the mine entrances. The strikers attacked the guards. "The mob got the worst of it—no weapons but fists being used," he reported, "we have had fire arms ready but kept them out of sight at all points." He alerted the sheriff and had a warrant issued for the ringleaders, who fled the county.

After five days the strike collapsed. Olmsted was not vindictive. He offered to pay in full any miner who wished to leave—more than two hundred accepted; many went to the Nevada Territory, where gold had been discovered. They were soon replaced—Olmsted had put advertisements in the San Francisco newspapers the day the strike broke out. He reduced the number of skilled miners and hired less expensive unskilled laborers at $2.40 a day, as well as Chinese workers, whom he paid only $1.75 a day.

He had weathered the first crisis. A few days later he went to San Francisco to greet his family. Mary arrived with an entourage: her seventeen-year-old cousin, Henry Perkins, who was to work as Olmsted's secretary; a maid; and an English governess for John, age eleven, Charlotte, nine, and Owen, now six—little Marion was two. It was a joyful reunion; Olmsted had been separated from them for six months.

Yet a cloud hung over the event. Olmsted had taken advantage of being in San Francisco to consult a physician about his "writing sickness." Dr. William Ayres was an old acquaintance from his Hartford youth. His diagnosis was alarming. He attributed Olmsted's distress to an enlarged heart. He advised living quietly and carefully, avoiding fatigue, and reducing writing and "brain-work" as much as possible. He told Olmsted that while his condition was not necessarily fatal, it was incurable—he would be an invalid for life.

In the absence of electrocardiographs and X-ray machines, identifying heart disease was a matter of guesswork. In fact, John Jenkins and William Van Buren, Olmsted's old friends on the Sanitary Commission and both experienced physicians, disagreed with the prognostication. Olmsted reasonably pointed out that Ayres—not they—had examined him. He trusted Ayres, whom he had known a long time, and he had no reason to doubt his diagnosis. He was shaken. "I am sadly damaged," he informed Bellows. His only consolation was that as manager of the Mariposa Estate he could "accommodate my own work to my strength," as he put it. "I can live here a quiet life & give the children a fair education," he wrote Vaux. In the same vein, he wrote his father, "I have had my full share of bustling life and shall be better content to live quietly for the rest or die where I am, than most men are."

Ayres's prescription had one beneficial result: for the first time in more than a decade Olmsted slowed down. He gave up the compulsive habit that he had fallen into while at the Sanitary Commission of working late into the night and rising at noon. He ate regularly—Mary saw to that. He stopped writing and dictated letters and reports to Henry Perkins. He learned to pace himself. He and Mary went riding every afternoon, often accompanied by the children on their donkeys—Kitty, Fanny, and Beppo. Evenings were spent at home. Mary read history to the children; John played his violin. Later, Olmsted rented a piano.

The landscape of Bear Valley may have been desolate, but the spring was delightful—warm, dry days and cool nights. Everyone thrived as a result of the healthy climate and the outdoor life. The children lost their sickliness; Mary relaxed. "There is a great dearth of incidents in our life here," she wrote a friend, "so that I can only tell you that we live comfortably and that strange as it may seem, time does not hang heavily on our hands."

Frederick and Mary had never had a real honeymoon; in their five years of marriage, vacations had been infrequent. Now when Olmsted went on a tour of the Estate, Mary, who had become a skilled horsewoman, accompanied him. "We went in a carriage with a servant on horseback, camped at night, put saddles on the horses in the morning and rode through the gulches and over the hills where a wagon couldn't approach. . . . It was very rough riding & the weather pretty warm, but we both enjoyed it and collected a heavy pack-load of quartz samples for closer examination & assay at home. . . . Mary is getting a quick eye for quartz, and the children are all becoming experts with the 'pan.' " It was an American version of *The Swiss Family Robinson*.

There were visitors. One was Benjamin Silliman Jr., a Yale professor of chemistry and geology like his father, whose classes Olmsted had briefly attended. Silliman, a leading authority on petroleum, was in California to evaluate oil properties on behalf of New York investors. Olmsted invited him to visit the Mariposa Estate and hired him to compile an evaluation of its gold-mining potential. Silliman was optimistic and endorsed Olmsted's plans in glowing terms. Another visitor was Henry Whitney Bellows. His protégé Starr King, the dynamic twenty-two-year-old pastor of San Francisco's First Unitarian Church and the Sanitary Commission's chief fund-raiser, had recently died of diphtheria. Bellows had come to California as a temporary replacement. He spent two days in Bear Valley in June. Despite his continued reservations about Olmsted's retreat from civic duty, Bellows could not help but be impressed by his friend's new life. "He is a kind of little monarch here," he wrote back to his colleagues on the Sanitary Commission, "has his own horses & servants at command, is universally well-spoken of & respected—conquered in that strike business, has reduced wages, improved comfort among the men, retains the best workmen . . . & on the whole is much better situated than I feared to find him."

Olmsted had intended to build a new house for his family, not in Bear Valley but farther south on the Princeton plateau, where it was cooler. Mary brought the architectural plans, prepared by Vaux after Olmsted's notes. Olmsted decided that Marion House, as they named it, would now have to wait until the Estate turned a profit. As an interim measure, he converted his spacious office into combined working and living quarters. Bellows described it thus:

> I am sitting in Olmsted's office writing at his table, while he with cap on, is this moment examining various specimens of gold-bearing quartz, with true official expertness. The Map of the Mariposa estate hangs in large proportions on the wall; also a naval & military map of the United States & Bancroft's Pacific states; a table covered with charts of the

mines; a long American Flag is folded on the floor (it was flying yesterday in honor of my arrival.) The office is carpeted with brussels. It is one of a long suite of rooms, built over the *Company* Store, giving 8 or 10 large apartments—which Mr. O. has fitted up in a most comfortable and tasty manner for the accommodation of his family.

To Bellows, and to Olmsted's other friends in the East, the distant Mariposa Estate seemed like a form of exile, a detour—if not an actual cul-de-sac—in a promising public career. That is not what Olmsted thought. "I never was happier, in the present, in my life," he wrote his friend Godkin. He had been married almost five years, yet this was the first time he had been able to spend a long, uninterrupted period with Mary and the children. He had always found his satisfaction in work and work-related friendships. First Central Park, later the Sanitary Commission, had engaged his entire attention; his family had always come second. Now that changed.

Olmsted first encountered Bear Valley in October. Winter and spring were benign. With July came the searing heat of summer. California was in the middle of a two-year drought. The trees wilted and the desiccated foothills turned brown and dusty. The weather became insupportable. In July the family set out for the higher and cooler terrain of the Sierra Nevada. The party included the governess, Miss Errington; the German housekeeper, Meta; and the cook, Bell, a black man; as well as William Ashburner and his wife. There were ten horses, eight mules, and two donkeys. They traveled forty miles to the South Fork of the Merced River, a place called Clark's. Here they camped for several weeks in an uplands meadow (now called Wawona) on a ranch belonging to Galen Clark. He was an affable New England–born explorer and frontiersman who had discovered the nearby Mariposa Big Tree Grove. Olmsted called him the "doorkeeper of the Yo Semite," for his ranch served as a stopping point for visitors traveling to the valley.

Clark took Mary and Olmsted to see the giant sequoias. It was a five-hour ride, but worth it, as Mary recounted:

> I know of no simile to convey to you an idea of the effect these trees produce on one. The color of the bark is that of light tan bark and the sides are in great fluted lines. They are like cathedral columns or gigantic organ pipes. We spread our blankets down in a fern brake where the del-

icate leaves of the ferns growing up five feet or more were between us and the camp fire and an opening among the tree-tops let in the star light from the almost black sky. As the fire lighted up the giant tree, the effect was sublime and kept one awake in spite of the fatigue of the day.

Olmsted returned to Bear Valley for two weeks to attend to business and inspect the construction of the new stamp mill. When he came back, the party left Clark's and followed the Merced eight miles up into the Yosemite Valley. The valley had been discovered by white men thirteen years earlier, and thanks to visiting writers, photographers, and painters, it had become well-known. Starr King, an enthusiast of landscapes, wrote a book about Yosemite in 1860. The photographer Carleton E. Watkins visited the valley a year later and published a series of widely distributed stereoscopic views. The month before Olmsted arrived in Bear Valley, the painter Albert Bierstadt spent two months sketching Yosemite. The resulting monumental paintings—*Domes of the Yosemite* and *Valley of the Yosemite*—were instant popular successes. Bierstadt was accompanied by Fitz-Hugh Ludlow, a writer whose description of Yosemite appeared in the *Atlantic* in June 1864.*

They pitched their tents opposite the 2,425-foot Yosemite Falls, the highest waterfall on the continent. The majestic scenery made a strong impression on Olmsted:

> We are camped near the middle of the chasm on the bank of the Merced, which is here a stream meandering through a meadow . . . like the Avon at Stratford—a trout stream with rushes & ferns, willows & poplars. The walls of the chasm are a quarter of a mile distant, each side—nearly a mile in height—half a mile of perpendicular or over-hanging rock in some places. Of course it is awfully grand, but it is not frightful or fearful. It is sublimely beautiful, much more beautiful than I had supposed. The valley is as sweet & peaceful as the meadows of the Avon, and the sides are in many parts lovely with foliage and color. There is little water in the cascades at this season, but that is but a tri-fling circumstance. We have what is infinitely more valuable—a full moon & a soft hazy smokey atmosphere with rolling towering & white fleecy clouds.

---

*Olmsted read Ludlow's article, "Seven Weeks in the Great Yo-Semite," and judged his overwrought and bombastic description "an abomination."

Willa Cather would later make a distinction between wilderness and landscape. The American West, she wrote, is "a country still waiting to be made into a landscape." The unique and affecting charm of Yosemite, as Olmsted perceptively noted, is that it is both wilderness *and* landscape. The craggy vastness of the chasm is older than any human presence, yet the valley floor appears comfortably domesticated. Olmsted appreciated this curious contrast; he and Vaux had created precisely this effect in Central Park, where the wilderness of the Ramble was side by side with pastoral meadows.

The Olmsted party camped in Yosemite until the beginning of October. They went on picnics and walked in the surrounding forest. Under the tutelage of Miss Errington the children looked for fossils. Mary indulged her hobby of rock collecting. Olmsted and John made a six-day excursion into the High Sierra. They were guided by William Brewer of the California Geological Survey, which was mapping the area. Olmsted was not fit enough to hike and was obliged to ride, yet they managed to reach the top of a previously unclimbed 12,764-foot peak. The Geological Survey customarily named mountains after prominent explorers and scientists, and Olmsted chose Mount Gibbs, in honor of his chemist friend Oliver Wolcott Gibbs.

The family resumed its life in Bear Valley. Although Olmsted felt better after his mountain holiday, he was not entirely cured. "I find the old symptoms returning as soon as I come back to the desk," he wrote his father. "I am very well so long as I don't think," he wrote Knapp. That was hyperbole: Olmsted might stop himself from writing, but not from thinking. He was drawn into public life. The hard-fought presidential election of 1864 embroiled Mariposa County as it did the rest of the country. Lincoln appeared vulnerable. He had put Grant in command of all the Union armies. Grant fought Lee for six bloody weeks in Virginia but was unable to defeat him. The war, now in its fourth year, appeared unwinnable. The Democratic candidate was the embittered General George McClellan. He ran on a platform suggesting a cessation of hostilities with the South and a negotiated peace. Olmsted, who staunchly supported Lincoln, wrote a long letter to the *Mariposa Weekly Gazette* titled "The Manager of the Mariposa Estate Defines His Position." The tables turned a few months before the election. Atlanta finally fell to Sherman's army, and General Philip Sheridan defeated the Confederates in the Shenandoah Valley. Lincoln was elected. In Mariposa County, Secessionist sentiment proved impervious to Olmsted's rhetoric and Lincoln was narrowly defeated.

Earlier the U.S. Congress passed an unnoticed but historic act. The legislation, introduced by Senator John Conness of California, granted the Yosemite Valley and the Mariposa Big Tree Grove to the State of California "for public use, resort and recreation . . . inalienable for all time." This was the beginning of what would become the National Park System. In September Governor Frederick Low of California appointed a commission to survey the valley and to recommend how the land grant should be managed. The Yosemite Commission included Josiah Whitney, the head of the California State Geological Survey, several prominent Mariposa County business leaders, William Ashburner, and Galen Clark. Low was the nominal chairman, but the Commission's real head was Frederick Law Olmsted. He was a natural choice, known to Low, who was also a Unionist, to Whitney, and, of course, to Ashburner and Clark. As manager of the Mariposa Estate he was an important figure in the county. Above all, he was a nationally recognized expert on parks.*

The same month that he was appointed to the Yosemite Commission, Olmsted was hired to lay out the grounds of a cemetery in Oakland. Mountain View was to be San Francisco's premier cemetery, following the model of rural cemeteries such as Greenwood and Laurel Hill. The consulting fee of several thousand dollars was welcome, but in this case money was not the prime motivation. Olmsted was challenged by the site: two hundred acres in the Oakland Hills, overlooking San Francisco Bay. The treeless, hilly terrain was quite unlike anything he had encountered in the East. Since coming to California he had begun to appreciate the Western landscape. Mountain View was an opportunity to explore its difference. It was also his first independent landscaping commission.

"I am going to lay out a burying ground near here & it is a great comfort for me to have that object," he wrote Knapp, "other than the heartsickening waiting on gold, which, so far, don't come." Eventually the gold did come. In October the Princeton mine hit a rich vein and gold production increased substantially. The company stock rose in value. It appeared that, at last, the Mariposa Company had turned the corner.

---

*That summer, Olmsted was awarded an honorary master of arts degree by Harvard University.

Olmsted, too, prospered. "I am for the present making money pretty fast for such a vagabond as I am," he wrote his father. His annual salary was a regal $10,000 (about $300,000 in modern dollars), but since his contract specified that he be paid in gold—which was worth more than greenbacks—his real salary was as much as twice that amount. He was finally able to pay off his debts. In January 1864, only three months after his arrival, he was even able to invest $2,500 with his stockbroker in San Francisco. In April he increased this to $4,000. He was a conservative investor. He avoided the volatile mining industry, although he expected California in general—and San Francisco in particular—to prosper. He bought stock in a steamship company, the state telegraph company, and a San Francisco water company. "I look therefore to enterprises which are related to the whole of this field or large parts of it as likely *ipso facto* to be safe, (if well managed and free from excessive competition)," he wrote Godkin, who had asked him to make some investments on his behalf. In July Olmsted assured him: "The mining stocks here have fallen on an average more than one half since I wrote, but the stocks I recommended have not fallen on an average at all. I have made from 2 to 3 per ct a month on all my investments." By the end of the year, the value of his investments was $6,000.

Looking back over the last year at Bear Valley, Olmsted was content. His health had improved. Prosperity, public recognition, a role in civic affairs, new creative endeavors, a happy family life: he could not have asked for more.

Olmsted Shortens Sail

ON THE EVENING OF JANUARY 6, 1865, two visitors from San Francisco called at the manager's office in Bear Valley. John Fry was an agent of the Bank of California, which handled the affairs of the Mariposa Estate. He was accompanied by a representative of Dodge Brothers, a San Francisco provisioner and the Estate's largest creditor. Fry informed an astonished Olmsted that the Mariposa Company in New York had refused payment on its outstanding debt of sixty thousand dollars. Consequently, the Bank of California would no longer honor Mariposa Company checks. Fry himself had just spoken with the sheriff in Mariposa to initiate legal proceedings. He was courteous but firm. He was here to attach the property of the Mariposa Estate.

Olmsted protested that there must be some misunderstanding. He showed the pair his accounts. They agreed that everything seemed in order. He appealed to Fry to suspend legal proceedings until he, Olmsted, had a chance to discuss the situation with the officers of the bank in San Francisco. He was sure that he could straighten things out. Fry agreed. Olmsted quickly arranged to depart. "My impression is that Mariposa will float over this bar," he assured Mary. But he did take one precaution. Before leaving, he collected four thousand dollars' worth of gold bullion, as well as some instruments, and gave himself a bill of sale amounting to almost the full value of a year's salary. He thought that the bank had been unnecessarily hasty, but he prepared for the worst.

He arrived in San Francisco late at night. He immediately met Darius Mills, the bank's president, and William Ralston, the cashier, whom he had telegraphed from Stockton. They, too, were courteous and assured Olmsted that their actions were not a reflection of their regard for him. He would continue to enjoy their full confidence, respect, and friendship. But the Mariposa Company was another matter. They darkly alluded to a "great Wall Street swindle." They told him that they had no choice but to act quickly to protect their shareholders. As far as they were concerned, Olmsted's employers were as good as bankrupt.

Olmsted knew that the Mariposa Company's cash reserves were low. He had been directed to undertake extensive—and expensive—improvements, and in 1864 his operating costs exceeded income by about $300,000. This deficit was to have been paid from cash reserves. But unforeseen, a previously unknown creditor of Frémont's had contested the title to the Estate. The claim was settled out of court for $300,000 in gold. The company used current gold production to pay its debts; during October and November, production had been high, but in December the rich vein ran out. Mariposa was caught short.

Temporary liquidity problems were common in the mining business. What had panicked Mills and Ralston was a recent scandal. In December 1864 Opdyke had brought a libel suit against his old political adversary Weed Thurlow, who had published an article alleging that Opdyke had misused public funds as mayor. The trial lasted several weeks and attracted enormous publicity. Opdyke lost his suit and emerged with his reputation severely tarnished. During the trial, the defense charged that Opdyke and his partners had shortchanged Frémont when they bought the Mariposa Estate. The charge was calculated to gain the sympathy of the jury since Frémont was a popular public figure. However, he denied that he had been cheated; on the contrary, he admitted that he had underrepresented the Estate's indebtedness at the time of the sale! This revelation coming on top of Opdyke's humiliation rattled Mariposa investors. Frémont testified on December 21. On December 28 the value of the stock, which had been $45 when Olmsted arrived in California, dropped to $30; by January 2 it had tumbled to $19.

Olmsted, who was unaware of the trial, assumed that the Mariposa Company was solid.* He persuaded Mills and Ralston to wait a few days until he could contact his superiors. He telegraphed the Mariposa president for advice and assistance. The response was "a sort of bunkum message from Mr Hoy, amounting simply to 'don't worry.'" Stalling for time, Olmsted negotiated an agreement whereby the Bank of California would

---

*Godkin wrote Olmsted describing the trial—"there is a tremendous libel suit going on here between Weed (Thurlow) & Opdyke, from which it plainly appears that one is as great a scoundrel as the other." But Olmsted did not receive the letter until the end of January.

receive all gold produced by the mines in exchange for granting a grace period of one hundred days before taking legal action.

Meanwhile in New York, the disgruntled Mariposa shareholders voted down the board's proposal to float a half-million-dollar bond issue. Olmsted was left in the dark about this, as he was about the other developments. Still hoping for some reprieve, he worked mightily to make the best of a worsening situation. He felt an obligation to the creditors and to his subordinates, particularly Pieper and Martin. The mines had to be kept open. This was not easy. Olmsted had been called an autocrat, yet on this occasion he showed himself a persuasive mediator. At one point, the unnerved bank attached the company stores. The miners, unpaid and deprived of supplies, refused to work. Olmsted immediately wrote a public letter to the men explaining the situation, and with Pieper's help, managed to calm them down. From San Francisco, he made arrangements with the sheriff, who was now effectively managing the Estate, to reopen the stores. Crisis followed crisis. In February the men who were owed back pay occupied one of the mines. Olmsted defused that situation, too, and convinced the bank to postpone collecting on the debt and to pay the miners.

Weeks turned to months. Olmsted stayed in San Francisco, but still no word came from New York. It dawned on him that he was on his own. At first he remained upbeat, explaining in a letter to Mary:

> We have lived so very happily of late, & you & the children are doing so well, I shall be disposed to stay as long as possible at Bear Valley. It will not be easy for us to shorten sail to the degree that it will be required if we go East. But although we should probably have to manage a good deal closer than we ever have before, I feel less anxiety about it than usual—less oppressive anxiety. The truth is I have enjoyed the last few months so much, that I think I have [been] sufficiently well charged with caloric to bear a little cold weather, if necessary, without breaking my heart or my temper—and I hope it is the same with you. A certain degree of health and of luxury does tend to limit your discontent, a fact which I don't think before last summer—autumn—I ever made any progress of faith in. "What I mean to say, is" that I have an increased and increasing positive respect for you as well as a decreased disrespect for your occasional perversities. You will think that I am sick that I write this—but I am, however that may be, very happy in our experience of late.

Despite his warning to Mary about having to manage "a good deal closer than we ever have before," Olmsted's financial situation was far from desperate. True, with the Estate in virtual receivership, he was not currently being paid a salary. Moreover, his lawyer had advised him that the bill of sale he had issued himself before leaving Bear Valley was "tomfoolery" and would not withstand legal scrutiny. On the other hand, he had good news from Morris Ketchum. The previous year Olmsted had deposited the one hundred shares of Mariposa stock he had received as annual pay in Ketchum's bank. Ketchum had had the foresight to sell the shares in November, when they were still worth $36. As a result, Olmsted personally lost nothing in the Mariposa collapse.

Olmsted and Ketchum had a special understanding. Before Olmsted left New York, Ketchum had approached him with a proposal. If Olmsted would provide him with advance information of mining discoveries and shortfalls, in return he would buy and sell Mariposa stock on Olmsted's behalf. Olmsted agreed. This was long before insider trading was outlawed, but the arrangement does cast a shadow on Olmsted's probity. Or rather, it suggests that Strong was mistaken: Olmsted did have a mercenary nerve. He was not a novice in business and understood that he needed Ketchum's help if he was to succeed financially. Their agreement lasted until May 1864, when the prudent Ketchum stepped down as a trustee of the Mariposa Company.

Olmsted's account with Ketchum, Son & Company contained seven thousand dollars; with his California investments, he had accumulated thirteen thousand dollars. Nevertheless, he had no intention of dipping into his savings—he needed income. An opportunity soon presented itself. "I have another landscape gardening nibble," he wrote to Mary in Bear Valley, "and shall do all I can to hook it, for Miller's sake." Edward Miller was a Central Park surveyor whom Olmsted had brought to Mariposa to work on the irrigation canal. With all improvements on the Estate halted, Miller had nothing to do—and no salary. He joined Olmsted in San Francisco.

Their first project was Mountain View Cemetery. The trustees had approved the design and planned to dedicate the cemetery in May. Miller laid out the first phase—about twenty acres. The notion of landscaping suitable to an arid climate had absorbed Olmsted. He realized that he could not hope to replicate a conventional rural cemetery. "You must then look to an entirely different way of accomplishing the end in

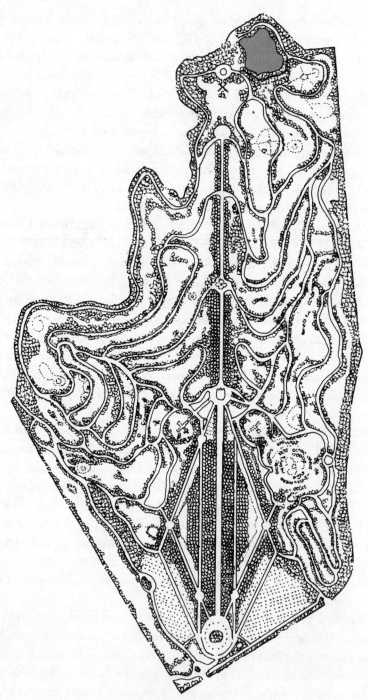

Mountain View Cemetery, Oakland, California (1865).

view, and to entirely different measures from those made use of in the East," he counseled his clients. Instead of attempting picturesque variety in the planting, he identified five tree species that flourished in the arid, windswept Oakland Hills. He was sure that the combination of vertical and horizontal foliage would have the desired effect. "The brooding forms of the coppices and the canopy of the cedars would unite in the expression of a sheltering care extended over the place of the dead, the heaven-pointing spires of the immortal cypress would prompt the consolation of faith," he wrote in the report that accompanied his plan.

The plan of the cemetery was original. The hillside site consisted of a flat area flanked by slopes. He placed a perfectly straight, cypress-lined avenue on the level portion. The avenue was divided in three by *ronds-points,* at the center of which stood monuments and fountains. From each *rond-point* a curvilinear system of pathways followed the contours of the slopes and led to the burial plots. The plots were surrounded by hedges "to give an appearance of greater seclusion and protection to the graves within the family lots than they would have if directly open to view from the carriage ways."

Walking down the central avenue of Mountain View Cemetery today, one can appreciate the wisdom of his solution. The formal allée is a solemn, ceremonial, *public* gesture that is a fitting contrast to the graceful curved paths that lead to the intensely *private* individual graves. Unfortunately, the hedgerows were not planted and the beautiful seclusion that Olmsted sought is absent. Nevertheless, his original intention remains. "No place of burial is satisfactory to us," he wrote, "which does not exhibit, besides evidence of respect paid by individuals and families to the memory of their own dead, evidences also of respect paid by the community of the living to the community of the dead." What he created at Mountain View was neither a garden nor a park but a city ... of the dead.

There were other landscaping projects. He was approached by the trustees of the College of California, who owned a large tract of land in the hills north of Oakland. They wanted an English-style park beside the future campus, but he was skeptical that this could be done. "It is an accursed country with no trees & no turf and it's a hard job to make sure of any beauty," he wrote to Vaux. Characteristically, Olmsted proposed to redesign the entire master plan. While the trustees were deliberating, he set Miller to work on smaller jobs. Mills, the president of the Bank of California, asked Olmsted for advice on landscaping a large tract of land on the San Francisco peninsula. This led to a commission from George Howard, a trustee of the Bank who owned a country estate outside San Mateo. Olmsted visited the site and prepared a report and a plan that he sent to Mary with the following instructions:

> I want you to prepare & insert a detail of planting the mounds—substituting what you like for what I have written. You will see I shirked it— partly because not competent partly because I could not remember the names of what I did think best.
>
> I think myrtles, fuschias & jessamines should be added. Forsythia & roses? On the West side would bananas come in with Magnolias or what? Would oranges or lemons come in before the rocks on the turf— directly in front of the verandah? I want one or two very nice shrubs there—quite distinct, exotic & aristocratic. Revise the whole if you can so much favor me, & then superintend Henry's copy of it. Let him make two copies & send one as soon as possible.

Olmsted was more interested in the big picture than in the details and always willing to delegate. It is revealing that in this case Mary was his collaborator. He obviously trusted her judgment. They must have spent much time talking about gardening; his directions are in a kind of shorthand, another sign of the closeness of their marriage.

"Take an interest in the Howard plan if you can," he instructed. "Remember there is money in it—a little & a penny earned will buy almost as much . . . as a penny saved." These commissions were a useful small source of income—and they kept Miller busy—but Olmsted was still not pursuing a career in landscape architecture. He saw business opportunities everywhere. Following Silliman's advice, he invested in several oil properties. He secured the financial backing of the sympathetic Bank of California and formed his own company to explore for oil. Ralston, the bank's cashier, was helping to launch a joint-stock company that owned vineyards in the Sonoma Valley. He invited Olmsted to join him. Olmsted's responsibility was to prepare the prospectus. "I was called upon to advise about the executive organization of a new corporation last week," he wrote to Godkin, "and sat down and in an hour drew up a complete scheme—wholly original—and did it so easily & satisfactorily to myself & had so much confidence that it would be better than anything else that had been talked about, that the idea has impressed itself upon me that this is my true business."

His oil company sank a well near Santa Cruz, did not find oil, and was soon disbanded; the winery raised money but did not prosper. He did not suffer financially in either case. His other schemes were mere shots in the dark. He briefly considered buying a morning newspaper in San Francisco and invited Godkin to come West and help him run it. Godkin thought that this was precisely the type of strenuous activity that his friend should avoid and admonished him: "I don't think that you are sufficiently conscientious or shrewd about your health." Olmsted suggested to Bellows that they start a national association of bookbuyers, a sort of book-of-the-month club. That, too, came to nothing.

On April 9, Palm Sunday, Olmsted attended church. It was exactly three months since he had left Bear Valley. During the service he was attacked by a deep melancholy:

> ... singing Glory! Hallelujah! with a great congregation and looking at the great flag of victory held over us, though of all with whom I ever had conscious sympathy of hope and prayer for this day I stood alone—and my heart cried back stronger than ever to my poor, sad, unhopeful brother, who alone of all the world, ever really knew me and trusted me for exactly what I was and felt, & tho' I felt more than ever how thoroughly strangers to my real self everybody here is, and how for any purpose that my heart has had in my past life, completely disabled and dead I am—yet it seemed as if you and some others were singing Glory! Hallelujah! too, & that there might be a capacity of life in my dead bones even yet.

Olmsted wrote this heartfelt passage that evening in a letter to Frederick Knapp. He poured out his soul to his friend, from whom he had not heard for six months. He felt himself abandoned by his father, Godkin, Vaux—even Knapp—none of whom had mentioned the Mariposa business in their letters. (They were probably embarrassed to allude to such a public failure.) He was alone in a strange city. He missed his family. He had seen Mary only once—she had just returned to Bear Valley after spending a week with him. What weighed most heavily on him, he wrote Knapp, was that he had provided so poorly for her and the children. He had tried—tried hard—to find other sources of income, but he had to admit that he had failed.

"When Olmsted is blue, the logic of his despondency is crushing and terrible," George Templeton Strong once wrote in his diary. Strong was perceptive. It seems likely that Olmsted suffered from chronic depression. This lifelong affliction typically manifests itself periodically, and at different intensities. Early symptoms include insomnia and an inability to concentrate, read, and write. That was probably what had happened to him while he was working on Central Park, at the end of his tenure with the Sanitary Commission, and during the previous year in Bear Valley.

"The great flag of victory" that Olmsted referred to was the fall of Richmond. Lee's army was in retreat and Union victory appeared imminent. In fact, almost exactly at the same time as Olmsted was singing "Glory! Hallelujah!" in San Francisco, Lee was formally surrendering to Grant at Appomattox. The good news buoyed Olmsted's spirits: "I can hardly contain myself with thanksgiving." Lincoln's assassination six days later appalled him. "At any rate the nation lives and is immortal," he wrote Knapp, "and Slavery is dead. Enough for us."

It was now mid-April and Olmsted's hundred-day deadline was up. He had managed to pay off the Bank of California, but the Estate still owed a considerable sum—$58,000. He did not know what to do; he had run out of ideas. He was dispirited. He also just wanted to get the creditors off his back and wash his hands of the entire Mariposa business. Whatever loyalty he had felt to his employers had gone—they had simply abandoned him. He made a drastic decision and signed over the entire Estate to the principal creditor, Dodge Brothers. The lease would run until the remaining debt was repaid; Dodge Brothers would operate the mines, collect the gold bullion, pay workers, and compensate the other creditors.

The later investigation of the U.S. commissioner into the affairs of the Mariposa Company characterized the decision to lease the Estate to Dodge as a "stupendous folly." In his low state of mind Olmsted had made an ill-considered judgment; Dodge Brothers mercilessly exploited the Estate to its own benefit (eventually, the Mariposa Company regained possession). The federal commissioner did not question Olmsted's integrity, but he advised that he should have retained ownership of the Estate and paid off the debt by selling property and milling equipment at auction. He noted Olmsted's lack of experience in mining and criticized the wisdom of some of his expensive improvements, but concluded that "the fundamental mistake was in the instructions given to Mr. O. to explore, open up and work as many veins as possible.... The plan of the company's organization, and the scale of its projected operations, were such as to invite every chance of ruin."

But that was hindsight. On April 20 Olmsted finally made his way back to Bear Valley. According to the terms of the agreement, he would no longer be manager, but he would "retain a duty of observation, access to books &c. & control of expenses." He was allowed to keep his living quarters, furniture, books, and personal effects.

A Heavy Sort of Book

WHATEVER HAPPENED to the Mariposa Company, Olmsted's tenure at the Estate was over. Even if the company recovered, it could never again afford a ten-thousand-dollar-a-year manager. Yet he did not pack up and leave. He decided to stay at least until the end of September, which would conclude his second year of service. This was partly a question of pride. He was also being practical. If he stayed, he had a slim chance of being paid—he had telegraphed New York with a request for five thousand dollars. The cost of living in Bear Valley was high; Mary had been obliged to let two of the servants go. Still, he was not unhappy to remain even at his own expense. The children were healthy; he and Mary enjoyed their outdoor life. When it got hot, they planned to return to their idyllic summer camp in the mountains. That would give him time to complete the Yosemite report, which was his personal responsibility.

The long-term future was uncertain. "I wish you could find some commission business in which you and I could engage together," he wrote Godkin, who was still trying to get "the paper" off the ground. What Olmsted had in mind was something "wherein a little capital would go a good way and be safe." Alternatively, he thought himself suited to be president of a railroad company, head of a news wire service, or editor of a newspaper. He considered the Foreign Service. "I have had ever since I have been in this burnt country, a real craving for the English climate. Mary has the same and agrees to live on bread and cheese for a year if I will get the consulship to any slushy old town where there are donkeys to let," he confessed. He was open to almost any career—except landscape architecture. Miller was still in San Francisco working on the cemetery and preparing to survey the College of California site, but Olmsted considered these projects as merely sidelines.

One thing, at least, was sure. He would leave California. It was not only the arid climate. After three months in San Francisco, he had concluded that without more capital his chances of making his fortune in the West were limited. "There are men of high position who would like to make use of me," he wrote Godkin, "but it is only because they think that I could get capital for them in New York—get up stock companies, of the Mariposa model, for the development of California property of questionable value, which I wouldn't if I could." The inference that Mariposa had been "of questionable value" is unmistakable, although Olmsted could not bring himself to admit that the whole Mariposa affair may have been an outright swindle from the start, as many people in New York—including Godkin—believed.

The management of the Estate was now firmly in Dodge Brothers' hands, and Olmsted found himself with free time. In the afternoons the family would ride to the top of Mount Bullion. There, beside a cool spring and with a magnificent view of the Yosemite Valley, they would have tea. The children would play among the spring flowers while he and Mary worked on a garden plot. Mornings found him at his writing desk. He was pleasantly surprised to discover that he was able to write for several hours a day. As long as he slept well and exercised regularly, the symptoms that had plagued him the previous year did not reappear. He sent an annual report to the Company explaining his handling of the Estate's debts. He also started to record everyday life in Bear Valley. He wrote about the different sorts of people: the Indians who lived on the edge of town, the Chinese and Mexican workers, and the American miners. Here is his description of a particular Kentucky gambler:

> He has a cigar in his mouth, a Colt's revolver in one pocket, a Geneva watch in another and scores of machines and many hundreds of hands have been employed in preparing his apparel. When freshly and mildly stimulated, he has a very active mind and a ready utterance. It is not unlikely that tomorrow morning, after he has taken a warm bath, his cognac and soda water, coffee and one or two after breakfast drams [I shall] again hear him discoursing, as I did this morning, with indignant eloquence on "the mockery of justice, the debasement of the ermine, the ignorance of law, the degrading of demagogueism, the abominable infidelity by _____!" of a recent decision of a Court with regard to the rights of colored people in public conveyances, reported in a San Francisco newspaper. In twenty minutes he will have made use of words pri-

marily prepared for him by Saxon, Roman, Greek, Sanscrit and I know not what other brains. Then again he will pass under my window humming a hymn of Handel, or I shall find him at the Post Office sitting in an arm chair, made for him in New Hampshire, and reading a novel first written in France, translated in England and printed for him in Boston. He will have been served before the day is over by your work and by mine and by that of thousands of other men, and yet will think of nothing so often or so intensely as the "cursed luck" by which he is served no better. And what will he do for us? Play a game of billiards with you or take a hand at cards if you want amusement, and if he wins money in this or any other way of speculating he will use it "generously." Within a year by pledging his word to drink no more he induced a poor hard worked widow to become his wife, having been previously the father of several children of different colors for [whose] maintenance or education he has never worked an hour or concerned himself a moment. He is [a] tall and large framed white man of English stock, born in a state of society which he speaks of [as] "the highest reach of civilization."

Olmsted lived in California at the beginning of the period that Hollywood would represent—and distort—in the motion-picture western. Nothing is remotely glamorous in his description of the indolent Kentuckian. This rugged individualist is portrayed as a social parasite and a bigot; in a subsequent passage he is unfavorably compared to the hardworking Chinese, whom he disdains. (Olmsted was dismayed to find racist prejudice extended to Chinese, Mexicans, and Indians.) Yet the gambler is neither a savage nor a rustic. He is what today would be called a consumer—of ideas as well as goods. Olmsted found life in Bear Valley primitive, but he was aware that the American frontier revealed something else, indeed, a curious paradox.

I was not prepared to find in a region so remote from the great centres of civilization so little of rural or backwoods simplicity. The English speaking people are no more unsophisticated here than in Piccadilly or St. Giles. Even the farmers have more commonly the carriage, style and manners of unfortunate horse jockeys and dissipated market men than of solid, steady and frugal countrymen. Go where you will on the mountains, the hills or the plains, wherever the slightest trail has been formed or the smallest sign of industry—mining, mechanical or agricultural—is to be found, you may also find empty sardine boxes, meat, oyster and fruit cans, wine, ale, olive and sauce bottles, with playing cards and torn leaves of novels, magazines and newspapers, more commonly New York newspapers, but sometimes French, German or English.

Olmsted titled these notes "A Pioneer Community of the Present Day." They were part of an ambitious project of long duration. Three years earlier he had written to his father: "I have been for some time accumulating notes and materials for a book." This was immediately after he had returned from his Sanitary Commission tour of the Midwest with Knapp. During that trip he compiled a lengthy travel diary. In it he documented his experiences in a slovenly hotel in Cincinnati, encounters with passengers on Mississippi steamboats, and vignettes of urban life in St. Louis, Chicago, and Cleveland. These travel diaries were part of a "whole caseful of notes" that included newspaper clippings, magazine articles, and background reading that he had been collecting for several years. During that spring in Bear Valley, he started to put these notes into order.

This book would not be a travel account. "I am cogitating a heavy sort of book on Society in the United States—the influence of pioneer-life—& of Democracy," he wrote to Godkin shortly after arriving in California. Olmsted's ambition was to write a comprehensive study of the state of civilization in America. Today the word *civilization* is most commonly used in reference to the distant past, as in "pre-Columbian civilization." In nineteenth-century America *civilization* was not an archaeological term; it referred to contemporary society. Moreover, as used by Olmsted, it described an enlightened state of virtuous and intellectual development. "Civilization is, in fact, the best condition of mankind," he had written in *A Journey in the Back Country*, "and the steps by which mankind have arrived at civilization do not need to be retraced to find morality, respectability or happiness."

The opposite of civilization is barbarism. Olmsted was greatly influenced by Horace Bushnell's famous public lecture "Barbarism the First Danger." Olmsted was at Sachem's Head at the time, so he probably didn't hear it but read it in a pamphlet. "Nothing is more certain," Bushnell wrote in a passage that Olmsted copied into his notes, ". . . than that emigration or a new settlement of the social state involves a tendency to social decline. There must in every such case be a relapse toward barbarism, more or less protracted, more or less complete." Bushnell certainly had in mind the Irish and European immigrants who were then arriving in large numbers in the Eastern cities, but he was no nativist. American history had always been a process of accommodating transplanted immigrant races who had left behind "all the old roots of local love and historic feeling, the joints and bands that minister nourishment," he wrote. Hence the importance of educational, civic, and religious institutions. But the settler on the Western frontier, unlike the uprooted European immigrant in the East, did not have the benefit of civilizing influences.

Bushnell placed his hopes in the power of religion to reform society; Olmsted was less sanguine about the prospects for civilization in the United States. He recognized the fragile situation of American society. He had already observed that one of the chief evils of Southern slavery was that it hindered the development of civilized communities, not only among the slaves but also among the slave owners. His experiences in west Texas had taught him that the conditions of life on the frontier were likewise far from propitious. This perception hardened during his stay in California. Pioneering required self-reliance, yet self-reliance often degenerated into self-indulgence and greed. Self-reliance was also accompanied by an exaggerated sense of personal honor, lawlessness, and profligacy. Bear Valley did not display that sense of solidarity that was engendered by civic institutions. When social and political organizations were formed, their purpose was merely "You stand by me & I will stand by you," as he put it. Self-interest did not equal community. "You must imagine for yourself what the condition of society is under these circumstances. It is nowhere; there is no society. Any appearance of social convenience that may be found is a mere temporary and temporizing expedient by which men cheat themselves to believe that they are not savages."

Olmsted planned to expand Bushnell's thesis. He would examine not only the frontier but also the large Eastern cities, previous immigrants as well as current Western settlers. As in the past, he based himself on personal observation and "facts." Previously, he had relied on newspapers and government reports; this time he conceived a quantitative analysis. He had always been fascinated by statistics. He required the Central Park police to keep detailed crime records. The first Sanitary Commission report of demoralization among Union troops depended heavily on statistics. He subsequently hired the actuary Ezekiel Eliott and made record-keeping the keystone of the Commission. Supplies were tracked from warehouse to battlefield. Patients were documented as they were admitted into hospitals. The Commission regularly published a hospital directory that eventually listed six hundred thousand names. (The directory kept track of medical histories and enabled families to locate their wounded and dead relatives.) Olmsted established a Bureau of Vital Statistics that tabulated the reports submitted by the sanitary inspectors. These published results "added more new and valuable facts to the science of vital statistics than any other contribution at any time," according to a contemporary encyclopedia. Olmsted took advantage of the Bureau of Vital Statistics to compile a social survey. At his own expense, he had a questionnaire circulated among more than *seven thousand* Union wounded. The data described family backgrounds as well as personal habits and attitudes. He hoped to discover how immigrants were altered by living in America, and how they differed from native-born citizens. "What are the habits, & what is the mental & moral condition of men in the United States whose character & habits have been chiefly influenced by European conditions, & what of those whose character & habits have been much affected by American conditions?" It was a grand scheme. He intended nothing less than to find what made Americans American.

Calvert Vaux Doesn't Take No
for an Answer

IN THE BEGINNING OF JUNE 1865, Olmsted received news from Godkin: "the paper" was to become a reality. A wealthy Philadelphia abolitionist named James Miller McKim had come forward as financial backer. The first issue would appear in July. Olmsted wrote a congratulatory letter. His advice to Godkin reflected both his own sense of isolation as well as his current preoccupation with the subject of civilization. "Your paper needs to be, peculiarly, a substitute to thousands of men situated as I am, as my lawyer twelve miles away is, as numerous clergymen are, for a cultivated companion.... Do recollect that except at a very few points there is no cultivated *society* in America, but a great many intelligent men & women, to whom a newspaper may well be the only substitute for whatever, in a society more elaborately civilized, keeps a man's common-place cultivation alive."

Two weeks later, with the heat of summer coming on, Frederick and Mary set off on a two-week excursion to Yosemite. In August, on another visit to the valley, they joined a large party led by Schuyler Colfax, a Republican Indiana congressman and Speaker of the House of Representatives. Colfax, who was making an official tour of the newly established overland mail route to California, was accompanied by newspaper correspondents from New York and Chicago, and by Samuel Bowles, a Massachusetts newspaper editor. Olmsted particularly wanted to meet Bowles, for he considered his *Springfield Republican* to be one of the best papers in the country. Bowles was a staunch Unionist and had been a supporter of Lincoln. Like Olmsted, he had a nervous disposition and a tendency to overwork. He had undertaken the trip with Colfax in the hope of restoring his failing health. Olmsted warned Bowles about indulging his "habit of mental intemperance" and admonished him to work less. Olmsted offered himself as an example: "I do know that I ought to be sent to an inebriate Asylum—and I do try to treat myself a little as a drunkard ought to treat himself."

The group camping at Clark's ranch that August also included several Yosemite commissioners—Galen Clark, William Ashburner, and George Coulter, a local businessman. Olmsted called an impromptu meeting of the Yosemite Commission to present a draft of his final recommendations. Olmsted may also have invited the Speaker of the House and the journalists to attend, for he would want to address such a distinguished audience. (Bowles did cover the Yosemite Commission in the *Springfield Republican*.)

Olmsted began his presentation by describing the scenery of the valley. He emphasized that the effect on the visitor did not reside in any single feature—the cliffs, waterfalls, meadows, or streams. "The union of the deepest sublimity with the deepest beauty of nature, not in one feature or another, not in one part or one scene or another, not any landscape that can be framed by itself, but all around and wherever the visitor goes, constitutes the Yo Semite the greatest glory of nature," he explained. This was his first point: Yosemite consisted of a series of linked experiences. These had to be preserved in their entirety.

The wealthy classes in Europe and elsewhere had always reserved for themselves the places of greatest scenic beauty; in a democracy this could not be allowed to happen, he said. The first aim of the Commission was to ensure that Yosemite and the Big Tree Grove did not fall into private hands. However, that was not enough, he argued. "It is necessary that they should be laid open to the use of the body of the people." This was his second point: Yosemite should be made easily accessible to the public.

He proposed the construction of a forty-mile-long stagecoach road to link Galen's ranch with the town of Mariposa, and to provide access to the Big Tree Grove. He had already had a survey of the road prepared. It followed a scenic route that would provide vistas and interesting views and included campsites. He recommended that a narrow carriage road should go up one side of the valley itself and return on the other. There would be turnouts and resting spots at frequent intervals. (This is, in fact, what exists in Yosemite today.) He assumed that most people would be camping but recommended the construction of five cabins that would be let to tenants with the provision that one room be reserved as a free resting place for visitors. Tents and camping gear would be available for rental; the prices for provisions would be controlled by the Commission.

Olmsted had no illusion about the number of future visitors. "It is but sixteen years since the Yosemite was first seen by a white man, several visitors have since made a journey of several thousand miles at large cost to see it, and notwithstanding the difficulties which now interpose, hundreds resort to it annually," he wrote in the report. "Before many years, if proper facilities are offered, these hundreds will become thousands and in a century the whole number of visitors will be counted by millions." His estimate was almost exactly correct; annual attendance at Yosemite Valley and the Mariposa Big Tree Grove first surpassed 1 million in 1954.

Olmsted was aware of the financial benefits of mass tourism; he referred to Switzerland and Bavaria as successful examples. Yet his prime motive in opening up this natural area to the public was not economic. Modern environmentalists often perceive a conflict between the preservation of wilderness and the demands of recreation. For Olmsted, recreation—or rather, re-creation—was paramount. When he discussed the recuperative power of natural scenery, he literally meant healing. He believed that the contemplation of nature, fresh air, and the change of everyday habits improved people's health and intellectual vigor. "The enjoyment of scenery employs the mind without fatigue and yet exercises it, tranquilizes it and yet enlivens it; and thus, through the influence of the mind over the body, gives the effect of refreshing rest and reinvigoration of the whole system."

Years earlier, Olmsted had envisioned Central Park as a surrogate Adirondack landscape where ordinary people could get away from their urban surroundings. Now he described Yosemite—a real wilderness—as a kind of public park, indeed, a national park.* Yosemite opened his eyes to an exciting new possibility: the experience of scenery, whether manmade or natural, could be a powerful *civilizing* force. This important insight undoubtedly arose from his recent writing about American society as well as his visits to the valley. The two strands of thought that had been preoccupying him for more than a decade finally came together. It is an important moment: he has realized that he might combine his interests in social reform and landscaping. This discovery could not have

---

*Yosemite, at this point, belonged to the State of California, but Olmsted suggested that it be thought of as "a trust from the whole nation."

come at a more opportune time. As he was writing his book and working on the Yosemite report, he was also debating with Calvert Vaux—and with himself—about whether he should return to New York to resume his landscaping career.

The debate had started six months earlier when Olmsted was in San Francisco dealing with the Estate creditors. Vaux had written to him about a new park—in Brooklyn. Several years before Brooklyn had purchased land and hired none other than Egbert Viele, late of Central Park, to prepare the plan. Although his design had been approved, the outbreak of war had interrupted further progress. The board of park commissioners was headed by James S. T. Stranahan, a former state congressman and a wealthy building contractor. Stranahan had been instrumental in commissioning Viele but now had doubts about the unimaginative plan. Seeking a second opinion, he had contacted Vaux.

Vaux accompanied Stranahan to the site on the outskirts of the city. He observed two major liabilities. One was Flatbush Avenue, which divided the park in two. The other was the city reservoir that stood on the smaller of the two parcels. On the spot, Vaux suggested a clever alternative: sell the awkwardly shaped smaller parcel and buy land on the other side of the avenue. This would create one large, continuous tract of about five hundred acres—half again as large as the original proposal. Viele planned only a small pond; Vaux's proposal could accommodate a real lake. He shrewdly pointed out that at forty acres it would be twice as large as the lake in Central Park. Stranahan seemed to like the idea, Vaux wrote excitedly in his letter. It appeared likely that Viele would, once again, be thwarted.

Olmsted was impressed. "Your plans [Vaux had included a sketch] are excellent, of course, you don't play with it but go at once to the essential starting points, and I hope the Commissioners are wise enough to comprehend it." Yet he was not enthusiastic about Vaux's suggestion that they work together on the park. He assured Vaux that much as he would like to do it, it was impossible. His health was poor, and he was liable to suffer a breakdown at any time. He had to think of his family; he did not believe that landscape gardening could provide him with a decent living.

This was the time when Olmsted, alone in San Francisco, was in the depths of his depression. Vaux must have sensed this, for he ignored the rejection. Four months later he wrote that Viele's plan had been set aside and the state legislature had approved the purchase of additional land for the projected park. Stranahan had not made any firm offer but he was "nibbling." "Never say die," Vaux wrote, "we may have some fun together yet." Two days later he sent a second, longer letter in which he stated: "I shall tell [the Brooklyn park commission] that I intend to ask you to go into it with me anyway & I will write to you what bargain I make." In an attempt to assuage Olmsted's financial worries, Vaux wrote that they had a slight chance of being rehired as consultants to Central Park.

Olmsted, now back in Bear Valley, replied. He confessed that he felt himself deficient in botany and gardening and resisted being called an artist, as Vaux had done in his last letter. He admitted that Central Park was dear to him: "There is no other place in the world that is as much home to me. I love it all through & all the more for the trials it has cost me." Yet he remained immovable. "I should like very well to go into the Brooklyn park, or anything else—if I really believed I could get a decent living out of it—but in landscape work in general I never had any ground for supposing that I could. You used to argue that I might hope to— that's all. I could never see it." This was not altogether unreasonable on Olmsted's part since he would have to rely entirely on landscape work for his income, whereas Vaux had his architectural practice.

Vaux was doing his best to convince his ex-partner, but he was laboring under a severe constraint. Communication was maddeningly slow. The telegraph was useful only for brief messages—and it often broke down. It took two or even three months for letters to make the round-trip. Undeterred, Vaux wrote letter after letter, not waiting for answers. He wrote on May 10 and 12. On May 20 he advised Olmsted that he had decided not to mention him to the board until Olmsted had made a firm decision. The commissioners wanted a plan by the end of the year, so Olmsted still had plenty of time to make up his mind. On May 22 the flurry of letters continued. This time, Vaux wrote about Central Park. Green appeared to be in trouble. He had asked Vaux to return to the park. Vaux had insisted on a formal request from the board and added that he would have to consult Olmsted. Things were coming to a head.

At the end of June, Olmsted was still undecided. "Mr. Vaux has made me a handsome offer to return and help him lay out the Brooklyn park," he informed his employee Miller, "but I cannot leave California at present." On July 31 Olmsted received yet another letter from Vaux, dated June 3. It contained Vaux's strongest plea yet. He asserted again that

Olmsted's true vocation lay in the world of landscape art, not administration. He reminded Olmsted of their fruitful partnership. Vaux admitted that he would never have entered the Central Park competition alone because of his "incapacity." "I feel it no less—I will not say no less, but very little less—now, and enter on Brooklyn alone with hesitation and distrust not on the roads & walks or even planting, which Pilat would have to attend to but in regard to the main point—the translation of the republican art idea in its highest form into the acres we want to control." For the proud Vaux, this was a heartfelt admission.

Olmsted was touched by Vaux's candor. He wrote a reply the next day. "If I don't wholly adopt or agree with all you say, at least I respect it very thoroughly and feel that I have not altogether done justice to your position heretofore," he admitted. Olmsted agreed that what they had done in Central Park—and what he himself was doing in California—was much more than horticulture. It *was* art. It was, however, a particular kind of art. At one point he referred to it as "sylvan art." "The art is not gardening nor is it architecture," he wrote. It was certainly not "landscape architecture." "If you are bound to establish this new art," he wrote Vaux, "you don't want an old name for it."*

This was quibbling, and Olmsted knew it. At this time he was completing the Yosemite report. Vaux's impassioned reminder that Olmsted's true calling lay in the field of landscape gardening struck a responsive chord. Olmsted could finally no longer resist. He agreed to return but wrote that he would not leave until the fall. He had too much unfinished business: the landscape projects, Yosemite, his investments. He also still hoped to get some money from the Mariposa Company. Lest this sounded vague, he assured Vaux that he was ready to leave sooner if necessary: "I mean to hold myself as free as possible, and to have my business so I can wind it up in a hurry." He mailed the letter (the telegraph lines were down) just before leaving for Yosemite with the Colfax party.

---

*Twenty-five years earlier, John Claudius Loudon had published a book titled *The landscape gardening and landscape architecture of the late Humphry Repton, esq. being his entire works on these subjects*. According to landscape historian John Dixon Hunt, this is the first documented use of the term *landscape architecture*.

Loose Ends

A FEW DAYS AFTER returning from Yosemite to Bear Valley, Olmsted traveled alone to San Francisco to wind up his business affairs. On the way he fell seriously ill with what he thought was cholera. He was in bed for five days. He saw the owners of Mountain View Cemetery and collected his $1,000 fee for completing the first phase of the project. He also met the trustees of the College of California, who engaged him to survey the site and prepare a master plan; they would pay $1,000 in gold and $1,500 in land. He and Edward Miller spent ten days making a survey and sketching out the basic plan.

The site of the future college was a monotonous, scrubby hillside in Oakland. Olmsted proposed dense planting to limit the immediate views. To preserve the tranquillity of the college, he chose a location apart from the village plots that had already been laid out in a simple gridiron. The area surrounding the college buildings was divided into several neighborhoods of large, wooded residential lots. The winding roads resembled country lanes. A low, well-irrigated dell in front of the college buildings was the only turfed area. Olmsted recommended against building student dormitories and proposed that students rent rooms in the village or, if residences were needed, that they should take the form of large houses. He explained to the trustees that the overall arrangement of the college was intentionally picturesque rather than formal. This would blend with the desired character of the neighborhood, and it would also allow easy expansion and modification.

Olmsted was developing his own method of working, which was not based on a theory of design or a predetermined set of aesthetic rules. He thought things out from a practical point of view, carefully planning after firsthand observation of the topography and the landscape. He combined functional organization, site planning, urban design, landscaping, and gardening. And art. (Vaux had been right about that, Olmsted was an artist.) When he presented his ideas to the trustees, they accepted them enthusiastically and instructed him to proceed and develop the plan. They did not take up any of his suggestions for naming the college town, however. He proposed "Bushnell," among others; instead, they decided on "Berkeley," in honor of the Irish bishop and philosopher.

The detailed plans for Mountain View Cemetery and the report and plans for the College of California would be completed later by Miller, who had agreed to accompany Olmsted to New York. Olmsted intended to divide his fees with Vaux; he would not be returning to the partnership empty-handed. He also had a third project in mind. He wanted to "drive the San Franciscans into undertaking a park," he wrote Vaux in his last letter. To that end he wrote an article that appeared in the *San Francisco Daily Evening Bulletin*. In "The Project of a Great Park for San Francisco" he argued strenuously that all major cities deserved an important park. To critics who said that building such a park was too expensive, he responded that the longer the matter was put off, the more costly land acquisition would become. He hoped that with the aid of influential friends such as William Ashburner and Frederick Billings, a trustee of the College of California, the city fathers might be convinced to undertake the park and to award the commission to Olmsted and Vaux.

While he was still in San Francisco, Olmsted received a telegram from Godkin's benefactor, James McKim.

You are chosen general secretary American freedmen's aid union salary seven thousand (7,000) bellows and godkin advising answer.

The Freedmen's Aid Union combined several voluntary societies whose interest was the welfare of freed slaves. Olmsted had often talked and written about the subject. He was well qualified for the position; Bellows and Godkin clearly thought so. Yet two days after receiving the offer, Olmsted wrote to his father, "I have no intention of accepting it. I am not fit for any duty requiring much writing or exciting labor." No doubt his recent illness had unnerved him. Nevertheless, he must have been intrigued by the offer, for despite his previous commitment to Vaux he left the door open. The telegram had already been delayed almost a month. Hoping for an explanatory letter, Olmsted decided to wait for the next delivery of his forwarded mail from Bear Valley before answering McKim.

A week later the mail arrived—nothing from McKim, but a letter from Vaux. It contained two announcements: the Board of Commissioners of Prospect Park had passed a resolution to hire Vaux for one year to make a plan and oversee the work (the fee was $7,500); and the Executive Committee of Central Park had appointed Olmsted & Vaux "Landscape Architects to the Board." The firm was to receive $5,000 per annum, and $5,000 as back pay for services already rendered. Vaux was elated but worried; Olmsted's letter with his decision to return had not yet reached him. "I should be satisfied with the result if I felt well assured of your real cooperation," he wrote. "As I said before, my main perplexity all through has been in this direction." If Olmsted had any doubts, the opportunity to work on his beloved Central Park dispelled them. He immediately sent two telegrams. One was to Vaux, assuring him of his intention to return to New York; the other was to McKim. It said simply, "I decline."

Shortly after, disturbing news arrived over the telegraph. His New York banker, Ketchum, Son & Company, had been forced to close its doors. Edward Ketchum—the "Son"—had embezzled $5 million. Olmsted, who had earlier requested that his account be transferred to San Francisco, was on tenterhooks. He eventually learned that the $6,400 had been transferred the day before the firm failed! His total loss amounted to one hundred shares of Mariposa stock, worth about $1,200. He felt "as if I had just come out from a cold bath."

Olmsted stayed another week in San Francisco arranging his affairs—he left more than $12,000 invested in California securities—and returned to Bear Valley. He planned to embark on a steamship that was sailing for Nicaragua (the Nicaragua route was cheaper than the Panama route). While he and Mary were packing, a telegram arrived from his friend Howard Potter in New York. Olmsted had granted Potter power of attorney and asked him to approach the Mariposa owners on his behalf. Potter's message was unambiguous: "No funds here yet no satisfactory assurances obtainable." Olmsted had waited for nothing. He left the Mariposa Estate on October 2, 1865, just a few days short of two years since he had arrived.

*   *   *

It was the spring of 1996 when I visited Bear Valley. Scant evidence remained that this was once the headquarters of the mighty Mariposa Estate. A small standing section of stone wall and traces of foundation were all that was left of Oso House, which had burned down years ago. I could only guess where the company store had stood. On the hillside I could see a handful of houses, one of which was obviously abandoned, the roof sagging, the windows boarded up. Bear Valley had not prospered. A sign by the two-lane highway listed the current population as seventy-five. There was a general store with two gas pumps. "Last Chance for Gas! No Service at Bagby," the sign indicated. Bagby, five miles away on the Merced River, had been the northernmost point of the Mariposa Estate. The only other commercial buildings were a restaurant and "Mrs. Trabucco's Mercantile," advertising antiques and gifts. It was Sunday, and only the general store was open. I felt hot and dry and bought a bottle of soda and drank it outside in the shade of the porch. Rising to the east was the bulk of Mount Bullion, covered with scrubby growth. The grass between the clumps of trees was already burnt yellow by the sun. The view was cheerless. Frederick and Mary were happy here, but they could not have been sorry to leave.

A MAGNIFICENT
OPENING

Calvert Vaux, June 1868.

We are neither of us old men you know. To me it seems & always has seemed a magnificent opening. Possible together, impossible to either alone.

—CALVERT VAUX TO FREDERICK LAW OLMSTED (1865)

Olmsted and Vaux Plan
a Perfect Park

THE TRIP HOME proved exhausting. It involved an uncomfortable carriage ride to Lake Nicaragua, crossing the lake by small steamer, and descending a rapids-infested river by stages to the Atlantic. Bad weather stranded them on the coast for a week. In all it took them forty-one days. In New York, Frederick and Mary settled in a boardinghouse—it would be several months before their furniture and possessions arrived from Bear Valley (by ship around Cape Horn). They had congenial company there—Charles Brace, who was still directing the Children's Aid Society, his wife, Letitia, and their children were also lodgers. Boarding was more expensive than renting, but there was no time to set up a proper household. Olmsted, Vaux & Company, Landscape Architects—Olmsted had conceded the title—required his immediate attention. The fledgling firm shared space with Vaux and Frederick Withers's architectural office at 110 Broadway. (Withers also was a partner in Olmsted, Vaux & Co.) Draftsmen were put to work completing the plans for the two California projects: Mountain View Cemetery and the College of California.

The Brooklyn park board expected a preliminary plan and a report by the end of the year. Vaux had offhandedly characterized the park to Olmsted as "an easy affair & a short job." That was a gross understatement, yet in a sense, Vaux was right. Thanks to his own timely suggestions, the Brooklyn park had none of the complications of Central Park. The proposed site was not an elongated rectangle but a generously proportioned diamond shape, a mile and a half long and about a mile wide. It was unencumbered by unsightly water reservoirs. No transverse roads would be required. In a word, it was perfect. Olmsted and Vaux were

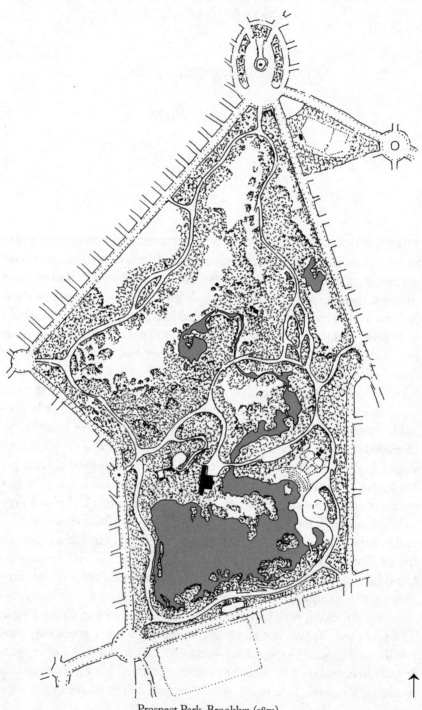

Prospect Park, Brooklyn (1871).

fully aware that this commission represented a unique opportunity, and they convinced the board to extend the deadline by almost a month.

They submitted the preliminary plan as well as a report. The report is a remarkable document, not simply a technical description but an extended essay on urban parks. It begins by emphasizing that the purpose of such parks is to provide "the feeling of relief experienced by those entering them, on escaping from the cramped, confined and controlling circumstances of the streets of the town; in other words, *a sense of enlarged freedom* [emphasis in original] is to all, at all times, the most certain and the most valuable gratification afforded by a park." Yet parks are more than scenery, the report emphasizes, they are social spaces "for people to come together for the single purpose of enjoyment, unembarrassed by the limitations with which they are surrounded at home, or in the pursuit of their daily avocations, or of such amusements as are elsewhere offered." Olmsted and Vaux admit that there is a conflict between the desire to create a pastoral landscape to contrast with the urban surroundings, and the need of large numbers of people to enjoy avocations and amusements. The purpose of their plan is to bring these disparate elements into one harmonious whole.

The report began by laying out the theory behind park design, but the actual plan was also a response to the particular place. One of the site's chief attributes, from a landscape gardener's point of view, was the presence of a large number of mature trees. "These trees are in two principal divisions, between which a space of two or three hundred feet in width is found, of undulating ground, not wholly ungraceful, and now mainly covered with a ragged turf." This undulating ground—at the north end of the site, closest to the built-up part of Brooklyn—became the so-called Long Meadow, three rolling pastures, stretching out a full mile in a graceful curve. The southernmost third of the site was flat farmland. This was the location of the lake, already identified in the sketches that Vaux had sent to Olmsted in California. Between the meadow and the lake was the remnant of a heavily wooded, ancient moraine. Across this treed, hilly ground Olmsted and Vaux laid out woodland paths and a meandering forest brook. "Although we cannot have wild mountain gorges, for instance, on the park, we may have rugged ravines shaded with trees, and made picturesque with shrubs, the forms and arrangement of which remind us of mountain scenery." The brook, "taking a very irregular course, with numerous small rapids, shoots and eddies, among rocks and ferns," was part of an elaborate waterworks. A steam engine pumped water from a deep well to a reservoir that fed the entire system of brooks, ponds, and lake.

The shoreline of the lake was varied with inlets and large and small islands, one of which served as the site for a music pavilion. The island pavilion was the focus of a semicircular space for concertgoers, and a formal garden. The lake narrowed into a little bay, at the head of which stood the Refectory. It was one of the few structures in the park, other than several bridges and rustic pavilions and arbors. Olmsted and Vaux proposed that museums and other educational buildings be erected on land belonging to the city on the other side of Flatbush Avenue.

The curved sweep of the meadows and the shape of the lake were both carefully delineated to produce an impression of great size, a technique Olmsted derived from Capability Brown's park at Trentham. In an even more overt imitation of an English country estate, Olmsted and Vaux also included a deer paddock. Yet the mood of Prospect Park was not British; it was simple and robust in a way that can only be called American. The pavilions, shelters, and lookouts were intentionally rustic. The two iron bridges were more like works of sturdy engineering than the refined filigree of Central Park's Bow Bridge. One of the large bridges (no longer extant) was timber; another was built out of boulders. Many of the smaller footbridges were constructed out of rough-hewn logs. Such exaggerated ruggedness, as well as the extraordinary feeling of expansiveness—the "sense of enlarged freedom"—demonstrated by the open spaces, was undoubtedly inspired by Olmsted's encounter with the Western landscape and Yosemite Valley.

Although some of the scenic effects were influenced by the British landscape tradition, the focus of this American park was the public.

> . . . in a park, the largest provision is required for the human presence. Men must come together, *and must be seen coming together* [emphasis added], in carriages, on horseback and on foot, and the concourse of animated life which will thus be formed, must in itself be made, if possible, an attractive and diverting spectacle.

Three different systems of circulation accommodated carriages, horseback riders, and pedestrians. Yet, unlike in Central Park, here the roads and walkways could be kept well apart. The carriage drive, for example, was largely restricted to the perimeter of the park, allowing the interior to be uninterrupted landscape. The absence of transverse roads likewise allowed Olmsted and Vaux to create large stretches of meadow and water.

Vaux had proposed that the park should have a "principal natural entrance." On the preliminary sketches he had sent to Olmsted, he noted that the majority of people coming from Brooklyn would arrive at the northern tip of the park. At the intersection of Flatbush and Vanderbilt Avenues he had drawn an oval plaza—now Grand Army Plaza—the one formal element in the park. The plaza both signaled the presence of and provided a transition to the park. The visitor moving through Prospect Park would experience a sequence of three different landscapes. First, the open, sunny, gently rolling meadows; next the dark, hilly, brooding wood; lastly the idyllic lake. Grass, woods, and water—the Brownian trilogy—were "the three grand elements of pastoral landscape for which we were seeking," wrote Olmsted and Vaux in their report.

The division of labor between the two partners was the same as before, with Olmsted doing most of the writing and Vaux overseeing the drawing. But Vaux's voice can be heard in the text, just as Olmsted undoubtedly influenced the design. Vaux had become an accomplished planner, judging from his masterly early reorganization of the site; Olmsted, after working independently on landscape projects in California, had more confidence in his artistic skills.

They had come a long way in the eight years since Greensward won the competition. Central Park is an impressive achievement for two neophytes, but it is the work of beginners. Its many different parts barely hold together—they are simply fitted into the awkward rectangle, side by side. There is no narrative thread. Prospect Park is different. Its elements demonstrate, with startling clarity, both variety *and* unity. Each has its own character yet interacts with its neighbor. Each also has a meaning. Laurie Olin describes Prospect Park as "a meditation on post–Civil War America": a transcendental vision of a unified, peaceful country, in which the meadows represent agriculture, the wooded terrain is the American wilderness, and the lakeside terrace and its more refined architecture, civilization. Neither Olmsted nor Vaux anywhere enunciates this compelling vision, but then artists are often reticent about their work. And there is no doubt that they did view Prospect Park as a work of art. In a section of the report titled "The Artistic Element in the Design of a Park," they unequivocally spelled out their vision:

A scene in nature is made up of various parts; each part has an individual character and its possible ideal. It is unlikely that accident should bring together the best possible ideals of each separate part, merely considering them as isolated facts, and it is still more unlikely that accident should group a number of these possible ideals in such a way that not only one or two but that all should be harmoniously related one to the other. It is evident, however, that an attempt to accomplish this artificially is not impossible. . . . The result would be a work of art, and the combination of the art thus defined, with the art of architecture in the production of landscape compositions, is what we denominate landscape architecture.

The Board of Commissioners considered Olmsted and Vaux's plan for several months. It had state approval to enlarge the boundaries of the park according to Vaux's proposal, but it had not formally adopted the change, so it took its time making the consequential decision. Meanwhile Olmsted received a letter from Mayor Henry P. Coon of San Francisco, authorizing him to plan a park for the city. In slightly more than a month, he had a preliminary report in the mail.*

Olmsted called on the city fathers to set their sights high. San Francisco would not remain merely a gold-rush town, he wrote, it would grow into an important city. The park "should be a pleasure-ground second to none in the world." He conceded that the dry climate of the Bay Area—it did not rain for six months of the year—and the windswept terrain represented a considerable challenge. Under such difficult circumstances, could San Francisco really expect to have a great city park? "I think that it can," he answered unequivocally.

The plan for the "public pleasure grounds" had several parts. Olmsted had observed that small gardens did well in protected and well-watered places in San Francisco. He identified a sheltered valley in an undeveloped part of the city near Buena Vista Hill where he situated an intimate park. Roads circled the park, but the main pleasure drive was a four-mile route that he called "the promenade." The promenade ran for several blocks parallel to Market Street, turned at an angle onto the line of Van Ness Avenue, and continued to the edge of San Francisco Bay. Here

*The San Francisco plan appears to have been solely Olmsted's work; the report was signed by him on behalf of Olmsted, Vaux & Co.

Olmsted proposed a plaza, a band pavilion, and a landing quay to serve as the "sea-gate of the city."

The first leisure promenades in European cities were on top of abandoned city fortifications. These promenades came to be known as *bollevarts*, or boulevards, after the German *bollwerk* (bulwark). Olmsted reversed the historic configuration and depressed the promenade in a trench, twenty feet below ground. The sloped embankments, sheltered from the prevailing east-west winds, were to be heavily planted with a variety of flowering plants, shrubs, and small trees. Along the 152-foot-wide base of this leafy, man-made ravine ran a central pedestrian mall flanked by bridle paths and carriage drives. City streets crossed on bridges and periodically connected to the promenade by ramps. It is difficult to judge something as unprecedented as a sunken linear park; it might have been beautiful—or claustrophobic. But the bold originality of Olmsted's solution is impressive. Impressive, too, is his foresight. In the next forty years San Francisco would grow from forty thousand to four *hundred* thousand.

The city fathers expected a version of Central Park. Instead, they got a plan that reconfigured a large part of the city for what must have seemed to many a distant future. They were unprepared for such an farsighted and expensive venture. Mayor Coon sent Olmsted his consulting fee—five hundred dollars—but advised him that it was unlikely that his proposal would be implemented. "I like the plan myself," he wrote, "but find at present great opposition to it." The pleasure garden and the sunken promenade were never built.*

The unrealized San Francisco pleasure garden does not loom large in Olmsted's oeuvre, yet it represents a turning point in his career. More was involved here than landscaping; the park and promenade were conceived on the scale of an entire city. The ability to think on a large scale, to project himself into the future, and to quickly master broad issues were skills Olmsted acquired while he was directing the United States Sanitary Commission, managing the Mariposa Estate, and chairing the Yosemite Commission. All these projects depended on his ability to digest and organize large amounts of information, and to integrate diverse require-

---

*Five years later, work began on a city park that did not incorporate any of Olmsted's proposals; Golden Gate Park, half a mile wide and more than three miles long, was a larger version of Central Park.

ments. All involved planning in time as well as space. Even Yeoman's first foray into journalism, which was an attempt to understand an entire region, was a useful preparation for Olmsted's adopted role of city planner.

After four months the Prospect Park board appointed Olmsted, Vaux & Co. landscape architects as well as superintendents of the actual construction. The annual fee was eight thousand dollars. Olmsted and Vaux assembled an experienced team: the engineer-in-charge was Joseph P. Davis; his assistants, John Bogart and John Y. Culyer, were both Central Park alumni (Culyer had also worked for the Sanitary Commission); the faithful Edward Miller, who had accompanied Olmsted from California, was appointed assistant architect. For various reasons, none of them was immediately available, so the burden of the initial organization fell on Olmsted. He loved it.

> We have put four hundred men at work and are getting on very nicely. I did not much like the ground at first, but it grows upon me and my enthusiasm and liking for the work is increasing to an inconvenient degree, so that it elbows all other interests out of my mind. When the organization is complete, I shall control this tendency better but at present it is necessary by personal vigilance to make good defects, therefore I give myself up to it. I get very tired every day but it agrees with me & I am in better health than I have been for several years.

Part of Olmsted's evident pleasure was due to the degree of managerial freedom he enjoyed. James Stranahan's methods were not those of Andrew Green. On June 16, 1866, Stranahan called a meeting of the board, and an appropriations bill, based on Olmsted's estimates, was discussed and passed. Then the commissioners adjourned for the summer, leaving all management decisions in Olmsted's hands. Earlier that summer, the Olmsted family had moved from Manhattan to Staten Island.* They rented a house in the town of Clifton, conveniently close to Vanderbilt's Landing, where the ferries from New York and Brooklyn docked. Olmsted commuted to Brooklyn daily.

Work began on July 1. By the middle of August, Olmsted had things

---

*That same summer, Tosomock Farm was—finally—sold. It proved not to have been a poor investment, after all. Bought for thirteen thousand dollars, it sold for more than twenty thousand dollars.

running smoothly. He and Mary took a three-week vacation. The family spent some time in Ashfield, Massachusetts, at the summer home of Charles Eliot Norton. Norton, who was currently editing the *North American Review* with James Russell Lowell, and Olmsted had become friends. Another guest was Samuel Bowles, the newspaper editor. From Ashfield, Frederick, Mary, and the children went to Walpole, New Hampshire, to visit Henry Bellows. They traveled north to Franconia Notch in the White Mountains, which Olmsted had last visited with his father, twenty-eight years earlier. It was more crowded than before. "We felt a little cheated of our enjoyment of the mountains by the crowd of infidels—philistines—which occupied them," he complained in a letter to Norton. They continued their trip by train to the Canadian border and finally reached Quebec City and the nearby object of their northern excursion, the dramatic Montmorency Falls.

Work on the park proceeded quickly. By the onset of winter, the plaza was graded as well as the first of the three meadows. The bridle paths and carriage drives in the northern part of the park were surveyed and their foundations completed. In their first progress report to the board, submitted on January 1, 1867, Olmsted and Vaux were upbeat. They promised to "enlarge the scale of operations in the Spring, with entire confidence, based upon the experience we have now had, in the ability and zeal with which we shall be sustained, not only by the gentlemen whom we have named [the engineering team], but by all who are engaged in the service of your Board."

Metropolitan

SHORTLY AFTER OLMSTED ARRIVED in New York from California, Godkin asked him to become associate editor of his weekly newspaper, now in full swing. Olmsted accepted. Godkin, in turn, was delighted. He informed his stockholders that "[Olmsted's] reputation is such that his connection with the paper would, I am satisfied, strengthen it with the public, and there is no person whose judgment and sagacity in journalism as in other fields I esteem more highly."

As associate editor, Olmsted solicited articles, corresponded with contributors, and set policy. "We go over all the editorial matter together," wrote Godkin, "so that he is in fact, as well as in name, responsible for all it contains." Olmsted was listed among the "regular or occasional contributors." Authors were not identified, so it is difficult to attribute specific articles to Olmsted. A reference in "The Week" to *A Journey Through Texas* must have originated with him; an editorial titled "The Progress of Horticulture" reads like Olmsted; the slightly cranky "Why Are Our Railroads not Luxurious?" reminds me of his earlier complaints about Southern hotels. Olmsted's editorial voice—if not, indeed, his pen—was probably responsible for "Health in Great Cities" in the May 11, 1866, issue, as well as an earlier editorial titled "The Future of Great Cities."

The Nation—as the paper was called—consisted of thirty-two densely packed pages of reporting, opinion, and criticism, and sold for fifteen cents.* Each issue began with a section titled "The Week," which reviewed the national press and commented on the events of the previous seven days. This was followed by editorials, articles, literary notes, poetry,

---

*Starting on May 1, 1866, Godkin and Olmsted experimented with two installments of sixteen pages that appeared on Tuesdays and Fridays. After two months they reverted to a single weekly edition.

and book reviews. There were several regular features: letters from London and Paris; "The South As It Is," written by a traveling correspondent obviously inspired by Yeoman; and a "Financial Review" column (preceded by a carefully worded disclaimer). Some of the people who wrote for the journal at this time included Longfellow, Lowell, Henry James, and John Greenleaf Whittier, as well as Norton, Bellows, and Charles Brace. The tone of the self-styled "Weekly Journal of Politics, Literature, Science, and Art" was progressive, bright, opinionated. It was not a runaway commercial success, but it quickly established itself as an influential periodical. " 'The Nation' is a weekly comfort and satisfaction," Norton wrote Godkin. "I hear nothing but good of it. Emerson . . . spoke to me last week in warmest terms of its excellence, its superiority to any other journal we have or have had."

The working capital for *The Nation* had been raised among forty stockholders. These included fervent abolitionists who became displeased with Godkin and Olmsted's moderate stance on Reconstruction and threatened to withdraw their support if the editorial direction did not change. In July 1866 Godkin, unable to mollify them and unwilling to alter his politics, took preemptive action. He liquidated the publishing company, raised new funds, and paid off the investors. He then formed a new company with only three owners: himself (holding three-sixths of the shares); the original backer, James Miller McKim (two-sixths); and Olmsted (one-sixth). This placed control of the paper in the hands of the two editors, something advocated by Olmsted. But his tenure as associate editor was short-lived. As the summer wore on and Prospect Park and other work consumed more and more of his time, he withdrew from the world of journalism that he loved so dearly. He did continue as part-owner of the *Nation* for another five years and remained lifelong friends with Godkin.

Olmsted still found time for extracurricular activities. In January 1867 he joined several friends, including Howard Potter, to mount an effort to combat a disastrous famine in the Southern states. He had been critical of Southern society, but now that the war was over, he felt a different sense of responsibility. As a member of the executive committee of the Southern Famine Relief Commission, he wrote the reports and used his newspaper contacts to raise public awareness and support. At this time he also learned his plans for Yo Semite had been sabotaged. He had left a copy of the final report with his fellow commissioners, who were to submit it to the governor. Without informing Olmsted, they decided that his recommendations were too expensive and shelved the report. He resigned in disgust.

The Nation carried several pages of advertisements. Next to William Bradbury's Pianos and B. T. Babbit's medicinal Saleratus was the following announcement:

Olmsted, Vaux & Co.,
LANDSCAPE ARCHITECTS.

The undersigned have associated under the above title for the business of furnishing advice on all matters of location, and Designs and Superintendence for Buildings and Grounds and other Architectural and Engineering Works, including the Laying-out of Towns, Villages, Parks, Cemeteries, and Gardens.

FRED. LAW OLMSTED,
CALVERT VAUX,
FRED'K C. WITHERS.

Towns, villages, parks—an ambitious range of services. In fact, the business of Olmsted, Vaux & Co. included all this. The firm undertook a dozen large commissions during its first two years of operation. The plans for the College of California were completed although work did not begin immediately (a few years later the college ran into financial difficulties and the Berkeley site was transferred to the newly established University of California, which did not adopt the design). Olmsted and Vaux drew up campus plans for the new Massachusetts Agricultural College in Amherst and designed a layout for a residential subdivision in Long Branch, New Jersey. They prepared preliminary reports for major parks in Newark and Philadelphia. But Prospect Park consumed their greatest energy. In the report that accompanied their initial plan, Olmsted and Vaux spelled out the range of their ambition:

> We regard Brooklyn as an integral part of what to-day is the metropolis of the nation, and in the future will be the centre of exchanges for the world, and the park in Brooklyn, as part of a system of grounds, of which the Central Park is a single feature, designed for the recreation of the

whole people of the metropolis and their customers and guests from all parts of the world for centuries to come.

This struck a chord with James Stranahan, the president of the board. An exceptionally farsighted individual, he would, a few years later, be one of the prime movers behind the Brooklyn Bridge. He would also serve as vice president of the commission that led to the creation of Greater New York. He encouraged Olmsted and Vaux to expand the scope of their planning and examine how streets leading to the park could be improved. In their second annual report they concluded that it would be expensive for the city to widen streets in the already occupied areas west and north of the park, but that such improvements could economically be undertaken on unbuilt suburban land. Even if an approach road were not built immediately, they observed, "the ground might be secured and the city map modified with reference to its construction in the future." This suggestion intrigued Stranahan and the board. Public meetings were held. A topographic survey was made. Olmsted and Vaux were requested to prepare more detailed studies.

Their next report (1868) began by arguing that the chief advantage of Brooklyn was its capacity to grow. "The city of New York is, in regard to building space, in the condition of a walled town," they wrote. "Brooklyn is New York outside the walls." They foretold a change in the functional organization of the city: a greater separation between the center, which would be devoted to business, and the residential neighborhoods in the suburbs. This peripheral growth would make access to the countryside difficult, increasing the need for recreational space within the city.

The report observed that "the present street system, not only of Brooklyn but of other large towns, has serious defects for which, sooner or later, if these towns should continue to advance in wealth, remedies must be devised, the cost of which will be extravagantly increased by a long delay in the determination of the outlines." The chief drawback, according to Olmsted, was the undifferentiated grid plan with its network of intersecting, uniform streets. He had already spelled out his opposition to this characteristic nineteenth-century device in his report on San Francisco. "On a level plain, like the city of Philadelphia, a series of streets at right-angles to each other is perfectly feasible, and the design is as simple in execution as it appears on paper," he had written, "*but even where the circumstances of site are favorable* [emphasis added] for this formal and repetitive arrangement, it presents a dull and inartistic appearance, and in such a hilly position as that of San Francisco, it is very inappropriate."

Olmsted and Vaux proposed modifying the grid. Their solution was a new kind a street, part avenue and part green space. They called it a "Parkway." The parkway was a 260-foot-wide avenue divided into five traffic lanes, each separated by a row of trees. The two outside lanes were reserved for commercial vehicles and gave access to the residential lots facing the parkway; the central carriageway was reserved for recreational traffic. Between the carriageway and the service roads were shaded pedestrian malls. Olmsted and Vaux also proposed that the next streets on each side of the parkway be widened to one hundred feet. These streets would be planted with double rows of trees so that "the house lots of these streets will be but little inferior to those immediately facing the Parkway." In the rear of these lots they introduced a service lane, "convenient sites for stables being thus provided." In total, this arrangement cut a 1,400-foot-wide green swath through the dense city.

The inspiration for the Brooklyn parkways is the Avenue de l'Impératrice (now the Avenue Foch) in Paris. The avenue opened in 1855; Olmsted saw it three years later in the company of its designer, Jean-Charles-Adolphe Alphand. The 330-foot-wide avenue, which led from the Place de l'Étoile to the Bois de Boulogne, incorporated a central carriageway flanked by a pedestrian mall on one side and a bridle path on the other. Side roads gave access to the villas that lined the avenue.

The Brooklyn parkways resembled the Avenue de l'Impératrice in cross section but not in length. The Parisian avenue was relatively short—only four-fifths of a mile. The Brooklyn parkways—like the San Francisco promenade—ran for several miles. One extended from Prospect Park to Coney Island, a distance of about six miles. Another, of similar length, connected the park to Fort Hamilton overlooking the Narrows. Here the report proposed a "marine promenade." A third parkway was to reach the Ridgewood Reservoir, in the hills east of the city. The most ambitious parkway extended to Ravenswood, opposite present-day Roosevelt Island. The island would provide an easy crossing of the East River by means of a ferry or a bridge.

> ... connection may thus be had with one of the broad streets leading directly into the Central park, and thus with the system of somewhat similar sylvan roads leading northward, now being planned by the Com-

missioners of the central park. Such an arrangement would enable a carriage to be driven on the half of a summer's day, through the most interesting parts of both of the cities of Brooklyn and New York, through their most attractive and characteristic suburbs, and through both their great parks; having a long stretch of the noble Hudson with the Palisades in the middle distance, and the Shawangunk range of mountains in the background, in view at one end, and the broad Atlantic with its foaming breakers rolling on the beach, at the other.

Two of the parkways were built: Ocean Parkway, connecting Prospect Park to Coney Island, and Eastern Parkway, stretching from Prospect Park as far as Crown Heights. The Ravenswood parkway was not realized. Although the grand vision of a pleasure drive stretching from the Palisades to the Atlantic Ocean remained stillborn, the parkway idea caught the imagination of the citizens of Brooklyn. Over the next fifty years, the city built more than thirty-eight miles of parkways.

The Narrows, New York

Thursday, June 20, 1867

It is late afternoon on a warm summer's day. A steady stream of vessels fills the strait between Long Island and Staten Island, where the Hudson River spills into the Atlantic Ocean. Stolid square-riggers and graceful fore-and-aft schooners plow the choppy waters. Fast brigs and California clippers heel over in the brisk wind. A dark cloud of smoke from a transatlantic side-wheeler rises among the billowing sails. There are dozens of small vessels: coastal lighters, fishing boats, and steam-driven tugs towing heavily laden barges. All are headed in or out of Upper New York Bay, one of the great natural harbors in the world.

Well away from this traffic, a small rowboat makes its way along the Staten Island shore. Olmsted, in shirtsleeves, is sitting in the stern munching an apple. His lean face is deeply tanned from days spent outside, supervising work on the park. A sailor's cap covers his balding head; it makes him look younger than his forty-five years. John, a sturdy boy with the delicate features of his father, is rowing. His brother Owen, a chubby nine-year-old, is curled up in the bow, sound asleep.

Towels and wet swimming costumes are draped over the bench. Olmsted has made it a summer habit to return home early, several afternoons a week, to take the two boys swimming. They have spent the last hour happily splashing about, and now they are returning home to Clifton. He treasures these little outings. While they were in California, he got used to spending time with the children. The previous year, his landscaping practice kept him away from home more than he liked, and he is being careful not to fall into his old work habits. He enjoys being on the water. It reminds him of boyhood summer holidays and boating on the Connecticut River with his brother. John was about fourteen then, too, he thinks, looking fondly at his stepson pulling intently on the oars.

The Narrows are less than a mile wide, and Fort Hamilton is clearly visible across the water. Beyond the commanding bulk of the fortification he can make out the rising ground that is Mount Prospect. The park commands most of his attention these days. The workforce has grown to more than a thousand men. They are making swift progress: the first of the three meadows is almost complete, and by the fall it will be open to the public. He is worried about damage to the new planting, but he cannot refuse the insistent Stranahan—it is thanks largely to him that the work on the park is going so smoothly.

"A little harder on the starboard oar, John," he directs. "Try to keep Bedloe Island over my right shoulder." The boat swings slightly as the boy dutifully alters direction. Olmsted notices the smoke from a paddleboat—the ferry from Brooklyn. He was on board a few hours ago after spending most of the day at the park. He finishes his apple and throws the core far into the water. A noisy group of seagulls swoops down, attracted by the splash. Owen wakes up, stretches, and sits up, looking across the bow of the rowboat.

"Look!" he cries excitedly, and waves.

Olmsted can see Mary and the two girls—Charlotte and little Marion— about a hundred feet away. He regards the small figure of his wife with affection. He is glad to see that she has come down to meet them—the sun and air do her good. Her health is finally improving. Last November she gave birth to a child. After a difficult delivery, the baby, a boy, lived only a few hours, not even long enough to be given a name. Mary's recovery was slow—she is thirty-seven, after all, already old for childbearing, and this was her sixth child. She is so brave, he thinks. He was too worried about Mary to grieve for his nameless son, yet he feels the loss. Although he loves John and Owen, he had hoped for a boy of his own.

He takes off his sailor's cap and halloos to the figures on the shore.

A Stopover in Buffalo

OLMSTED, VAUX & Co. prospered. The partners planned a zoological garden near Central Park and a college campus in Maine. The Brooklyn park commissioners asked them to look at Washington Park, which was dilapidated and needed a thorough overhaul. Olmsted's friend Potter owned land in New Jersey and wanted landscaping advice; so did Francis George Shaw, George Curtis's father-in-law, who had an estate on Staten Island. Andrew Dickson White, the first president of the university founded by Ezra Cornell in Ithaca, consulted them about a new campus. The trustees, who had approved a plan whose chief feature was a formal quadrangle, resisted Olmsted's proposal for a more irregular layout. He enlisted the help of his friend Charles Eliot Norton to influence the university president.

Norton, too, had become a client. He wanted to subdivide his family estate in Cambridge and engaged Olmsted to draw up the plans. During one of Norton's visits to New York, they resumed their discussion of Olmsted's book on American civilization. With Norton's help, he continued to accumulate research material. He was making slow progress— he did not have enough time. The daunting task of collating the statistics from the Sanitary Commission—more than eight thousand completed forms had to be classified and analyzed—remained. He wrote to Frederick Knapp asking him to undertake the task. Olmsted planned to work on the manuscript during his summer vacation.

But the summer of 1868 proved to be one of Olmsted's busiest. In August he received a letter from William Dorsheimer, who had written two years earlier for advice about a public park for the city of Buffalo. Now, as head of a private committee of leading citizens, he was extending a formal invitation. Buffalo was one of the ten largest cities in the United States. It had prospered because of the Erie Canal and was now

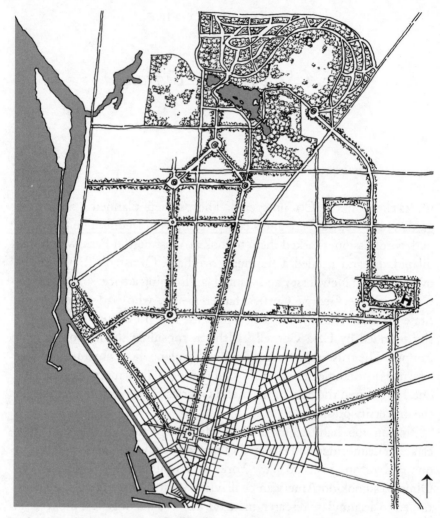

Buffalo, New York (1876).

a grain-handling port as well as an important meatpacking and iron-manufacturing center. Olmsted, who was leaving that weekend for Chicago, immediately altered his travel plans to include a stopover in Buffalo.

He was accompanied on this trip by one of his employees, a young engineer named John Bogart. On Sunday, August 16, they arrived in Buffalo, where they met Dorsheimer, who forthwith took them on a quick tour of several potential sites. He was the U.S. district attorney for northern New York State and, like Olmsted, a member of the Century Association. During the war he had served as a colonel and been active in the Sanitary Commission. Olmsted was impressed by his no-nonsense approach. "The business opened at once & promisingly," he wrote Mary in one of his regular letters. He agreed to make a presentation to Dorsheimer's committee on his way back from Chicago.

Olmsted and Bogart returned to Buffalo exactly one week later. Olmsted discovered that he was to address a public meeting of two hundred civic leaders the following Tuesday. The meeting would be chaired by former president Millard Fillmore, who lived in Buffalo. Fillmore was not just a figurehead. As president, he had actively supported A. J. Downing's plan for a public grounds in Washington, D.C. This august Buffalo assembly was expecting "to hear an address on the matter of a public park from the distinguished Architect of the N.Y.C.P. Fred Law Olmsted Esqr," Olmsted wrote to Mary. He and Bogart got down to work. On Monday morning, they drove out to the sites. They made a quick survey and dug test pits to ascertain the nature of the ground; by nightfall they were half-done. They completed the work the next day. That evening Olmsted spoke at the meeting. He had contracted a cold on the train and had a sore throat, but managed to talk for an hour, he wrote to Mary, "with tolerable smoothness and I should think with gratifying results. At any rate the men who started it were very much pleased & encouraged."

Dorsheimer's committee had reason to be pleased. Olmsted did not merely give a general talk about cities and public parks, he sketched out a specific park plan for Buffalo. He had been shown three alternative sites. The largest, in an undeveloped area four miles north of the city, was 350 acres. The second site, about two miles from the center of town, was much smaller, 35 acres. It occupied a dramatic bluff overlooking the mouth of the Niagara River. The third site was located on high ground and afforded a panorama of the city and Lake Erie.

Olmsted proposed that the city acquire not one but all three sites. The large tract would be made into what he called the Park. He pointed out that the undulating ground and profusion of trees would require little beautification; Scajaquada Creek, which flowed through the valley, could easily be dammed to create a lake. The riverside park he called the Front. It would have a promenade and a waterfront terrace that could be used for civic ceremonies. The third park would be the Parade; it would serve for more active recreation. The three sites approximated the shape of a huge baseball diamond, with downtown Buffalo at home plate, the Parade at first base, the Park at second, and the Front at third. The distance between the "bases" was two to three miles. Olmsted proposed parkways and tree-lined avenues to link the parks with each other—and with the downtown. In two hectic days, he had conceived this extraordinary tour de force—the outlines not of a park, but of an ambitious park *system*. If carried out, this master plan would govern the growth of Buffalo for years to come.

"I did a deal of talking privately & publickly [*sic*]—was cross examined &c & got thro very well," Olmsted wrote Vaux, who was then in England. Olmsted enclosed a newspaper clipping that described the evening's proceedings. "At least the project was advanced materially, I was told, & they will go to the Legislature in January for a Commission." Dorsheimer's committee, at its own expense, engaged Olmsted to prepare a preliminary report, which he submitted on October 1. Since Vaux did not return to America until November 16, this early work can definitely be attributed to Olmsted. He emphasized the need for a far-reaching solution. "We should recommend that in your scheme a large park should not be the sole object in view, but should be regarded simply as the more important member of a general, largely provident, forehanded, comprehensive arrangement for securing refreshment, recreation and health to the people." The Park was a version of Prospect Park, with a large meadow and a lake. The idea of parkways was based on the plans that Olmsted and Vaux were carrying out in Brooklyn. Yet the scale and extent of the project were unprecedented in their work. Olmsted's interest in city planning had its genesis in his proposal for San Francisco; in Buffalo, he was given the opportunity to put it all together.

Buffalo had been planned in 1804 by Joseph Ellicott, the brother of Andrew Ellicott, collaborator and successor of L'Enfant in Washington. The focus of the plan was a large square—later named Niagara Square—from which eight avenues radiated like the spokes of a wheel. Olmsted admired Ellicott's design. His proposal refined rather than altered the street pattern. He planned to widen several of the major streets to one hundred feet to create treed avenues. Among these was Delaware Avenue, which became the main approach from Niagara Square to the Park. From the Park, a mile-long, two-hundred-foot-wide parkway would lead to a large *rond-point* on the scale of the Place de l'Étoile in Paris. From this circle, two additional parkways would radiate to two more formal squares.

The Parisian influences in Olmsted's proposal are obvious. They are at odds with his later reputation as a proponent of winding streets and picturesque planning. He was nothing if not pragmatic. Indeed that was the strength of this plan. It is not a geometric diagram nor a theoretical construction imposed on the city. Unlike his San Francisco plan, it does not depend on a single idea. Nor, despite his respect for Ellicott, did Olmsted produce a version of European neo-baroque planning such as would later be revived by the City Beautiful movement. He was no historicist. Instead, his highly original plan was a complex and refined network of parks, parkways, avenues, and public spaces that represented a degree of sophistication in city planning previously unknown in the United States. He distributed parks throughout the city to make recreation space more accessible. Elsewhere, broad avenues and parkways brought trees and greenery into the congested grid of streets. In Buffalo, Olmsted showed how the burgeoning American industrial city could be made livable.

CHAPTER FORTY

Thirty-Nine Thousand Trees

DURING THAT BUSY SUMMER of 1868, Olmsted and Bogart had gone from Buffalo to Chicago to meet Emery E. Childs, the president of the Riverside Improvement Company. The company intended to subdivide sixteen hundred acres into residential plots. They had only five days to meet Childs, tour the site, discuss possible plans, and negotiate the terms of a contract. Childs told Olmsted that he wanted to start building that fall. Olmsted agreed to write without delay a preliminary report that would be used to attract investors. He was confident, for in his usual quick manner he had already seized on the major limitations and opportunities of the site. He described these to Mary in a letter that he wrote while returning home on the train:

> The motive is like this: Chic. is on a dead flat. The nearest point having the slightest natural attractions is one about 9 miles straight back— West. It is a river (Aux Plaines) or creek 200 ft wide, flowing slowly on limestone bottom, banks generally sandy & somewhat elevated above the prairie level & about 10 ft above low water with sandy slopes & under water a little limestone debris. As a river not very attractive, but clean water 2 or 3 ft deep, banks & slopes rather ruggard [*sic*] & forlorn in minor detail but bearing tolerable trees—some very nice elms but generally oaks mostly dwarf. The sandy, tree-bearing land extends back irregularly, so that there is a good deal of rough grove land—very beautiful in contrast with the prairie and attractive. 1600 acres of land including a fair amount of this grove but yet mainly rich flat prairie have been secured, & the proprietors are now secretly securing land in a strip all the way to Chicago—for a continuous street approach—park-way. I propose to make the groves & river bank mainly public ground, by carrying a road with walks along it & to plan village streets with "parks" & little

openings to include the few scattered motes [hillocks] on the open ground. An excellent R.R. passes through it & a street R.R. parallel with the park way is projected.

Olmsted was aware of the risk involved in working with a land developer—he described the project in a letter to Vaux as "a big speculation." It was expected that the sale of the 2,450 building lots would generate profits of up to $7 million—an immense sum. The agreement that Olmsted drew up in Vaux's absence specified that they were to be paid $15,000 in installments before the end of the year. The payment was to be in the form of building lots "to be selected by Olmsted, Vaux & Co.," or in cash if lots were not available. The fee for the execution and supervision of the project amounted to the princely sum of $112,500, likewise paid in lots.

Only five days after returning to New York, Olmsted finished his report for Childs. In addition to elaborating the points he had already made to Mary, he discussed the connection between suburb and city. He conceded the importance of the twenty-minute railroad link (the first out-of-town station of the Chicago, Burlington & Quincy Railroad was located in the center of the property). Yet he argued that the railroad "at best affords a very inadequate and unsatisfactory means of communication between a rural habitation and a town either for a family or for a man of business." What was needed was a pleasure drive to the city—in effect, a suburban parkway. He found the present form of the proposed road inadequate. He recommended acquiring a strip of land two hundred to six hundred feet wide and predicted that this promenade would become a major Chicago attraction. He estimated that construction of the parkway would cost $4 per foot of lot frontage. He pointed out that thanks to the enhanced value of the lots, which would sell for between $30 and $60 per foot of frontage, the parkway would more than pay for itself.

Olmsted, never bashful when it was necessary to sell a client on an idea, painted this enticing picture of the parkway:

Having a means of communication with the city through the midst of such a ground, made gay and interesting by the movement of fine horses and carriages, and of numbers of well-dressed people, mainly cheerful with the enjoyment of recreation and the common entertainment, the distance would not be too great for the interchange of friendly visits, for the exercise of hospitality to a large circle of acquaintance, or for the enjoyment of the essential, intellectual, artistic, and social privileges which specially pertain to a metropolitan condition of society.

He understood that a potential drawback to suburban living was isolation. Later planners conceived suburbs as a means of escaping the city. Olmsted did not see it this way. The parkway was an essential link. For him the "metropolitan condition" included cities *and* suburbs.

By 1868, suburbs were a well-established part of the metropolitan life of New York and Boston. The earliest suburbs grew up around existing villages such as Clifton on Staten Island, or Brookline outside Boston. The first formally planned suburban community was Llewellyn Park, begun in 1853 on a four-hundred-acre site in West Orange, New Jersey. The architect Alexander Jackson Davis with Eugene Baumann devised a picturesque layout according to Downing's principles. Childs, an Easterner, must have been familiar with Llewellyn Park. That was probably his chief reason for approaching Olmsted, Vaux & Co.—who better to design a beautiful "villa park" than the preeminent park builders of the day? Olmsted, who had known Davis since the time he had asked him to design a house for Sachem's Head, admired Llewellyn Park; when he was planning the College of California, he wrote to Vaux: "I propose to lay [it] out upon the Llewellyn plan." But now he was dead set against the idea. He pointed out to Childs that not only was the flat site unsuited to a park, but that parks and suburbs were different. "The essential qualification of a park is *range,* and to the emphasizing of the idea of range in a park, buildings and all artificial constructions should be subordinated," he wrote in his report. "The essential qualification of a suburb is domesticity, and to the emphasizing of the idea of habitation, all that favors movement should be subordinated." (The latter quality is precisely what makes Olmsted's suburb so different from late-twentieth-century suburbs, with their obsessive focus on movement and the automobile.)

Olmsted's objections were also practical since the projected building lots were much smaller than in Llewellyn Park: most were half an acre instead of three. Domesticity required a plan that accentuated the particularity of each house and yet created a harmonious relationship between the different houses, which would be close together. Not that common needs were ignored. There were ball fields and croquet grounds, an island in the river was designated a picnic ground, and in addition to the 160-acre park on both sides of the river, several commons, groves, and greens were scattered throughout the suburb. Together with the streets and roads, public areas constituted almost a third of the total area of Riverside, as the project came to be named.*

Riverside was based on a grid, but not a simple rectilinear grid. "We should recommend the general adoption, in the design of your roads, of gracefully-curved lines, generous spaces, and the absence of sharp corners," Olmsted wrote. "The idea being to suggest and imply leisure, contemplativeness and happy tranquillity." With the exception of Quincy and Burlington Streets, which were parallel to the railroad tracks and bordered by three hundred small lots, there were no straight streets in Riverside, only winding roads.† Today curvilinear suburban layouts have become a cliché and are usually so poorly executed that it is easy to dismiss Olmsted's achievement. To understand what he was getting at, one must see Riverside for oneself. The streets curve gently, just enough to break the monotony of endless open vistas. The judicious location of street trees, the careful design of sidewalks and common green areas, the variety of open and closed views, all contribute to the contemplativeness and happy tranquillity that he sought. Olmsted once described suburbs as combining the "ruralistic beauty of a loosely built New England village with a certain degree of the material and social advantages of a town." Riverside was the first fully realized rendering of this American ideal: a compromise between private and public, between domesticity and community, between the city and the country.

In the summer of 1930, some sixty years after Riverside was begun, a visitor wrote:

> If a stranger were blindfolded, whisked to the heart of Riverside, Illinois, and then permitted to look about, he would probably never suspect that he was standing in a prairie oasis and that just beyond the confines of his vision lay gangster-ridden Chicago and all the endless gridiron

*Olmsted did not like the name Riverside, but even with Mary's help, failed to provide an acceptable substitute. On the other hand, he probably was responsible for several of the road names: Downing, Repton, Loudon, Kent, and Uvedale (Price), as well as Audubon (after the great ornithologist), Bartram (after the American botanist), and Shenstone (after the eighteenth-century British landscape gardener).

†Olmsted distinguished between "streets," which were urban and straight, and "roads," which were rural and winding.

Riverside, Illinois (1868).

and monotony of the Western Chicago region. After he had seen the long curving Common with an elm-arched road on each side, and the attractive houses already of some age, facing the Common and set well back from the road in the midst of trees and shrubs, the stranger would doubtless believe that he was in a New England village.

Longwood Common and Scottswood Common do resemble New England town greens, and the associations evoked by the irregular plan and the tree-lined roads were not accidental. Like Lancelot Brown, Olmsted adapted his design to the capabilities of a site, but when these were absent or skimpy, as they were in the featureless Illinois prairie, he was not averse to creating scenic effects. He dammed the Des Plaines River to allow swimming and pleasure boating. The elm-arched roads and the attractive groups of trees and shrubs that the 1930 visitor to Riverside admired were Olmsted's work, too. He planted no less than seven thousand evergreens, thirty-two thousand deciduous trees, and forty-seven thousand shrubs.

Best-Laid Plans

ALTHOUGH THE OPPORTUNITIES to plan a comprehensive park system for a major city and to lay out a large suburban community from scratch came to Olmsted by chance, there was nothing accidental about what he produced. He was not, of course, a trained planner. For Olmsted, the lack of formal education was no more of a disadvantage in his planning than it had been in his landscaping. His ability to look far ahead served him well. "It should be well thought of that a park exercises a very different and much greater influence upon the progress of a city in its general structure than any other ordinary public work," he advised the city fathers of Buffalo, "and that after the design for a park has been fully digested, a long series of years must elapse before the ends of the design will begin to be fully realized." Unlike many later planners initially trained as architects, he did not approach planning as an extension of architecture. "Let your buildings be as picturesque as your artists can make them. This is the beauty of a town," he once wrote. "Consequently, the beauty of the park should be the other. It should be the beauty of the fields, the meadow, the prairie, of the green pastures, and the still waters." He was concerned with beauty but he did not try to impose his aesthetic vision on the city as a whole. "We cannot judiciously attempt to control the form of the houses which men shall build," he wrote in his Riverside report. "We can only, at most, take care that if they build very ugly and inappropriate houses, they shall not be allowed to force them disagreeably upon our attention when we desire to pass along the road upon which they stand. We can require that no house shall be built within a certain number of feet of the highway, and we can insist that each householder shall maintain one or two living trees between his house and his highway-line."

Olmsted's city planning was influenced by the book that he was writing. Its working title was now "The Pioneer Condition and the Drift of

Civilization in America." In March 1868 he drew up a new outline with six chapters. The first, largely complete, described the frontier society of Bear Valley. The others would deal with the effects of immigration, the results of the Sanitary Commission survey, life in large cities, and countervailing tendencies.* As he saw it, the "drift" of American civilization was toward mediocrity, even barbarism, but not inexorably so. "Nothing is decided as yet," he wrote. There were "civilizing currents" in American society, not the least of which was concerned individualism: a "lively sense of the personal interest and the personal property of every man in those things which benefit communities."

"The Pioneer Condition" was a hopelessly ambitious project for someone as busy as Olmsted. He never finished it. He last wrote on the subject in late 1868 or early 1869. In one of the remaining fragments he posed the questions:

> Rich men and poor men, Rich communities and poor communities. Penetrate the lacquer and which is which? Where is there trustworthy evidence of true prosperity? Who is it that is successful? What is healthy growth & what is diseased monstrosity?

The last question was a reference to American cities and towns, which, like the American frontier, were changing. "The recent rapid enlargement of towns and withdrawal of people from rural conditions of living is the result mainly of circumstances of a permanent character," he told a meeting of the American Social Science Association, of which he was a founding member. He did not deplore the change; he had seen too much of rural life to romanticize it. Moreover, he understood the attraction of city life. "Compare advantages in respect simply to schools, libraries, music, and the fine arts," he told his fellow social scientists. "People of the greatest wealth can hardly command as much of these in the country as the poorest work-girl is offered here in Boston at the mere cost of a walk for a short distance over a good firm, clean pathway, lighted at night and made interesting to her by shop fronts and the variety of people passing." He knew that "the poorest work-girl" was unlikely to be drawn to the fine arts, but he added that this was merely a question of education— another essence of city life.

---

*Olmsted corresponded with Knapp about tabulating the results of the Sanitary Commission survey, but no work appears to have been done.

Olmsted gave up writing his book at the time he realized that town planning could be an effective way of promoting what he called "healthy growth." Unlike modernist city planners of the 1920s, Olmsted was neither a radical nor a utopian; he believed that it was possible "to realize familiar and traditional ideals under novel circumstances." This attitude appealed to civic leaders, businessmen, and politicians alike and explains why his planning proposals were easily accepted. (He was also a good salesman.) It took Dorsheimer's citizens' committee and the Buffalo city council less than a year to mobilize legislative support. Olmsted, Vaux & Co. were hired to oversee the work. The final plan adhered to the concepts that Olmsted had sketched out in his Buffalo talk. Vaux designed a boathouse in the Park, a pavilion in the Front, and a large grandstand for a thousand spectators in the Parade. The work would continue over the next seven years until Buffalo became, as Olmsted proudly wrote to Waring, "the best planned city, as to its streets, public places and grounds, in the United States if not in the world." For decades, these parks and parkways guided the growth of what subsequently became known as the City of Elms. It would take the automobile, urban renewal, and a less sensitive generation of planners to undo Olmsted and Vaux's achievement.

Childs, true to his word, started construction at Riverside immediately. Olmsted, Vaux & Co. opened a field office headed by their partner, Frederick Withers. The firm received several architectural commissions. The initial plan did not show a town center—people were expected to do their shopping in downtown Chicago. Later, Withers did design a commercial block with stores and offices near the railroad depot. The town's water tower, a striking structure that resembled a medieval German keep, was built by William LeBaron Jenney, the young military engineer whom Olmsted had met during the siege of Vicksburg. Jenney, who practiced architecture and landscape gardening in Chicago, was responsible for the hotel and several houses in Riverside—including his own.

Construction was progressing, but Olmsted, Vaux & Co. was having difficulties with its client. Olmsted suspected that the value of the building lots they were receiving in payment was inflated; the developer's position was that he was basing his calculations on the final land value. However, sales were slow. Childs announced the founding of Riverside Female University, "which will be completed for use at the commencement of the Fall term next year." No university materialized. He declared that the parkway to Chicago would be finished in four months—another exaggeration. Olmsted, Vaux & Co. bore the brunt of the developer's financial troubles. "We have had to commence legal proceedings twice to hold our own position as Superintendents in a satisfactory way," Olmsted wrote a friend. Nevertheless, he called Riverside "the most interesting of all the undertakings we have been connected with," and he stayed on.

Shortly before Olmsted's first visit to Riverside, the Illinois legislature debated a bill to create a large public park in Chicago. Although the idea of a park had been in the air since the founding of the city, it had recently come to the fore with the publication of an ambitious park scheme in the *Chicago Times*. Two of the most vocal supporters of the park bill were Ezra B. McCagg, a wealthy lawyer, and William Bross, the lieutenant governor of Illinois. Both men had been influenced by Olmsted. McCagg, who had been president of the local branch of the Sanitary Commission, met him during the war; the two had discussed Chicago's need for a park. Bross met Olmsted when he visited the Yosemite Valley with the Colfax party. As he later recalled, they spent most of their time together in conversation about Central Park. "Both Colfax and Olmsted agreed with me that nothing was needed to make Chicago the principal city of the Union but a great public improvement of a similarly gigantic character." The intention to create a rival to Central Park was a measure of Chicagoans' lofty ambition.

The park bill did not pass. The advocates of the park proposed new legislation, this time not for a single park but for a system of parks and parkways spread across the entire city. This tactic successfully broadened public support and the bills were enacted. Three separate park commissions were created, each responsible for a different part of the city. There was no master plan. The northern division incorporated the partially completed Lincoln Park. The western division included three parks— Humboldt, Garfield, and Douglas; Jenney was to be the landscape architect. The southern division, the site of the original proposal, was the largest of the three. Called South Park, it was the centerpiece of the Chicago park system.

Shortly after the legislation was passed, Olmsted contacted the newly appointed South Park commissioners. A year later, Olmsted, Vaux & Co. was hired to plan South Park. The fee was set at $15 per acre, or more than $15,000, $2,500 to be paid immediately. With cash in hand and a major commission in their pockets, Olmsted and Vaux no longer had to put up with Childs's chicanery. His latest scheme was to build his own house in the middle of Long Common. "I am shocked and pained to hear that such a suggestion could for a moment be entertained," Olmsted wrote to Childs. "I entreat you to give it up." Childs relented, but this was the final straw. At the end of April, Olmsted, Vaux & Co. and the Riverside Improvement Company parted ways. The planning of the suburb was complete, and the landscaping, roads, drains and sewers, and gas and water lines were well advanced. Supervision of the construction passed to Jenney.

South Park was a challenge. Larger in area than Central Park, it was made up of three distinct parts: a 593-acre piece of land along Lake Michigan (now Jackson Park); a 372-acre rectangle of prairie about a mile inland (now Washington Park); and a 600-foot-wide strip linking the two. The land beside the lake was low-lying and marshy and too windswept for large trees to grow; the inland site was flat and featureless. Altogether, the "capabilities" of the site appeared distinctly inauspicious. Olmsted and Vaux described their solution in the report that they submitted with their plan:

> There is but one object of scenery near Chicago of special grandeur or sublimity, and that, the lake, can be made by artificial means no more grand or sublime. By no practical elevation of artificial hills, that is to say, would the impression of the observer in overlooking it be made greatly more profound. The lake, may, indeed, be accepted as fully compensating for the absence of sublime or picturesque elevations of land.

The unifying motif of South Park was water. Olmsted and Vaux proposed dredging the swampy land next to Lake Michigan to create an intricate system of lagoons and waterways for boating and swimming. The shore would be dotted with shelters and landings. They named this area the Lagoon Plaisance. Olmsted and Vaux foresaw that this part of the park, with its dramatic waterfront and unique lagoons, would become a major attraction. They planned a thousand-foot pier for ferryboats to bring pleasure seekers from the center of the city, six miles away.

Olmsted and Vaux called the long strip of parkland the Midway Plaisance and planned a mile-long canal along its length. Pleasure rowers in the summer—and skaters in the winter—could thus start in the Lagoon Plaisance and travel all the way to the inland portion of the park. The canal ended in a series of small ponds called the Mere. The Mere was the focus of the so-called Upper Plaisance, which included a deer paddock, a children's play area, playing fields, picnic areas, a music stand, and a refectory pavilion. Making the best of the flat, open site, they turned the rest of the inland park into an immense meadow—the Southopen Green—also useful for parades and athletic events. One of the commissioners, examining the drawing of the meadow, said, "I don't see, Mr. Olmsted, that the plans indicate any flower beds in the park. Now where would you recommend that these be placed?" Olmsted's promptly replied, "Anywhere outside the park."

The idea of an aquatic park had no antecedents either in Olmsted and Vaux's work or in anyone else's. Like the Ravine in Prospect Park—although on a vastly enlarged scale—it represented the deliberate introduction of a "theme" into a public park, in this case Lagoons of the Tropics. Vaux had never seen the tropics, but Olmsted had. Eight years earlier, on his way to California, he had crossed the Isthmus of Panama and had been overwhelmed by the landscape. "After my excitement was somewhat tempered," he wrote at the time to Ignaz Pilat, the head gardener at Central Park, "I naturally fell to questioning how it was produced, and whether, with materials that we can command in the temperate regions, we could to any marked degree reproduce it." What interested Olmsted was not the different vegetation, nor even the general appearance of tropical scenery, but the emotion it aroused in him. "If my retrospective analysis of this emotion is correct, it rests upon a sense of the superabundant creative power, infinite resource, and liberality of Nature—the childish playfulness and profuse careless utterance of Nature." It was this playfulness that he wanted to achieve at South Park, although he was realistic about the means:

> You certainly cannot set the madrepore or the mangrove at work on the banks of Lake Michigan, you cannot naturalize bamboo or papyrus, aspiring palm or waving parasites, but you *can* set firm barriers to the violence of wind and waves, and make shores as intricate, as arborescent and as densely overhung with foliage as any. You can have placid and limpid water within these shores that will mirror and double all above it as truly as any, and thus, if you cannot reproduce the tropical forest in all its mysterious depths of shade and visionary reflections of light, you can secure a combination of the fresh and healthy nature of the North with the restful, dreamy nature of the South.

Playfulness was fitting for the Lagoon Plaisance. In contrast to Central Park and Prospect Park, which were largely intended for passive leisure, much of South Park was destined for active recreation. The difference had less to do with a change in Olmsted and Vaux's idea of what a city park should be than with the difference in the natural settings of Chicago and New York. The surroundings of New York—and Brooklyn—offered many sites where people could picnic, swim, and play games. This was not the case in Chicago. The Chicago River was an industrial thoroughfare; the windblown shore of Lake Michigan—an inland sea—was inhospitable in its natural state; and the flat prairie offered few attractive settings. The pleasure grounds in South Park would rectify this situation.

Henry Hobson Richardson

SHORTLY AFTER OLMSTED RETURNED to New York from California, he met a young man who would become not only one of his closest friends but also his most esteemed colleague: Henry Hobson Richardson. Richardson, the son of a successful New Orleans businessman, was born and raised in Louisiana, graduated from Harvard, and was sent to Paris in 1859 to study architecture at the École des Beaux-Arts, only the second American to do so (he was preceded by Richard Morris Hunt). When the outbreak of the Civil War abruptly cut off his financial support, he came back to Boston, where his fiancée lived. Richardson, who was sixteen when he left New Orleans, was not an avowed secessionist. He may have stayed in Boston, but he felt uncomfortable taking an oath of allegiance to the Union when his younger brother had just quit Harvard to enlist in the Confederate army. He returned to Paris and continued his studies at the École des Beaux-Arts, supporting himself by working in an architect's office.

Six months after the end of the war, he returned to the United States. The ambitious young man who had spent six years learning both the theory and the practice of architecture was eager to start his career and settled in the commercial capital of the country, New York (he never again returned to New Orleans). He spent an uneventful year doing small jobs for decorators and builders. Then, thanks to a college friend, he entered a competition to design a church in Springfield, Massachusetts. "That is all I wanted," he said gleefully on learning that he had won, "*a chance.*" He could now marry his faithful fiancée—Julia Gorham Hayden, the daughter of a Boston physician. They settled in a rented cottage on Staten Island. Soon after the birth of their first child (there would be six in all), with the financial help of his father-in-law, Richardson started building a large, wood-shingled house for his new family—in Clifton, where Olmsted lived.

Olmsted recollected the first time that Richardson came to his home. A pile of rough tracings was on Olmsted's desk, which prompted Richardson to observe:

The most beguiling and dangerous of all an architect's appliances was the T-square, and the most valuable were tracing-paper and india-rubber. Nothing like tracing over tracing, a hundred times. There was no virtue in an architect more to be cultivated and cherished than a willing spirit to waste drawings. Never, never, till the thing was in stone beyond recovery, should the slightest indisposition be indulged to review, reconsider, and revise every particle of his work, to throw away his most enjoyed drawing the moment he felt it in him to better its design.

This was Olmsted's own view.

In early 1868 Olmsted offered Richardson an architectural commission. The previous year, Alexander Dallas Bache, Olmsted's old friend from the Sanitary Commission, had died. Bache's colleagues wanted to erect a cemetery monument and asked Olmsted to recommend an architect. It might appear odd that Olmsted picked a neophyte rather than his seasoned partner Vaux, but the commission was small—the construction budget was two thousand dollars—and Olmsted may have wanted to give an aspiring practitioner a helping hand.

Not that Richardson needed the work. By now he was designing three churches, an addition to the Century Association, and two large residences. One of these was for William Dorsheimer. Since Olmsted had just met Dorsheimer at the time, he probably recommended Richardson. This was not a small commission—when it was completed, Dorsheimer's house was one of the finest on Buffalo's stylish Delaware Avenue. Olmsted's recommendation was a sign of his growing confidence in the young architect.

It was easy to like Richardson. An admiring female acquaintance described him: "He was of good height, broad-shouldered, tall-chested, dark complexion, brown eyes, dark hair, parted in the centre, and had the look of a man in perfect health and with much physical vigor. He wore his clothes, which fitted him well, with an indescribable air of ease." Richardson shared Olmsted's admiration for Paris, his love of domesticity and family life, and his devotion to work.* Still, they were an odd pair:

---

*Richardson also had a physical impairment: he stuttered.

the forty-six-year-old New Englander who had written so scathingly about the South, and the thirty-year-old Southerner whose family had been slave owners.

On July 20, 1870, Olmsted published a letter in the *New York World* about the future of Staten Island. He summarized his recommendations to the Staten Island Improvement Commission, which the state had created in reaction to the malaria epidemics that regularly broke out on the island. The Commission, impressed by Olmsted's call for a comprehensive study, hired him. Olmsted assumed that the future of the island, which was still largely farmland, would be as a residential suburb of New York. Yet he found that "the district is much less healthy, and the pleasure with which a family, having any feeling for natural beauty, can reside in it is not nearly as great as it was twenty years ago." Here was a "suburban district of great beauty, declining in value of real estate apparently because of being brought nearer to town, and this, at a period when in other directions suburban real estate has been advancing five and ten fold in value!" Part of the problem was undoubtedly the prevalence of malaria, which his report proposed to eradicate by constructing drainage systems, flood courses, and flood regulators.* Olmsted understood that to attract city dwellers Staten Island had to offer more than a healthy environment. The report proposed a far-reaching plan to improve the island's roads; two large water preserves and conservation areas combined with public recreation lands to guarantee the quality of the natural environment; and improvements to the ferry service to encourage commuting. People who moved to the suburbs wanted space. "If the interior land should be cut up into smaller plots than an acre," Olmsted warned, "most people will prefer to pass a little more time on the public conveyances, and go farther." The report referred to Riverside and recommended quarter-acre house lots near the ferry landings, and lots of up to five acres in the interior of the island.

Staten Island covered sixty square miles—this was in effect America's first regional plan. Olmsted approached this new task with characteristic thoroughness. He consulted no fewer than seventeen local physicians.

---

*Malaria was thought to be caused by "bad air," related to dampness and poor drainage. Standing water does, in fact, serve as a breeding ground for malarial mosquitoes, but this relationship was not discovered until 1897.

He compiled appendices on sanitary geology, the results of soils and water-quality tests, a report by an engineer on improving ventilation in the ferryboats, and an extract of a French evaluation of a British steam-powered road locomotive. He sought the advice of experts in many disciplines: public health, geology, chemistry, engineering, and veterinary science. He drew on his wide range of professional contacts: his old adversary at the Sanitary Commission John Newberry, now teaching geology at Columbia College; William LeBaron Jenney's engineer partner, L. Y. Schermerhorn; and a British engineer, George Radford, who was overseeing the construction of the Buffalo parks for Olmsted, Vaux & Co. But the idea of regional planning was simply too novel—his recommendations were never acted upon.

Olmsted had made two demands of the Commission: first, the work should be adequately compensated (the Commission agreed to pay $1,200 for the study); second, he would not do the work alone. He proposed a team consisting of "three gentlemen, residents of the island, who now occur to me qualified by their professional education, training and experience to advise the Commission." The crucial public health issues were handled by Dr. Elisha Harris, who had been a cofounder of the Sanitary Commission and in New York had recently organized the first free public vaccination program for smallpox. Drainage and road construction were the responsibility of a civil engineer named Joseph Trowbridge. The third expert was H. H. Richardson. What he contributed to the study is not exactly clear—there is a brief mention of house design. In his letter to the Commission, Olmsted described Richardson as "a gentleman trained in the most thorough French technical school familiar with European roads and Sanitary Engineering and of highly cultivated tastes with a strongly practical direction." Although Richardson was both cultivated and practical, this made the young architect sound like a graduate of the great French civil engineering school, the École des Ponts et Chaussées.

The following year Olmsted and Richardson collaborated again. Richardson was appointed architect for the State Asylum for the Insane in Buffalo. The site being adjacent to the largest of Olmsted and Vaux's parks, they were asked to advise on the location of the buildings and the layout of the grounds. Olmsted surveyed the site with Richardson and prepared a landscaping plan. The vast asylum occupied Richardson for the next five years.

Richardson's congenial personality, his social credentials and Parisian background, and his rigorous Beaux-Arts training attracted clients. He also began to show real originality. In 1870 he won a competition for the Brattle Square Church in Boston. This design is generally considered a breakthrough in his architectural development, the first building in which he adopted the Romanesque style that he would make his trademark. Richardson's talented assistant on the church was Charles Follen McKim (whose father, James Miller McKim, had financed *The Nation*). Richardson, like Olmsted, attracted able collaborators. The frieze of the beautiful tower was sculpted by Frédéric-Auguste Bartholdi (who would later design the Statue of Liberty); the interior was to be decorated by the New York muralist and stained-glass maker John La Farge. Thanks to La Farge and Olmsted, Richardson took on a red-haired young man who would soon become his chief assistant—Stanford White.

Olmsted had been introduced to architecture by Vaux, who was solidly grounded in the picturesque High Victorian tradition of Ruskin. Vaux's work, while often of high quality, was derivative. Richardson was a different sort of architect—not only better trained, but interested in finding a different, simpler mode of architectural expression. In that regard, he and Olmsted were kindred spirits. But Richardson's creative talent was largely intuitive—he was not an intellectual. He also lacked Olmsted's broad experience of American culture and society. That was the real reason that Olmsted had invited his young friend to be a part of the Staten Island study—to further the latter's education.

Olmsted's Dilemma

BETWEEN AUGUST 1868, when Olmsted started to work in Buffalo, and March 1871, when the plans for South Park were completed, Olmsted and Vaux's practice grew. They prepared a second study for the Fairmount Park Commission in Philadelphia, started to build city parks in New Britain, Connecticut, and Fall River, Massachusetts, and planned park systems for Albany and Hartford. The work in Brooklyn continued—and expanded: they were commissioned to build a large parade ground next to Prospect Park, to landscape Tompkins Square, and to lay out a brand-new park on the grounds of Fort Greene; Ocean Parkway was completed and work started on Eastern Parkway; the planting and architectural embellishment of Prospect Park required both partners' full attention. There were more residential subdivisions—one in Needham, Massachusetts, and another on a beautiful nine-hundred-acre suburban site in Tarrytown Heights, New York—and campus work at Vassar and Amherst. Many of these projects produced only reports; others resulted in complete plans; some—New Britain, Riverside, and Buffalo—were under construction. Olmsted also had several personal clients such as the Staten Island Improvement Commission, Cornell University, and Quartermaster General Meigs, whom he advised on landscaping national cemeteries for the war dead.

It should have been a triumphant period for Olmsted. The landscape practice that he and Vaux had begun only five years before was a success. There had been setbacks such as Riverside, but Prospect Park—their masterpiece—was nearing completion, the Buffalo park system was progressing smoothly, and Chicago's South Park promised to seal their reputations as the preeminent landscape architects in the country. Still Olmsted was dissatisfied. He relished taking on new and challenging commissions, but the pressure of having to produce plans and reports for so many impatient clients began to make themselves felt. He started to feel inadequate, which was usually a sign that he was overdoing it. "I am poorly qualified for a great deal of the work which I feel myself impelled to regard as coming to me as a duty," he wrote his friend Kingsbury. He felt harried. "The very hardest of [my work] I cannot possibly perform, to satisfy my sense of duty under ordinary everyday conditions—in my office subject to interruptions & with all the distractions of constant complicated demands of a host of people." He found himself taking work home. "I wish I could meet what I think to be my duties to the public & to my family with less work," he complained.

He resented being drawn away from his family, all the more so as he was now the father of a new baby—a son—born the year before and christened Henry Perkins after Mary's father. Olmsted cherished his domesticity. Here is his description of a typical Sunday at Clifton:

> I am longer at breakfast & get a better one than usual. I read two Sunday newspapers, I smoke after breakfast as I usually do not. Being on the coast & near shipping, I reciprocate their courtesy & pay the day the compliment of hoisting my ensign or seeing the children do it. I play with the children more. Generally late in the day I go out with some of them—in summer we go rowing—sometimes drive back on the island—go to the Brewery & I treat them to sangaree [sangria] or a little beer; in winter I have been to the skating ponds with them. My wife generally goes with us. She has often been—at least more than once or twice—to the Brewery. Sometimes we go picnicing either by boat to the Long Island shore or to the high woods by wheels.

But he added, "I wish these excursions were more frequent, but I rarely get through or get too tired to go on further with my work till near sunset, & it is too late for anything but a row."

Olmsted and Vaux shared the work. They developed the designs together, then Olmsted wrote the reports and Vaux and his draftsmen produced the plans. Vaux also supervised the design of any park structures such as bridges and pavilions. Yet the collaboration was unequal, for Olmsted devoted considerably more time to the partnership than Vaux, who also carried on an architectural practice. Between 1868 and 1871, Vaux and Withers designed and built three large hospital complexes and about a dozen private residences, including one for E. L. Godkin. Vaux's most celebrated client was the noted landscape painter Frederic Edwin

Church, who commissioned a remarkable Islamic-Moorish villa over-looking the Hudson River.

The responsibility for overseeing the landscaping and planning pro-jects increasingly fell to Olmsted. His subordinates were engineers who supervised topographic surveys, drainage, and road construction, and landscape gardeners who attended to planting. But he oversaw the work and visited the sites—in Chicago, Buffalo, and scattered all over New England. Since he dealt with the clients, they wanted to see only him. Olmsted signed the preliminary Buffalo report with the name of the firm, but when it was published by the Commission, it was given the title "Mr. Olmsted's Report." He was the one to whom people talked, whose recommendations they wanted to hear. He was also the one who drummed up business.

Olmsted thought that he was carrying an unfair share of the firm's work, but did not know what to do about it. He almost quit. "I feel myself so nearly desperate that I have to school myself against the danger of some foolish undertaking—such as putting all I can get together in a farm, cutting the world and devoting myself to asceticism. But against extreme lunacy in this way my wife makes a pretty strong bar." Mary, who had had her fill of farming, would have nothing to do with the idea; he had to find some other solution. Olmsted discussed his predicament with his friend Samuel Bowles in Springfield, Massachusetts, where Olmsted was advising two of Bowles's friends on landscaping (obviously part of Olmsted's problem was that he couldn't say no). Bowles, who shared Olmsted's tendency to overwork, suggested that he move to the country, not to be a farmer but to work as an independent landscape con-sultant "not tied to any architectural firm." The idea of striking out on his own intimidated Olmsted. "You write in view of one horn of my dilemma," he wrote Bowles on his return to New York. "I want more assistance and, even if there were no ties of sentiment & obligation I have not courage enough left to dispense with V's cooperation."

Mary and the children usually spent the summers away from Staten Island. That September Olmsted joined them in Lake George. The month's vacation did not lift his spirits. He was still undecided about his future. "I am looking in earnest for some less irritating & exasperating method of getting a living than that I have lately followed," he wrote to Kingsbury on October 8, 1871, the very day the great Chicago fire broke out. Olmsted, who was in Chicago a month later, wrote a long article for

The Nation. He mentioned that one of the less obvious but equally cata-
strophic effects of the fire was the destruction of "important papers, contracts, agreements, and accounts, notes of surveys, and records of deeds
and mortgages." Among these were all the plans and records for South
Park, including the nearly completed assessment rolls. It would take
months of painstaking work to recover this information. In any case, it
seemed unlikely that construction of the park would begin soon; rebuilding downtown Chicago meant that the pleasure ground would be put on
hold. Tropical lagoons and thousand-foot piers would have to wait.

In addition to their professional practice, Olmsted and Vaux continued
their on-again, off-again relationship with Central Park. They were
appointed "Landscape Architects," a title that proved largely honorific as
their advice was rarely sought. In May 1870 William "Boss" Tweed
pushed through a new city charter that supplanted the park board by a
Department of Public Parks; Olmsted and Vaux were named "advisors"
and "Chief Landscape Architects." This turned out to be merely window
dressing, too. Over their protests the Tweed administration spent large
amounts of money "improving" Central Park—planting flowers, clearing
undergrowth, building a zoo. After six months Olmsted and Vaux's positions were abolished.

   The Tweed regime did not last long. A year later, thanks in large part
to the perseverance of Andrew Green, who was now city comptroller,
Tweed was indicted and the so-called Tweed Ring collapsed. Henry
Stebbins, who had headed the Board of Commissioners during Central
Park's early years, was brought back. Olmsted was delighted: "The
appointment of Stebbins as Pres^t, of Green as Treasurer (which he
declines) and of O. & V. as Landscape Archts. Advisory, is the public vin-
dication of the Old Board." Olmsted and Vaux also secured the appointment of Frederic Edwin Church as a park commissioner; his presence
would ensure that in the board's deliberations "the art element should be
recognized."

   Olmsted and Vaux were paid a joint salary of six thousand dollars per
year (later increased to ten thousand dollars). Their official title was now
"Landscape Architects and General Superintendents," but their roles
soon diverged. Vaux busied himself with architectural matters such as
designing the Boathouse. Olmsted, directing the Bureau of Design and
Superintendence, turned his attention to repairing the damage and dis-

repair caused by the neglect and poor management of the previous administration. "The Park has suffered great injury," he wrote, "which it is even now impossible wholly to retrieve through the neglect of timely thinning of the plantations and the maltreatment of the last year and a half." He loved Central Park. He threw himself wholeheartedly into the job. He fired off letters to Stebbins, memoranda to park supervisors, and lengthy directives to the keepers and gardening staff.

In May 1872 Stebbins went to Europe on business and Olmsted was elected acting president and treasurer of the Department of Public Parks. He took full advantage of his authority. He initiated an inquiry into the advisability of lighting the park at night and opening it to the public. He issued a handbill publicizing park activities for children. ("At the Dairy and the Great Hill there is turf on which young children are allowed to play, and shaded seats; fresh, pure and wholesome milk is furnished at 5 cts. a glass, and bowls of bread and milk for children at 10 cts.") He recommended a reorganization of the park police. (The first murder in Central Park occurred in October 1872.)

During that summer Olmsted received an unexpected offer. The Liberal Republicans had nominated Horace Greeley as their presidential candidate in the 1872 election. A dissenting faction, of which James Miller McKim was a member, proposed an alternative slate and nominated Olmsted as its vice-presidential candidate. This was all done without Olmsted's knowledge and he refused the nomination, even publishing an announcement to that effect in the *New York Evening Post*. Privately, he wrote McKim, "It appeared to me in the highest degree absurd." Nevertheless, he admitted, "I am surprised & gratified that it is so well received."

On October 24 Stebbins returned from Europe. To be acting president, Olmsted had resigned his position as landscape architect and general superintendent, leaving Vaux alone in that role. Now Olmsted and Vaux requested Stebbins to change the earlier working arrangement. Henceforth Olmsted would be "Landscape Architect" and Vaux "Consulting Landscape Architect" to better reflect their respective responsibilities. They informed Stebbins that separate appointments would be necessary as they were no longer business partners. A week earlier, they had signed the following agreement:

> It is hereby mutually agreed between Fredk. Law Olmsted and Calvert
> Vaux that the partnership heretofore existing under the name of Olm-

sted and Vaux Landscape Architects (which has for some months been inoperative in reference to Central Park) shall now close so far as new work is concerned, and that all outstanding engagements on joint account shall be as soon as practicable be adjusted to this date.

Olmsted had overcome whatever qualms he had had about striking out on his own. I can't help but see Mary's hand in this. She could be fully as impulsive as Frederick, and she would have pressed for a decision. She had never warmed to Vaux. She would have encouraged her husband to make a break. Vaux, too, was at a turning point. He had severed his partnership with Withers a few months earlier and now had a new partner: Jacob Wrey Mould. Two important commissions for the New York Park Department had since come their way: the new Museum of Natural History, on Manhattan Square adjacent to Central Park, and across from it the new Art Museum on the east side of the park. When completed, the Museum of Natural History would be the largest building in the United States; the Art Museum (now the Metropolitan Museum of Art) was to be the foremost cultural institution of the city. Building these two civic monuments would make Vaux the leading architect in New York.

It was an amicable break. They agreed to work together again should the opportunity arise; for many years Olmsted kept a photograph of Vaux in his office. But both men wanted to go it alone. The partnership that had begun fourteen years earlier with Greensward was over.

Alone

As THE WORK on Prospect Park wound down and his responsibilities for Central Park increased, Olmsted found living on Staten Island inconvenient; he had already spent the previous winter in Manhattan with friends. Now he also needed an office of his own. He bought a five-story brownstone on the north side of West Forty-sixth Street, and his family moved there in November 1872. His office was a large room on the first floor overlooking the rear garden. The rest of the house was the family quarters. A suite of rooms was set aside for Olmsted's father and stepmother.

Mary and Frederick were still unpacking when a letter came from his half brother Albert. Albert casually mentioned that their father had slipped on an icy walk and broken his hip. Alarmed, Olmsted caught the first train to Hartford. He arrived that evening to find his eighty-one-year-old father in pain from the injury but otherwise in good spirits. In the morning, seeing that the situation was not serious, Olmsted returned to New York. The next day he received a telegram from Albert confirming that their father was doing well. A few hours later a second telegram indicated that he had taken a turn for the worse. Again, Olmsted hurried to Hartford. His father greeted him with a smile: "Why! Who's this? Fred? So you've come back!" But he appeared "dreadfully older than the day before"; according to the doctor, there was no hope. John Olmsted died at one o'clock the next morning, calmly and without struggle, surrounded by his wife, his daughter Mary, and his two sons.

Shortly before his death, John Olmsted had appointed Frederick and Albert trustees and executors of his estate. He willed his house and "a fair provision for its maintenance" to his wife; he divided the balance of his property, which consisted of mortgages, railroad bonds, and manufacturing stocks, equally among the four children. (Olmsted estimated each would get an annual income of fifteen hundred dollars).* Among his father's private papers Olmsted discovered a file of old newspaper clippings going back twenty years, including Yeoman's letters, book reviews, and articles about Olmsted's landscaping work. He was touched by this evidence of paternal pride. "He was a very good man and a kinder father never lived," he wrote Kingsbury.

His father's death signaled the beginning of a difficult year. Olmsted's next trial was at Central Park. Seeking to cut costs, the board called for a reduction in the number of park police, or keepers. To stretch his resources Olmsted devised what he called a "round system." He required keepers to make a tour of the entire park three times a day, and to check in at predetermined locations following a schedule. This meticulous routine was unpopular and produced complaints. The keepers' cause was taken up by the press, and the ensuing public furor obliged Olmsted to write a long, defensive report explaining his actions to the public—and to the board. The board, unconvinced, voted to create a separate division of Police (as well as of Landscape Gardening), severely limiting his authority. Olmsted, who still considered himself superintendent, protested; Stebbins, siding with him, resigned his presidency. The board backed down and withdrew its proposals. Yet it did not stop questioning Olmsted's authority on a variety of matters. At the end of the summer, frustrated, he impetuously asked Salem Wales, the new president, to relieve him of his responsibilities as landscape architect. The board tabled his letter and immediately sent a telegram asking him to stay on. Mollified, he agreed.

The very next day, Jay Cooke & Co., a leading New York bank, failed. During the following week several other large banks would go out of business, and the Stock Exchange closed until the end of the month. The so-called Panic of 1873 produced more than five thousand bankruptcies across the country. Olmsted's position with Central Park was secure, but the panic did affect his practice. Work on South Park in Chicago had been limping along under the independent supervision of Horace Cleveland, who had worked for Olmsted and Vaux on Prospect Park—now it

---

*Mary Ann Olmsted contested the will and accused her son and stepson of dishonesty during the probate hearings. The will was upheld, and relations between Olmsted and his stepmother never healed.

virtually ceased. The Tarrytown Heights Land Company, for whom Olmsted and Vaux had planned a nine-hundred-acre residential subdivision to rival Riverside, declared bankruptcy. The roads and villages that Olmsted had so carefully fitted to the beautiful hilly terrain would never be built; moreover, the company shares that he had taken in lieu of fees were worthless.*

The overwork, the quarrels on the park, and the belated emotional stress of his father's death finally had their effect. The following month Olmsted succumbed to a serious depression; this time he could not read at all. He spent all of four months recovering. It could not have been an easy convalescence—incapacitated in a darkened room and unable to work. All he could think of was his father's death, his breakup with Vaux, his problems on the park, his failed commissions, his future.

When Olmsted was low, he often reached out. When he was finally able, he wrote to friends: Knapp, Brace, and Katharine Wormeley (with whom he had continued to correspond since their days on the hospital ships). His letter to Brace, written a few days before Christmas, is particularly gloomy, reflecting his sorry mood. Olmsted's hero, John Stuart Mill, had died earlier that year; "May my last end be like his," he wrote. He admired Mill's agnosticism; evidently Olmsted's illness had not made a believer of him. In his present state his writing became more tortured than usual. "Suppose a man who sees things so far differently from the mass of ordinary healthy men is thereby classed as of defective vision, as of diseased men," he wrote Brace. "Then I have not a doubt that I was born with a defect of the eye, with a defect of the brain."

He missed his friend Richardson. Richardson had won a prestigious competition to design Trinity Church in Boston, and since most of his work was now in New England, he moved to Brookline, a Boston suburb. He and Olmsted now saw each other only occasionally.

Later that summer of 1874, Olmsted asked Richardson to design a memorial arch for Buffalo's Niagara Square. By then he had recovered his eyesight and returned to work. He continued to work at Central Park. Tying up loose ends, he and Vaux submitted an annual report to the Brooklyn Park Commission. It turned out to be their last—following the financial panic, the city could no longer afford their services. New com-

---

*The Panic of 1873 also brought the Riverside Improvement Company to insolvency; it would be another twenty years before Riverside was complete.

missions came to Olmsted: the grounds of a hotel in Saratoga Springs, the Hartford Institute for the Insane, a cemetery in Syracuse, and the commons in Amherst. He was assisted by Jacob Weidenmann, a Swiss-born architect and landscape gardener who had previously worked for him on Prospect Park. In May 1874 the two men formally agreed to work together on selected projects. "Mr. Olmsted and Mr. Weidenmann can at all times be commanded for any business of their common profession," the public announcement read. Olmsted was back.

The Mall, Central Park

Saturday, May 23, 1874

The double rows of American elms, planted fourteen years earlier, create a green tunnel. Sunlight filters through the canopy of new leaves and throws dappled patterns of light and shade on the gravel walk. It is a beautiful day, the Mall is crowded: ladies in voluminous skirts and colorful hats; Irish nurses in bonnets and white aprons, pushing baby carriages; gentlemen in frock coats and top hats; a few young clerks in stylish broadcloth suits; the children in a variety of dress, miniature versions of their parents. It is a decorous crowd; tomorrow—Sunday—is when working people have a holiday and attendance will be even larger.

At the north end of the Mall, on the west side, is the bandstand. Mould has pulled out all the stops for this design. The raised platform is covered by a Moorish-style cupola, dark blue and covered with gilt stars. It is topped by a sculpture of a lyre. The roof is supported by crimson cast-iron columns. The band-stand is unoccupied—the Saturday-afternoon concerts start next month. The annual summer series is so popular—up to forty-five thousand people attend—that the park board has provided extra seating and has taken the unprece-dented step of allowing listeners to sit on the grass. Not everyone admires these free concerts. "The barriers and hedges of society for the time being are let down," sniffs the Times, "unfortunately also a few of its decencies are forgotten."

The barriers of society are not altogether absent. Across the Mall from the bandstand is a broad concourse where the wealthy park their carriages and, separated from the lower orders by a long wisteria arbor, listen to the music in comfortable isolation. Beside the concourse stands a large one-story building with a swooping tiled roof and deep, overhanging eaves. Originally the Ladies

Refreshment Pavilion, it has recently been converted into a restaurant called the Casino.

Mary and Marion Olmsted come out of the Casino, followed by Frederick carrying little Henry. Charlotte is not with them, she is visiting friends. John is at Yale and Owen is in school with Knapp.

"That was a wonderful lunch, my dear," says Mary Olmsted. "Shall we walk down to the lake?"

The footpath, skirting the concourse and the entrance to the arbor, leads down to a small plaza. They pass the unusual fountain with its rotating arms that spray water into the air and join the throng of people on the Mall. There is little to distinguish the Olmsteds from the other strollers. Mary, fashionably dressed, lace at her throat, her brunette hair covered by a comely bonnet, is carrying a parasol. Twelve-year-old Marion is in a short crinoline skirt, white socks, and buckled shoes. She would like to skip ahead, but she walks obediently beside her mother. Olmsted is wearing a light-colored jacket, a dark vest and matching trousers, and a broad-brimmed hat. His drawn face and the pallor of his skin attest to the previous year's illness. His limp is more apparent as he carries his three-year-old boy.

The main carriage drive of the park runs beside the plaza. As usual, a crowd has gathered here to stare at the prancing horses and the smart carriages, hoping to catch a glimpse of someone rich or famous. The Olmsteds do not pause but descend a broad staircase that leads to an arcade beneath the drive. The vaulted tunnel is covered by glazed Minton tiles that Mould has imported from Staffordshire. The extravagant colors of the tiles and the shapes of the arches are intended to evoke Granada, according to the effervescent Englishman. Olmsted finds it overdone—and why Granada?—but the public seems to like the exotic effect.

They emerge into the bright sunlight, on a large terrace beside the lake. Directly in front of them is the new fountain. It consists of two superimposed basins, the upper basin topped by a bronze statue of an angel, wings outswept, holding a lily.

"Why, Mary, don't you think that Mrs. Stebbins has done a creditable job?" says Olmsted.

He has known the sculptor Emma Stebbins, sister of his colleague Henry Stebbins, for a dozen years. He likes The Angel of Waters, *which refers to the miraculous Biblical Pool of Bethesda in Jerusalem. The double metaphor of the nation healing itself after the war and parkgoers recovering from the stress of city life appeals to him.*

He puts Henry down, takes his hand, and leads him a short distance to one of the stone benches that ring the terrace. Olmsted allows himself a rare cigar and contemplates the scene. They are sitting beneath one of the two flagpoles from which long gonfalon pennants are suspended. The placid surface of the lake stretches out in both directions. The terrace serves as a landing, and a group of people are waiting to board a rented boat, a long craft with a canvas roof. Several smaller rowboats are on the water as well as a graceful black gondola. It is a real one, from Venice, a gift from John Gray, one of the commissioners. Olmsted can see the Ramble across the lake. The foliage that he and Pilat planted is fully grown and hides Vista Rock, now the base of the Belvedere Castle.

The Ramble appears unkempt to his eye. The trees badly pruned, or not pruned at all; unthinned evergreens choking one another. His gardening force is inadequate. It's difficult to convince the board that the park requires constant care, especially now that it has become so popular. The park keepers have recorded more than 10 million visits for each of the last three years. Ten million!

Henry tugs at his father's sleeve. "He wants to feed the swans," says Mary. "Why don't you take him. Marion and I will wait here."

They walk across the terrace. A keeper in a long gray uniform coat recognizes Olmsted and salutes.

"Good afternoon, sir. Fine day. Everything in order."

"More Interesting Than Nature"

Olmsted's status as the preeminent landscape architect in the country was confirmed when he was invited to lay out the grounds of the United States Capitol in Washington, D.C. The invitation came during his prolonged incapacitation. He managed to submit a preliminary report by the following January. A few months later, Congress voted to proceed, appropriated the money, and placed Olmsted in charge.

Between the Capitol and the rising Washington Monument lay Downing's park, unfinished and already severely compromised by the intrusion of the Smithsonian Institution and the tracks of the Washington & Alexandria Railroad. Thus the civic space that should have been the focus of the national capital lacked both coherence and dignity. As was his custom, Olmsted wanted to expand the scope of his work and proposed to develop a comprehensive plan for the entire area. Not wanting to appear forward—but not willing to leave judgments about design to politicians—he called for an oversight committee made up of prominent landscape architects, including his friend Horace Cleveland of Chicago, and William Hammond Hall, who was building Golden Gate Park in San Francisco. Congress was reluctant to undertake the expensive task of replanning the national capital and instructed Olmsted to confine himself to the fifty acres on Capitol Hill.

L'Enfant's original plan showed the Capitol facing west across a square toward the Potomac. The final plan for Washington, drawn by his successor, Andrew Ellicott, moved the building closer to the brow of the hill and located the square on the other side. The result was an architectural contradiction: the building faced the square, which was the formal entrance and the site of important public ceremonies such as presidential inaugurations, but it turned its back on the Washington Monument and the Executive Mansion. Olmsted proposed to restore L'Enfant's concept, so that "what has been considered [the Capitol's] rear will be recognized as its more dignified and stately front." He did this by adding a monumental terrace and broad steps descending the west flank of Capitol Hill. On the east side of the building he laid out a drive lined by tulip trees, a pair of fountains, and a large open plaza in front of the building. These improvements were designed in the neoclassical spirit of Latrobe and Bulfinch's Capitol. Only farther from the building did Olmsted resort to a more naturalistic landscaping of turf and clumps of trees, arranged to create selected vistas of the immense dome. The work proceeded slowly. Olmsted refused to be hurried and spent time—and money—on preliminaries such as soil preparation and drainage. The two-hundred-thousand-dollar budget proved insufficient, and it was a decade before Congress appropriated funds for the terrace.* This project would involve him for years to come.

New York was the foremost city on the North American continent, famous for its size—1 million people—its wealth, its grand buildings, its elevated trains, and, of course, its Central Park. So, when Montreal, the largest city in Canada, decided to build a public park, it turned to Olmsted. He was, at first, reluctant. He was occupied with Capitol Hill, the Central Park administration, and several smaller landscaping projects. "I was not eager to take it," he later recalled.

Montreal was small by American standards—only 120,000 people— but attractively sited on an island in the St. Lawrence River. The most striking natural feature of the city was Mount Royal, a 735-foot-high mass of traprock, about a mile long and half a mile wide, that rose in the middle of the island. Montreal and its suburbs stretched between the river and the rocky escarpment of the mountain; no buildings were on Mount Royal itself, which was divided into several large estates. The city had spent more than a million dollars to acquire these parcels, until it owned almost the entire mountain—430 acres. This was where Olmsted was to lay out a park. The site was another reason for his reluctance: "diffidence in my ability to do justice to so unusual a problem."

Nevertheless, he agreed to go to Montreal. As he expected, the hilly site was hardly ideal for a park. Yet the rugged slopes were picturesque,

---

*Olmsted's architectural assistant on the Capitol was Thomas Wisedell, a young British architect whom Vaux had recruited to work on Prospect Park.

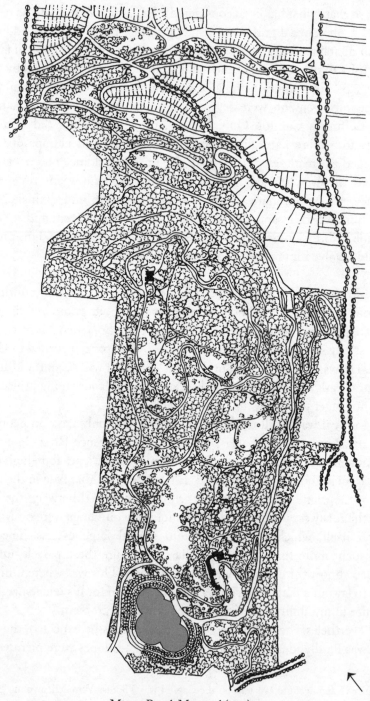

Mount Royal, Montreal (1877).

and the views were extraordinary. From the heights of the mountain one could see the entire city with its dozens of church spires, the great river, several curiously shaped hills that punctuated the flat St. Lawrence lowland, and far away, the ranges of the Green Mountains and the Adirondacks. He was intrigued. "I would observe that the distant prospects in all directions, offer such controlling attractions that some of them, being commanded from nearly all parts of the ground, the immediate local landscape conditions are of much less consequence than they usually are in pleasure grounds, and that it is not undesirable that they should be subdued in character," he wrote the commissioners on his return to New York. He accepted the job.

His design was straightforward. "It would be wasteful to try to make anything else than a mountain of it," he advised the commissioners. What impressed Olmsted was the diversity of the mountain site. He divided it according to topography, vegetation, and soil into eight distinct areas, to which he gave his customarily evocative names. The Piedmont and the Côte Placide were gently sloping ground at the eastern base of the mountain; the Underfell was a treed area located immediately below the Crags, a dramatic cliff; Cragsfoot was steep and heavily wooded; Upperfell, near the mountaintop, and Brackenfell, lower down, had rocky outcroppings and clumps of trees, the Brackenfell being distinguished by its richer soil and cover of ferns; the Glades was an attractive meadowlike area adjacent to the Upperfell.

Mount Royal was Olmsted's first major urban park since his break with Vaux. It represents a departure from Prospect Park. Instead of using "the three grand elements of pastoral landscape" (meadows, forest, water) and manufacturing scenic effects, he based his design on the site's intrinsic scenic characteristics. Having identified these qualities, he set out to either heighten their advantages or mask their shortcomings. He treated the undramatic Côte Placide as "a little park district" and laid out a residential neighborhood of 270 residential lots. His idea was to sell lots to help pay for the park. He planted vines and low shrubs in the Crags to make the cliff appear higher. He thinned out trees in the poor soil of the Upperfell and thickened the forest of the Brackenfell. He did little in the Glades, which already resembled a mountain meadow. Olmsted paid great attention to the carriage drives. They should be integrated into the slope to create the minimum disturbance and should be gently—but not uniformly—graded, "so that a good horse, with a fair load, can be kept moving at a trot without urging in going up hill, and without holding back in going down."

"Regard the work to be done in your behalf on the mountain as primarily a work of art," Olmsted urged the commissioners. The landscaping of Mount Royal required no less artifice than Prospect Park, but it was artifice of a different order, simpler in its effects, more naturalistic in its means. Here, for example, are his detailed instructions for landscaping the freshly excavated edges of the drives:

> You can shape the banks at once in such desirable forms as frost, and rain, and root growths might chance to give them after many years. You can do more. You can, by a little forecast, make them at one point bolder and more picturesque in contour by a fitting buttress of rock than nature, working alone, would be able to do. By inserting little pockets of leaf-mould about this rock, and proper seeds or plants, you can then prevail upon nature to dress it with characteristic mountain forms of foliage and bloom, more interesting than nature would, in a century, otherwise provide. You can put in the way of immediate growth behind this rock a broad dark mass of low mountain pine, or pensive, feathery and brooding hemlock, educated to a character which nature, left alone, gives to one of its species in a thousand, to supply the degree of canopy and shadow which will be the most effective for your purpose. And, this being done, you are finally relieved of the nuisance and expense which the natural washing down of your abrupt bank would have otherwise entailed.

The work did not go smoothly. The park commissioners were ordinary city councilors with no particular qualifications for overseeing the construction of a park. "They address the other members of the Council with no authority of their own in the matter," he complained. They were tardy in providing him with a topographic survey, then rushed ahead to build a drive to the mountaintop, even before his own plan was complete. Eighteen months after commencing, Olmsted had to alter his design for a small lake in the Glades to accommodate a twenty-acre reservoir demanded by the City Council. He was further delayed by inaccurate information about the park's boundaries. Nevertheless, he presented the finished plan in October 1877. He titled the drawing simply "Mount Royal," for "the term park, as applied to the mountain, should be discarded, and its older, more dignified, and wholesomely suggestive appellation preserved and emphasized."

Olmsted wrote his final report in 1881. It would be another eight years before Mount Royal was finished. John Nolen, who would become one of the most accomplished town planners in the United States, wrote about the park in 1906. He called it "one of the most successful designs in the history of landscape architecture. And why? Because the conditions were understood and appreciated and made the basis of the improvements, and these improvements are but the application of a new and original manner of old art principles. The result is a public park that is convenient and beautiful, and that becomes more and more satisfying each year." Nolen saw Mount Royal in its prime. Despite Olmsted's exhortations, subsequent generations of city officials did not treat his work as art. The residential area on the Côte Placide was never realized. A belvedere and a chalet were built, but not where specified on the plan, and not according to Wisedell's rustic designs. The top of the mountain, which was to have had a lookout tower, was overwhelmed by an eighty-three-foot-high illuminated cross. The reservoir that Olmsted had unwillingly integrated into the plan was never built; however, in the 1930s a kidney-shaped, masonry-edged pond was added to the Glades. Beside it stands a modernistic pavilion, the Canadian counterpart to the hideous Wollman Rink in Prospect Park.

And yet. When I lived in Montreal, I would often walk up the long carriage road of Mount Royal—now closed to all vehicles except the occasional horse-drawn calèche—through the dark-forested Underfell and beneath the imposing Crags. I didn't know the names and I didn't give the scenery much thought—I was usually deep in conversation or, if alone, lost in reverie. The mountain was a popular retreat. During the summer the faculty and staff of the school of architecture where I taught gathered in the Glades for an annual picnic. In the winter the snow muffled all sound and it was easy to imagine myself in the Rockies. I would never have described Mount Royal as a "prophylactic and therapeutic agent of vital value"; it was just a place to go when I was feeling particularly happy or sad or solitary or sociable. The Mountain was a part of Montreal—and apart; natural and magical; healthful and healing.

Olmsted in Demand

OLMSTED AUGMENTED his annual salary of six thousand dollars from the New York Department of Public Parks by private consulting fees—five thousand dollars for Mount Royal, fifteen hundred for the U.S. Capitol, and income from smaller commissions. He landscaped the Schuylkill Arsenal in Philadelphia, and an army depot in Jeffersonville, Indiana; he prepared master plans for Trinity College in Hartford and Johns Hopkins University in Baltimore; he laid out the grounds of the McLean Asylum outside Boston. Weidenmann was a partner in some of these projects, and Olmsted occasionally called on Radford for engineering advice and on Wisedell for architectural support. He also had a new assistant, John Charles Olmsted. John joined him in June 1875 after graduating from college. He had intended to be a doctor like his father and had studied at Yale's Sheffield Scientific School. Of his own volition he changed his mind and decided to become a landscape architect. Olmsted arranged for him to spend two summers working as a surveyor in Utah and Nevada. Owen, who was accepted at the Columbia School of Mines, also had a summer job as a surveyor—in Maine. Little Henry was only five; it was too early to know where his talents lay.

In the summer of 1875, Olmsted convinced Richardson, who had never taken a vacation in his life, to join him on a "Cook's Tour" of upstate New York, Quebec, and New England. The two men with their wives traveled to Buffalo, whose park system was almost complete, and saw Niagara Falls. The next stop was Montreal and Mount Royal. From there the party traveled to Quebec City and visited Montmorency Falls. They returned home through the White Mountains. Richardson later referred to the trip as his "wedding journey," and he enjoyed himself like a "school-boy," according to Olmsted. The two friends took turns playing tour guide to Mary and Julia, Olmsted pointing out sites of scenic beauty and Richardson describing buildings of architectural interest.

During the trip, Olmsted and Richardson discussed their current preoccupation: the New York State Capitol in Albany. This building, designed by Thomas Fuller, the British architect of the recently completed Parliament Buildings in Ottawa, had been under construction for six years. Things had not gone well. The $4 million budget was depleted and the walls had barely reached the second floor. An alarmed state legislature had formed an investigatory commission chaired by William Dorsheimer, who had recently been elected lieutenant governor. When the Commission decided it needed outside architectural advice, Richardson's name naturally came up. So did that of Leopold Eidlitz, a well-known New York architect. The third member of the architectural advisory board was Olmsted. Dorsheimer valued his judgment, as did Richardson and Eidlitz. "Mr. Olmsted . . . was associated in this Board upon equal terms with the two architects," explained Mariana Van Rensselaer, "because of his practical familiarity with their art and his long experience with large public undertakings."

The three men were charged with examining the design as well as the construction of the Capitol. They found that while the foundations and basement were structurally sound, the building had defects. They argued that the style of the unfinished exterior—Italian Renaissance—was ostentatious and costly; they proposed that the building be finished in the simpler Romanesque style. Since the report included architectural drawings, the proposed changes obviously undermined Fuller. This produced a public outcry as many architects attacked the board for its lack of propriety in criticizing a fellow professional. The legislature dithered, but in the end Dorsheimer prevailed. The hapless Fuller was dismissed and the contract was awarded to the architectural advisory board. The experienced Eidlitz was the senior partner and designed the Assembly chamber and the central tower; Richardson was responsible for the Senate, the Court of Appeals, and the library; they collaborated on the exterior. Olmsted dealt with the terraces and the landscaping.*

*   *   *

---

*That year, Richardson christened his sixth child Frederick Leopold William as a tribute to his partners and his supportive patron.

On January 1, 1874, New York annexed approximately twenty square miles from southern Westchester County. The question of how this largely rural area, called the Twenty-third and Twenty-fourth Wards (approximately half of what is now the Bronx), should be developed was put into the hands of the Department of Public Parks. Olmsted was called on to prepare a master plan. He worked with John James Robertson Croes, an engineer employed by the department. Olmsted saw this first major expansion of the city as an opportunity to rethink the Commissioners' Plan of 1811, as he and Vaux had already tried to do in their plan for Washington Heights. In his opinion, the Manhattan grid had several drawbacks. The standardized two-hundred-foot-deep blocks constrained the size of buildings. "If a proposed cathedral, military depot, great manufacturing enterprise, house of religious seclusion or seat of learning needs a space of ground more than sixty-six yards in extent from north to south, the system forbids that it is built in New York." Since all the building lots could not be less than one hundred feet deep, smaller, cheaper lots were precluded. Nor were the deep lots particularly efficient. "There are many houses not much wider than the hovels of other cities, which yet have sixty or seventy feet of depth, and fifty to sixty feet of height." Lastly, the rectilinear grid could not be adjusted to changes in topography.

> Even on a flat alluvial site, like that of Chicago, it is essentially wasteful and extravagant. In proportion as a site is rugged and rocky it is only more decidedly so; not simply because in this case it involves greater unnecessary cost, but because variety of surface offers variety of opportunity, and such an undertaking often deliberately throws away forever what might otherwise be distinctive properties of great value.

The new master plan divided the annexed area into four parts. The village of Morrisania, which had already started to adopt the Manhattan grid, was the commercial center of the new district. Farther north, in an area called West Farms, Olmsted and Croes laid out moderately dense residential neighborhoods. The area west of the Riverdale Road, a rugged promontory overlooking the Hudson, was to be an exclusive residential suburb. "What is meant by treating the district as a suburb," Olmsted explained, "is, that the development of a distinctly suburban and picturesque character should everywhere be kept frankly in view as a source of wealth, and that the roads should be adapted to a population living less densely, and with which pleasure driving and walking are to be, relatively to heavy teaming, more important than in the streets of the compact city." The agricultural northern part of the Twenty-fourth Ward was to be a relatively low-density suburb similar to Tarrytown Heights.

Croes designed a railway system linking the new wards to the city, and circling the entire area. This was an important ingredient of their plan. The rail lines were carefully planned to take advantage of the topography and to avoid grade crossings; tracks were either depressed below street level or carried above on bridges. Planning rail lines and streets simultaneously was unusual in the nineteenth century; tracks were typically laid long after the streets were built, requiring expensive expropriation and causing disruption of the city fabric and traffic. "A judicious laying out of the annexed territory requires a certain effort of forecast as to what the city is to be in the future," Olmsted wrote in the preliminary report. "In this respect, there is a great danger in attempting too much as in attempting too little." What is striking about the Bronx plan is how circumspect it is. There are no grand parkways or ronds-points. At first glance, it appears almost conventional.

Olmsted had learned to be cautious. In 1873, shortly after his breakup with Vaux, the Northern Pacific Railway had asked him to plan the new city of Tacoma, its western terminus in the Washington Territory. With the assistance of Radford, he produced a plan artfully adapted to the hilly site. The avenues curved sinuously across the slopes; the perpendicular narrower streets ran uphill. All the lots were served by lanes. The main street terminated in a park overlooking Puget Sound. It was an elegant solution. Yet the client was aghast. A contemporary observer summed up the reaction: "The most fantastic plat of a town that was ever seen. There wasn't a straight line, a right angle or a corner lot. The blocks were shaped like melons, pears, and sweet potatoes. One block, shaped like a banana. . . . It was a pretty fair park plan but condemned itself for a town." Actually, almost all the individual building plots were conventionally rectangular, and the curved and doglegged streets would have reduced construction costs. Yet the railroad directors would have none of it. They found themselves a surveyor who laid out a simple grid.

In the Bronx plan, Olmsted avoided anything that would scare his client. Yet his simplicity was deceptive. The subtle adjustments to the current policy of continuing the Manhattan grid produced a very different urbanism. The new parts of Morrisania had long blocks oriented

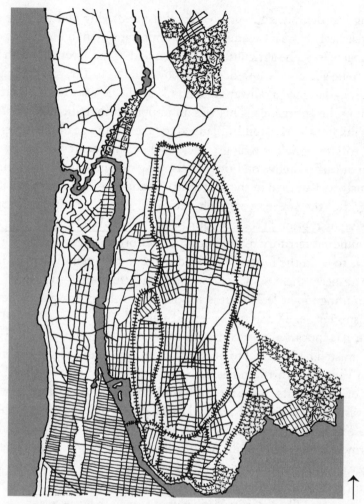

Twenty-third and Twenty-fourth Wards, New York (1877).

north-south instead of east-west, so that all houses got some sun. West Farms consisted of a patchwork of grids whose slightly shifting orientation created variety, the same kind of variety that makes such cities as New Orleans and San Francisco interesting. The picturesque suburban layouts were derived from earlier projects, but what makes the Bronx plan unusual is that Olmsted showed how areas of low, medium, and high density could be combined into a seamless whole that would be "the plan of a Metropolis; adapted to serve, and serve well, every legitimate interest of the wide world; not of ordinary commerce only, but of humanity, religion, art, science, and scholarship."

The adjustment of streets to terrain and the integration of rail lines and streets would save money in the long run, but would require large, immediate investments. This proved a stumbling block. Andrew Green, the city comptroller, had inherited a depleted treasury from the Tweed era. He would not approve spending money on surveying and buying rights-of-way in the new wards when downtown Manhattan, where the majority of New Yorkers lived, urgently needed public investments. Even Henry Stebbins, who generally supported Olmsted, balked. More than a year's work had come to naught.

It is hard to fault Green's logic. He simply did not have the money. But even had the money been available, the farsighted plan may still not have been approved. Most New Yorkers accepted the standardized grid of their city. It may not have been beautiful but it was expedient. There was no need, Stebbins pointed out, for anything more "fanciful."

"I Shall Be Free From It on the 1st of January"

IN 1874 WILLIAM H. WICKHAM, a Democrat with Tammany connections, became mayor of New York. The *New-York Times* observed: "The Park is still a prize which Tammany—'reconstructed' Tammany—yearns to get into its possession. It will always be the coveted booty of the Democrat organization, and we are sometimes inclined to think that the success of the designs upon it is only a question of time." Wickham's first move was to get rid of Andrew Green, the upright and incorruptible comptroller, known—not altogether affectionately—as Handy Andy. When Green's term was up, Wickham appointed John Kelly, another Tammany man. The following year the composition of the four-man Central Park board also changed drastically: three of the four Democrats were now Tammany supporters. Olmsted soon felt the effect, as he later recounted in a memoir:

> There were symptoms such as this: that, while observing great cere-
> mony of politeness with me, there were three of [the commissioners]
> whom I was never able to get to meet me on the Park (nor on any
> park). . . . Twice an appointment was actually made; and each time the
> commissioner failed to keep it, afterwards courteously apologizing. . . . I
> myself received from without the board several warnings, both direct and
> indirect. . . . Threats were made in such a manner as to leave me in no
> doubt that it was intended to guard against a public accountability for
> them. . . . I knew that my movements were being furtively dogged, and I
> presumed that they were so with a view to obtaining pretexts upon
> which to urge my removal.

This unpleasantness caused Olmsted to consider a leave of absence. He thought of going to Europe. He wasn't really running away; he was returning to his professional roots, as he had done before. He had another reason. In early September 1877 he had sent John, now twenty-five, to spend several months in England and France. The trip was to be part of his apprenticeship. To that end Olmsted had given him six pages of instructions, "to be read over and committed substantively to memory while at sea, re-read in London and again in Paris." John was to examine parks and public grounds, zoological gardens, park structures, and architecture in general. Olmsted expected "full notes and . . . careful & specific reports" about the parks. "This is not discretionary," he added firmly. He was explicit about what he wanted John to look at: how older parks such as Birkenhead and Hyde Park had aged; what replanting was being carried out; what measures were taken to facilitate nighttime use; did older park structures look picturesque, or merely "forlorn and shabby?" John was to keep his eye out for "any substitute for the common French edging of iron," and for a fifteen-foot-diameter fountain for one of the Buffalo parks. Olmsted listed useful contacts: in Liverpool, Alfred Field (his neighbor in Staten Island who had moved back to England); in London, Sir William Hooker, the superintendent of Kew Gardens, and William Robinson, an author and landscape gardener; in Paris, Frédéric-Auguste Bartholdi, and the American sculptor Augustus Saint-Gaudens, who was honeymooning in France. John was also to call on Olmsted's friend Edouard André, a talented young landscape architect who had been the assistant of the great Alphand, builder of the Bois de Boulogne. When André had been in New York, Olmsted had shown him around Central Park and Prospect Park. Now he would return the favor.

Olmsted soon realized that he may have overdone the planning. "I know that it is feasible to do it all but I think perhaps you will be obliged to work too hard," he wrote shortly after John's departure. He advised him to watch his health and ease up if he felt fatigued. When he arrived, John dutifully reported his activities, writing long letters every two or three days. Olmsted reciprocated. "[Your letters] are in all respects admirable and give us great pleasure," he wrote. He informed John of his increasingly precarious situation on Central Park and his plan to take a leave. He also encouraged John to study hard since he would probably be obliged to earn a living on his return.

Except for a hurried visit to Paris and the English countryside, John spent most of the first two months in London, much of it in the South Kensington Museum, reading books on architecture. He stopped touring parks and reporting on landscape matters. He wrote dreamily of his plans to study architecture. On December 1 Olmsted wrote a seventeen-page letter scolding John for "drifting with the currents of personal ease and habit." He admonished him to devote more time to direct observation. "There are hundreds of structures which you have seen in a month which incontestably contain more worthy results of human study and labor and are higher monuments of art, each of them, than is to be found in all the churches on this continent or than all the architects and schools of architecture can in all your lifetime place before you." Olmsted insisted that landscape architecture offered the greatest chance for John's future. His reasoning was pragmatic: "The chances of the good will of my business, when I am dead or superannuated, to any one capable of making it amicable, are equivalent in value to a moderate fortune . . . worth more than all else I can leave my family."

Olmsted was unsparing in his assessment of John's talent. "You are not a man of genius in art. A man of less artistic impulse I never knew," he wrote. "You have no care to produce anything—to carry to perfect realization any conception. Consequently as you have insisted on making yourself an artist, you must spend great labor, years of study with little satisfaction of any worthy ambition. Of all this I thoroughly warned you." This was needlessly harsh. Olmsted's problems with the board had made him irritable; now John bore the brunt of this discontent. Still, Olmsted's anxiety was real enough, even if his prescription was bad-tempered. He was afraid that his shy, introverted stepson would drift from one occupation to another, much as he himself had done. Moreover, he was counting on John's help in his landscaping business. He was writing as a concerned father, but also as a demanding teacher. Olmsted took the long view, and he did not allow himself—or John—to have any illusions. "Don't be so cowardly as not to face your necessities with good will, or so silly as to make believe that you are what you would simply like to be," he counseled. Despite the criticisms, Olmsted continued to supply John with an abundance of money, and he made it clear that the final decision would be John's own.

Two weeks later Olmsted returned from a business trip to find several long letters from John, more than eighty pages of detailed reporting on his activities in London. They showed that Olmsted's outburst had been hasty. "It is evident that there was little occasion for the long letter which I wrote on the text of certain expressions of despondency and evidencies of fatigue & temporary embarrassment," he wrote sheepishly. It is a measure of John's docile nature—and of his closeness to his stepfather—that they patched it up. "I agree to what you say as to my capacity and artistic impulses," John wrote, but added "that I shall never produce artistic work ... I am not so sure of and that remains to be proved."* The rest of their voluminous correspondence—more than fifty letters exchanged during four months—continued a candid discussion of the best way for John to acquire "art wisdom."

At one point John even suggested that he might return to New York and become Olmsted's surrogate at the Park Department, "with the understanding that I was to be directed by you unofficially." The suggestion was only half-serious; "I am, on the whole, inclined to think that you will not be compelled to leave," he wrote. Olmsted was not so sure. He continued to make plans for his European trip, strengthened now in the conviction that his presence would help John acquire the firsthand knowledge that was so essential to his further education.

In December Olmsted received an anonymous letter containing a newspaper clipping with a marked passage stating that "disgraceful charges" were pending against him. These became public soon enough. Comptroller Kelly announced that he was suspending Olmsted's salary, for the reasons that "Mr. F. L. Olmsted, Landscape Architect ... renders little or no service in that capacity; that his duties outside the City of New York render his absence necessary and frequent, that he had been absent from his duties for twenty-six days during the month of October, and that the parks are in that state of completion that the services of an architect can be dispensed with." The threat contained in the last statement was unmistakable.

Olmsted felt this public humiliation keenly. "It will not be thought surprising that I should have had sleepless nights, or that at last I could not keep myself from over-wearing irritation and worry," Olmsted later recalled of this stormy time. "The resulting depression, acting with an extraordinary prostration from the great heat of the summer, and the recurrence of an old malarial trouble, brought me, late in the season, to a condition comparable to that often produced by a sun-stroke, perhaps of the same nature." His doctor advised a vacation. On December 15 Olm-

---

*In fact John had taken drawing courses while in college and was an accomplished draftsman.

sted wrote John about his impending dismissal and reiterated his plan to
come to Europe. He thought he needed a rest first: "I shall go at once to
some quiet place, perhaps on the Devonshire coast, with pleasant short
walks and interesting scenery & take lodgings for a month." The next
day he changed his mind and wrote that he thought it likely that "after 10
days at sea with tolerable weather I shall have gained enough to be able at
once to begin active diversion." By Christmas he was sure his days with
the Parks Department were numbered. "I shall be free from it on the 1st
of January," he wrote. He looked forward to making an extended European tour with John. He originally thought of visiting only England,
France, and Germany, but the ambitious itinerary he sketched out to
John also included Belgium, Holland, Switzerland, Austria, and Italy.
"Think it well out and be prepared to see what is most valuable to be seen
by us in the route," he instructed John, and added the practical advice:
"You will want a small steel tape (10, 20 or 30 ft.) & a pocket rule in feet
and inches, a good traveling lantern & candles & compact sketching
materials. Your luggage must be light and handy. Examine guide books
with care & buy discreetly if there is occasion."

The day after Christmas, Olmsted officially requested an unpaid
three-month leave of absence. He did not expect a favorable response,
but the leave was immediately granted. He was to sail for England on
January 9, 1878. On January 5 the board passed the following resolution:

> *It is therefore Resolved,* That the Bureau of Design and Superintendence
> [Olmsted's department] . . . is hereby discontinued, and the offices con-
> nected therewith are abolished; and it is further
> *Resolved,* That the Hon. F. Law Olmsted . . . is hereby appointed
> "Consulting Landscape Architect" to the Commission, his services to
> be paid for out of the appropriate fund from time to time, as they are
> availed of.

It was cleverly done. Olmsted was not exactly fired, nor could the
board be accused of acting behind his back. The commissioners offered
to meet him on the following Wednesday, the very day he was scheduled
to sail. They correctly guessed that he would not postpone his trip.
Before embarking, Olmsted wrote them a letter asking that the decision
concerning his position on the park be deferred until his return, and that
his longtime assistant in the Bureau, Howard Martin, be put in charge
during his absence. He must have known that the requests would be

denied. Norton wished him Godspeed: "I am glad you are going abroad, for I believe, as well as hope, that a vacation in Europe will do you good."

Olmsted landed in Liverpool, revisited Birkenhead Park, and met John in London. From there they set out on their journey, more or less adhering to Olmsted's original itinerary. They went to Antwerp, Brussels, The Hague and Amsterdam, spending one or two days in each city, only long enough to visit the public park, zoo, or botanical gardens that Olmsted had deemed worthy of study. From Frankfurt, John wrote his mother, "He seems to have enjoyed what he has seen very much and so far as his conversation shows has not been worrying about things in New York." They continued to Munich, Venice, Florence, Pisa, and Como, and skipping Switzerland, arrived in Paris in mid-March.

They spent several days in Paris before returning to London. Edouard André accompanied them about the city parks, introduced them to his friends, and took them to the opera. He was finishing an encyclopedic tome on landscape gardening, *L'Art des Jardins*. André greatly admired American parks and included a plan of Central Park as well as drawings of the Brooklyn parkways and the lake at Prospect Park. In an introductory section on public parks, he singled out Olmsted.

> If ever an artist had the good fortune to design a future city and was given carte blanche, I would suggest that he study the very beautiful plans for the city of Buffalo (United States) designed by the skillful American landscape architect, Monsieur F. Law Olmsted. In his plan, different parts of the city are linked by an uninterrupted system of parks and landscaped avenues that are laid out in the grandest and most practical fashion.

Olmsted enjoyed seeing old friends, but the trip had not greatly improved his health. His depression continued. A portrait photograph taken in Paris shows a worn fifty-five-year-old, face expressionless, eyes puffy from lack of sleep. He continued to feel exhausted and even complained to John that "the disease, whatever it is, has certainly been making steady progress and I have sunk rapidly within the last few days." French doctors examined him. They found that he had a slight heart condition, some symptoms from his old bout with malaria, and a "slightly disordered" nervous condition. Not surprisingly, the state of his mental health eluded them. They found "no pronounced disease of any of the organs or tissues of his body . . . [and] expressed no alarm whatsoever at his condition," John, who was understandably perplexed at his father's condition, wrote his mother. "He has formed no idea what he will do in returning or whether he will be able to work at all," John added. "He seems almost to have convinced himself that he is permanently broken down."

It was another month before they sailed back to New York. They were home by the end of April; Olmsted had been away four months, not three. In his absence, his friends had rallied support. A letter protesting his removal appeared in the *New York World*. It had fifty signatories, including businessmen, publishers, politicians, writers, and artists. Missing was Calvert Vaux. He was miffed because the *New York Tribune* had published a long letter from Godkin referring to Olmsted as the sole designer of Central Park. Vaux sent a strongly worded letter of protest to the newspaper. Mary had Owen publish an acknowledgment of Vaux's "equal share" in Central Park. Privately, she fumed at Vaux's "chivying English disposition." Finally Vaux published a letter supporting Olmsted. "Father thinks Mr. Vaux's letter very handsome," John wrote to his mother, "though it seems to me he gave *you* a very unnecessary amount of worry by doing so." Not that any of this mattered. In the end the protests had no effect. Olmsted's tenure at Central Park was finally over.

STANDING FIRST

H. H. Richardson, c. 1884.

Frederick Law Olmsted, c. 1890.

Charles Eliot Norton, undated.

Of all American artists, Frederick Law Olmsted, who gave the design for the laying out of the grounds of the World's fair, stands first in the production of great works which answer the needs and give expression to the life of our immense and miscellaneous democracy.

—CHARLES ELIOT NORTON (1893)

An Arduous Convalescence

FOR THE FIRST TIME in a dozen years, Olmsted was entirely cut loose from the responsibilities and political intrigues attached to Central Park. Yet he was not in a position to enjoy his freedom. His previous bouts of depression—during his early tenure at Central Park, waiting alone in San Francisco, and following the death of his father—had been followed by progressively longer periods of recovery. Such was the case now. Leaving the office in John's hands, he and Mary passed the next two summers in Cambridge, Massachusetts, with Fanny and Edwin Godkin. Olmsted was not entirely idle, however. While there, he collaborated with Richardson on several small projects. He also worked with Charles Sprague Sargent, a self-taught horticulturist who was Asa Gray's successor as director of Harvard's Botanical Garden and had asked Olmsted to help him plan the university's Arnold Arboretum. In Cambridge, Olmsted often met Charles Eliot Norton, who was now professor of art history at Harvard. Olmsted and the New York State Survey's director, James T. Gardener, had earlier written a report recommending the creation of a scenic reservation around Niagara Falls. When the state legislature hesitated, Olmsted, Norton, and Gardener together organized a petition. Thanks to Norton's wide circle of literary friends, the signatories included Emerson, Longfellow, Francis Parkman, and Oliver Wendell Holmes, as well as John Ruskin and Olmsted's boyhood hero, Carlyle.

It sounds like an arduous way to convalesce, yet according to his own demanding standards, Olmsted was merely puttering about. In June 1879 he wrote to André: "I am doing but little professionally, my most important active work being the Capitol Grounds in Washington." That was not quite accurate. While he was still with Central Park, he had been contacted by Charles Dalton, of the newly formed Boston Park Commission. Dalton, a Boston businessman, was another Sanitary Commission alumni.

He invited Olmsted to Boston and solicited advice informally. The Commission's final report—written by Dalton—recommended several parks connected by parkways. Olmsted's influence was unmistakable, and he expected to prepare the final plans. Yet on returning from his European trip with John, he was disappointed to find that the commissioners had held a park design competition in his absence. To add insult to injury, he was being invited to be one of the judges. He declined. He referred to the Central Park competition, which had produced so much bad feeling. He also expressed his doubts about the value of a competition for something as subtle as laying out a park. Yet he shrewdly left the door open:

> No aid I could give in the selection of a plan to receive your premium would materially lessen either class of objections to the competition, which I have indicated. Advising your choice I should place myself in a leaky boat with you. Keeping out of it I retain a professional position in which it is possible I may yet be of service to you.

The twenty-three entrants included Robert Morris Copeland, who had participated in the Central Park competition. He fared no better this time; the five-hundred-dollar prize was awarded to an amateurish design by a local florist. As Olmsted had foreseen, the embarrassed commissioners asked him to step in. He sketched out his ideas and was offered a long-term contract: two thousand dollars a year for three years to design and oversee the construction of the park. Olmsted, leery after the debacle of the competition and still smarting from Central Park, was careful to spell out that he would be working as a private consultant, not as a city employee.

The park site was one hundred acres adjacent to Back Bay, a fashionable residential neighborhood built on land recently reclaimed from the Charles River Basin. This low-lying area received the sewage outflow of Muddy River and Stony Brook and flooded at high tide; it became a fetid, muddy flat as the water receded. The problem, Olmsted quickly realized, was not how to design a park: "The central purpose of this work is simply that of a basin for holding water, as an adjunct of the general drainage system of the city." In collaboration with the city engineer he devised a plan that diverted the sewage into underground conduits and solved the tidal problem by creating an artificial salt-grass marsh, traversed by a winding stream. This was not scenic design. "The object of this crookedness," he explained, "is to prevent the surface of the water from being raked by the wind for any considerable distance and consequently to prevent a swell from forming." The stream banks were further protected against erosion by being gently sloped; three water-gates controlled the tidal flow from the Charles and the outflow of the two creeks.

Drives were laid out at the edges of what Olmsted pointedly called an "improvement." (At his insistence, the so-called park was officially renamed Back Bay Fens.) Smaller roads led to boat landings at the water's edge so the winding stream could be used for recreation. Olmsted recommended that Richardson design the two main bridges. Thus was a work of engineering transformed. It was not intended to be a work of art—which is probably why Olmsted didn't mention it to André—it was to appear as undisturbed nature within the city.

The supportive commissioners and the city council approved the final plan in timely fashion. Construction began soon after. Encouraged by this unaccustomed cooperation, Olmsted turned to the problem of the Muddy River itself, the boundary between Boston and the small town of Brookline. The project took shape as the result of a question he had asked the city engineer.

"What are your plans for dealing with the Muddy River above the Basin?"

"We have none."

"What are you likely to have there eventually—a big conduit of masonry to carry the flood, several miles in length, and intercepting pipes for the sewerage from both sides?"

"That is not unlikely."

"Such arrangement will be very costly and will be delayed many years because of its cost. Meantime and before many years the Muddy River valley will be very dirty, unhealthy, squalid. No one will want to live in the neighborhood of it. Property will have little value and there will grow up near the best residence district of the city an unhealthy and pestilential neighborhood."

"All that is not impossible."

"Why not make an open channel there and treat the banks of it as we are going to treat the banks of the Basin. Would that not be an economical move?"

"I don't see but it would."

"Then the roads leading up that valley to Jamaica Pond would be the beginning of a Park-way leading from the Back Bay to the Arboretum and West Roxbury Park."

"They might be."

"Suppose then that we put our two professional heads together again and see if we can't make a practicable plan for that purpose and get the city to adopt it."

"Agreed."

Olmsted did not work on any more large urban plans after the rejection of Tacoma and the failure of his Bronx proposal. He understood that Americans were simply not willing to make the sort of long-term public investments required by city planning. Pragmatically, he restricted his efforts to what city administrations were willing to do: parks, parkways, and drainage systems. But he did not lose sight of his goal. The Fens and the Muddy River improvement were not conceived as individual projects, they were means to civilize the city.

25 Cottage Street, Brookline, Massachusetts

Friday, February 25, 1881

The Richardson home stands on a wooded, two-acre lot in rural surroundings. The front of the Federal-style farmhouse is rather grand with a two-story-high porch and tall pillars that might recall the plantation architecture of Richardson's Louisiana if the ground were not blanketed with a coat of fresh snow. Attached to the rear of the eighty-year-old house is a recently built, one-story annex. The low, flat-roofed wing houses the architect's office.

It is early morning and the workrooms have not yet filled up with the dozen or so young men who are Richardson's assistants. Olmsted, who is staying with the family for a few days, is alone in the narrow drafting room. Wooden drawing files line the walls; large trestle tables are spread with plans. He walks down an aisle next to a row of alcoves. Each alcove contains a stool and a drawing table. Illumination is provided by a window and a wall-mounted gasolier on an extendible arm. Each alcove can be closed by a curtain hanging from a track on the ceiling. Olmsted likes the practical simplicity of the compact work spaces, which are affectionately known as coops.

He has risen early this morning, but he has slept well and feels refreshed.

After four years he has almost recovered from the illness that afflicted him that last summer he was employed on Central Park. He is still officially the "Consulting Landscape Architect," even if no one ever consults him. Of course, he is better out of it. He deliberately stays away from New York, delegating the office management to John, who has turned out to be a valuable assistant. Avoiding overwork has helped his recovery. It reminds him of the advice he gave to his friend Samuel Bowles, years ago, to beware of his "habit of mental intemperance." Poor Bowles—he died a month before his fifty-second birthday, while Olmsted was in Europe.

He strolls around the room. The unfinished drawings on the drafting tables attest to the variety—and quantity—of his friend's commissions: a city hall, a beautiful library, another town hall, several railway stations. He looks closely at the drawings of a rustic gate lodge for a large estate owned by Frederick Lothrop Ames, whose wealthy family has been Richardson's most generous patron. Ames, Richardson, and Olmsted have spent many hours planning the grounds of the estate. Richardson has sought Olmsted's advice on many of these projects, which is one of the reasons for his presence in Brookline. Another is to meet with Charles Sprague Sargent, whose estate is across the street from Richardson's house. Thanks to the energetic Sargent, who is a Brookline park commissioner, the Muddy River Park was recently approved by Brookline and Boston; work has already begun on the Fens. Now Olmsted and Sargent are discussing ways to convince Harvard to make the arboretum a part of the city's growing park system.

Olmsted finds what he has been looking for. He sits down to examine a drawing pinned to the table. It shows a large country house. The building stands on a base of rubble walls and is entirely covered in wood shingles. The design is unusually plain, devoid of ornament and decoration. The client is Dr. John Bryant, Olmsted's son-in-law, who has recently married Charlotte. Olmsted was concerned for moody Charlotte's future and is pleased with the marriage. He is looking forward to laying out the grounds, which are by the sea in Cohasset, Massachusetts.

"There you are, Olmsted. Good morning," booms a familiar voice.

Richardson is wearing a capacious tweed ulster that emphasizes rather than hides his considerable girth. This is no longer the slender youth whom Olmsted met fifteen years ago; he now weighs close to three hundred pounds. His monumental proportions attest to his prodigious appetite for food and drink. With his dark, wavy hair parted in the middle, a full beard, and his sparkling eyes, he cuts a Falstaffian figure. Olmsted knows that despite his appearance of bonhomie, Richardson is far from healthy. He suffers from a hernia that sometimes incapacitates him for months on end. During these periods he directs his practice from the second-floor bedroom. This morning, however, he is mobile and beams with good humor.

"I see that you're looking at B-B-Bryant's house. It's simple, but I think it has turned out well. We will start building in the spring."

"You're kind to do this for Charlotte and John. I can see that you're busy."

"We are that," Richardson answers contentedly. "Charles Eliot of Harvard College liked Sever Hall so much that he has been talking about a new building for the l-law school." He speaks in fast bursts, but still occasionally stutters. "If we get the job, I may have to bring in more boys to help me. I want to build a large space over here with skylights where we can exhibit drawings and beyond it a private studio for myself." His arm sweeps out, describing his plans. "With a big fireplace-brr, it's cold in here. Why don't we go in the house. My morning walk has given me an appetite. I do believe that cook has made a special b-breakfast in your honor."

Olmsted notices a pool of melted snow at Richardson's feet.

"Don't tell me that you were outside. It must have been hard going with the snowfall we had during the night."

"Not at all. The town has a man who plows the streets. Didn't you hear his team passing by the house this morning?"

"This is a civilized community!" Olmsted exclaims. "Brookline appeals to me—I ought to live here. I've thought about it a lot. The Boston parks are going well and I will be busy with them for years. There's nothing to hold me in New York, and the longer I stay away from the city, the better I feel."

"That's what I k-keep telling you! Do what I did. Move. But not till we've had breakfast."

Fairstead

In the summer of 1881 Olmsted put his New York house up for rent. He, Mary, and the children moved to a leased house in Brookline. Added to the attractions—the civility of the town, friendships, greater professional opportunities, a return to his New England roots—was the escape from New York. The reminders of his personal defeat weighed heavily on him. "You can have no idea what a drag life has been to me for three years or more," he wrote to Brace. "I did not appreciate it myself until I began last summer to get better. The turning point appears to have been our abandonment of New York." Three years!

He did not leave quietly. After settling in Brookline, he wrote a pamphlet telling his side of the Central Park affair. *The Spoils of the Park: With a Few Leaves from the Deep-laden Note-books of a "Wholly Impractical Man"* appeared the following year. The tone was sarcastic rather than bitter. He included many examples of the political patronage, corruption, and sheer ignorance that had marked his tenure in the Department of Public Parks.

> The president once notified me that a friend of his was to come before the Board as spokesman for a "delegation" of citizens, to advocate the introduction of a running-course on the Park.* He would ask me to explain some of the objections to the project, but hoped that I would do so in a way as little likely to provoke the gentleman as possible, as he had great weight in politics, and it would be in his power to much embarrass the Department. I followed these instructions as I best could; but it was impossible for me not to refer to the landscape considerations. At the first mention of the word the gentleman exclaimed, and by no means "aside," "Oh, damn the landscape!" then, rising, he addressed the presi-

*There were constant efforts—resisted by Olmsted and Vaux—to introduce into Central Park a running-course, or speedway, where drivers could race their carriages.

dent to this effect: "We came here, sir, as practical men, to discuss with your Board a simple, practical, common-sense question. We don't know any thing about your landscape, and we don't know what landscape has to do with the matter before us."

Who was this practical blockhead? Olmsted did not name names. Nor did he refer to his feuding with Green or the behind-the-scenes maneuvering of board members and supposed friends. As he explained to Brace, "Consideration of the responsibility of several men of good standing for some of the more atrocious bargains obliged me to steer as delicately as possible." But without scandalous details *The Spoils of the Park* did not cause a stir. Olmsted received congratulatory letters from many of his professional friends—Waring, Eidlitz, Potter, Weidenmann, Cleveland; Norton offered to buy a hundred copies to send to his friends. But the pamphlet did not make much of an impression on the public.

In October 1881 Frederick and Mary received a disturbing telegram from Owen that his health was "very low." Owen was then living in Montana. Clarence King, whom Olmsted had hired as a young man to carry out the first survey of Yosemite, had helped Owen to start a cattle company (with financial assistance from Olmsted). Owen was attracted to the venture not least because, like his father, he was physically frail. He hoped the outdoor life of a rancher would improve his health. It had the opposite effect. John hurried West to fetch his ailing brother, but Owen died in Albany, New York, before reaching home. On top of this calamity, Olmsted fell from his horse and suffered a broken breastbone, which laid him up for several weeks.

It was not an auspicious start to their new life in Brookline. Yet the town agreed with them. Brookline had seven thousand inhabitants. It had maintained its rural character and resisted annexation by Boston, attracting many wealthy and successful families as well as people of more modest means. It was a quintessential nineteenth-century suburb, a true "borderland," lying between town and country. The rolling, wooded hills recalled the leafy Hartford of Olmsted's childhood. "I enjoy this suburban country beyond expression," he wrote Brace, "and in fact, the older I grow, find my capacity for enjoyment increasing. We have had great trials & agitations in the last year but the result on the whole has been with all tranquilizing. I am to turn sixty with two grandsons.*

---

*Charlotte had borne two children since her marriage.

He looked like a grandfather now, for he had grown a full beard that, like his hair, was turning white. When his father had turned sixty, he sold his business and retired. Olmsted was reasonably well-off—he could afford to live in Brookline—but he was not in a position to stop working. In any case, it was not his character. Feeling renewed in health, his spirits lifted, he threw himself back into his profession.

He was hired to plan a new campus for Lawrenceville School, near Princeton, New Jersey. Here was an opportunity to implement an idea that he had first proposed to the trustees of the College of California, almost twenty years earlier. At that time he had envisaged student residences "having the general appearance of large domestic houses, and containing a respectably furnished drawing-room and dining-room for the common use of the students, together with a sufficient number of private rooms to accompany from twenty to forty lodgers." The headmaster of Lawrenceville School, James Cameron Mackenzie, thought along the same lines. The Lawrenceville "student houses" proved so successful that the arrangement has survived to the present. The brick buildings were designed by the accomplished Boston architects Peabody and Stearns, who also built masters' residences, a chapel, and a large stone classroom building in a Richardsonian-inspired Romanesque style. The sturdy brick architecture is handsome, but what impressed me as I walked about the school grounds was the sweet simplicity of the Circle, which forms the green commons of this little school village.

Richardson asked Olmsted to collaborate with him on more projects: the Oakes Ames Memorial Town Hall in North Easton, Massachusetts, with its remarkable Civil War cairn, which Olmsted planted with honeysuckles, wild roses, andromedas, and daphnes; the Quincy library; and no fewer than fourteen stations for the Boston & Albany Railroad. Olmsted did more than landscaping. In the case of the town hall he advised Richardson to build on a rocky outcropping in the center of town. According to Mariana Van Rensselaer, who knew both men, "Mr. Richardson . . . was constantly turning to Mr. Olmsted for advice, even in those cases where it seemed as though it could have little practical bearing upon his design. And where it could have more conspicuous bearing he worked with him as a brother-artist of equal rank and of equal rights with himself." Olmsted's taste for rusticity influenced the architect, who incorporated rough glacial boulders into some of his buildings. This made it hard to know exactly where the building stopped and the landscape

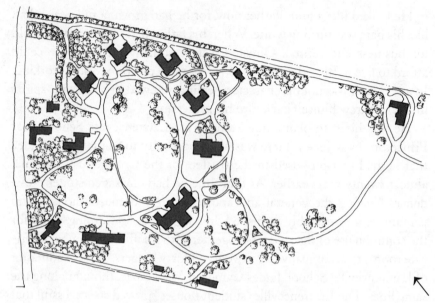

Lawrenceville School, New Jersey (1886).

began, an effect that Olmsted often sought. Richardson's habit, acquired when he was a student at the Beaux-Arts, was to cogitate a design problem before setting pencil to paper; Olmsted was his sounding board.

Olmsted's biggest project during this period was another public park. The city of Detroit wanted to create a park for summer excursions on an island in the Detroit River, Belle Isle. It was an unusual problem—to combine a Lido with a natural recreation area—and Olmsted produced an unusual solution. He placed the ferry dock at one end of the island. Here he concentrated the public establishments: a refectory, boathouses, a lookout tower resembling a lighthouse, playing fields, a racing oval, and exhibition grounds. He called this area the City Fair. The rest of the two-mile-long island was left in as natural a state as possible. A gently sloping beach controlled erosion of the shore. The woods of elm, oak, and hickory were thinned out to create meadows, the largest of which was eighty acres and could function as a parade ground. This minimalism was not simply a question of economy. The simplicity that had emerged in Mount Royal had become an aesthetic goal. To drain the marshy land of the low-lying island, he proposed a system of underground pipes leading into canals, which were emptied out by steam-operated pumps. The canals also served for pleasure boating. The most dramatic structure was a sixteen-hundred-foot-long roofed gallery that curved sinuously between the two boat piers. The two-story gallery was one of the first large buildings that he designed himself, and its flowing, organic shape is more adventurous than anything that even Richardson was doing at the time. Olmsted had definite ideas about architecture in his parks and was confident in his own ability. "In what may be termed the project of a design, I am stronger than most architects," he once boasted, "and I can work effectively & harmoniously to a result having unity of design with an architect, and can persuade & control and induce an architect to work harmoniously with me."

Olmsted was paid seven thousand dollars for Belle Isle, which included a supervision fee for three years. He and Mary must have felt financially secure since they decided to give up their rented house for more permanent quarters. Richardson suggested a building site next to his own house and offered to design a "beautiful thing in shingles." Instead, in the summer of 1883, they bought a seventy-year-old farmhouse nearby. Olmsted established his office in the front parlor, which he extended ten feet to accommodate a large drawing table; the second floor of the extension was a sleeping porch off his bedroom. From his window he could see the continuous green canopy formed by the trees on both sides of the road. On the southwest corner of the building he added a sunroom. The clapboard house was painted dark red with green trim. Olmsted—or more likely Mary, who often suggested the names for his projects—called the house Fairstead, the beautiful place.

Fairstead, a five-minute walk from the Richardsons', was in a neighborhood of rolling hills and twisting country roads. Like many nineteenth-century suburbs, Brookline had started as a summer resort, and it still contained large estates such as Sargent's Holm Lea. Olmsted's property was small, less than two acres. He set about to turn the grounds into a garden. Or, rather, a miniature park, for his approach to gardening was really a smaller version of his larger landscapes—a blend of opportunism and artifice. At the entrance he laid out a carriage turn and planted a Canadian hemlock in the circle. Immediately on the right of the circle was a natural depression dominated by a large outcropping. He built a craggy flight of steps leading down into the hollow and added a fieldstone arch to make a grotto. Rhododendrons, cotoneasters, dogwoods, and a profusion of vines completed the effect of a secret dell.

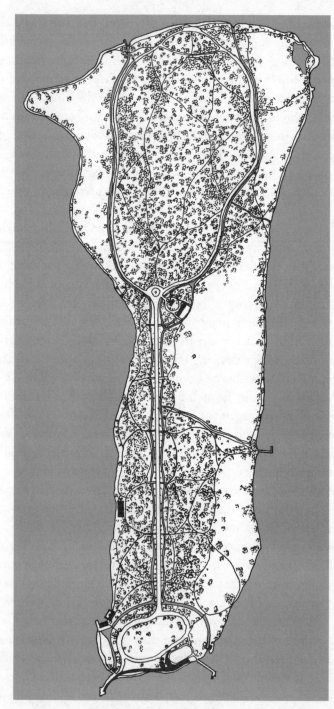

Belle Isle, Detroit (1883).

On the south side was the site of an old gravel pit. Here he laid out a path banked with pudding stone, planted mountain laurel, birch, ash, and cherry, and created a small version of the Ramble in Central Park. The rest was a lawn. In the middle he planted a single American elm. Olmsted disapproved of bedded flowers; instead he ringed the lawn with a rich composition of greens: trees, shrubs, ferns, and ground covers. Dark yews formed a background for lighter ostrich ferns. The hillside at the back of the garden was planted with larger trees: hemlocks, oaks, and Norway maples. He generally followed the instructions that he had once given a gardener: "to mix shrubs with the trees; to use shrubs to break the edges of the plantation; and to see that there were no sharp lines between groups of this and groups of that." A spruce-pole fence, covered in fast-growing climbers, ivy, and creepers, ringed the two sides of the property that were close to the road, and a rustic gateway marked the entrance.

There was nothing manicured about Olmsted's treatment of this sub-urban garden, far from it. "Less wildness and disorder I object to" was his philosophy. The most extreme example of this taste for wildness was the way he treated the house itself. He installed a grid of wire on the south and east walls and planted Chinese wisteria and bower actinidia. Soon the facade was entirely shrouded by a thick blanket of creepers and vines interrupted only by protruding window shutters and the striped canvas awning of the sunroom. Classical gardeners such as André Le Nôtre had extended architecture far into the landscape by means of terraces, reflecting pools, topiary, and geometric beds. Olmsted did the opposite—he made architecture disappear.

The improvements to Fairstead were carried out while Olmsted was traveling. John did much of the implementation. With his scientific college background, his European travel, and his exposure to a variety of projects, he was becoming skilled. In 1878 Olmsted had considered his apprenticeship complete and gave him an interest in the business. Nevertheless, John remained shy and withdrawn. When the family moved to Fairstead, he was thirty-one. Still unmarried, he lived with his parents.

The other Olmsted children at Fairstead were Marion and her thirteen-year-old brother. At the age of seven Henry had been renamed Frederick. Or, rather, Frederick Law. Olmsted had once reminded John that his most valuable legacy was likely to be the "good will of my business." How better to ensure the continuity of this goodwill than by having a "Frederick Law Olmsted" in the firm for years to come? Mary, a practical person, must have concurred in this extraordinary decision. Rick, as everyone called him, had no say in the matter. He would go into the family business, and he would do so bearing a famous name.

And Olmsted *was* famous. He now attracted a steady stream of clients and commissions. However, his old way of working was proving unequal to the demands of an expanding practice. John was a valuable colleague, but they needed more assistants. The first of these was Charles Eliot, a tall, lanky twenty-three-year-old who had taken courses in agriculture and horticulture after graduating from Harvard. He came highly recommended by Charles Eliot Norton, who had been one of his professors (and who was also a second cousin), and by the architect Robert Peabody, his uncle and Olmsted's neighbor and sometime collaborator. Eliot started immediately. "I am to go about with Mr. Olmsted, and am expected to gather the principles and the practice of the profession in the course of this going," he wrote a friend. "I am to be of what service I can, and this, if I am to judge by ten days' experience, will consist chiefly in doing draughtsman's work, making working drawings from preliminary design-plans, etc. I have already had a little journey with Mr. Olmsted to Newport and Providence, and learned much and enjoyed more."

A year later Eliot was joined by Henry Sargent Codman, a graduate of the Massachusetts Institute of Technology and the nephew of Charles Sprague Sargent. Codman and Eliot were from privileged backgrounds (Eliot's father was the president of Harvard). Olmsted was not a snob, but he understood that an important part of a landscape architect's job was "influencing men of means and enterprise" (as he once put it to John). To do this it helped to be one of them. He had his eye on both of these bright young men as future partners in the firm; for the moment they were "apprentices." Olmsted looked to Richardson for this model. Richardson treated his employees as both assistants and pupils, somewhat in the fashion of a Parisian atelier. Of course, most of his employees were formally trained—at the École des Beaux-Arts or at the Massachusetts Institute of Technology. Olmsted had to be more systematic. "We put them to such work as they can do in our office," he explained, "if we can find room for them, and they travel with us (at their own expense) and read under our advice for two or three years. After that they generally make a tour of foreign study." Olmsted the reluctant student had become a schoolmaster.

CHAPTER FIFTY

The Character of His Business

OLMSTED WAS SETTLED, surrounded by friends and colleagues, economically secure, and busy with work. Yet he still fell prey to occasional depression. He expressed his feelings in a letter to Brace. "You decidedly have the best & most worthily successful life of all whom I have known. The C. A. [Children's Aid Society] is the most satisfying of all the benevolent works of our time. I have done a good deal of good work in my way too but it is constantly & everywhere arrested, wrecked, mangled and misused & it is not easy to get above intense disappointment & mortification." Central Park continued to be plagued by politics. Vaux had been appointed landscape architect by the Parks Department in November 1881. His advice was ignored and he resigned; a year later, their old enemy Colonel Egbert Viele, who still maintained that Olmsted and Vaux had plagiarized his design, wheedled his way onto the Central Park board. Viele, a Democrat, was using the position as a stepping-stone toward a congressional seat. The future of Prospect Park was compromised when a new Brooklyn administration fired the indefatigable James Stranahan and abolished the park board. Mount Royal was still incomplete, due to a lack of funds. (In 1881 Olmsted published a pamphlet on the Montreal park hoping to influence the city council, but to no avail.) At Chicago's South Park, Cleveland had only managed to complete less than half of the inland site.

Olmsted's depression was underscored by several events. The previous year his stepdaughter Charlotte, who had grown woefully unstable after the birth of her third son, had to be institutionalized. Then Olmsted lost his two mentors—George Geddes, who had introduced him to scientific farming, and Henry Whitney Bellows, who had drawn him into the great national endeavor of the Sanitary Commission, both died. More unexpected was the death of his young architectural collaborator Thomas

Wisedell. Olmsted had also just read Brace's obituary of Friedrich Kapp, their faithful collaborator in the free-soil movement. "Instead of being shocked by the death of old friends, I wonder they could have lived till so lately," Olmsted reflected. "Most of all [I wonder] that I am still living," he added gloomily.

Brace forwarded Olmsted's letter to Frederick Kingsbury—the three often exchanged correspondence—and later sent Kingsbury's sensible reply to Olmsted.

> I enjoyed Fred O's letter, which I return. It's a pity he should attach so little importance to the much he has accomplished and so much to the little he has not succeeded in doing to his mind. No man ever comes up to his ideals who has any. And as for reputation, there are few men who have a more enviable one than Fred. Well known and highly respected in two hemispheres and in three departments of human effort, Literature, Philanthropy and Art. Most men would be fairly satisfied (if men ever are satisfied) with his position in either.
>
> He ought to be able thoroughly to enjoy the fruits of his labor, and I hope he still may be as he gets into a serener period of life if things go well with him.

"I am not sure however but that last is all gamon [sic] as I don't think life seems any serener with me as I grow older," Kingsbury added. Olmsted certainly had not grown serene. He was still hurt by public criticism. "I think it comes harder to an old man to be grossly insulted," he observed. Nor had he learned to accept professional setbacks. This is something that Charles Eliot Norton chided him about: "You are preaching truths above the comprehension of our generation. . . . Montreal indifference, New York degradation are conditions to be anticipated and therefore not to excite disappointment. . . . Your original success with the Central Park was an anomaly." Norton did not have a high regard for the public's taste. "You are compelled to throw your pearls before swine," he cynically observed, "and are fortunate if they do not turn and rend you for not giving them their favorite swill." This was not Olmsted's view. He maintained a constant—if guarded—optimism about people's ability to appreciate the scenic and restorative powers of landscape. That is why the failures rankled so.

Another element in Olmsted's discontent was the new type of consulting practice that he had established in Brookline. It was making heavy demands on his time. In the same letter to Brace, he complained:

I keep working as close to my possibilities as ever, my possibilities, never large, growing perceptively smaller with every year. John takes more & more off and I have two good young men as "pupils," but the character of my business becomes smaller & brings a greater multitude of diverse concerns to me & I get very weary of turning so often from one thing to another and of so many long & short expeditions.

The character of my business becomes smaller. He did not have less to occupy him than before. Quite the opposite. But instead of working on a small number of large commissions, as he had in the past, his practice now included a large number of small commissions. In the year 1884, for example, the Olmsted firm was involved in no fewer than sixteen private estates. It may appear odd for the designer of some of the largest public parks in the nation to be advising individuals, but he could not afford to turn down such work. Moreover, he had a real interest in domestic landscapes and paid as much attention to them as to the parks. One of the few magazine articles he wrote at this time described the landscaping of a small residential plot in a Western city.

He was experiencing the dilemma of running a consulting firm: he needed assistants to ease the burden of work, but he had to find more work to keep the assistants busy. Yet he refused to cut corners. He would not merely provide plans. His normal procedure for small domestic projects was to charge one hundred dollars (about three thousand dollars in modern dollars) for a visit and preliminary advice. "If what I advise is in a general way acceptable and it is desired that I should go further, I undertake a general guidance of the work to be done." There were additional charges for preparing drawings, purchasing plants, and overseeing the work, with intermittent visits over the following two or three years.

Not all these projects made the same claims on Olmsted's time, of course, but as senior partner he made most of the site visits; John, assisted by Eliot and Codman, managed the office. A business trip in May 1884 illustrates the demands of his far-flung practice. On Thursday he was in New York to meet the architect Charles McKim, who was now in partnership with William Rutherford Mead and Stanford White. McKim had a "capital client," a prominent New York banker with a country property near Ossining. They spent the day there; that evening Olmsted had a late supper with McKim in New York. On Friday he traveled to Trenton, New Jersey, where his firm was building a park. The man he had come to see was away, but Olmsted visited the suburban nursery where the plants for the park were being grown. He then went to nearby Lawrenceville, "where building seemed very backward and there was much apparent confusion," and met the head master. He was back in New York in time to catch the night train to Detroit, whose city council had just voted more than sixty thousand dollars to begin work on Belle Isle. He expected his stay to be brief; instead, he found a small crisis. The newspapers had reported that his proposed pier could not accommodate the draft of large ferryboats. Despite high winds, Olmsted personally accompanied a lumbering boat to the proposed location. "I was ill-treated," he complained, "the Ferry Company gave me their heaviest & deepest & most unwieldy boat." He proved that his plan was sound. From Detroit he went to Washington, D.C., to inspect the Capitol grounds, which were finally nearing completion. Withal, he still found time to send John planting instructions for a part of the Back Bay Fens. "Temple [a nurseryman] will probably be able to get but little periwinkle or moneywort & if so it had better be concentrated near the bridge where it will be looked down upon. The large-leafed sedum which grows in great patches at various points (as at North Easton, Cohasset & Wenham Lake) may be crowded—cheaply—upon all the rocks except close to the Commonwealth Bridge."

Olmsted may have complained to Brace about the character of his business, but as his letter to John suggests, private work served as an important testing ground for his ideas. Wenham Lake was an estate that he had been working on since 1880. The large property was on Wenham Great Pond in Beverly, Massachusetts, near Salem. For the house, a large informal affair built of fieldstone, brownstone, and shingles by Peabody and Stearns, Olmsted created a great platform overlooking the pond. The platform was part paved terrace and part lawn, edged by a curving wall of fieldstone and surrounded by heavy planting of shrubs and trees. The lawn extended two hundred feet to the south where a summer house overlooked a sunken flower garden.

When Olmsted visited the property in September 1881, initial landscaping had begun. He was unhappy with the general appearance. He wrote his client a long, forthright letter. "As the house was not in itself disappointing I finally conclude that the trouble lay in the suggestion of a quality of smugness in its surroundings." In short, the new landscape looked too genteel. He urged a simple solution: seed the entire area with pine and larch and then thin them out in a few years. The effect Olmsted aimed for was a "proper summer lodge, so placed in the midst and near the edge of a forest as to command an opposite forest over a sheet of water, with an oasis of ladies' ground strongly but rudely and in a forest fashion built in to the wild hillside with it."

Olmsted planned the entire 275-acre site of what would be called Moraine Farm. He designed the curving approach road, creating alternating views of meadows and forestland. He laid out three carriage drives through the picturesque wooded part of the site and beside the lakeshore. Drawing on his scientific-farming background, he installed forty acres of underground drainage pipes to improve the fields. The rest of the land was unsuited to farming. He planted conifers for future logging, experimenting with various species—European larch, Scotch and Austrian pine, and Norway spruce. White pines did well, and about sixty thousand were planted. Moraine Farm is now surrounded by suburban buildings, but the forest that Olmsted planted is still there; the fields that he drained continue to produce crops. The graceful approach road and the sweeping terrace and lawn likewise remain, a testament to their makers' skill and foresight and to their owners' diligent care.

The Sixth Park

THE FENS AND THE MUDDY RIVER IMPROVEMENT were part of a continuous park system. East of the Fens was Commonwealth Avenue, built in 1856 when a large portion of the Charles River was filled to create the Back Bay. The hundred-foot-wide avenue with a pedestrian mall running down the center terminated a mile away at the Public Garden and Boston Common, a colonial town green. West of the Muddy River Improvement was Jamaica Pond, a lovely seventy-acre body of water and a favored recreation spot for boating and skating. In time, the city acquired a narrow belt of land surrounding the pond. Half a mile away, to be linked by a parkway, was the hilly Arnold Arboretum, which, thanks to Sargent and Olmsted's efforts, was now included in the park system. And half a mile from the arboretum was the 527-acre site of what would soon be named Franklin Park (in honor of Boston's native son).

Boston's seven-mile-long park system became known as the Emerald Necklace. In 1884 the Park Commission asked Olmsted to turn his attention to the design of Franklin Park, the Emerald Necklace's brilliant pendant. He responded by spelling out his terms. This would be his sixth major park; he wanted to make sure that his responsibilities were understood. In Central Park he and Vaux were municipal employees, and in Prospect Park they managed the workforce. On the other hand, when they designed Chicago's South Park, they acted in an advisory capacity, as Olmsted also did in Montreal and Detroit. The latter arrangement secured independence from political pressures, but at the cost of giving up control over day-to-day implementation. With Franklin Park he hoped to combine the freedom of an external adviser with the authority of an architect-in-chief. He suggested that the city hire a superintending gardener who would be an employee of the city but "should receive orders for carrying on the work only from or through my office and reports of the gardening force to the Board should pass through my office." (Olmsted had someone in mind: William L. Fischer, the experienced head gardener of Central Park.) He demanded that "the question of the division of duty between the engineering force and the gardening force should be at all times subject to my decision." He asked the parks department to establish—and staff—a field office. His fee for preparing the plan was five thousand dollars, and he requested an additional thousand dollars a year for a renewable three-year engagement to "secure unity of design and be responsible for the final character of the work."

That was not a large design fee for a major park. Olmsted was aware that the Boston Park Commission was worried about costs. Franklin Park would be as large as Prospect Park, where the land had cost $4 million. Boston spent only $600,000 on land and wanted the construction cost to be similarly modest. Prospect Park had cost $5 million to build; Olmsted promised that the construction cost of Franklin Park would not exceed $1.5 million.

He did not see the strict economy demanded by the frugal Boston commissioners as a drawback. The artlessness that he had been perfecting since Mount Royal here came to the fore. There would be no complicated Adirondack ravines in Franklin Park, no elaborate rambles, no expensive lakes or lagoons.* Structures were few and unpretentious—there would be no Bethesda Fountain or Belle Isle gallery. Below Scarboro Hill there would be a small dairy; on Schoolmaster's Hill, Olmsted proposed a shelter for picnickers and a trellis-covered terrace. The buildings were rustic, with pudding-stone walls and thatched roofs. "Eccentric and quaint" was how he described them. The largest building in the park, likewise conceived by Olmsted himself, was a sprawling shelter with a huge overhanging roof.

The singularity of this park was to emerge from the site itself, which Olmsted described as having "the usual characteristics of the stony upland pasture, and the rocky divides between streams commonly found in New England, covered by what are called 'second growth' woods . . . not beautiful individually, but, in combination forming impressive masses of foliage. It not only contains no lake, permanent pool or stream of water, but it commands no distant water view. It includes no single

---

*The 1885 master plan had no water bodies. Following a citizens' petition, Olmsted added a series of brooks and pools flowing into a small pond.

natural feature of distinguished beauty or popular interest." This made it sound banal, but it was precisely the peaceful character of this scenery that appealed to him. The problem, as he saw it, was not to transform this undramatic landscape, but to enhance it. Just as he had made Mount Royal more mountainous, he would make this homely landscape more pastoral. He called it the Country Park.

> To sustain the designed character of the Country Park, the urban elegance generally desired in a small public or private pleasure ground is to be methodically guarded against. Turf, for example, is to be in most parts preferred as kept short by sheep, rather than by lawn mowers; well known and long tried trees and bushes to rare ones; natives to exotics; humble field flowers to high-bred marvels; plain green leaves to the blotched, spotted, and fretted leaves, for which, in decorative gardening, there is now a passing fashion. Above all, cheap, tawdry, cockneyfied garden toys, such as are sometimes placed in parks incongruously with all their rural character, are to be eschewed. But a poor, shabby, worn, patchy, or in any way untidy rurality is equally to be avoided with fragments of urban and suburban finery. In this respect the park is designed to be an example of thoroughly nice, though modest and somewhat homespun housekeeping.

The Country Park was two-thirds of Franklin Park; the rest he called the Ante Park. It was divided into several parts: the Playstead was a thirty-acre athletic field suitable for civic parades; the Little Folks' Fair was a children's area; in addition there were ball and tennis grounds, a refectory, a music amphitheater, a deer park, and a small zoological garden. The focus of the Ante Park was the Greeting, a long, formal promenade or alameda that resembled the Central Park Mall but was twice as long— half a mile—and combined pedestrian walks with carriage drives and bridle paths. Olmsted's study of European parks had convinced him that public parks and nighttime activities were not incompatible, and he suggested that the Greeting and the Playstead were to be "without underwood, and adapted, with electric lighting, for night as well as day use."

Public parks now had a variety of functions. Olmsted dealt with this by isolating areas for active recreation. The reason he gave was functional: the thin, hard soil of the Country Park did not lend itself to intensive use and "cannot, therefore, be prepared to resist the wear of athletic sports without undue expense." Yet the fundamental purpose was to preserve intact

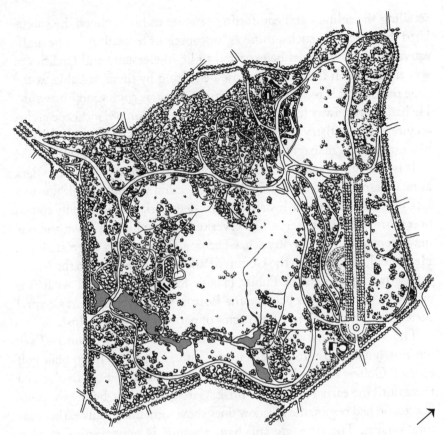

Franklin Park, Boston (1891).

the character of the Country Park: "To provide opportunity for a form of recreation to be obtained only through the influence of pleasing natural scenery upon the sensibilities of those quietly contemplating it."

Olmsted was no aesthete. In his report to the Boston Park Commission, after quoting several famous writers on the effects of rural scenery, he acknowledged that "there are some who may be inclined to question if a considerable degree of refined culture, such as is common only to the more worldly fortunate, is not necessary to enable one to enjoy the charm of rural scenery sympathetically with Wordsworth, Emerson, Ruskin, and Lowell." His answer was unambiguous. "To enjoy it intellectually, yes; to be affected by it, made healthier, better, happier by it, no." For Olmsted, the curative power of natural scenery was universal. Perhaps recalling the solitary and comforting rambles of his boyhood, he speculated that there was such a thing as "unconscious recreation." "The highest value of a park must be expected to lie in elements and qualities of scenery to which the mind of those benefiting by them, is liable, at the time the benefit is received, to give little conscious cogitation," he wrote. He had moved away from Vaux's narrow conception of landscape architecture as art. Artistry there was, certainly, but it was combined with city planning, urban management, public education, and public health.

It is difficult to judge Olmsted's Franklin Park today. The Ante Park as he designed it has disappeared. The Greeting was never built due to a lack of funds. A zoo was installed in the deer park and eventually spread over more than eighty acres. The Overlook shelter burned down and was never replaced; the Playstead has become the site of a large stadium. Heathfield, a meadow in the Country Park, was turned over to the Massachusetts Department of Public Health for a hospital; and what was originally a nursery has become the Boston Parks Department's central maintenance yard. All in all, 120 acres of parkland have been lost.

The vast meadow that was the centerpiece of the Country Park remains, but at a cost. It has been turned into an eighteen-hole public golf course.* Golfers are hardly as picturesque as the herd of sheep that grazed there until the early 1900s. On a brisk March afternoon, before the golfing season had begun, the meadow does show something of its earlier pastoral quality. The trees are still bare, the turf is only starting to turn green, yet the effect, while melancholy, is not unpleasant. Judging from old photographs, the planting around Scarboro Pond is not as lush as it used to be, but the gentle, framed view of the stone bridge designed by Richardson's firm remains. Still, Olmsted would be disappointed in our stewardship, I think. He worked so hard to convince his clients that they were building for posterity. In his report on Franklin Park he pointedly included the following quote from John Ruskin (ellipsis in the original):

> Let it not be for present delight, nor for present use alone; let it be such work as our descendants will thank us for, and let us think . . . that a time is to come when . . . men will say, *"See! this our fathers did for us."*

---

*The first use of the meadow for golf occurred as early as 1890. Ironically, the 1989 refurbishment of the golf course initiated the modern revival of Franklin Park, which during the previous three decades had been largely abandoned by middle-class users and had fallen into disrepair.

Fairstead, Brookline, Massachusetts

Monday, July 20, 1885

It is midday, and the family is gathered in the garden behind the house. John, an avid amateur photographer, is crouched behind a camera mounted on a tripod. He is squinting at the upside-down image on the back plate. Satisfied, he stands up and lets the black cloth drop.

"I'm ready. Please, nobody move. This is going to be an eight-second exposure."

The shutter clicks, time stops. He has posed his subjects reclining on the lawn under a tree. Rick is in the center of the little group. He is wearing a dark shirt and knickerbockers. His head has been shorn for the summer, which makes his protruding ears more prominent. Rick is attending Roxbury Latin School, preparing for Harvard. It will be his fifteenth birthday in four days but he looks glum. Marion sits to her brother's left. She is a serious young woman of twenty-three who already wears the grim pall of Victorian spinsterhood. There are two unidentified women—visitors or neighbors—a mother and daughter, perhaps. Olmsted, summery in seersucker jacket and pith helmet, lounges propped on one elbow. He wears glasses and is holding a letter. Mary is in the rear, leaning against the tree trunk. She is swathed in a long checkered dress, her face framed in a white scarf that is tied in a large bow under her chin. She is the apex of John's carefully arranged triangular composition, and her small figure completes this decorous New England Déjeuner sur l'herbe.

There is a second click followed by an audible sigh. Rick jumps up, the women brush the grass clippings off their skirts, and Olmsted slowly eases himself upright.

"Now I want one with John," orders Mary. "Show Rick how to operate the camera. Let's stand up for this one. Frederick, take that hat off, it makes you look like David Livingstone. Marion, you stand over here; John, you're on the other side."

John moves the camera and rearranges the setting according to his mother's instructions. He is a slender young man of thirty-two. He has grown a trim beard that emphasizes his long, delicate face and makes him resemble a figure in an El Greco painting, the effect now emphasized by his clasped hands. He, too, is wearing a seersucker jacket. He and Olmsted look like members of the same club or team, which, in effect, they are. Last year John became a full part-

ner in what is now called F. L. & J. C. Olmsted, Landscape Architects. Olmsted stands in the center, flanked by the two female visitors. Mary has placed herself in front of her husband. She is the smallest figure, but with her tablecloth of a dress and her arms determinedly akimbo, she dominates the picture. She appears good-humored, capable, entirely in control.

Mary is fifty-five, Olmsted sixty-three. He has let his hair and his beard go long. His blue eyes gaze evenly at the camera. He has a slight smile, and his face is ruddy from days spent outside. He looks healthy and relaxed. More than that, he looks at ease—with himself, and with the world.

And his world is uncommonly rich. There are Monday nights at Richardson's, when the architect gathers his apprentices and former pupils for talk, music, and plenty of food and drink. Sargent, who owns one of the largest estates in the town, has introduced the Olmsteds to Brookline society, and Norton has done the same in academic Cambridge. Olmsted has been elected to the exclusive Saturday Club, a Boston institution that convenes once a month for dinner and conversation. The members include such figures as Oliver Wendell Holmes, James Russell Lowell, William Dean Howells, and William James. Such men appreciate Olmsted's accomplishments as an editor, writer, abolitionist, and public servant. His Boston parks are known to all. Working close to home has meant less travel, and more time to spend at Fairstead, especially working in the garden. He has not had a proper garden of his own since Tosomock Farm (he does not count the tiny plot behind his brownstone in Manhattan). It is only two years since they moved here and everything is still raw. However, the fast-growing creepers and vines that he and John have planted are beginning to cover the fence and the walls of the house. The "wildness and disorder" that he favors will appear soon enough.

Olmsted Meets the Governor

OLMSTED AND JOHN PRESENTED their plan of Franklin Park to the park commission, but before a decision was made a new city government, composed for the first time of Irish Democrats, took office. Yankee patricians such as Norton feared the worst. The city council appointed a new park commission, which immediately annulled Olmsted's contract. However, they were merely flexing their political muscles, for a few weeks later Olmsted was reinstated under the old terms. The following year his plan was officially adopted.

Olmsted's success was marred by tragedy. Richardson had been diagnosed with Bright's disease (chronic nephritis), which affected his kidneys and contributed to his great weight. The prognosis was not good. In March 1886, recuperating from a recent attack of tonsilitis, he went to Washington. Olmsted, who was there on Capitol business, visited him in his hotel and found his friend in an alarming state. "His eyes were bloodshot, his face red, his forehead studded with beads of sweat," Olmsted recalled. "He spoke feebly, hesitatingly, and with a scarcely intelligible husky utterance." Olmsted urged him to return home immediately. Then a client of Richardson's came in. During the next hour, as he explained his drawings, Richardson became animated and seemed to regain his usual energetic demeanor. As he was leaving, Olmsted said, "Eidlitz asked me to let him know how I found you. I shall have to tell him, never better in your life." Both men laughed, but it was a hollow joke, and they knew it. When Richardson came back to Brookline, he took to his bed. Olmsted went to see him, but the doctor advised that he was too weak to receive visitors. A fortnight later Richardson was dead. "He passed away so quietly and softly that no one present knew when death occurred," recalled Olmsted. The funeral was held in Trinity Church. Olmsted noted that more than fifty of Boston's architects attended, as well as

McKim, White, and Saint-Gaudens from New York. Richardson was only forty-seven. "He never had as much to do; never had such assurance of his leadership and the public's grateful acceptance of it, never had been as strong and happy in his art as in his last days," Olmsted wrote Mariana Van Rensselaer. He could not get used to thinking of him as gone.

Henry Codman introduced Olmsted to Francis A. Walker, the dynamic president of the Massachusetts Institute of Technology, Codman's alma mater. Walker was currently advising Leland Stanford, the wealthy California railroad magnate. Two years earlier, Stanford's fifteen-year-old son had died of typhoid fever, and Stanford and his wife, Jane, had decided to found a university in memory of their only child. They had toured several Eastern universities, including Yale, Cornell, and Harvard. At MIT, Stanford tried to recruit Walker as his president. Walker declined but agreed to act as a consultant and now approached Olmsted. Would he be the planner of the new university? After an exchange of letters with Stanford, a deal was struck. Olmsted asked for—and received—the unprecedented sum of ten thousand dollars for preparing a preliminary plan. In late August 1886, accompanied by Codman and young Rick, Olmsted set out to meet Walker and Stanford in California, where the new university was to be built.

They took the train to Portland, Oregon, and then a stagecoach to San Francisco. Codman and Rick accompanied Olmsted to the Mariposa Big Tree Grove and stayed with Galen Clark, who, still hale, was now officially known as the "Guardian of the Yosemite Valley and Big Tree Grove." Since Stanford was busy, they made a train excursion to Los Angeles. Olmsted described the countryside to John. "The daylight part of the journey here is through the Mohavi desert, the most forbidding region I ever saw," he wrote. "The most interesting objects to us being forests of the yuccas, as large as our larger apple trees. But mainly, for hundreds of miles, great mountains, canons [sic] & plains almost bare of vegetation, waterless, hot—mercury nearly all day above 100°. There is nothing tropical in the general aspect of the country here and it appears barren except when cultivated, planted & watered." When they returned to San Francisco, Olmsted sent Rick and Codman on a tour of Santa Cruz and the Napa Valley and himself went to Palo Alto, Stanford's estate in the Santa Clara Valley.

Leland Stanford was a U.S. senator who had been governor of California, but he was best known for pushing to completion the first transcontinental railroad. An impressive, bearlike figure, he had amassed money, power, and land—over eight thousand acres on which he planned to build the university. The first order of business was to decide on a site for the future campus. Palo Alto rose from a flat plain into the foothills of the Santa Cruz Mountains. Olmsted recommended a hilly spot, imagining a larger and more picturesque version of Lawrenceville in the rolling landscape. Stanford would have none of it. He insisted that the university should be built on the plain. The willful railroad builder knew exactly what he wanted: not an academic village but something monumental and grand. "There is not any word half big enough for his ideas of what it is to be," Olmsted complained. But he went along. "The site is settled at last," he wrote John, "not as I had hoped."

A few days later Olmsted, Codman, and Rick left San Francisco. At Salt Lake City they split up, Codman and Rick continuing home and Olmsted making a long detour north, to Montana. His destination was his dead stepson Owen's property: the Running Water Ranches of the Lacotah Company, for which Olmsted had put up the money. He was dismayed by what he found. "It was a high interest speculation," he wrote John, "& the luck has not been with us." The cattle ranch was worth less than when it had been bought, although Olmsted hoped that a mild winter and better markets might increase its value.

Farther east he made another stop: the Niagara Falls commission in Buffalo. Much had happened since he and Norton had organized an international petition to create a reservation around the falls. After the petition failed to persuade the state legislature, they formed the Niagara Falls Association. This lobbying campaign finally led, in 1883, to the passing of a state bill and two years later a million-dollar bond issue to purchase land. Since William Dorsheimer had been appointed president of the board overseeing the project, Olmsted had every expectation of getting the job. But there was a snag. One of the five commissioners was none other than his old adversary Andrew Haswell Green. Green had vetoed Olmsted and proposed his own candidate: Calvert Vaux! Olmsted, smarting from Green's criticism, had been driven to write to Governor Hill of New York objecting to the insinuation that Vaux was the chief creative force behind Central and Prospect Parks—"our responsibility for the design of both parks is precisely equal." He had also bristled at Green's description of Vaux as Downing's student—"he was never a pupil in the ordinary sense," Olmsted correctly pointed out. To break the deadlock Dorsheimer had suggested that Olmsted and Vaux work together, but Green would not budge. Vaux had asked Olmsted if he would consider taking a subordinate role as "Consulting Landscape Architect." Olmsted, who was unwilling to play second fiddle, had remained noncommittal.

Now Olmsted was in Buffalo to assess the situation. He paid a "pleasant official call" on one of the commissioners, the state senator Sherman S. Rogers. Rogers told him that a plan would have to be prepared soon so that it could be included in the annual water legislation, but it was still unclear who would be given the commission. "I am sorry I don't see how I can give any time to it," Olmsted wrote John. He had been gone from Brookline for close to two months and was looking forward to returning home. In any event, he thought he had enough on his plate. "The Stanford matter will be a perplexing study," he cautioned his partner.

At this time Olmsted's "shop," as he called it, was reduced to three persons: himself, John, and Henry Codman. Charles Eliot, his apprenticeship complete, had left the previous year to travel in Europe. As he had with John, Olmsted provided him with the names of parks and gardens to visit, and with personal introductions. In return, Eliot dutifully sent a steady stream of letters containing reports and observations. He traveled all over Europe, including Scandinavia and Russia, for a year. On his return he declined to rejoin Olmsted's office to work on Stanford University; he was bent on striking out on his own. Olmsted, who had a high regard for his young pupil, wished him well and gave him the following useful advice: "You write easily, fluently, and in a critical way that is in demand. What you wrote offhand about the Italian Gardens—and about the Baltic parks, (in that last letter), and on various other matters you saw, would make a capital series of magazine articles, with a very little modification to the scale of a popular audience. . . . And, perhaps a book. Anything of the sort (to speak of the indirect profits) will be worth much more to you than advertising in the Nation, for example."

Olmsted and Walker each wrote a preliminary report for Stanford. Olmsted stressed the need to adapt the university to its unique climate. He knew that Stanford, who was born in Watervliet, New York, wanted a New England–style campus with large buildings set among lawns and trees. "If we are to look for types of buildings and arrangements suitable to the climate of California it will rather be in those founded by the wiser men of Syria, Greece, Italy, and Spain," Olmsted warned. Walker's report described the educational program. He recommended a "cottage system" for student housing, on the Lawrenceville model. His most novel suggestion was that the university be housed in one-story structures. "Mr. Olmsted and myself are fully agreed that, with proper architectural treatment, buildings of this character, made of massive stone, connected by an arcade, may be made singularly effective and picturesque."

As yet no architect had been chosen. Walker recommended Richardson's firm, now known as Shepley, Rutan and Coolidge. In his will, Richardson had directed that his practice be carried on by his young protégé Charles A. Coolidge, George F. Shepley (who was engaged to Richardson's daughter), and Charles H. Rutan, an engineer. Since Coolidge and Shepley were both MIT men (and Coolidge's mother was Walker's cousin), Walker's endorsement is easy to understand. Olmsted, who was on intimate terms with Coolidge and the others, strongly approved. He and Coolidge thus worked out the details of the master plan.

In the end the Stanford plan bore no resemblance to Lawrenceville School or to any of Olmsted's earlier campus layouts. Stanford and his wife, who also influenced the design, admired French neoclassical architecture, and they clearly expected a formal plan. Olmsted and Coolidge placed the arcaded buildings around a large quadrangle, positioning the memorial church (containing Leland Stanford Jr.'s tomb) on one side and the library on the other. They softened the all-over formality by opening the quadrangle to the south to provide a vista of the far-off foothills.

Coolidge took the models and plans to California, where he met with a cool reception. "The very quietness and reserve which we like so much in it is what they want to get rid of," Coolidge wrote Olmsted after a week of meetings with the Stanfords. As usual, Stanford was insistent. He wanted the quadrangle turned to offer its long, impressive side to the approach road; he wanted the church to be given pride of place opposite the entrance to the quadrangle, never mind the vista to the hills; lastly, he wanted a memorial arch marking the entrance, an arch huge enough to be seen from the beginning of the long approach road. Stanford had already scheduled the cornerstone-laying ceremony two weeks hence (on what would have been his son's birthday); he ordered Coolidge to revise the plans on the spot. Coolidge protested. "The Gov. replied a Landscape Arch't and an Arch't might be disappointed but he was going to have the buildings the way he wanted them."

In Brookline, Olmsted was furious. "There is a story to be told about the Stanford University which can be deferred until you come here," he informed Mariana Van Rensselaer. "The matter is going not very well." Nevertheless, the university was an extraordinary commission. At eight thousand acres, and with a budget that eventually exceeded $30 million, this was the largest project Olmsted had ever undertaken; indeed, it was the largest building project of its kind in the country. Stanford intended to create an entire town adjoining the university, with residential neighborhoods for the students and staff, as well as an arboretum. There promised to be work for years to come.

Olmsted and Vaux,
Together Again

WHILE COOLIDGE WAS in California trying to satisfy Leland and Jane Stanford, Olmsted was working on the Niagara Falls project. The board had finally overruled Green and appointed Olmsted and Vaux jointly as landscape architects. Olmsted was pleased that after seventeen years the Niagara reservation was to become reality. He did not feel ill will toward his old partner; he knew that Vaux had been manipulated by Green, as had happened before about Central Park. He was also aware that Vaux's career had not prospered since their breakup. Vaux had hoped that the simultaneous construction of the American Museum of Natural History and the Metropolitan Museum of Art would lead to greater things. He completed the first phases of the buildings, but when it came time to continue, his master plans were set aside and the jobs were given to others. In the case of the Metropolitan, the original design exhibited Mould's flamboyant touch, but for budgetary reasons the finished building was rather dull and was not well received. Mould and Vaux had broken up, and over the years Vaux's practice had dwindled. In the mid-1880s, Charles Loring Brace commissioned him to design a series of lodging houses and industrial schools for the Children's Aid Society. It was honorable work, honorably executed, but a far cry from the days when moneyed clients and great institutions had sought his services.

One of Vaux's last prominent clients was Green's friend Samuel J. Tilden, the former governor of New York and presidential candidate. When the Tilden house on Gramercy Park was complete, it was reviewed by the *Art Amateur*. "Mr. Vaux is a very good landscape architect," the critic wrote, "but he has apparently not been awake to what has been going on in domestic architecture in New York during the last few years."

What had been going on was a flowering of styles that were explicitly historical and monumental: Richardson's muscular Romanesque, Hunt's imposing French Renaissance, and McKim, Mead, and White's new classicism. Vaux's brand of High Victorian architecture had become old-fashioned.

The Niagara commissioners wanted the plan and report for their next year's February meeting, so Olmsted and Vaux got down to work. By the end of the year they had the main outline of the plan. Letters, drawings, and memoranda flew back and forth between Brookline and New York. It was like old times. "He helped me and I helped him" is how Olmsted described the process, "and at some points each of us crowded the other out a little." At the beginning of February, Vaux came to Fairstead to complete the drawings. Olmsted kept changing the text so often that Vaux worried they would not finish in time. "He can't take writing easily," John explained. "He must worry over it till the moment when it is delivered and he can alter it no more."

Olmsted worried over the report because he considered Niagara Falls "the most difficult problem in landscape architecture to do justice to, it is the most serious—the furthest above shop work—that the world has yet had." He believed that the overall natural context, the linked "passages of natural scenery," not any single dramatic feature, made Niagara—like Yosemite—special. Olmsted and Vaux wanted the visitor to experience not merely the spectacle of a mighty waterfall but also the "incomparable greater beauty of a kind in which nearness to the eye of illumined spray and mist and fleeting waters, and of the intricate disposition of leaves, with infinitely varied play of light and shadow, refractions and reflections, and much else that is undefinable in conditions of water, air, and foliage, are important parts."

Unlike Yosemite, which was a vast and relatively inaccessible area with a small number of visitors (about three thousand a year at that time), the reservation around Niagara Falls had as many as ten thousand visitors in a single day. Much of Olmsted and Vaux's report was devoted to planning the reservation so that the crowds of people could enjoy an intimate and natural experience. The reservation, as recommended by Olmsted's report to the New York State Survey, consisted of Goat Island, lying between the American Falls and the Canadian Horseshoe Falls, as well as a strip of land on the American side of the river. They laid out a carriage drive around the island, hidden in the trees and a hundred feet or so away from the water's edge. They believed that the best way to see the falls was on foot, and a system of pathways provided access to sites of particular interest—the Cave of the Winds, Luna Island, Porter's Bluff. They located a visitors' center and shelters for picnickers on the mainland (on the site of what had been an amusement park). No structures were to be on the three-hundred-acre island save for two forest pavilions.

"We are far from thinking that all that is required to accommodate the designed end is to 'let Nature alone,'" Olmsted and Vaux wrote. They discussed public safety, handicapped access, guide boards for walkers, and even ways to reduce vandalism. They proposed an inexpensive horse omnibus to take visitors around the island. They specified ways to protect the riverbanks from erosion and to conserve selected natural areas. In sum, they described a coherent and unified approach to planning a public nature preserve that was a pioneering model of sensible, balanced, and realistic environmentalism.*

In October 1887 Olmsted returned to California. The design of the university had become increasingly formal. A long avenue led from the railroad station to the mammoth memorial arch. Olmsted tried unsuccessfully to convince Stanford to hire Saint-Gaudens to sculpt the frieze of the arch; Stanford had never heard of Saint-Gaudens and was not interested. The Governor also had his own ideas about the grounds. Although he conceded to paving the quadrangle as Olmsted wanted, he insisted that elsewhere there be lawns rather than shrubbery. He did approve Olmsted's proposal to create a large arboretum that would be a showplace of native California trees as well as drought-resistant species from other parts of the world. Olmsted hired a forester, who established a nursery and transplanted thousands of seedlings. Then, after a year, Stanford had a change of heart and work on the arboretum stopped. As for the town to be planned north of the university, that project, too, was abandoned.

Stanford paid handsomely, yet he and his wife were the worst kind of clients: opinionated, willful, capricious. They brought back photographs of a Swiss hotel from a European vacation and instructed the architects

---

*The report and plan were submitted in 1887 and forwarded by the board to the state legislature. However, work did not begin for several years; it was overseen by Vaux. Vaux's biographer has speculated that Olmsted withdrew from later involvement with Niagara so that Vaux, who was financially strapped, might have a source of income.

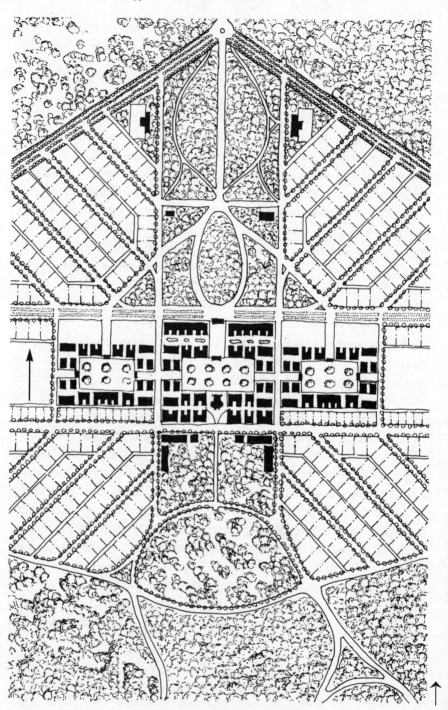

Stanford University, California (1888).

to use them as the model for a men's dormitory instead of the student cottages that Olmsted and Walker had planned. Coolidge, by now thoroughly browbeaten, went along. Jane Stanford's pet project was the university museum, which had been given pride of place at the entrance to the quadrangle. She decided that she wanted a replica of a building that her son had once admired in Athens, ignoring that a three-story, neoclassical structure would be out of place in the low, Romanesque quadrangle. Eventually, the museum grew too large for its site and had to be relocated elsewhere on the grounds.

A modern visitor may wonder at the incongruous mosaic mural adorning the main facade of Coolidge's memorial church. The mural was the result of yet another European visit by the Stanfords, this time to St. Mark's in Venice. This particular "improvement" was carried out without the architect's approval, since by then Shepley, Rutan, and Coolidge had been fired. Stanford gave the responsibility for carrying out their design to his wife's brother, Ariel Lathrop. Lathrop was also to oversee the landscaping work. Olmsted protested that his verbal agreement with Stanford was that the landscape superintendent, an experienced engineer named MacMillan, would answer directly to him. Lathrop ignored the objection. Matters came to a head in May 1890 when Lathrop summarily dismissed MacMillan. Olmsted wrote a long and conciliatory letter to Lathrop but to no avail. He then addressed Stanford: "I am too old a man to be reasonably asked to put aside all that I have learned of my business, because a man of Mr. Lathrop's training and habits has not learned as much." His complaint went unanswered. The impasse effectively marked the end of Olmsted's involvement with the project. Neither he nor Codman visited the building site again. When the university formally opened the following year, Olmsted, who had not been invited to the ceremony, wrote Stanford a congratulatory letter nevertheless. The latter responded coolly, "We are gradually improving the grounds in accordance with your plans."

It is easy to understand why Olmsted lost interest. Despite the agreeable effect of the low, arcaded buildings, the mating of Richardsonian architecture and excessively formal planning is awkward. What little remains of Olmsted's landscaping is not a success either. The eight large planted circles in the paved quadrangle struck me as clumsy—a rare case of an Olmsted landscape that appears contrived. He tried hard to accommodate himself to his client's wishes, but his heart wasn't in it.

When Jane Stanford completed the campus—after her husband's death—she had an inscription carved conspicuously across the facade of the church below her mosaic mural: ERECTED TO THE GLORY OF GOD AND IN LOVING MEMORY OF MY BELOVED HUSBAND LELAND STAN- FORD.* That was pretentious but accurate. The university had been the Governor's monument all along.

---

*When the church was rebuilt after an earthquake, the inscription was not restored (it survives today as a small plaque). The 1906 earthquake also destroyed the enormous memorial arch and Jane Stanford's museum. All the buildings erected under Coolidge's direct supervision remained standing.

"Make a Small Pleasure Ground and Gardens"

OLMSTED WITHDREW from Stanford without undue concern; he was in a position to be choosy. He had emphasized this in his last letter to Ariel Lathrop: "I am at this time (with my partners) the landscape architect of twenty works of considerable importance; that is to say, I do not include in that ordinary private grounds." He had also made sure Lathrop understood that Governor Stanford was not Olmsted's only wealthy client, mentioning that he was doing no fewer than three commissions for the Vanderbilt family. Lest Lathrop imagine that he was unduly impressed by the size of Palo Alto, Olmsted pointedly added that one of these commissions was an estate of six thousand acres.

The estate belonged to George Washington Vanderbilt. He was the son of William H. Vanderbilt, Olmsted's neighbor on Staten Island forty years earlier, who had recently died, leaving an estate of $200 million (6 billion in modern dollars). George, the youngest of eight children, inherited $10 million. In August 1888 he and Olmsted traveled to Lone Pine Mountain, outside Asheville, North Carolina, where Vanderbilt planned to build his country retreat. "I came to Asheville with my mother. We found the air mild and invigorating and I thought well of the climate," he told Olmsted. "I took long rambles and found pleasure in doing so. In one of them I came to this spot under favorable circumstances and thought the prospect fairer than any other I had seen." Vanderbilt explained that he had bought the land and over the years had amassed two thousand acres. "Now I have brought you here to examine it and tell me if I have been doing anything very foolish."

Olmsted agreed that the air was fresh and the views across the French Broad River to Mount Pisgah and the Great Smokies were splendid. "But the soil seems to be generally poor," he pointed out. "The woods are miserable, all the good trees having again and again been culled out and only runts left. The topography is most unsuitable for any thing that can properly be called park scenery," he concluded with characteristic bluntness. Vanderbilt, somewhat crestfallen, asked what he should do. Olmsted, drawing on his experience at Moraine Farm, had a ready answer. "My advice would be to make a small park into which to look from your house; make a small pleasure ground and gardens; farm your river bottoms chiefly to keep and fatten livestock with a view to manure; and make the rest a forest, improving the existing roads and planting the old fields."

Vanderbilt trusted Olmsted, who was also landscaping the family mausoleum on Staten Island, advising all three of Vanderbilt's sisters on improving their country estates, and laying out the grounds of his brother Frederick's summer house in Newport. George Vanderbilt, unlike his three brothers, had stayed out of railroading. Olmsted described the twenty-six-year-old bachelor as "a delicate, refined and bookish man, with considerable humor, but shrewd, sharp, exacting and resolute in matters of business." The suggestion that commercial forestry represented a good investment, that it was a dignified business for a gentleman, and could moreover serve as a national example appealed to Vanderbilt. After several months of deliberation, he happily agreed to Olmsted's proposal. Indeed, his enthusiasm for forestry was such that he soon expanded his holding—hence the "six thousand acres."

A tree nursery was started, topographic surveys of the property were commissioned, and plans were laid for a gravel plant and for a railroad spur to transport materials to the site. Superintendents were hired to oversee the construction, landscaping, and the nursery. These men were employed by Vanderbilt but answered directly to Olmsted. The grand plan that he had so quickly sketched out began to take shape.

Vanderbilt chose Richard Morris Hunt as his architect. Hunt had worked with Olmsted on the Vanderbilt family mausoleum. He had also built a mansion and a summer house for George's brother William and renovated George Vanderbilt's house in New York. Hunt is best remembered as the favorite architect of Gilded Age socialites, but his practice was varied. At this time, he had just completed the base for the Statue of Liberty and would shortly be chosen to supplant Vaux as architect for the Metropolitan Museum of Art. He had reached the pinnacle of his profession.

Hunt's first design was a conventional brick country house in the colonial revival style. The second version was larger, a rambling Tudor mansion of rough-hewn stone. "I very much like your new plan," Olmsted observed, "and your suggestions as to position, etc. satisfy." Hunt had not yet visited the site, and the busy architect had probably not paid the small commission much attention. This changed. Three months later, Hunt took Vanderbilt on a whirlwind tour of great houses in England and France. Evidently both men had set their sights higher.

Meanwhile Olmsted wrote a thirty-six-page report describing the chief landscape elements of Biltmore, as Vanderbilt would name his estate.* Olmsted discussed water supply, forestry, agriculture, a nursery, and an arboretum. A separate section was devoted to the three-mile carriage drive that would lead from the main road to the house. Olmsted intended the approach road to be an integral part of the landscape experience. It should have a "natural and comparatively wild and secluded character, its borders rich with varied forms of vegetation, with incidents growing out of the vicinity of springs and streams and pools, steep banks and rocks, all consistent with the sensation of passing through the remote depths of a natural forest."

Hunt and Vanderbilt returned from Europe in July, and in October Hunt delivered a large wooden model of the final design. The country mansion had become a palace with a banquet hall, a winter garden, and an indoor swimming pool; 250 rooms in all! The steeply pitched roofs and picturesque turrets and chimneys were inspired by châteaux such as Chambord, Chenonceaux, and Blois. Olmsted's challenge was to marry the degree of formality demanded by the French Renaissance architecture with the natural character of the approach road and the rest of the estate. It was not an easy task. "There are one or two points about which I am nervous," he confessed, "and this is because I am not quite at home when required to merge stately architectural work with natural or naturalistic landscape work." Nevertheless, he faced the challenge. He worked closely with the self-assured Hunt, five years his junior. Olmsted could be diplomatic and theirs was a smooth collaboration. "He has accepted every single suggestion that I have made and I have accepted every single sug-

---

*Olmsted devoted a section of his report to naming the estate. He discarded French Broad and suggested Broadwood; Vanderbilt toyed with Bilton but settled on Biltmore (Bildt was his ancestral town in Holland).

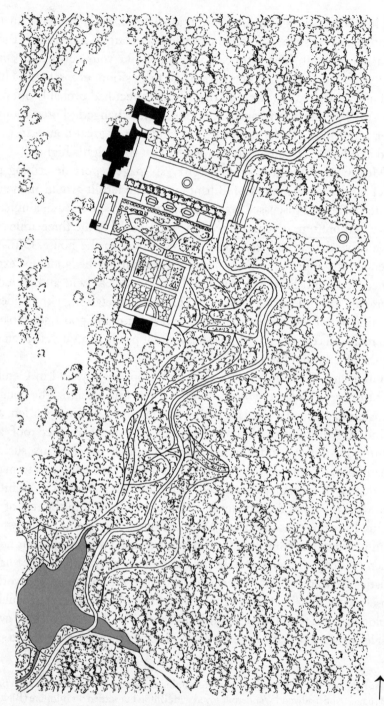

Biltmore Estate, Asheville, North Carolina.

gestion that he has made," Olmsted observed, "and I do not think that in the end there will be a note of discord in the combined work."

The design of the Biltmore grounds is unusual, both in the Olmsted oeuvre and in the history of landscape architecture. It is a successful—and entirely original—combination of two great landscaping traditions: French and English. The entrance court, for example, is a conventional neoclassical composition. The rectangle of grass, with a circular basin in its center, is bounded on two sides by rows of tulip trees; at one end the court is terminated by the main facade of the house, and at the other by a retaining wall with *rampes-douces*, gently ascending ramps, which lead to an upper terrace. Yet the arrival in the court is anything but conventional. The traveler, having negotiated the three-mile-long approach road, comes around a curve and is suddenly thrust into bright sunlight. He is at one end of the court, but not facing the house. Only after turning does the visitor see Hunt's impressive facade framed by the rows of tulip trees.

Stretching south from the end of the house is a vast rectangular platform resembling a bastion—Olmsted's idea. The surface of this terrace is gravel; there are no plants (originally there was a bowling green). In the far corner is a small, high-roofed pavilion. It looks like an afterthought. Olmsted argued hard to convince Hunt and Vanderbilt of the wisdom of this small architectural gesture. In fact, it is a masterstroke. The contrast between the domestic garden-house and the huge château is both unexpected and poignant. From this little aerie one looks out on the rolling pastures of the deer park, the forest (artfully improved by Olmsted), and the dramatic panorama of the Great Smoky Mountains.

Against the tall retaining wall of the terrace, facing east to the gardens, is a long arbor shaded by Japanese wisteria. The arbor overlooks a hillside on which Olmsted has created an unusual landscape. "A place out-of-doors is wanted which, attractive at all times in a different way from the terrace, will be available for a ramble" is what he told Hunt. The result does not resemble the Central Park Ramble, however; it is a manicured garden—part wild, part cultivated—with curving paths and evergreen shrubs. There are no flowers. (There is a four-acre walled garden for fruits, vegetables, and flowers nearby.) The function of the so-called Shrub Garden is to be a transition between the formal terraces and the increasingly naturalistic landscape that unfolds the farther one walks from the house. A series of paths leads through a forested vale and into a wooded glen. The gurgling sound of several rills adds to the charm. The footpaths crisscross the streams over bridges and stepping-stones. Eventually one arrives at a pond formed by a dam that creates a waterfall at the far side, almost hidden among the hemlocks. In only half an hour, one has passed from the French Renaissance to the dark primeval forest of the New World.

If Olmsted saw anything ironic about Yeoman returning to the South to lay out an estate for a wealthy Northerner, he did not comment on it. "We have a good deal of work now in the Slave States and it is most interesting to review the field of my former travels, as I often have an opportunity to do," he observed. "The revolution has been a tremendous one and I am well satisfied with the present results." Asheville was an example of this revolution, the town's development fueled by Northern investment in resort hotels. Vanderbilt's presence added to the prosperity. The construction of Biltmore employed hundreds of local laborers and craftsmen—many of them black. Vanderbilt founded a Young Men's Institute in Asheville and built Biltmore Village for the estate workers, where he would subsidize the schools (one for whites, one for blacks) and the churches.

Olmsted described Biltmore as "a private work of very rare public interest in many ways." He was thinking of the scientifically managed forest. Olmsted brought in Gifford Pinchot to oversee Biltmore's forest operations. He was a young American graduate of the École Nationale Forestière at Nancy and the first trained forester ever to hold such a position in the United States. Under Pinchot's direction Vanderbilt bought more than one hundred thousand acres of land to create Biltmore Forest.

Biltmore may have had aspects of "rare public interest," but it was chiefly the personal indulgence of a millionaire. There is no reason to apologize for Olmsted's involvement—there is no evidence that he ever did. The great seventeenth-century landscape architect André Le Nôtre created his masterpiece, the grounds of Vaux-le-Vicomte, for one of the richest men in France. Vanderbilt, hardly the richest man in the United States but surely among the most magnanimous, offered Olmsted the opportunity to build a great and uncompromising work of landscape art. Olmsted gratefully accepted. He oversaw the work personally, traveling to Biltmore several times each year. Once there he often spent five and six hours at a stretch in the saddle, put up with uncomfortable accommodations, and suffered from the altitude. He obviously thought that it was worth it.

Central Park, New York

It takes decades to realize the landscape architect's vision.
Patience and long-sightedness were among Olmsted's chief qualities.

The freshly graded Mall in 1863, shortly after completion
with rows of American elm saplings.

The Mall in 1894. The green canopy forms a solid archway over the promenade.

The Terrace in 1863, still under construction.

The completed Terrace in the 1880s, the fully-grown trees forming a solid backdrop.
The Bethesda Fountain, a symbol of healing, was added after the end of the Civil War.
The gondola is Venetian.

The Terrace in the 1920s, as popular as ever,
even though the fountain is not running.

The site of Central Park consisted of rocky outcroppings and swampy lowland.
The meadows, woods, and lakes, which Olmsted imagined as a poor-man's substitute
for Adirondack scenery, are entirely man-made.

Winter, 1866. The surroundings, visible through the sparse vegetation,
are largely rural. The lake was hurriedly completed and ice-skating
quickly became a popular pastime.

Winter, c. 1890. The trees hide the adjacent city,
except for the newly built Dakota apartment house.

In the early 1860s, the new landscape is still bare. The Marble Arch, which no longer exists, was the chief pedestrian entrance to the Mall.

Some twenty or thirty years later, the arch is beginning to be hidden by the vegetation. Architecture always took second place in Olmsted's parks.

By the early 1900s, the arcadian illusion is complete.
New Yorkers of all ages, classes, and races, gather in a meadow.

Lawrenceville School, New Jersey

*Frederick Law Olmsted's landscaping practice included not only public parks,
but also civic buildings, suburban subdivisions, private residences, and universities.
In 1883, he began designing a new campus for Lawrenceville School.*

The focus of the school is the Circle, shown here in 1885, shortly after completion.
Olmsted's design intention is hardly visible in this bare landscape.
He incorporated a few existing large trees into his design.

This photograph, taken about 1896, shows Olmsted's vision
of a New England village green starting to emerge.

By the 1950s, the school buildings
are almost entirely hidden among the trees.

Olmsted Drives Hard

IN JANUARY 1890 Charles Brace sent Olmsted a copy of his latest book. "It strikes me as your best work from a literary point of view," Olmsted replied, but "I do not see why you should say it is probably your last." He did not know that Brace, four years his junior, was seriously ill; he died that August. Olmsted mourned his lifelong friend. "His death was a shock to me," he wrote Kingsbury, "and the shock has been growing greater since." About himself, he was philosophical. "Of course, I am not planning to live longer," he wrote in another letter. He was approaching seventy. His beard, entirely white now, curled in disordered profusion. "What a good ancient philosopher you look like!" Norton wrote him, after seeing his portrait in *Harper's*. "But, indeed, what a good old philosopher you are!" It was one of those rare times that Olmsted was contented. "I enjoy my children. They are the center of my life; the other being the improvement of scenery and making the enjoyment of it available. Spite of my infirmities which do drag me cruelly, I am not to be thought of as an unhappy old man."

He was now the head of a national consulting business with as many as twenty employees. The firm, called F. L. Olmsted & Co., had a new partner: Henry Codman. After completing his apprenticeship he had spent most of 1889 in Europe, working in Paris with André and traveling as far as Morocco to study arid landscapes. Harry, as everyone called him, was a tall, burly young man with a dark mustache. Intelligent, energetic, and affable, he had just those qualities that Olmsted deemed necessary for a landscape architect. Harry shouldered some of the burden of traveling to project sites, while John supervised the apprentices, draftsmen, and clerks who worked in the new office wing that had been added to Fairstead. Olmsted thought that his firm was "much better equipped and has more momentum than ever before." He once observed that "I have all my life been considering distant effects and always sacrificing immediate success and applause to that of the future. In laying out Central Park we determined to think of no result to be realized in less than forty years." In enlarging his practice Olmsted took the same long view. John was in his thirties, Harry was twenty-seven, and Rick, who had decided to become a landscape architect, was just starting at Harvard. In one form or another Olmsted & Co. would stay in business a long time.

August 1890 found Olmsted and Codman in Chicago. They had been invited by the board of the corporation that was overseeing the construction of the World's Columbian Exposition, commemorating the four-hundredth anniversary of the discovery of the New World. Chicago had recently edged out St. Louis, Washington, D.C., and New York for the honor of hosting America's first world's fair. (Olmsted had been consulted on possible sites by New York and had taken part in a campaign to keep the fair out of Central Park.) The Chicago board wanted advice on the best site for the fair.

There were seven alternatives. For a variety of reasons the choice narrowed down to South Park, which Olmsted and Vaux had planned twenty years earlier. The obvious choice was Washington Park, the partly finished inland portion; so-called Jackson Park, by the lake, remained a barren marsh. To Harry, the lakeside site appeared desolate—"swampy, the surface of a large part of it not being materially above the surface of the lake at high stages of the water." Three months later they returned to Chicago to present their recommendation. Olmsted, who still considered Lake Michigan Chicago's only striking natural feature, had insisted on Jackson Park. John Olmsted once observed that "it was one of the greatest advantages that Father had that his employers usually grew to have such faith in him that they often were prepared to accept his recommendations without attempting to understand them." This was one of those times. At first the board balked, but after much discussion and debate it agreed. Olmsted was delighted. "We have carried our first point, that of tying the Fair to the Lake," he wrote John.

Olmsted had one particularly strong supporter, an unofficial adviser to the corporation named Daniel Hudson Burnham. Burnham was only forty-four but with his partner, John Root, was already one of the most successful architects in Chicago. Intelligent, charming, and, like Olmsted, largely self-made, Burnham was a dynamo. A contemporary described him as someone who "inspired confidence in all who came within the range of his positive and powerful personality."

The board appointed Burnham chief of construction, which effectively put him in charge; Root was named consulting architect; Olmsted and Codman were retained as consulting landscape architects.* The four worked together on the overall plan. They were a good team. Olmsted's experience balanced Burham's brashness. Burnham, a skillful planner, was always willing to concede in artistic matters to his partner, Root, a gifted designer. Codman was the youngest, only twenty-seven, but he quickly gained the respect of the Chicagoans. "Harry Codman's knowledge of formal settings was greater than that of all the others put together," Burnham later recalled. "He never failed."

The underlying concept originated with Olmsted and Codman. The major natural landscape feature of the fair would be water, not only Lake Michigan but also a system of basins, canals, and a lagoon. An existing stand of small oaks dictated the location of a large island in the center of the lagoon. The excavated earth would be used to create raised terraces on which the buildings would be constructed. In contrast to the naturalistic lagoon, the terraces would have hard edges and would surround a formal basin.

The arrangement of buildings around the basin was inspired by the last world's fair, the great Paris Exposition of 1889, whose monumental buildings had lined the central mall, terminating in Gustave Eiffel's tower. Root is generally credited with the design, but Olmsted and Codman undoubtedly contributed. After all, Olmsted was then working out the formal terraces of Biltmore, and Codman was familiar with the French exposition after his three months in Paris. While the buildings around the lagoon would be varied, those around the basin would be formal and monumental. The fair covered all of Jackson Park and stretched up the Midway Plaisance. Altogether, this extraordinarily ambitious scheme was four times larger than the Paris exposition.

The general principles of the plan were approved by the board. Burnham, who saw the fair as a great national event, proposed that a select group of prominent architects design the main buildings. With Olmsted's and Root's advice, a list was drawn up. Richard Morris Hunt was an obvious choice; so was Charles McKim of McKim, Mead & White, and Robert Peabody of Peabody & Stearns. George B. Post of New York

---

*Harry Codman probably negotiated the $22,500 fee; he had earlier convinced Olmsted to demand a hefty sum from Stanford.

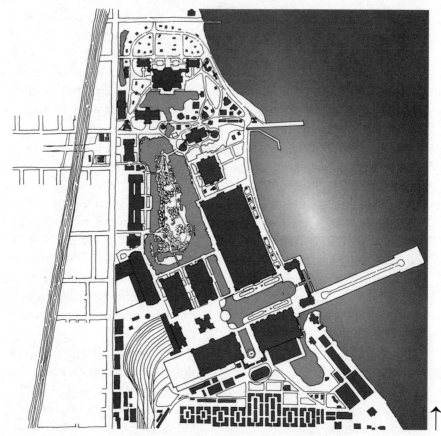

World's Columbian Exposition, Chicago (1893).

and Henry Van Brunt of Van Brunt & Howe in Kansas City were both highly respected practitioners. The five architects represented a close circle: Post and Van Brunt had been Hunt's pupils, and Howe and Peabody had been pupils of Van Brunt's; Hunt, McKim, and Peabody had all studied at the Beaux-Arts, and all three had worked with Olmsted.

At first the Easterners were standoffish. But Burnham's eloquence—and no doubt Olmsted's participation—won them over. Burnham then earmarked five Chicago architects—among them Louis Sullivan and Olmsted's friend Jenney. In January all the architects met in Chicago. A pall hung over the proceedings, as just after the meetings started John Root died of pneumonia. The architects assembled formed a committee that included Olmsted and Codman, and elected Hunt as their chairman. They gave a "cordial and unqualified approval to the plan as originally presented," Olmsted recalled. The Easterners would design the buildings around the basin, and the local architects, the buildings around the lagoon.

They returned with their sketches at the end of February. Olmsted and Codman were there; so was Augustus Saint-Gaudens, who had agreed to act as an artistic adviser to the fair and to aid in the selection of sculptors. Burnham described the scene:

> We had a breakfast for the visiting men. They were filled with enthusiasm. Charles McKim, with a good deal of repressed excitement, broke out, saying: "Bob Peabody wants to carry a canal down between our buildings." I said I would agree to that, even though it would cost something. . . . Next, Saint-Gaudens took a hand. He said the east end of the composition should be bound together architecturally. All agreed. He suggested a statue backed by thirteen columns, typifying the thirteen original States. All hailed this as a bully thing.

Olmsted recorded that "the general comradeship and fervor of the artists was delightful to witness & more delightful to fall into." At the end of this meeting, "Gussie" Saint-Gaudens made his famous comment to Burnham: "Look here, old fellow, do you realize that this is the greatest meeting of artists since the fifteenth century!"

The fair was to open on May 1, 1893. That left only two and a half years to transform the more than six hundred forlorn acres. By May 1891 the excavation of the lagoon, canals, and basins was complete. Supervision was complicated. At first, Olmsted and Codman directed the work from Brookline. At Burnham's urging, Codman spent more and more time on the site. He was joined by Rick, who worked for the summer as an unpaid assistant to the superintendent of construction.

Olmsted spent about half his time working on the fair, the rest on Biltmore and the firm's many other commissions. During this period he advised the Union Pacific Railroad on hotel sites in Utah, and real estate developers on subdivisions near Denver. He wrote a report on the National Zoo in Washington, D.C., and was consulted by the superintendent of West Point. He advised the governor of Alabama on the state capitol grounds, and the federal government on a nature reserve at Hot Springs, Arkansas.

That summer he was struck down by what he said was arsenic poisoning induced by new wallpaper in his bedroom; he also was fatigued from the continuous travel, and from the insomnia that plagued him. He spent the summer convalescing in Brookline. In early September he felt well enough to go to Chicago. Under Burnham's guidance rapid progress had been made. Most of the major buildings were under construction and planting had commenced. It normally takes decades to establish the landscape of a park; Olmsted and Codman had only two years and had to contend with unpredictable winter weather and the lake's fluctuating water level. They decided to use the first planting season for testing different varieties, and the second for replanting, repairing, and finishing.

The following March, Olmsted was in Chicago again. The winter had been mild and the planting could resume. For this Herculean task, he later estimated that the shores of the lagoons alone required "one hundred thousand small willows; seventy-five large railway platform carloads of collected herbaceous aquatic plants, taken from the wild; one hundred and forty thousand other aquatic plants, largely native and Japanese irises, and two hundred and eighty-five thousand ferns and other perennial herbaceous plants." Olmsted and Codman could not rely on local nurseries for this material. The majority of the cattails, rushes, irises, and pond lilies were collected from lakes, rivers, and swamps in Illinois and Wisconsin.

"I never had more before me or less inclination to lay off than now," Olmsted observed. His visit to Chicago was part of a trip that included stops in Biltmore, Knoxville, Louisville, and Rochester—2,700 miles in all. He continued to drive himself hard. Richardson, despite his fame, had died insolvent, bequeathing his widow only debts; Olmsted had no intention of leaving Mary in such a predicament.* That explains his willingness to accept commissions farther and farther afield, despite the long-distance rail travel that was becoming increasingly discomforting as he grew older. Now, feeling weak and not fully recovered from the previous summer's illness, he decided that the best restorative for him would be a European trip. Codman appeared to have matters well in hand in Chicago, so in early April Olmsted sailed for England. He was accompanied by Marion, who had never been abroad; Rick and Phil Codman,

---

*He estimated that he was putting aside more than a thousand dollars a year (about thirty thousand in modern dollars)—a considerable sum.

Harry's younger brother, who was an apprentice, were there as companions and pupils.

As in the past, a European trip was an opportunity for Olmsted to revisit parks. This time his schedule included tours only of England and France. The Chicago fair was uppermost in his mind, and he spent a week on the Thames trying out a variety of electric launches; he made notes about reeds and other waterside vegetation. In France, he discussed the Paris Exposition with André and visited the grounds. Many of the surviving buildings displayed polychrome decoration—the bright gayness appealed to him. "They show, I think, more fitness for their purposes, seem more designed for the occasion and to be less like grand permanent architectural monuments than ours are to be. I question if ours are not going to look too assuming of architectural stateliness and to be overbonded with sculptural and other efforts for grandeur and grandiloquent pomp." With an eye on Biltmore, he visited the new château at Chantilly and made a tour of the Loire Valley. He was impressed by the architecture but not by the landscaping. "All these châteaux that we have seen, looked at largely, appear dreary, incomplete and forlorn for want of adequate foliage furnishing."

Traveling with the young men and Marion was a pleasure. "I am having a great deal of enjoyment, and I hope laying in a good stock of better health," he wrote Mary. The latter goal was not realized. When he returned to England, he became ill. He spent three months sequestered in the home of an English physician who—like doctors in the past—could find no physical ailment. The sleeplessness—and the resulting fatigue—resumed. Nevertheless, he stayed on, touring, meeting people, taking notes. He returned home after an absence of six months. For the purpose of his health, the trip had been a failure. "More than a failure. I was more disabled when I returned than when I left."

Olmsted returned from Europe at the end of September 1892; by the next month he was in Chicago. Now Harry Codman was unwell, so Olmsted saw to the planting of the wooded island. After his European tour he was more than ever convinced that simplicity and naturalness were required as a counterpoint to the grandeur of the architecture, especially as it had been decided to paint all the buildings around the basin uniformly white. He instructed the gardening superintendent to increase the quantity of green foliage. "I fear that against the clear blue sky and the blue lake, great towering masses of white, glistening in the clear hot, summer sunlight of Chicago, with the glare of water that we are to have both within and without the Exposition grounds, will be overpowering." Olmsted counted on the wooded island to be a shaded oasis for tired fairgoers.

He was concerned about the fair since he saw it as an unparalleled opportunity to influence popular taste. Traveling between Brookline, Biltmore, and Chicago, and overseeing park projects in Milwaukee, Knoxville, and Kansas City, he could see that his work was "having an educative effect . . . a manifestly civilizing effect" on the American public. As a writer, reporter, and editor, he had always sought a large audience. Now he had one. Just as he taught landscaping to the young men who came to his office, in Chicago he was preparing a national lesson.

Abruptly his plans were thrown into confusion. On January 13, 1893, Harry Codman, who was recovering from an appendectomy, died. It was a hard blow for Olmsted. "I am as one standing on a wreck," he wrote to Pinchot in Biltmore, "and can hardly see when we shall get afloat again." He was in low spirits again: not only was his protégé dead, the most important project of his firm was in jeopardy. Despite a serious cold, he rushed to Chicago. There, a doctor warned him of pneumonia. That— and a blizzard—kept him from immediately attending to business. He wrote John a wretched letter. "It looks as if the time had come when it is necessary for you to count on me out. . . . I do think that we shall have to decide on throwing up a lot of our business. I am not to be depended on. . . . I say again common prudence requires that you should lay out your course, not counting on me. It is very plain that as things are we are not going to be able to do our duty here."

John, who knew his stepfather, took these dire predictions with a grain of salt. The firm weathered the blow of Harry's death. This was due in no small part to Charles Eliot, to whom Olmsted turned in his distress. Eliot came out to Chicago to help with the crucial final planting and finishing. He had been successful on his own, and his writing had gained him a reputation, but he enjoyed working with his old teacher on a large project. A month later F. L. Olmsted & Co. became Olmsted, Olmsted & Eliot.

The Fourth Muse

The Concert Hall,
Madison Square Garden, New York

Saturday, March 25, 1893

The flamboyantly ornamented room, designed by Stanford White, is decorated with evergreens and palms. Three crimson banners hang from the ceiling. Each bears a single word surrounded by a wreath of gilded laurel: "Painting," "Architecture," "Sculpture." Below the banners are round tables seating men in evening dress—the ladies are in the gallery. Over the clatter of cutlery and the clink of glasses floats the lively music of the Hungarian Band.

The occasion is a tribute to Daniel Burnham. There is a smattering of politicians, businessmen, and civic leaders, but the majority of those attending are in the arts: painters, muralists, sculptors, craftsmen, architects. Daniel Chester French, whose monumental statue adorns the fair's basin, is there; so is the actor Edwin Booth, the glassmaker Louis Comfort Tiffany, and the conductor Walter Damrosch. The literary world is represented by Charles Scribner, Parke Godwin, and E. L. Godkin. The novelist and influential critic William Dean Howells sits at the head table on the stage; so does Charles Eliot Norton, who has come down from Cambridge to give one of the toasts. Norton sits to the left of Hunt, who presides. Hunt, McKim, Saint-Gaudens, and the painter Francis D. Millet—who is Director of Decoration for the fair—are among those who have organized this event. Hunt, too, penned the droll dedication that appears in the program of toasts: "A director of faith is good; but since faith without works is dead, a Director of Works is better. The Daniel who now comes to judgment may safely be lionized."

The two-hour dinner has come to a close. While the guests are served coffee and cigars, the lights dim and stereoscopic slides of the exposition are projected on a large screen. Most of those present have not yet seen the fair, which opens in five weeks. The views are spectacular. Hunt's impressive Administration Building, which forms the gateway to the fair, has a dome larger than that of the Capitol; the arched steel hall of Post's Manufactures Building is a wonder—it is the largest roofed structure ever built; McKim's Agriculture Building, crowned by Saint-Gaudens's Diana (originally intended for Madison Square Garden), is a jewel. The white buildings, adorned with sculptures and murals, cast rippling reflections in the canals; Frederick MacMonnies's Columbian Fountain, the centerpiece of the great basin, sparkles in the sun; the planting in the lagoon is lush and tropical. The views are greeted with approval and much handclapping by the more than two hundred guests. The greatest applause comes with the final slide: an image of the Director of Works, Daniel Burnham.

Hunt, dignified, gray-haired, with a mustache and a spade beard, gets up slowly—he has arthritis. He says a few words of tribute, turns to Burnham, and removes a false bouquet of roses that stands in front of the guest of honor to reveal a massive silver loving cup. The foot-high vessel, designed by McKim, is engraved with the names of the 272 guests. Burnham pours an entire bottle of wine into the cup, drinks, and passes it up and down the table. The cup then circulates around the entire room. It is occasionally topped up with champagne, to the enthusiastic cheers of all assembled.

Hunt proposes a toast to Burnham. All in the room rise to their feet and lift their glasses. Then Burnham speaks. He is genuinely moved by the occasion. He praises the talent of his colleagues who have come together to create the fair and have worked so harmoniously and unselfishly together.

"You know who these men are. They sit with you tonight," he says, sweeping his hand around the room. "Each of you knows the name and genius of him who stands first in the heart and confidence of American artists, the creator of your own parks and many other city parks."

He pauses until the burst of applause dies down.

"He it is who has been our best adviser and our common mentor. In the highest sense he is the planner of the Exposition—Frederick Law Olmsted." This time the applause is deafening.

Burnham is not finished. "No word of his has fallen to the ground among us since first he joined us some thirty months ago. An artist, he paints with lakes and wooded slopes; with lawns and banks and forest-covered hills; with mountainsides and ocean views. He should stand where I do tonight, not for the deeds of later years alone, but for what his brain has wrought and his pen has taught for half a century."

Burnham was effusive. It was forty years—not fifty—since Olmsted had entered public life. But the accolade was on the mark. The fair was Olmsted's creation, and not merely because he had contributed so much to the design. "Make no little plans," Burnham is supposed to have said. Thinking big was something he and his generation had learned from Frederick Law Olmsted.

Yet the object of these encomiums was absent. Charles Eliot's pocket diary notes that the evening of the banquet Olmsted was with him in Washington, D.C. They were returning home from Atlanta, and because Olmsted could no longer sleep on trains, they stayed the night at the National Hotel. Eliot also notes that on the same day his partner sent two telegrams—one to Chicago, one to New York. Were these regrets for not attending the dinner? Olmsted's name—like that of John Olmsted—was engraved on the loving cup. The next day the *New-York Times* reported both Olmsteds among those present, suggesting that the reporter had used an official guest list. Possibly Olmsted was called away on urgent business at the last minute, or poor health prevented him from returning sooner (Eliot's diary entry for the twenty-sixth: "Mr. O. ailing"). Yet the letter that Olmsted wrote to John from Atlanta just before returning does not mention poor health or being rushed. On the contrary, it offhandedly refers to possible stops in Baltimore and Philadelphia. Of the Burnham dinner, nothing. (It is unclear if John attended the dinner.)

I am inclined to think that the sudden trip to Atlanta was merely a pretext—Olmsted missed the banquet on purpose. The dinner invitation he received read: "We desire to give [Burnham] a banquet in recognition of the great benefits to architecture, sculpture, and painting that have resulted from [his] connection with the Columbian Exposition in Chicago." The cover illustration of the program of toasts echoed the theme of the three crimson banners that hung over the banquet hall: three muses—sculpture, architecture, and painting—supporting a loving cup. The fourth muse, landscape architecture, was nowhere to be found!

If Olmsted was offended, he would not have made a fuss. But Burnham would have understood the real reason for his absence. That is surely another reason why he singled out Olmsted for such high praise— "he should stand where I do tonight"—mentioning him first, and speaking of him at length while making only brief references to the architects, painters, and sculptors. If Olmsted had absented himself on purpose, politeness would have required that he mention the reason at least to his close friend Norton. The Harvard professor of art history and one of the country's leading intellectuals had been invited to the dinner to speak on "Architecture, Sculpture, and Painting." Norton, whom someone once called a pessimistic optimist, was known to hold conservative, often curmudgeonly views about contemporary art, but he spoke highly of the fair. He closed with these pointed remarks:

> The general design of the grounds and of the arrangement of the buildings was in every respect noble, original and satisfactory, *a work of fine art not generally included in the list of poetic arts* [emphasis added], but one of the most important of them all to America—that of the landscape architect. Of all American artists, Frederick Law Olmsted, who gave the design for the laying out of the grounds of the World's fair, stands first in the production of great works which answer the needs and give expression to the life of our immense and miscellaneous democracy.

Eliot knew that Olmsted was frustrated by people's unwillingness to recognize landscape architecture as an art. Olmsted thought that this was chiefly because they confused it with what he called decorative gardening. According to him, landscape architecture involved composition and perspective in which details were subordinate to the whole, contrary to decorative gardening, which treated "roses as roses, not as flecks of white or red modifying masses of green." He considered landscape architecture akin to landscape painting, except that the landscape architect used natural materials instead of pigments. That, of course, was the root of the problem. Since the medium—as well as the subject—was nature itself, the public often failed to discriminate between the two. No one would think of altering a landscape on canvas, but a garden was different. "I design with a view to a passage of quietly composed, soft, subdued pensive character, shape the ground, screen out discordant elements and get suitable vegetation growing," Olmsted observed. "[I] come back in a year and find—destruction: why? 'My wife is so fond of roses;' 'I had a present of some large Norway spruces;' 'I have a weakness for white birch trees—there was one in my father's yard when I was a boy.'"

Long ago, he and Vaux had started calling themselves "landscape architects," hoping that this would set them apart from horticulturists and decorative gardeners. Olmsted was still dissatisfied with the term, but in the absence of an alternative, he used it. He was aware of his leading position in the field; he wanted respect for his profession. Shortly after the Chicago fair opened, both Harvard and Yale offered him an honorary doctor of laws. He thought it was "the queerest thing," but he accepted "because it gives a standing to my profession which it needs."

It was thus that Olmsted had high hopes for the Chicago exposition. "If people generally get to understand that our contribution to the undertaking is that of the planning of the scheme, rather than the disposition of flower beds and other matters of gardening decoration," he explained to Mariana Van Rensselaer, "it will be a great lift to the profession."

"Everywhere there is a *growing* interest in the Exposition," Olmsted wrote Burnham after the fair opened. "Everywhere I have found indications that people are planning to go to it. . . . There is a rising tidal wave of enthusiasm over the land." Go they did. During six months, more than 27 million visitors went, a huge number considering that the entire population of the United States in 1890 was only 63 million. The public was dazzled by the fair, by its size, its technology, and its monumental beauty. The critics, too, were complimentary. Naturally, the spectacular buildings around the basin—which people called the Court of Honor—attracted the most attention, but some appreciated the achievement of the overall plan. The perceptive architecture critic Montgomery Schuyler wrote: "The landscape-plan is the key to the pictorial success of the Fair as a whole. . . . In no point was the skill of Mr. Olmsted and his associates more conspicuous than in the transition from the symmetrical and stately treatment of the basin to the irregular winding of the lagoon."

Looking at old photographs of the fair in my battered copy of *Official Views of the World's Columbian Exposition,* I am struck precisely by the charming contrast between the natural landscaping of the lagoon and the formal terraces that surround the basin. Water is the unifying theme; there are boats everywhere. "We should try to make the boating feature of the Exposition a gay and lively one in spectacular effect," Olmsted explained to Burnham, on more than one occasion. Olmsted prohibited steam-powered boats as too large and too noisy and proposed electric launches instead. This technology was novel and largely untested in America. Olmsted overcame Burnham's initial reluctance and personally oversaw the design of the boats, insisting on brightly varnished wood-work and gaily striped awnings. He was concerned about safety, too, and permitted only craft that could be turned and stopped quickly, such as Venetian gondolas. There were other exotic craft. A replica of a Viking ship crossed the Atlantic from Norway; it was joined by a Japanese dragon boat, a Venetian skiff, and a whaling bark. Olmsted had replicas of the *Niña,* the *Pinta,* and the *Santa María* built and anchored them next to the Casino.

The comprehensiveness of his environmental design is astonishing. He introduced ducks, geese, and swans, "to supply a means of appropri-ate decoration and of pictorial interest to the interior waters of the Expo-sition," instructing that "a variety of color in the fowl is desirable." He explained: "The effects of the boats and the water fowl as incidents of movement and life; the bridges with respect to their shadows and reflec-tions, their effect in extending apparent perspectives and in connecting terraces and buildings, tying them together and thus creating unity of composition—all this was quite fully taken into account from the very first." Another of his ideas was to have a small fleet of birch-bark canoes, paddled by American Indians in buckskin shirts and moccasins. "The canoes would add a feature of interest to all observers, and most Euro-peans coming to the Fair would be glad to have a trial of them and to pay liberally for it," he assured Burnham. Here the chief of construction drew the line. Such frivolity belonged on the Midway—in Sitting Bull's Camp perhaps—not in the Court of Honor.

Olmsted did his best to liven the atmosphere of what the press had dubbed the White City. After the fair opened, he proposed that Burnham hire a squad of banjo players and other strolling musicians. "Why not skipping and dancing masqueraders with tambourines, such as one sees in Italy?" Olmsted asked. He also suggested having persons in native "heathen" costumes brought from the Midway Plaisance, which was the location of the amusement park, to the Court of Honor on Friday evenings.* "They would at least give spice and variety to the scene, and a picturesque element." But there was nothing frivolous about the Court of Honor, as far as Burnham, McKim, and the other architects were con-cerned. The temporary exhibition buildings were designed with an ambi-

---

*The Midway Plaisance was such a success that *midway* became a synonym for any area of a carnival or circus devoted to sideshows and other amusements.

tious goal. "The influence of the Exposition on architecture will be to inspire a reversion toward the pure ideal of the ancients," Burnham told a Chicago newspaper. Olmsted did not share this vision. On the contrary, he had been on the opposite side of a dispute with Hunt and Stanford White, who wanted to introduce classical monuments into Central Park and Prospect Park. Olmsted was uncomfortable with what he characterized as their doctrinaire fanaticism regarding classical architecture. Nevertheless, he respected their abilities and their sincerity. He explained his position to William Stiles, the editor of *Garden and Forest*, who was complaining about the classicists. "You know that these men of the enemy are my friends. . . . I have managed to work in hearty, active, friendly cooperation with them. . . . At Biltmore we have managed to reconcile the requirements of Hunt in his Renaissance buildings with a generally picturesque natural character in the approaches. . . . There has not been the slightest break of harmony between us." Similarly in Chicago, Olmsted continued, he combined the "formal stateliness that our architectural associates were determined to have in the buildings" with natural scenery and "succeeded to their satisfaction." "A sufficient explanation of the apparent anomaly," he added, "is that there is a place for everything."

A place for everything. Olmsted's vision had room for the tropical ambience of the lagoon and the great sweep of cobbled beach beside Lake Michigan; for the refinement of the Court of Honor and the vulgarity of the Midway; for the diversity of the state pavilions and the sedate Palace of the Fine Arts. That was the chief difference between Olmsted and the architects. They wanted to create order out of chaos. He wanted to accommodate order *and* chaos.

Dear Rick

THE FAIR, THE EUROPEAN TRIP, Codman's death, had taken a lot out of Olmsted. He was starting to feel his age. A letter he wrote to John from Biltmore shows his frame of mind: indecisive, anxious, unsure of himself.

I am doubting some whether Eliot had better come here now or wait till February when, if living, I must come again. It should depend on the state of work elsewhere. I should think that by the end of next week I should be ready to start for Atlanta. Have you no doubt of the expediency of my going on to Louisville, to Chicago, Detroit, Buffalo, Rochester? It is a long and risky journey for me. I am not quite sure of the plan we had in view when I left. Was it that Manning [the firm's horticulturist] should go the round with me? or Eliot, or both? Am I needed at Kansas City? It is so long since I have been at Louisville that I shall be lost there if I go alone. You must send me the names of the people whom I shall need to renew acquaintance with. At this moment I cannot recall one. At Chicago they seem to have got away from me.

Whatever qualms he had about a long trip, Olmsted was eager to go to Atlanta. "With reference to your future business it is very desirable to make the firm favorably known at the South and 'extend its connections' as the merchants say," he advised John. The business in Atlanta involved the Kirkwood Land Company, which he had been advising for three years. The company planned to build a residential subdivision on fifteen hundred acres, four miles from downtown Atlanta in an area later known as Druid Hills. Olmsted had recommended that a "convenient, rapid, agreeable and popular means of communication . . . be provided between the city and some central point on the property." As in Riverside, he proposed a parkway, this time incorporating an "electric road"—that is, a trolley-car line. The parkway wound its way through a series of increasingly bucolic parks and man-made water bodies; the residential streets led away from this green corridor into the wooded hills. He completed the plan in 1893, although work was delayed until 1905 because of financial difficulties.

Olmsted's main concern was still Biltmore. The deadline for the completion of construction was Christmas 1895. By the end of 1893 the limestone walls of the house had risen to the second floor and the landscaping was well advanced. Hundreds of visitors came to tour the construction site, confirming Olmsted's claim that Biltmore would generate great public interest. "It is far and away the most distinguished private place, not only of America, but of the world," he assured John and Eliot, who did not share his enthusiasm for the project. Olmsted pointedly reminded his partners that while they stood at the forefront of the profession as far as public parks were concerned, "We have been unfortunate with *private places*. We have had no great success, have gained no celebrity. . . . The more important that we make a striking success where a chance is given us. *This* is a place and G.W.V. is a man, that we must do our best for."

The following year Rick finished Harvard, graduating magna cum laude—Olmsted's concerns that his high-spirited son was not academically inclined proved unfounded. He was extremely fond of Rick. "I like him very much," he confessed to Norton, "and he is affectionate and confiding, to me, more than boys generally to their fathers, I think." Olmsted encouraged Rick to become a landscape architect and set him a high goal. "I want you to be prepared to be a leader of the van . . . to make L.A. respected as an Art and a liberal profession." Yet when Rick graduated, he was not invited to join the firm. Instead Olmsted arranged a surveying job for him in Colorado. He considered that despite his twenty-four years Rick needed toughening (Olmsted lamented his own lack of formal education, but he firmly believed in learning from experience). He also wanted to broaden Rick's horizons. "The more you see—the more parts of our country and the more varied topographical and climatic conditions you have opportunity to carefully observe even from [railroad] car windows, the larger will be your professional capital," he wrote him. In the same letter Olmsted told his son that he had arranged for him to complete his apprenticeship at Biltmore.

Olmsted left Rick at Biltmore in November 1894. Two days before Christmas, Olmsted sat down in his Fairstead office to write him a letter.

The twenty-one dense pages took him three days to complete. Part of the letter contained touching personal advice, revealing as much about the father as about the son.

> Are you gaining any in the art of putting yourself to sleep when you will—the art of which Napoleon and Grant were equally masters? Are you going regularly to church—to what; and are you training yourself to avoid a critical view of it & cultivating devoutness & the childlike religion which Christ advanced in spite of the theological wrangling of the clergy? Do you succeed in avoiding theological disputes with Mr. McNamee [Vanderbilt's agent]? Are you helping Mr. Pinchot in his negro Sunday School? . . . Are you getting any practice in shooting, fishing or hunting . . . Have you shot a wild turkey?
>
> Are you going to any balls, or dances? Are you punctual and regular in your social—"society"—dates? Are you making acquaintances at the Hotels? . . . There are several nice people living within a few miles of you and you must not neglect social duties or opportunities. Recognize yourself & be sure that you are recognized as a gentleman of Society. Be punctilious & exacting with yourself in all those rites and forms and manners by which gentlemen and ladies recognize a gentleman.

The chief purpose of the letter, like the "instructions" that Olmsted had furnished John on his European trip, was to lay out a program of self-study. "Keep it all the time well in mind that you are now in a school of which you are yourself the headmaster," he wrote. "Do not neglect to think . . . how this ward of yours (F.L.O. Jr.) is to be educated." While emphasizing that Rick should take the opportunity to learn as much as possible about all aspects of the work that was being carried out at Biltmore, Olmsted was adamant on one point. "Your school for nearly all wisdom in trees and plants and planting is Biltmore." Chauncey D. Beadle, the estate's nurseryman, was to be Rick's tutor. "I am as ready to give Beadle a tuition fee of a thousand dollars as I was to give it to Harvard College," he assured his son. (Rick was not yet an employee of the firm; he received an allowance from his father.) *"If you don't get it now you never will,"* he cautioned. "Book knowledge can not be made to answer this purpose. Knowledge that you can pick up in the office will not suffice."

Olmsted considered his own lack of botanical knowledge a severe limitation, one that he insisted should not afflict Rick. "I want you not merely to be better fitted in this respect than I have been," he wrote, "but enough better to make good to the world what of the art of my profession I have been unable to supply." He signed the letter "Frederick Law Olmsted, Senior," to further emphasize his point. It was to Frederick Junior—to him alone—that he was passing the baton.

Rick had studied zoology at Harvard, but he found memorizing plant names tedious. Nor was he able to establish a rapport with Beadle, who did not have the time—or the inclination—to take the neophyte under his wing. Altogether, Rick was discouraged. Olmsted was unmoved. "I shall not take you into this office until you are much better grounded in trees and shrubs than any one here now. . . . If you think it impracticable, the sooner you give up the profession the better." He immediately added: "But I know *it is not impracticable,* and I *insist* on your making yourself an expert nursery man." Olmsted apologized for being so blunt. He recalled that his own career had suffered from his father's indulgence. That made him frank, he explained. Rick, too, was candid. He turned obstinate. The prospect of years of botanical study did not attract him, he wrote. If a knowledge of plants was really essential to being a landscape architect, "then I am compelled to answer, with pain and regret, after the most serious and thorough thought, that I believe I would better enter upon another career." He mentioned teaching, engineering, and architecture.

"You seem to me to have very much of my character," Olmsted wrote his son, "you are weak where I am weak; you are strong where I am strong." That was partly true. Rick had Olmsted's ease with people; he was athletic; he had been publisher and editor of his school's newspaper. All the month of January the letters flew back and forth between Brookline and Biltmore. "Stick to it. Get the better of your difficulties. Conquer them as a man." "It is too late to turn back," Olmsted admonished. In one respect Rick was not his father's son: he was not headstrong. In the end, he agreed to persist with the "botanical and horticultural drudgery." Olmsted was pleased but remained firm: "I should be disposed to keep you at Biltmore five years, rather than have you fail." But he reassured him that he was "anxious to get you under training here before I die."

In February Olmsted returned to Biltmore, accompanied by Mary. They planned to be there until early May, but Vanderbilt asked them to stay longer. He had commissioned John Singer Sargent to paint portraits of Hunt and Olmsted. Sargent depicted Hunt standing on the front terrace with the house in the background. He placed Olmsted in the forest, surrounded by dogwood, laurel, and rhododendron. The life-size, full-length portraits, which today hang in the second-floor living hall of Biltmore House, are poignant. Hunt looks self-assured, but his gaunt features show the stress of the disease that would kill him only two months later. Olmsted, leaning heavily on his stick, appears in ruddy good health and at ease. In fact, he was troubled. He had been unusually cantankerous the previous week; his treasured arboretum was not going well.

Olmsted loved trees. "If man is not to live by bread alone, what is better worth doing well than the planting of trees," he had once written. He had an elaborate arboretum in mind for Biltmore, "a finer, more beautiful, more distinguished and more useful museum of living trees than any now existing in the world." The mild climate of Biltmore would allow the collection to include both Southern and Northern indigenous varieties, of which he had already purchased four thousand seedlings. It took him four years to elaborate this plan. Finally, in December 1893, he submitted a report to the impatient Vanderbilt. Olmsted's intention was to lay out the arboretum on two sides of a long road. The trees would be displayed like pictures in an art gallery: "Water-side trees by the lake; Ash, on the fertile well-drained meadow; Magnolias in the dingles opening southward; Oaks on the higher upland, and so on." Two specimens would be planted near the road; behind these would be a small group of the species; farther back still, a full acre of growth would exhibit the species under forest conditions. He wanted the nine-mile-long arboretum road to serve several purposes at once: as a tree museum, a catalog of forestry resources, and a pleasure drive.

Olmsted was no tree expert. He counted on Charles Sprague Sargent of the Arnold Arboretum to help him identify and organize the specimen trees. Sargent agreed, then backed out—he considered it inadvisable to put a scientific collection under private ownership. Pinchot the forester, Beadle the nurseryman, and Manning the horticulturist were not much help—each had his parochial interest; only Olmsted had the vision of the whole. "I must yet for a time keep the plan before me as a sculptor keeps his work under damp cloths, in a plastic form," he told Vanderbilt. The design was mostly in his head, and his powers were flagging. "Father does not keep track of the details of this affair," Rick wrote to John. "When he went over the road 'in detail' with Manning there was little more than general consideration of the groups. . . . I hope the firm as represented by you and Eliot knows a great deal more about the Arboretum than Father does."

In truth, Olmsted had been having trouble with his memory. In one embarrassing incident, he had confused the planting layout of the tulip trees along the two sides of the entrance court. "If Rick had not been with me and had not privately set me right I should have shown the fact in a flagrant way to Mr. Vanderbilt," he admitted to John. This slip—not the first—confirmed his suspicion that he could no longer rely on his memory. "I think it my duty to tell you this at once in order that you may take measures to guard the business from possible consequences. . . . I see that I ought no longer to be entrusted to carry on important business for the firm alone." This time John was alarmed and hurried to Biltmore to accompany his parents home. They left before the portrait was complete. Sargent asked Rick, who was Olmsted's size, to put on his father's suit and coat and stand in while he finished the portrait.

Sunset

OLMSTED SPENT THE REST of the spring at Fairstead. He still went downstairs to the office. He was lucid, but continued to be forgetful. One day he wrote three separate but identical letters to Vanderbilt, "each without slightest memory of previous letter," an employee recalled. When Eliot found this out, he wondered if similar things had been getting out before. He and John decided that it was necessary to get their partner away from the office, at least for a time.

For several years Mary and Marion had been spending summers in a rented cottage in the village of Sunset on Deer Isle, Maine. They were often joined by Rick and John but rarely by Olmsted, who did not like the makeshift living arrangements in what he called the "little shebang." In August Mary asked him to accompany her to Sunset. He agreed, expecting a short stay, yet after two weeks there was no talk of returning home. "I am still here because Mother and Marion seem to have arranged that I should be," he wrote Rick, "but I can't say that I am enjoying myself or that it does not continue to be hugger-mugger." August turned to September and Mary insisted that they stay longer. She and John feared that if Olmsted returned to Brookline, he would want to be involved in the office. To satisfy him, John regularly kept him informed of the firm's activities. Olmsted, with time on his hands, sent long advisory letters, causing John to testily demand that he read the reports more carefully "before you write your daily [!] letter to us." He also warned his stepfather that "your failing memory will in time necessitate some slight readjustment of firm matters but you need not give it further thought for some weeks to come."

Olmsted suspected that he was the victim of a ruse, but he was resigned. "A queer situation it seems to me," he wrote Eliot, "but for the present I accept it and am trying to make the poor best of it." Rick was still in Biltmore and wrote frequently. Olmsted cherished these letters.

"Nothing goes as far to lift me out of the feeling of desolation," he wrote. "It is the assurance that you are taking up what I am dropping." He was coming to terms with his situation. His forgetfulness was not improving—it was getting worse. It seemed likely that he would not recover. Characteristically, he did not delude himself. All his life he had faced reality; he did so now. "Keep me here as long as you can," he told Mary. In a moving letter to Eliot he confessed his anguish. All he asked was not to be entirely cut off from the firm.

> I am grateful for your letter of 23ᵈ. I hardly need say that I have been passing the bitterest week of my life, resentment gradually giving way to a realization of the truth. In my flurry I have done some things which I would not do now and for which I am sorry. If I can be treated in the spirit suggested by your letter: if I can continue to live at home, and, especially, if I can, in any humble and limited way, be useful to you for a short time longer, it will be a great comfort to me. You cannot think how I have been dreading that it would be thought expedient that I should be sent to an "institution." Anything but that. My father was a director of an Insane Retreat, and first and last, having been professionally employed and behind the scenes in several, my dread of such places is intense. . . . It was perhaps right to deceive me as I was deceived when brought here, but further dealings with me in that spirit—with any deception—will greatly aggravate my misfortune. Dealt with frankly and kindly I hope to be able to cultivate a spirit of Christian withdrawal.

The next day his meekness disappeared. Mary found him in a dreadful state. "He makes us very nervous he is so violent," she wrote John. "Do not tell any one that your father's state is pitiful," she ordered him. "Let us keep it to ourselves as long as we can. Else his name will be useless to the business." She was not hard-hearted. Her husband's name was his chief legacy, as he himself had pointed out. It had to be protected. He would have approved.

Mary did her best. Yet as her husband's behavior became increasingly erratic, it was difficult to carry on in remote Sunset. Marion, already high-strung and further upset by her father's behavior, was not much help. Two weeks after the violent outburst they all returned to Brookline. The local doctor diagnosed premature old age brought on by overwork, complicated with "melancholia." He directed that Olmsted should stay away from the office and recommended a sojourn in England, whose damp weather would do him good, he assured Mary. She and Marion would accompany him. Olmsted wrote a final letter to Rick. "My doctors wish me to think that I am to be cured," he observed wryly. He continued to worry about Biltmore: "As I am drawn away from it and realize more and more the finality of this withdrawal, the intenser grows my urgency to be sure that what I have designed is to be realized." He was overjoyed when Rick returned to say good-bye, and they prevailed upon him to accompany them. The party left in mid-November.

As the Olmsteds sailed, a cruel accident befell Calvert Vaux. Seventy-one, now employed as a landscape architect by the New York Parks Department, he was living in Bensonhurst. On November 19, 1895, he disappeared during a dense fog while on his morning walk beside Gravesend Bay. It was feared that he might have fallen into the water, and his drowned body was found three days later. When Mary received the news in England, she burned the letter, afraid of its effect on Olmsted (she told him later).

Rick rented a house in Lymstone, Devonshire, and engaged a nurse. At his father's request Rick paid a visit to Kew Gardens and later briefly stopped in Paris before returning home in late December. Olmsted wrote John a long letter describing Rick's activities in England, instructing him about Rick's education, and giving advice about Biltmore and the firm's future. He commented only briefly on his own state of mind: "I am going down hill rapidly. I am much depressed but try not to show it." His condition was worsening, the confused and sometimes violent spells recurring with greater frequency. The doctor's prognosis was bleak. "He gives up all hope of improvement for your father," Mary informed Rick bluntly, "and says that all we can do is to stave off the more active form of inflammation and hope for simple imbecility."

Olmsted was probably a victim of some form of dementia. The progress of this disease is gradual, often measured in years. In its early stages it manifests itself as mere forgetfulness, which is why it is difficult to diagnose. As the disease advances, abnormal deposits of protein destroy the nerve cells in the brain and memory fades further, causing a gradual descent into bewilderment and confusion. Typically, the patient has good days and bad. Belligerence and paranoia can develop in extreme cases. Olmsted, who once wrote to Rick from Sunset complaining that John was plotting a coup to take over the firm, exhibited all these symptoms.

A few months later, when Olmsted became unmanageable, Mary was obliged to consign him to a sanitarium. She and Marion, exhausted by the ordeal, were now free to travel. They toured southern England and went to London. Mary eventually sent Marion, who was increasingly distraught, home.* Without consulting her sons, she took power of attorney over her husband's affairs. She ordered John and Rick to oversee the construction of a house on forty-six acres of land that she had earlier purchased on Deer Isle. John wondered what his mother would do with herself in such a remote place. "If she had some good-natured talkative darky servants it might be some relief but a solitary white woman servant won't be gay." Knowing that she would not be swayed, John hired an architect—the talented William Ralph Emerson—and put Rick, who was now an employee of the firm, in charge of the project.

When Mary and Olmsted returned from England in July, accompanied by a housekeeper and a male nurse, they went straight to Maine. The house, a large affair with eight bedrooms, was not yet finished. They lived in tents, which reminded Mary of Yosemite. They moved in before the winter. The comfortable house (which Mary named Felsted), the invigorating climate, the view of Penobscot Bay, and the calm surroundings did not have the desired effect. Olmsted continued his downward spiral. In March 1897 Felsted received tragic news from Brookline. Charles Eliot had died suddenly of meningitis. At first, Olmsted was agitated and wanted to return. He could not sleep for three days. Then, just as quickly, he forgot the whole business.

Only Olmsted's close friends were aware of his plight; as far as everyone else was concerned, he had merely withdrawn from public life. In time the clients of the firm had become used to dealing with John Olmsted and Charles Eliot. When Eliot died, John invited Rick to become his partner. By then there was no need to continue the pretense and they renamed the firm Olmsted Brothers. Their business did not decrease; far from it, they found themselves more in demand than ever. The seeds that their father had sown across the country sprouted and bore fruit. In time the Fairstead office expanded and became the largest landscape architecture practice in the country, probably in the world.

Olmsted was to live at Felsted less than two years. Rick, who visited regularly, finally concluded that nothing more could be done. The very

*Before returning to the United States, Mary traveled to France, stayed in Paris, and visited John Hull Olmsted's grave in Nice.

thing that his father feared most could not be postponed. In September 1898 the family moved Olmsted to McLean Asylum in Waverly, about four miles from Brookline. There, the great landscape architect lived in a cottage surrounded by grounds that he himself had designed.

In one of his last letters to Rick, Olmsted had directed his son personally to take charge of the Biltmore arboretum. Rick had not become skilled in trees and plants, and the complicated work confounded him. Vanderbilt lost interest in the project, and the arboretum's fate was sealed in 1900 when, financially squeezed, he stopped all new work on the estate.* Rick was only twenty-seven when he became a partner in the firm—the period of apprenticeship that his father had anticipated was relatively brief. Nevertheless, he soon eclipsed his older half brother. "John is John & must be taken as he is made," Mary once wrote, "most excellent but clumsy." Rick, on the other hand, was outgoing and convivial. And he had the famous name. In short order he blossomed. In 1898 he was appointed landscape architect to the Boston Metropolitan Park Commission, a regional organization that Eliot had helped to found. Rick followed his father's admonition to "make L.A. respected as an Art and a liberal profession." In 1899 he helped to establish the American Society of Landscape Architects. In 1900 Charles W. Eliot invited him to Harvard to create the country's first curriculum in landscape architecture; two years later he was appointed the Charles Eliot Professor of Landscape Architecture. The following year Rick achieved national prominence when President Theodore Roosevelt appointed him with Daniel Burnham to the Senate Park Commission. The Commission, which eventually included McKim and Saint-Gaudens, was charged with replanning the center of Washington, D.C.† In a few short years Rick truly had become the "leader of the van." Sadly, by then Olmsted was no longer able to appreciate that the last great project of his life had come to fruition just as he had hoped—and planned.

On Thursday, August 27, 1903, the McLean Asylum telephoned Fairstead with the news that Olmsted, now eighty-one, was unconscious and

---

*Biltmore Forest did fulfill Olmsted's hopes. It was the location of the first forestry school in the United States and eventually became Pisgah National Forest.
†The guiding force behind this project was Senator James McMillan of Michigan, who, twenty years earlier, had approached Olmsted to design Belle Isle.

breathing heavily. Death was imminent. Mary, John, and Rick rushed to Waverly. They were told it was a question of a few hours at most. When Olmsted's state remained unchanged, John took his mother home. Frederick Olmsted died at two o'clock the next morning with Rick at his bedside.

Two days later the *New-York Times* published a full-column article under the headline "F. L. OLMSTED IS DEAD: End Comes to Great Landscape Architect at Waverly, Mass." It was eight years since he had dropped out of public life, but he was not forgotten. Soon letters and telegrams would arrive in Fairstead from friends, colleagues, and clients: André, Kingsbury, Burnham, Vanderbilt. When Charles Eliot Norton, who was at his summer house, heard about it, he wrote Rick a tender note:

> I have felt much for you during the past week. Though the death of your Father comes as a relief in its freeing him from all that made his last years sorrowful to himself and sad to those who loved him, it brings home to you the sense of loss and change. . . . You can, however, have nothing but happiness in looking back on the years of his life. Few men have done better service than he, service beneficent not only to his own generation, but to generation after generation in the long future.

The funeral was held at Fairstead the following Monday. Only family members attended: John and Rick; Olmsted's half brother Albert and his wife; Charlotte's husband, John, and their two children; and Olmsted's cousin Fanny. "It was a meager unsatisfactory service in proportion to the few who came to it," noted John Olmsted sadly. Mary had wanted it that way. She herself stayed away; her farewells had been said long ago.

Prospect Park, Brooklyn

Thursday, August 7, 1997

It is mid-afternoon. The trees throw long shadows across the rolling surface of the Long Meadow. There are a few small groups of people sitting under the clumps of trees that break up the green sward. A woman and a man, deep in conversation, are walking across the meadow toward Swan Boat Lake. The woman is the administrator of the park. I am the man. She is showing me around.

We reach a path that skirts the lake—a pond, really—and enter the trees. It is quiet, and we can hear the sound of falling water. A dozen paces later, through an opening in the trees, I glimpse a little tableau. At the far end of a still pool a spring gushes out of a rocky outcropping. The outcropping is only a few feet above the water's level, creating a little cataract that splashes noisily onto a large boulder. From the pool a stream rushes beneath the rustic footbridge on which we are standing. Just before the stream tumbles into the pond, it swirls around a vertical rock.

We continue down the curved path beside the pond. The shimmering expanse is bordered by trees on one side and the meadow on the other. A turn brings us once more into the dark woods. We cross another footbridge over a gurgling stream. The path turns into a mountain track, carved into an almost vertical, rock-strewn slope. We stop to look down where the slope descends to the stream, which has widened as it courses through a deep glen. "That's the Ambergill," she says. "Olmsted loved these old English names."

We pass a row of potted shrubs ready for planting, a reminder that this entire section of the park is being restored. Over the years it had fallen into disrepair, the spring dried up, the brook silted solid, the pond overgrown with weeds. Now, boulder by boulder, seedling by seedling, tree by tree, it is being rebuilt. I can see stacks of pipes and piles of crushed stone among the trees. The site must have looked much the same during its construction 130 years ago.

The path turns sharply right, bringing us to the edge of a ravine. The water is not yet running in this part of the restoration. When it does, the Ambergill will course through a narrow defile and fall eight feet into the ravine. At the far end, the torrent will disappear beneath huge boulders that appear to have tumbled into the cleft of the ravine. The boulders form a cyclopean bridge that carries the path farther into the forest. In the other direction, a flight of roughly dressed stone steps rises steeply up the hill.

This entire sequence—the spring, the pond, the glen, the ravine—occupies a tiny space; the straight-line distance that I have walked is barely a thousand feet from beginning to end. Yet so skillfully did Olmsted and Vaux lay out the path, engage the senses, mask distances, and direct attention from one event to another, that I have entirely forgotten that just over the brow of the hill lies Long Meadow and beyond it Flatbush Avenue.

We retrace our steps through the dark glade and alongside the shimmering water until we reach the comforting green swathe of the meadow, a clearing in the distance. The administrator is describing the work that yet needs to be done. I am glad that the park is in such good hands. But half my mind is else-

where, still in the man-made little piece of Adirondack mountains, hearing the forest sounds, walking the sun-dappled path among the swaying trees.

I have visited many Olmsted parks. Most, like this one, are being tended, cared for, restored. That pleases me for these really are precious, historic places— as precious and historic in their way as Chartres Cathedral or the Acropolis. Unlike old buildings, however, these places are not historical relics. Timeless, I want to say. But I well know that they are rooted in a particular time and place, and in the minds of particular men. What ambition, what effort, what devotion.

See! this our fathers did for us.

OLMSTED'S DISTANT EFFECTS

Frederick Law Olmsted making notes in the snow, c. 1890.

Distant Effects

THE FIRST BIOGRAPHY of Frederick Law Olmsted appeared while he was still alive. Written by Mariana Griswold Van Rensselaer, it was published in the October 1893 issue of the popular *Century Illustrated Monthly Magazine.* Van Rensselaer had the advantage of a long friendship with her subject, and she was an astute critic of the arts; her *Henry Hobson Richardson and His Works* (Boston: Houghton Mifflin, 1888) is both appreciative and insightful. Unfortunately she never undertook a full-length biography of Olmsted. No other biographer came forward in the years following Olmsted's death. Between February and July 1906, Wilson Eyre's *House and Garden* magazine published four illustrated articles on selected Olmsted projects (including Mount Royal). They were written by John Nolen, then studying landscape architecture under Frederick Law Olmsted Jr. at Harvard and soon to become one of the country's most accomplished town planners.

The closest thing to an Olmsted biography was edited by Rick together with Theodora Kimball, who was then the librarian of Harvard's department of landscape architecture, where Rick continued to teach until 1914. *Frederick Law Olmsted, Landscape Architect, 1822–1903,* which carried the long subtitle, *Forty Years of Landscape Architecture; Being the Professional Papers of Frederick Law Olmsted, Senior* (New York: G. P. Putnam's Son's, 1922), was followed by a companion volume, *Central Park as a Work of Art and as a Great Municipal Enterprise, 1853–1895* (New York: G. P. Putnam's Son's, 1928). For many years this collection of correspondence, reports, biographical fragments, and chronological highlights remained the chief source of firsthand information about Olmsted's life.

In 1931 the writer and architectural critic Lewis Mumford published *The Brown Decades* (New York: Harcourt Brace, 1931) in which he devoted much of a chapter to Olmsted. Mumford's perceptive appreciation of Olmsted's position in nineteenth-century America was not widely shared. In fact, by then the man whom Mumford described as having "almost single-handed laid the foundations for a better order in city building" had slipped into almost total obscurity. Part of the reason, paradoxically, was Rick's success. After replanning Washington, D.C., he helped found the National Park Service and advised on the management of Yosemite. He came to dominate the planning field, serving as president of both the American Society of Landscape Architects *and* the American Institute of Planners. His Brookline firm (John died in 1920) laid out world's fairs, college campuses, urban parks, private estates, and residential suburbs across the United States. He had long since dropped the "Junior" from his name—*he* was now the famous Olmsted.

Olmsted had resisted attempts to reprint *The Cotton Kingdom,* yet for the first half of the twentieth century if he was remembered at all, it was as a chronicler of the antebellum South. *A Journey in the Seaboard Slave States, with Remarks on Their Economy* (including a biographical sketch by Rick) was republished by G. P. Putnam's Sons in two volumes in 1904; Putnam's reprinted *A Journey in the Back Country* in 1907. *A Journey Through Texas* was reprinted much later (Austin, Texas: Von Boeckmann-Jones Press, 1962). The first serious reassessment of Olmsted's Southern reporting was Broadus Mitchell's *Frederick Law Olmsted, a Critic of the Old South* (Baltimore: Johns Hopkins University Press, 1924). Although Mitchell's work has factual errors, it remains a perceptive appraisal. Edmund Wilson's profile of Olmsted as a critic of the South in *Patriotic Gore* (New York: Oxford University Press, 1962) is likewise worth reading. But the breakthrough, as far as Olmsted reaching a broader audience, occurred earlier with the appearance of a new edition of *The Cotton Kingdom* (New York: Alfred A. Knopf, 1953), edited with a thoughtful introduction by the noted historian Arthur M. Schlesinger Sr. This version remained in print for twenty years and was reissued in slightly altered form in 1984. Incidentally, the availability of *The Cotton Kingdom* has directed attention away from Olmsted's original newspaper accounts. That is a shame, for the reports that appeared in the *New-York Daily Times* (and a few in the *New York Daily Tribune*) are fresher and more vivid than the heavily augmented and twice-summarized (and overwritten) versions that make up *The Cotton Kingdom.*

When Schlesinger was writing his introduction, he consulted a previously unavailable source of information. In 1947–48 Rick had given his father's personal and business correspondence and other family records to the Library of Congress. The approximately twenty-four thousand items formed the basis of the Frederick Law Olmsted Papers and were later augmented by additional material from the Olmsted office (Rick continued to practice until 1950; he died in 1957). It is a remarkable archive. Olmsted, to put it mildly, was a pack rat. He saved everything: personal and business letters, travel diaries, ticket stubs, clippings, expense sheets, drafts of reports, fragments of writing. Sadly, no correspondence exists before he was eighteen; it was probably lost in the fire that destroyed the barns at Tosomock Farm, where Olmsted had stored many of his possessions while he was in Bear Valley. Nor are there significant surviving personal or business papers of Calvert Vaux. In 1977 the Frances Loeb Library of Harvard University's Graduate School of Design acquired the papers of John C. Olmsted (from his daughter Carolyn), including many letters that throw interesting new light on the relations between father and stepson.

A register of the Frederick Law Olmsted Papers was prepared in 1963, but not until 1975 was the entire collection microfilmed (on no fewer than sixty reels). By then America was well on its way to rediscovering Frederick Law Olmsted. In 1967 Henry Hope Reed and Sophia Duckworth's *Central Park: A History and a Guide* (New York: Clarkson N. Potter, 1967) and Clay Lancaster's *Prospect Park Handbook* (New York: Greensward Foundation, 1967) appeared. These popular works both underlined the pivotal roles of Olmsted and Vaux. Edited collections of Olmsted's landscaping and planning reports were published, notably *Landscape into Cityscape: Frederick Law Olmsted's Plans for a Greater New York City* (ed. Albert Fein, Ithaca, N.Y.: Cornell University Press, 1967) and *Civilizing American Cities: Writings on American Landscapes* (ed. S. B. Sutton, Cambridge, Mass.: MIT Press, 1971). The sesquicentennial of Olmsted's birth—1972—was marked by an exhibition organized and directed by William Alex at the Whitney Museum of American Art titled "Frederick Law Olmsted's New York." The exhibition, and an accompanying book of the same name by Elizabeth Barlow and Alex (New York: Praeger, 1972), further heightened public awareness. The first full-length life of Olmsted appeared the following year, *FLO: A Biography of Frederick Law Olmsted* (Baltimore: Johns Hopkins University Press, 1973) by Laura Wood Roper. Roper had written several articles on Olmsted, including "Frederick Law Olmsted and the Western Texas Free-Soil

Movement" (*American Historical Review,* October 1950), the excellent "Frederick Law Olmsted in the 'Literary Republic' " (*Mississippi Valley Historical Review,* December 1952), and " 'Mr. Law' and Putnam's Monthly Magazine" (*American Literature,* March 1954). Her book is a model of the scholarly biography. Roper had the added benefit of talking with Rick at length and was the first researcher given access to the Olmsted papers by the family. A second biography, Elizabeth Stevenson's *Park Maker, a Life of Frederick Law Olmsted* (New York: Collier Macmillan, 1977), was published a few years later.

The availability of the Frederick Law Olmsted Papers has given rise to an extraordinary project of the Johns Hopkins University Press: *The Papers of Frederick Law Olmsted.* The intention of the editors is to publish the most significant of Olmsted's letters, writings, and reports. Twelve volumes are projected; seven have appeared at the time of writing: *The Formative Years, 1822–1852* (ed. Charles Capon McLaughlin, 1977); *Slavery and the South, 1852–1857* (ed. Charles E. Beveridge and Charles Capon McLaughlin 1981); *Creating Central Park, 1857–1861* (ed. Charles E. Beveridge and David Schuyler, 1983); *Defending the Union, 1861–1863* (ed. Jane Turner Censer, 1986); *The California Frontier, 1863–1865* (ed. Victoria Post Ranney, 1990); *The Years of Olmsted, Vaux & Company, 1865-1874* (ed. David Schuyler and Jane Turner Censer, 1992); and *Writings on Public Parks, Parkways, and Park Systems* (ed. Charles E. Beveridge and Carolyn F. Hoffman, 1997). Begun by a redoubtable Olmsted scholar, Charles Capon McLaughlin, and now under the overall editorship of Charles E. Beveridge, this monumental series, intelligently annotated and exhaustively researched, represents an invaluable aid to anyone interested in Olmsted, including this author.

Exhibitions and books are one thing, but what revived Olmsted's reputation among the general public was the rehabilitation of Central Park. During the years after World War II, the park steadily deteriorated: the grounds became overgrown, buildings were abandoned, the Bethesda Terrace was neglected and covered in graffiti. The general dilapidation—as well as fear of crime—kept the public away, and Central Park became an embarrassing eyesore. In December 1980 Mayor Edward Koch announced the formation of the Central Park Conservancy, a private fund-raising body. Together with park administrator Elizabeth Barlow Rogers, this group was responsible for rebuilding and restoring the park. The restoration was done with as much historical accuracy as possible, and a new generation of New Yorkers rediscovered the beauty of Greensward. The renewal of other parks followed: not only the ravine area of Prospect Park, but also Boston's Franklin Park and the Louisville park system.

The entire story of Central Park is told in Roy Rosenzweig and Elizabeth Blackmar's *The Park and the People: A History of Central Park* (Ithaca, N.Y.: Cornell University Press, 1992), which is particularly good on the origins and early days of the park. David Schuyler's *The New Urban Landscape: The Redefinition of City Form in Nineteenth-Century America* (Baltimore: Johns Hopkins University Press, 1986) is a review of the impact of Olmsted's planning ideas, and the same author's *Apostle of Taste: Andrew Jackson Downing 1815–1852* (Baltimore: Johns Hopkins University Press, 1996) is a useful biography of Olmsted's chief predecessor. William Alex's *Calvert Vaux: Architect and Planner* (New York: Ink, Inc., 1994) is a good source of visual material on the park projects that Olmsted and Vaux designed together; Francis Kowsky's *Country, Park, & City: The Architecture and Life of Calvert Vaux* (New York: Oxford University Press, 1998) provides a sympathetic view of the Olmsted–Vaux partnership. Melvin Kalfus's psychobiography, *Frederick Law Olmsted: The Passion of a Public Artist* (New York: New York University Press, 1990), is highly speculative but contains some interesting background research. Lee Hall's *Olmsted's America: An "Unpractical" Man and His Vision of Civilization* (Boston: Bulfinch Press, 1995) sheds little new light on its subject.

A number of authors have written about specific Olmsted landscaping projects. Cynthia Zaitzevsky's *Frederick Law Olmsted and the Boston Park System* (Cambridge, Mass.: Harvard University Press, 1992) is an exemplary account that examines in admirable detail the working methods of the Olmsted firm. One does not have to agree with M. M. Graff's criticisms of Olmsted (she is a Vaux fan) to find useful nuggets in *Central Park, Prospect Park: A New Perspective* (New York: Greensward Foundation, 1985). John M. Bryan's *Biltmore Estate: The Most Distinguished Private Place* (New York: Rizzoli, 1994) provides an account of the building of this remarkable estate. Olmsted's trials are recorded in *The Founders and the Architects: The Design of Stanford University* (Stanford: Stanford University, 1976) by Paul V. Turner. The garden at Fairsted is described in detail by Mac Griswold in "Fairsted: A Landscape as Olmsted's Looking Glass" (*Arnoldia*, summer 1996). *Viewing Olmsted* (Montreal: Canadian

Centre for Architecture, 1996), the catalog of a photographic exhibition, offers several evocative—and many unusually idiosyncratic—views of selected Olmsted parks by three well-known photographers.

A number of scholarly articles have dealt with Olmsted's ideas about parks and landscaping, notably Geoffrey Blodgett's "Frederick Law Olmsted: Landscape Architecture as Conservative Reform" (*Journal of American History,* March 1976), Laurie Olin's "Form, Meaning and Expression in Landscape Architecture" (*Landscape Journal,* fall 1988), George L. Scheper's "The Reformist Vision of Frederick Law Olmsted and the Poetics of Park Design" (*The New England Quarterly,* September 1989), and Anne Whiston Spirn's "Constructing Nature: The Legacy of Frederick Law Olmsted" (in *Uncommon Ground: Toward Reinventing Nature,* ed. William Cronon, New York: W. W. Norton & Company, 1995). It would be ungrateful of me not to mention the short essay that sparked my own interest in Olmsted, Roger Starr's "The Motive Behind Olmsted's Park" (*The Public Interest,* winter 1984).

An excellent introduction to Olmsted's landscape work is Charles E. Beveridge's lavishly illustrated *Frederick Law Olmsted: Designing the American Landscape* (New York: Rizzoli, 1995), whose beautiful photographs of parks and gardens by Paul Rocheleau are almost as good as being there. Almost, but not quite. When I started to think of writing about Olmsted, Laurie Olin told me, "Always look at the work first." I have tried to follow his advice and have visited Mountain View Cemetery in Oakland, Central Park, Prospect Park, Mount Royal, Riverside, Boston's Emerald Necklace, Fairstead in Brookline (now the Frederick Law Olmsted National Historic Site), Lawrenceville School, Smith College, Moraine Farm, and Biltmore Estate, as well as Hartford, Sachem's Head, Staten Island, Fairstead (which is now a National Historical Site), Bear Valley, and Yosemite. Walking over the grounds that Olmsted shaped, experiencing the scenic views that he created, sitting under the trees that he planted, has been one of the added pleasures of writing this book.

A Selected List
of Olmsted Projects

FREDERICK LAW OLMSTED AND CALVERT VAUX

1858–76	Central Park, New York, N.Y.
1860–74	Hartford Retreat for the Insane, Hartford, Conn.
1865	College of California, Berkeley, Calif.
1866	Columbia Institution for the Deaf and Dumb, Washington, D.C.
1865–95	Prospect Park, Brooklyn, N.Y.
1867	Seaside Park, Bridgeport, Conn.
1867–73	Cornell University, Ithaca, N.Y.
1867–86	Fort Greene Park, Brooklyn, N.Y.
1868	Parade Ground, King's County, Brooklyn, N.Y.
1868	Tompkins Park, Brooklyn, N.Y.
1868–74	Eastern and Ocean Parkways, Brooklyn, N.Y.
1868–87	Riverside residential community, Ill.
1868–89	Riverside Park, New York, N.Y.
1868–1915	Delaware Park, The Parade, and The Front, Buffalo, N.Y.
1869–71	Walnut Hill Park, New Britain, Conn.
1870–72	Tarrytown Heights residential community, N.Y.
1870–95	South Park, Chicago, Ill.
1870–1914	South Park, Fall River, Mass.
1870–1920	Downing Park, Newburgh, N.Y.
1871	New York State Asylum for the Insane, Buffalo, N.Y.
1876–89	Morningside Park, New York, N.Y.
1879–95	State Reservation at Niagara Falls, N.Y.

FREDERICK LAW OLMSTED

1864–65 Mountain View Cemetery, Oakland, Calif.
1865–67 San Francisco Public Grounds, Calif.
1870–88 Staten Island Improvement Commission, Staten Island, N.Y.
1872–75 McLean Asylum grounds, Waverley, Mass.
1872–86 Parkside subdivision, Buffalo, N.Y.
1872–94 Trinity College, Hartford, Conn.
1873–93 Mount Royal Park, Montreal, Canada
1873 Tacoma Land Company, Tacoma, Wash.
1874–81 Yale University, New Haven, Conn.
1875–78 Twenty-Third & Twenty-Fourth Wards, New York, N.Y.
1875–94 U.S. Capitol grounds, Washington, D.C.
1878–1920 Back Bay Fens, Boston, Mass.
1879–97 Arnold Arboretum, Boston, Mass.
1880–93 Muddy River Improvement, Boston, Mass.
1881–84 Bridgeport Parks, Bridgeport, Conn.
1881–1895 Belle Isle, Detroit, Mich.
1881–1921 Franklin Park, Boston, Mass.
1883–1901 Lawrenceville School, Lawrenceville, N.J.

FREDERICK LAW OLMSTED WITH JOHN CHARLES OLMSTED AND HENRY SARGENT CODMAN (+1893)

1884–92 Brookline Hill subdivision, Brookline, Mass.
1886–1914 Stanford University, Palo Alto, Calif.
1886–90 Planter's Hill and World's End subdivision, Hingham, Mass.
1887–96 Wilmington Parks, Wilmington, Del.
1888–93 World's Columbian Exposition, Chicago, Ill.
1890–95 Essex County Parks, Essex County, N.J.
1890–1906 National Zoological Park, Washington, D.C.
1890–1912 Genesee Valley Park, Rochester, N.Y.
1891–95 Louisville Parks, Louisville, Ken.
1891–1909 Biltmore Estate, Asheville, N.C.
1891–1909 Smith College, Northampton, Mass.
1892–94 Bloomingdale Asylum, White Plains, N.Y.
1892–1905 Druid Hills residential community, Atlanta, Ga.
1893–1895 Wood Island Park, Boston, Mass.

CHARLES ELIOT (+1897), JOHN CHARLES OLMSTED (+1920), AND FREDERICK LAW OLMSTED JR.

1895–99	Washington University, St. Louis, Mo.
1895–1912	Royal Victoria Hospital, Montreal, Canada
1895–1927	Bryn Mawr College, Bryn Mawr, Penn.
1896–1922	Mount Holyoke College, South Hadley, Mass.
1896–1932	Vassar College, Poughkeepsie, N.Y.
1897–1914	Roland Park, Baltimore, Md.
1897–1924	Audubon Park, New Orleans, La.
1900–06	Brown University, Providence, R.I.
1901–1910	University of Chicago, Chicago, Ill.
1901–1930	Seattle Parks, Seattle, Wash.
1902–12	Williams College, Williamstown, Mass.
1902–20	University of Washington, Seattle, Wash.
1903	Lewis and Clark Exposition, Portland, Oreg.
1903–19	Johns Hopkins University, Baltimore, Md.
1904–05	Portland Parks, Portland, Me.
1906–08	Spokane Parks, Spokane, Wash.
1907–21	New Haven Improvement Commission, New Haven, Conn.
1908–25	Boulder Improvement Association, Boulder, Co.
1909	Alaska-Yukon-Pacific Exposition, Seattle, Wash.
1909–12	Battery Park, Charleston, S.C.
1909–31	Forest Hills Gardens residential community, Queens, N.Y.
1909–31	Pittsburgh Civic Commission, Pittsburgh, Penn.
1910–11	Dayton Parks, Dayton, Oh.
1911	San Diego Exposition, San Diego, Calif.
1912–13	Newport City Improvement, Newport, R.I.
1914–31	Rancho Palos Verdes residential community, Palos Verdes, Calif.
1925–26	Philadelphia Sesquicentennial Exposition, Philadelphia, Penn.
1925–31	Harvard Business School, Cambridge, Mass.
1925–32	Haverford College, Haverford, Penn.
1925–65	Duke University, Durham, N.C.
1927–35	Fort Tryon Park, New York, N.Y.
1929–32	Notre Dame University, South Bend, Ind.
1932–33	Morris Arboretum, Philadelphia, Penn.

According to the invaluable *The Master List of Design Projects of the Olmsted Firm 1857–1950* (Boston: Massachusetts Association for Olmsted Parks, 1987), "between 1857 and 1950 the firm participated in some way in 5,500 projects."

ACKNOWLEDGMENTS

I am grateful to the following for their advice, help, and useful counsel: Amy Brown, Tom Comitta, Paula Deitz, Jeremiah Eck, Drew Faust, Arleyn A. Levee, Ian McHarg, Rollins Maxwell, Henry Hope Reed, William Rawn, and especially Laurie Olin. Eva Burns, M.D., thoughtfully offered a psychiatrist's perspective. Jace Gaffney kindly suggested what became the title of this book. William Alex of the Frederick Law Olmsted Association was gracious with his time. Several people generously showed me around Olmsted works: Tupper Thomas, Administrator, and Christian Zimmerman, Landscape Architect, of the Prospect Park Alliance; Frances G. Beatty, Senior Landscape Architect of Boston Parks & Recreation; George and Mimi Batchelder of Moraine Farm; and Michael S. Cary, Head Master of Lawrenceville School.

Libraries and librarians are always helpful, but I would like to single out Mary Daniels, Special Collections Librarian of the Frances Loeb Library of the Harvard University Graduate School of Design, for guiding me through the John C. Olmsted Collection. Helpful, too, were: Marilyn M. Love, archivist of Lawrenceville School; Deborah Husted Koshinsky of the Architecture and Planning Library, SUNY Buffalo; Cynthia Van Ness of the Buffalo and Erie County Public Library; and the staff of Interlibrary Loans of the Van Pelt Library of the University of Pennsylvania. During the long writing of the book I was able to count on the helpful assistance of several able research assistants: Kate Howarth, Kiet Ta, Phuc Tran, Jason Kim, and David Bagnoli. Shawn Seaman skillfully drew the plans of Olmsted projects.

Alexandra Truitt did an outstanding job researching photographic material. Steve Boldt is a copy editor par excellence. Iris Tupholme and Nicole Langlois at HarperCollins in Toronto were helpful. Susan Moldow of Scribner was as supportive a publisher as one could ever hope to have.

My editor, Nan Graham, can discuss ideas and parse sentences with equal enthusiasm—and skill. Carl Brandt lent his attentive agent's ear. John Lukacs generously took time off from his own writing to review mine. My wife knows how much this book owes to her, so I will only say, "Thank you, Shirley."

NOTES

ABBREVIATIONS

FLOP: Frederick Law Olmsted Papers, Manuscript Division, Library of Congress, Washington, D.C.
JCOC: John C. Olmsted Collection, Frances Loeb Library, Graduate School of Design, Harvard University.

SCHEMES
Chapter One: "Tough as nails"

19   "a vigorous, manly fellow . . .": Frederick J. Kingsbury, "Biographical fragment," c. 1904, FLOP.
19   "His face is generally very placid . . .": Katharine Prescott Wormeley, *The Other Side of War; with the Army of the Potomac. Letters from the Headquarters of the United States Sanitary Commission during the Peninsular Campaign in Virginia in 1862* (Boston: Ticknor & Company, 1889), 63.
19   "All the lines of his face . . .": *Letters of Charles Eliot Norton,* ed. Sara Norton and M. A. DeWolfe Howe (Boston: Houghton Mifflin, 1913), 264.
20   "They tried a mob . . .": Frederick Law Olmsted to John Olmsted, March 11, 1864, FLOP.
20   "He is an extraordinary fellow, . . .": George Templeton Strong, *Diary of the Civil War, 1860–1865,* ed. Allan Nevins (New York: Macmillan, 1962), 304.
21   "He looks far ahead, . . .": Henry Whitney Bellows to James Miller McKim, August 18, 1865, Henry Whitney Bellows Papers, Massachusetts Historical Society, Boston.
22   "the main object . . .": Frederick Law Olmsted to Montgomery Cunningham Meigs, August 2, 1870, FLOP.
22   "nursery rows could be planted . . .": Ibid.

Chapter Two: Frederick goes to school

23   "When I was three years old . . .": Frederick Law Olmsted, "Autobiographical fragment," undated, FLOP.
24   "He was at bottom . . .": Frederick Law Olmsted to John Charles Olmsted, January 29, 1873, FLOP.
25   local eminence . . .: see Richard Hofstadter, *The Age of Reform: From Bryan to F.D.R.* (New York: Random House, 1955), 135.

25 "prayed to God . . .": Frederick Law Olmsted, "Autobiographical fragment," undated, FLOP.

26 One biographer has suggested . . .: see Charles Capen McLaughlin, "His Life Work," *The Papers of Frederick Law Olmsted, Vol. I, The Formative Years 1822–1852*, ed. Charles Capen McLaughlin (Baltimore: Johns Hopkins University Press, 1977), 4.

27 "I was active, . . .": Ibid., n. 8, 110.

Chapter Three: Hartford

28 "I was strangely uneducated, . . .": *Frederick Law Olmsted, Landscape Architect, 1822–1903*, ed. Frederick Law Olmsted Jr. and Theodora Kimball (New York: G. P. Putnam's Sons, 1928), 69.

29 "I see certain advantages . . .": Frederick Law Olmsted to Frederick Newman Knapp, October 8, 1866, FLOP.

30 "A boy . . . who . . .": Ibid.

30 "the attention of his friends . . .": The *Times*, October 3, 1835.

31 "refinement of America": see Richard L. Bushman, *The Refinement of America: Persons, Houses, Cities* (New York: Alfred A. Knopf, 1992).

32 "It is highly gratifying . . .": *Connecticut Courant*, September 25, 1832.

32 "The town is beautifully situated . . .": Charles Dickens, *American Notes* (New York: Oxford University Press, 1985), 66–69.

33 "It came to me after a time . . .": Frederick Law Olmsted, "Autobiographical fragment," undated, FLOP.

33 "a notable influence . . .": Ibid.

33 "He was very fond . . .": Frederick J. Kingsbury, "Biographical fragment," c. 1904, FLOP.

34 "I was but nine . . .": Frederick Law Olmsted to Mariana Griswold Van Rensselaer, June 17, 1893, FLOP.

Chapter Four: "I have no objection"

36 "the pupil of a topographical engineer, . . .": Frederick Law Olmsted, "Autobiographical fragment," undated, FLOP.

36 "When fourteen I was laid up . . .": Ibid.

37 "Because of an accident . . .": *Frederick Law Olmsted, Landscape Architect, 1822–1903*, ed. Frederick Law Olmsted Jr. and Theodora Kimball (New York: G. P. Putnam's Sons, 1928), 69.

37 "Advised to give up . . .": Ibid., 4.

37 "went to NYK . . .": John Olmsted, Family Record, Expense Memorandum Books, FLOP. This discrepancy is pointed out in Melvin Kalfus, "In Memory of Summer Days: The Mind and Work of Frederick Law Olmsted" (Ph.D. diss., New York University, 1988), appendix C, 623.

38 "fitting for college . . .": "Memorandum of 'notable events in Fred's life,' from diary of John Olmsted with some additions (all as to dates later than 1857), by Mary Cleveland Olmsted," undated, JCOC.

38 "If you will not go back . . .": John Olmsted to Frederick Law Olmsted, September 27, 1838, FLOP.

39 "I am very pleased . . .": John Olmsted to Frederick Law Olmsted, October 7, 1838, FLOP.

39 "decently restrained vagabond life, . . .": Frederick Law Olmsted, "Autobiographical fragment," undated, FLOP.

40 "Please send us some . . .": Frederick Law Olmsted to John Hull Olmsted, July 7, 1840, FLOP.

Chapter Five: New York

42 "Placed at sixteen . . .": Mariana Griswold Van Rensselaer, "Frederick Law Olmsted," *Century Illustrated Monthly Magazine* 46, no. 6 (October 1893): 861.

42 "perhaps being tired . . .": Frederick J. Kingsbury, "Biographical fragment," c. 1904. FLOP.

42 "I have no recollection . . .": John Olmsted to Frederick Law Olmsted, September 27, 1838, FLOP.

43 "Bizarre and not very agreeable,": Richard Reeves, *American Journey: Traveling with Tocqueville in Search of Democracy in America* (New York: Simon & Schuster, 1982), 315.

43 "commercial habits . . .": Alexis de Tocqueville, *Journey to America*, ed., J. P. Mayer, trans., George Lawrence (New York: Harper & Row, 1988), 203.

44 Estimates of loses . . .: Hawthorne Daniel, *The Hartford of Hartford* (New York: Random House, 1960), 74.

45 "Oh, how I long to be . . .": Frederick Law Olmsted to Mary Bull Olmsted, March 20, 1841, FLOP.

46 "The business is such that . . .": Frederick Law Olmsted to John Hull Olmsted, August 29, 1840, FLOP.

47 "Ally has the difficulty . . .": Frederick Law Olmsted to John Olmsted, March 16, 1865, FLOP.

Chapter Six: A year before the mast

48 "Ol will go to China . . .": Frederick Law Olmsted to John Hull Olmsted, December 7, 1842, FLOP.

48 "We must come down . . .": Richard Henry Dana Jr., *Two Years Before the Mast: a personal narrative of life at sea* (New York: World Syndicate Publishing Company, 1907), 279.

48 It is possible that Olmsted . . .: see Melvin Kalfus, "In Memory of Summer Days: The Mind and Work of Frederick Law Olmsted," (Ph.D. diss., New York University, 1988), n. 22, 245.

49 "it might almost be true . . .": Frederick Law Olmsted to John Hull Olmsted, December 7, 1842, FLOP.

50 "It grieves me very much . . .": Frederick Law Olmsted to parents, August 6, 1843, FLOP.

51 "a sailor's life is . . .": Richard Henry Dana Jr., *Two Years Before the Mast: a personal narrative of life at sea* (New York: World Syndicate Publishing Company, 1907), 39.

52 "After resting myself . . .": Frederick Law Olmsted to Maria Olmsted, November 30, 1843, FLOP.

53 "Home! home! . . .": Frederick Law Olmsted to John Olmsted, December 27, 1843, FLOP.

54 "A more discontented, . . .": Frederick Law Olmsted to parents, August 6, 1843, FLOP.

55 "much more cause . . .": Frederick Law Olmsted to John Olmsted, September 24, 1843, FLOP.

55 "It's perfectly *ridiculous* . . .": Frederick Law Olmsted to John Hull Olmsted, December 10, 1843, FLOP.

Chapter Seven: Friends

56 "What a shivering idea . . .": Frederick Law Olmsted to Charles Loring Brace, August 4, 1844, FLOP.

57 "It's no wonder you got . . .": Frederick Law Olmsted to John Hull Olmsted, May 31, 1844, FLOP.

58 "In study I am wonderfully . . .": Frederick Law Olmsted to Frederick J. Kingsbury, June 12, 1846, FLOP.

59 "The effect of the ice . . .": Frederick Law Olmsted to Abby Clark, January 18, 1845, FLOP.

60 "For myself, I have every reason . . .": Frederick Law Olmsted to Charles Loring Brace, June 22, 1845, FLOP.

61 "A most uncommon set . . .": *The Life of Charles Loring Brace: Chiefly Told in His Own Letters,* ed. Emma Brace (New York: Charles Scribner's Sons, 1894), 27.

Chapter Eight: Farming

63 "I walked down in earnest . . .": Frederick Law Olmsted to Charles Loring Brace, February 5, 1846, FLOP.

63 "Had a good time, . . .": Ibid.

64 "right smack & square . . .": Frederick Law Olmsted to John Hull Olmsted, March 27, 1846, FLOP.

64 "You lifted me a good deal . . .": Frederick Law Olmsted to Elizabeth Wooster Baldwin, December 16, 1890, FLOP.

64 "Why, bless you, . . .": Frederick Law Olmsted to Charles Loring Brace, March 27, 1846, FLOP.

66 "This has been a good place . . .": Frederick Law Olmsted to Charles Loring Brace, July 30, 1846, FLOP.

67 "Does Miss (you know) . . .": Frederick Law Olmsted to Frederick J. Kingsbury, June 12, 1846, FLOP.

67 "You ask who Sara . . .": Frederick Law Olmsted to John Olmsted, July 1, 1846, FLOP.

67 "I will think and act right, . . .": Frederick Law Olmsted to Frederick J. Kingsbury, August 22, 1846, FLOP.

68 "So have we endeavored, . . .": Thomas Carlyle, *Sartor Resartus* (New York: Dent, Dutton, 1973), 219.

68 "Produce! Produce! . . .": Ibid., 148–49.

68 "the greatest genius . . .": Frederick Law Olmsted to John Olmsted, August 12, 1846, FLOP.

69 "Fred went off in great style . . .": John Hull Olmsted to Frederick J. Kingsbury, March 16, 1847, FLOP.

70 *Inside, Olmsted sits* . . .: Frederick Law Olmsted to Charles Loring Brace, October 12, 1847, FLOP.

70 *"grossly licentious . . ."*: Joel Eliot Helander, *Oxpasture to Summer Colony: The Story of Sachem's Head in Guilford, Connecticut,* (Guilford, Conn.: Joel E. Helander, 1976), 187.

71 *"Do you think I shall . . ."*: Frederick Law Olmsted to Frederick J. Kingsbury, August 22, 1846, FLOP.

71 *"Setting out bushes, . . ."*: Joel Eliot Helander, *Oxpasture to Summer Colony: The Story of Sachem's Head in Guilford, Connecticut,* (Guilford, Conn.: Joel E. Helander, 1976), 190.

Chapter Nine: More farming

74 "I intend to set . . .": Frederick Law Olmsted, "Queries on Sea-Coast Agriculture," *The Horticulturist,* August 1847: 100.

74 "Shall have a better . . .": Frederick Law Olmsted to Frederick J. Kingsbury, September 23, 1847, FLOP.

74 "make quite a pretty show . . .": *Frederick Law Olmsted, Landscape Architect, 1822–1903,* ed. Frederick Law Olmsted Jr. and Theodora Kimball (New York: G. P. Putnam's Sons, 1928), 85.

75 "The farm generally pleases . . .": Frederick Law Olmsted to John Hull Olmsted, February 16, 1847, FLOP.

75 "There had been some vague . . .": John Hull Olmsted to Frederick J. Kingsbury, March 1848, FLOP.

76 "for the consideration . . .": Guilford Land Records, vol. 37, 181.

77 "Father bought it, . . .": John Hull Olmsted to Frederick J. Kingsbury, March 1848, FLOP.

77 "for the interest . . .": Frederick Law Olmsted to John Olmsted, March 12, 1860, FLOP.

77 Another letter makes . . .: see Broadus Mitchell, *Frederick Law Olmsted: A Critic of the Old South* (Baltimore: Johns Hopkins University Press, 1924), 54.

78 "Just wear your feet out, . . .": *The Life of Charles Loring Brace: Chiefly Told in His Own Letters,* ed. Emma Brace (New York: Charles Scribner's Sons, 1894), 59.

78 "Just the thing . . .": Frederick Law Olmsted to Frederick J. Kingsbury, July 16, 1848, FLOP.

79 "Frederick was at this time . . .": *Frederick Law Olmsted, Landscape Architect, 1822–1903,* ed. Frederick Law Olmsted Jr. and Theodora Kimball (New York: G. P. Putnam's Sons, 1928), 79.

79 "Thus, with a few strokes . . .": Ibid., 86.

79 developed as Seaside Estates . . .: Margaret Boyle-Cullen, "The Woods of Arden House," *The Staten Island Historian,* April-June 1954: 15.

80 "We believe [the society] . . .": Frederick Law Olmsted, "Appeal to the Citizens of Staten Island," December 1849, FLOP.

Chapter Ten: A walking tour in the old country

82 "In five years . . .": Frederick Law Olmsted to Frederick J. Kingsbury, October 14, 1848, FLOP

82 "He is in the direct . . .": John Hull Olmsted to Frederick J. Kingsbury, March 1848, FLOP.

82 "I want somebody . . .": Frederick Law Olmsted to Frederick J. Kingsbury, October 14, 1848, FLOP.

82 "Fred is reading Macaulay ...": John Hull Olmsted to Frederick J. Kingsbury, February 10, 1849, FLOP.

82 "The Modern Painters improves ...": Frederick Law Olmsted to John Hull Olmsted, February 10, 1849, FLOP.

83 "I have got very intimate ...": Frederick Law Olmsted to John Hull Olmsted, February 24, 1849, FLOP.

83 "There are a lot of books ...": *Frederick Law Olmsted, Landscape Architect, 1822–1903*, ed. Frederick Law Olmsted Jr. and Theodora Kimball (New York: G. P. Putnam's Sons, 1928), 73.

84 "I exceedingly fear ...": Frederick Law Olmsted to John Olmsted, March 1, 1850, FLOP.

84 he would spend about $300 ...: *Frederick Law Olmsted, Landscape Architect, 1822–1903*, ed. Frederick Law Olmsted Jr. and Theodora Kimball (New York: G. P. Putnam's Sons, 1928), 5.

85 "I did not mean ...": Frederick Law Olmsted to John Olmsted, March 1, 1850, FLOP.

86 "two of the very greatest ...": Ibid.

86 "There we were ...": Frederick Law Olmsted, *Walks and Talks of an American Farmer in England* (Ann Arbor, Mich.: University of Michigan Press, 1967), 59.

87 "A gentle undulating ...": Ibid., 97.

JOSTLING AND BEING JOSTLED
Chapter Eleven: Mr. Downing's magazine

91 "American education ...": Lewis Mumford, "The Renewal of the Landscape," *The Brown Decades* (New York: Harcourt, Brace, 1931), 85.

92 "I began life as a ...": *Frederick Law Olmsted, Landscape Architect, 1822–1903*, ed. Frederick Law Olmsted Jr. and Theodora Kimball (New York: G. P. Putnam's Sons, 1928), 83.

92 "Everybody at home ...": Frederick Law Olmsted to Charles Loring Brace, November 12, 1850, FLOP.

92 "I am disappointed ...": Frederick Law Olmsted to Charles Loring Brace, January 11, 1851, FLOP.

93 "I was glad to observe ...": Frederick Law Olmsted, "The People's Park at Birkenhead, near Liverpool," *The Horticulturist*, May 1851: 225–26.

94 Downing wrote a lead essay, ...: Andrew Jackson Downing, "The New-York Park," *The Horticulturist*, August 1851: 345–49.

94 "gardening had here reached a perfection ...": Frederick Law Olmsted, "The People's Park at Birkenhead, near Liverpool," *The Horticulturist*, May 1851: 225.

95 "Suspicious, distrustful, often ...": Frederick Law Olmsted, "A Voice from the Sea," *American Whig Review* 14, December 1851: 526.

Chapter Twelve: Olmsted falls in love and finishes his book

96 "I doubt if I shall ...": Frederick Law Olmsted to Charles Loring Brace, January 11, 1851, FLOP.

97 "upon intimate acquaintance ...": Ellen K. Rothman, *Hands and Heart: A History of Courtship in America* (New York: Basic Books, 1984), 111–12.

97 "moments of indifference ...": Karen Lystra, *Searching the Heart: Women, Men, and*

Romantic Love in Nineteenth-Century America (New York: Oxford University Press, 1989), 181.

97 Men considered the engagement . . .: Ellen K. Rothman, *Hands and Heart: A History of Courtship in America* (New York: Basic Books, 1984), 157.

97 he met Emily . . .: Mary Cleveland Olmsted, "Biographical fragment," undated, FLOP.

97 "Pray tell me what . . .": John Olmsted to Sophia Hitchcock, October 28, 1851, Letters of Mrs. Page, Archives of American Art, National Collection of Fine Arts, Washington, D.C.

99 "Odd-looking vehicles . . .": Frederick Law Olmsted, *Walks and Talks of an American Farmer in England* (Ann Arbor, Mich.: University of Michigan Press, 1967), 79–80.

100 "not a town have we seen . . .": Ibid., 225.

100 "a splurgy, thick book, . . .": Frederick Law Olmsted to Frederick J. Kingsbury, October 17, 1852, FLOP.

100 "one farmer's leg . . .": Frederick Law Olmsted, *Walks and Talks of an American Farmer in England* (Ann Arbor, Mich: University of Michigan Press, 1967), xv.

100 "one of our original . . .": Review of *Walks and Talks of an American Farmer in England, The Horticulturist,* March 1852: 135.

101 "Here is a book of travels . . .": Ibid.

101 "natural and unprejudiced impressions . . .": Review of *Walks and Talks of an American Farmer in England, American Whig Review,* March 1852: 282.

101 "our farmer observes . . .": Review of *Walks and Talks of an American Farmer in England, Cummings Evening Bulletin,* October 23, 1852: 2.

101 "eminently popular, . . .": Review of *Walks and Talks of an American Farmer in England, Harper's New Monthly Magazine,* December 1852: 138.

101 "His sketches of landscape, . . .": Review of *Walks and Talks of an American Farmer in England, The Horticulturist,* January 1853: 43.

Chapter Thirteen: Charley Brace intervenes

103 "If you could get . . .": Frederick Law Olmsted to Charles Loring Brace, January 11, 1851, FLOP.

103 "I anticipate your most . . .": *The Life of Charles Loring Brace: Chiefly Told in His Own Letters,* ed. Emma Brace (New York: Charles Scribner's Sons, 1894), 142.

104 "A wild stormy day . . .": Ibid., 61–62.

105 "It does *not* mean, . . .": Ibid., 68.

106 "natural right, . . .": Frederick Law Olmsted, *Walks and Talks of an American Farmer in England* (Ann Arbor, Mich.: University of Michigan Press, 1967), 240.

106 "The law of God . . .": Ibid., 241.

107 "Before, this slavery . . .": *The Life of Charles Loring Brace: Chiefly Told in His Own Letters,* ed. Emma Brace (New York: Charles Scribner's Sons, 1894), 117.

107 "Why won't you . . .": Ibid., 57.

107 "After reading your letter . . .": Ibid., 112.

107 "shoot a man . . .": Frederick Law Olmsted to Frederick J. Kingsbury, October 17, 1852, FLOP.

108 "observations on Southern Agriculture . . .": Ibid.

Chapter Fourteen: Yeoman

113 "I can't write . . .": Frederick Law Olmsted to Charles Loring Brace, February 8, 1853, FLOP.

113 "He [Olmsted] tenaciously . . .": Edmund Wilson, *Patriotic Gore: Studies in the Literature of the American Civil War* (New York: Oxford University Press, 1962), 221.

114 "I was deeply influenced . . .": *New-York Daily Times*, February 25, 1853.

114 "I have raised hay, . . .": Ibid., April 28, 1853.

114 "On the other side, . . .": Ibid., June 14, 1853.

115 "intelligent gentleman, . . .": Ibid., February 16, 1853.

115 "Many people at the North . . .": Ibid.

116 "Although he probably has . . .": Ibid.

116 "No man can write . . .": Ibid.

116 "I did not intend . . .": Ibid., March 17, 1853.

117 "I shall be able . . .": Frederick Law Olmsted to Charles Loring Brace, December 22, 1852, FLOP.

117 "It would only make . . .": *New-York Daily Times*, March 30, 1853.

117 "how, without quite destroying . . .": Frederick Law Olmsted, *The Cotton Kingdom: A Traveler's Observations on Cotton and Slavery in the American Slave States* (New York: Alfred A. Knopf, 1953), 48.

118 "Do you work any niggers? . . .": Ibid., 171.

118 "Louisiana or Texas, . . .": Ibid., 230.

119 "have their standard . . .": *New-York Daily Times*, April 28, 1853.

120 "The negroes are . . .": Ibid., March 30, 1853.

120 "Slavery in Virginia, . . .": Ibid.

120 "If I was free, . . .": Frederick Law Olmsted, *The Cotton Kingdom: A Traveler's Observations on Cotton and Slavery in the American Slave States* (New York: Alfred A. Knopf, 1953), 262.

121 "I cannot see how . . .": *New-York Daily Times*, February 13, 1854.

121 "Yet, mainly, the North . . .": Ibid.

121 "Hurrah for gradual Emancipation . . .": Frederick Law Olmsted to John Olmsted, August 12, 1846, FLOP.

Chapter Fifteen: A traveling companion

122 "There is no city . . .": *New-York Daily Times*, September 14, 1853.

122 "They are generally very pretty, . . .": Ibid.

124 "decidedly the best reports . . .": Ibid., February 13, 1854.

124 "[The *Times*] sends . . .": *Savannah Republican*, February 22, 1853.

124 "designed to gloss . . .": *New-York Daily Times*, February 13, 1854.

124 "[My] motive for . . .": Frederick Law Olmsted, *A Journey Through Texas; or, A Saddle-Trip on the South-Western Frontier: with a Statistical Appendix* (New York: Mason Brothers, 1859), v.

125 "they do not seem . . .": Frederick Law Olmsted to Charles Loring Brace, December 1, 1853, FLOP.

126 "We are traveling about, . . .": Frederick Law Olmsted to Anne Charlotte Lynch, March 12, 1854, FLOP.

Chapter Sixteen: The Texas settlers

128 "There was also *pfannekuchen*, . . .: *New-York Daily Times*, March 31, 1854.
130 "Educated, cultivated, . . .": Ibid., April 4, 1854.
130 "In Neu-Braunfels . . .": Ibid., April 14, 1854.
131 "And such a State, . . .": Ibid., June 3, 1854.

Chapter Seventeen: Yeoman makes a decision

132 "a deep notch of sadness": Frederick Law Olmsted, *A Journey in the Back Country* (New York: Mason Brothers, 1860), 11.
134 "I should *probably* . . .": Frederick Law Olmsted to John Olmsted, March 13, 1855, FLOP.
135 "I regret to be left . . .": John Hull Olmsted to Bertha Olmsted, May 6, 1855, FLOP.

Chapter Eighteen: "Much the best Mag. in the world"

137 "The best writers . . .": Frederick Law Olmsted to John Olmsted, May 28, 1855, FLOP.
138 "I can't well write . . .": Frederick Law Olmsted to Edward Everett Hale, August 23, 1855, FLOP.
139 "I suppose that you . . .": Ibid.
140 "There can be little . . .": Frederick Law Olmsted to John Olmsted, December 9, 1855, FLOP.
141 "I am much worried . . .": Frederick Law Olmsted to John Olmsted, November 8, 1855, FLOP.
141 "singularly fair, . . .": Review of *A Journey in the Seaboard Slave States*, *North American Review*, July 1856: 278.
141 "the most complete . . .": Harriet Beecher Stowe, "Anti-Slavery Literature," *Independent*, February 21, 1856: 57.
141 "Mr. Olmsted observes . . .": Review of *A Journey in the Seaboard Slave States*, *Household Words*, August 23, 1856: 138.

Chapter Nineteen: Abroad

143 "What I chiefly hope . . .": Frederick Law Olmsted to Joshua Dix, August 3, 1856, FLOP.
143 "How Ruffianism in Washington . . .": *New-York Daily Times*, July 10, 1856.
144 "I would not like to have . . .": Frederick Law Olmsted to Joshua Dix, August 3, 1856, FLOP.
144 "there should be no more purchases . . .": *The Papers of Frederick Law Olmsted, Vol. II, Slavery and the South 1852–1857*, ed. Charles E. Beveridge and Charles Capen McLaughlin (Baltimore: Johns Hopkins University Press, 1981), 389, n. 4.
144 "one of the partners . . .": Mary Cleveland Olmsted to John Charles Olmsted, August 17, 1916, JCOC.
145 "Owing to the pressure . . .": Frederick Law Olmsted, *A Journey Through Texas; or, A Saddle-Trip on the South-Western Frontier: with a Statistical Appendix* (New York: Mason Brothers), iii.
146 "my best book . . .": Frederick Law Olmsted to Mariana Griswold Van Rensselaer, June 17, 1893, FLOP.
146 "First: Slavery educates, . . .": Frederick Law Olmsted, *A Journey Through Texas; or,*

A Saddle-Trip on the South-Western Frontier: with a Statistical Appendix (New York: Mason Brothers, 1859), xvi–xvii.

147 "Any further extension . . .": Ibid., xxviii–xxix.

148 "The German colonies . . .": Review of *A Journey Through Texas*, *North American Review*, April 1857: 565.

148 "The time to guard . . .": T. H. Gladstone, *The Englishman in Kansas: or, Squatter Life and Border Warfare* (New York: Miller & Co., 1857).

149 "The creditors exonerated Curtis . . .": Frederick Law Olmsted to Frederick J. Kingsbury, April 26, 1857, FLOP.

151 "I am delighted to hear it, . . .": Frederick Law Olmsted, "Passages in the Life of an Impractical Man," undated. FLOP.

Hitting Heads
Chapter Twenty: A change in fortune

155 "For the past sixteen years . . .": Frederick Law Olmsted to the President of the Commissioners of the Central Park, August 12, 1857, FLOP.

156 "a practical farmer, . . .": Roy Rosenzweig and Elizabeth Blackmar, *The Park and the People: A History of Central Park* (Ithaca, N.Y.: Cornell University Press, 1992), 128.

156 "I desire very simply . . .": *The Papers of Frederick Law Olmsted, Vol. III, Creating Central Park 1857–1861*, ed. Charles E. Beveridge and David Schuyler (Baltimore: Johns Hopkins University Press, 1983), 78.

156 "The subscribers earnestly recommend . . .": *Frederick Law Olmsted: Landscape Architect, 1822–1903*, ed. Frederick Law Olmsted Jr. and Theodora Kimball (New York: G. P. Putnam's Sons, 1928), opp. 120.

157 "having had time . . .": Frederick Law Olmsted to John Hull Olmsted, September 11, 1857, FLOP.

157 "on the whole, . . .": Ibid.

157 "I shall try the frank, . . .": Ibid.

Chapter Twenty-One: The colonel meets his match

160 "I have got the park . . .": Frederick Law Olmsted to John Olmsted, January 14, 1858, FLOP.

160 "It appears we are not . . .": John Hull Olmsted to Frederick Law Olmsted, November 13, 1857, FLOP.

160 "In his death . . .": John Olmsted to Frederick Law Olmsted, November 28, 1857, FLOP.

160 "I have never known . . .": John Hull Olmsted to Frederick Law Olmsted, November 13, 1857, FLOP.

Chapter Twenty-Two: Mr. Vaux

161 "living with my partner . . .": Frederick Law Olmsted to John Olmsted, January 14, 1858, FLOP.

162 "Being thoroughly disgusted . . .": M. M. Graff, *The Men Who Made Central Park* (New York: Greensward Foundation, 1982), 15.

163 "I was just in mind . . .": Frederick Law Olmsted to Mariana Griswold Van Rensselaer, June 11, 1893, FLOP.

163 "There was something else . . .": Ibid.

163 "If successful, I should not . . .": Frederick Law Olmsted to John Olmsted, January 14, 1858, FLOP.

164 "We do not find . . .": *New-York Daily Times*, May 13, 1858.

Chapter Twenty-Three: A brilliant solution

165 "broad reaches of park . . .": Andrew Jackson Downing, "The New-York Park," *The Horticulturist*, August 1851: 347.

166 "but by no means . . .": Calvert Vaux and Frederick Law Olmsted, "Description of a Plan for the Improvement of the Central Park, GREENSWARD," FLOP.

167 "The great charm . . .": Calvert Vaux, *Villas and Cottages* (New York: Harper & Brothers, 1864), 51.

167 "winter gardens of glass, . . .": Andrew Jackson Downing, "The New-York Park," *The Horticulturist*, August 1851: 347.

167 "Buildings are scarcely . . .": Calvert Vaux and Frederick Law Olmsted, "Description of a Plan for the Improvement of the Central Park, GREENSWARD," FLOP.

168 "the established character . . .": *New-York Daily Times*, April 30, 1858.

169 It has been suggested . . .: See, for example, M. M. Graff, *Central Park, Prospect Park: A New Perspective* (New York: Greensward Foundation, 1985), 29.

170 "Together they had all . . .": Mariana Griswold Van Rensselaer, "Frederick Law Olmsted," *Century Illustrated Monthly Magazine* 46, no.6, October 1893: 863.

Chapter Twenty-Four: A promotion

171 "I was technically not . . .": Frederick Law Olmsted to Calvert Vaux, November 26, 1863, FLOP.

172 "What artist so noble . . .": Frederick Law Olmsted to the Board of Commissioners of the Central Park, May 20, 1858, FLOP.

173 "He shall be the chief . . .": *New-York Daily Times*, May 18, 1858.

174 "The time will come . . .": Frederick Law Olmsted to the Board of Commissioners of the Central Park, May 31, 1858, FLOP.

175 muslin banners reading . . .: Henry Hope Reed and Sophia Duckworth, *Central Park: A History and a Guide* (New York: Clarkson N. Potter, 1967), 20.

176 "very full and thorough . . .": *New-York Daily Times*, May 13, 1858.

177 "Your successor at the helm . . .": George E. Waring Jr. to Frederick Law Olmsted, October 17, 1859, FLOP.

177 "It is one great purpose . . .": Frederick Law Olmsted to the Board of Commissioners of the Central Park, May 31, 1858, FLOP.

Chapter Twenty-Five: Frederick and Mary

178 "Don't let Mary suffer . . .": John Hull Olmsted to Frederick Law Olmsted, November 13, 1857, FLOP.

179 "I feel just thoroughly . . .": Frederick Law Olmsted to John Olmsted, September 23, 1859, FLOP.

180 "full particulars of its construction, . . .": Frederick Law Olmsted to the Board of Commissioners of the Central Park, December 28, 1859, FLOP.

180 "I find that the simplicity . . .": Frederick Law Olmsted to Sir William Jackson Hooker, November 29, 1859, FLOP.

181 "In hollow lanes . . .": Uvedale Price, *Essays on the picturesque, as compared with the sublime and the beautiful*, vol. I (London: J. Mawman, 1810), 25.

181 "the best private garden . . .": Frederick Law Olmsted to the Board of Commissioners of the Central Park, December 28, 1859, FLOP.

182 "standard formula of artificial water, . . .": Nigel Everett, *The Tory View of Landscape* (New Haven: Yale University Press, 1994), 39.

182 "public and private grounds . . .": Frederick Law Olmsted to the Board of Commissioners of the Central Park, December 28, 1859, FLOP.

182 "greatly improved health . . .": Ibid.

Chapter Twenty-Six: Comptroller Green

183 "Few landscapes present . . .": *Frederick Law Olmsted: Landscape Architect, 1822–1903*, ed. Frederick Law Olmsted Jr. and Theodora Kimball (New York: G. P. Putnam's Sons, 1928), 66.

184 The accompanying text . . .: *The Central Park: Photographed by W. H. Guild, Jr. with descriptions and a historical sketch by Fred. B. Perkins* (New York: Carleton, 1864).

184 "Much better than any other public work . . .": Frederick Law Olmsted to Charles Loring Brace, December 8, 1860, FLOP.

185 "to act as treasurer, . . .": Edward Hagaman Hall, "A Short Biography of Andrew Haswell Green," *Ninth Annual Report, 1904, of the American Scenic and Historic Preservation Society* (Albany, N.Y., 1904), 154.

186 "It is quite expensive . . .": Andrew Haswell Green to Frederick Law Olmsted, November 12, 1860, FLOP.

186 "The best conceptions of scenery, . . .": Frederick Law Olmsted to the Board of Commissioners of the Central Park, January 22, 1861, FLOP.

188 "Only as they were leaving, . . .": Frederick Law Olmsted to John Olmsted, October 21, 1860, FLOP.

Chapter Twenty-Seven: King Cotton

190 "I will not here conceal . . .": Frederick Law Olmsted, *A Journey in the Back Country* (New York: Mason Brothers, 1860), 6–7.

190 "I do not see . . .": Ibid., 7.

191 "I do not now say . . .": Ibid., 8.

191 "It would be presumptuous . . .": Ibid.

191 "No more important contributions . . .": Review of *A Journey in the Back Country, The Atlantic Monthly*, November 1960: 635.

191 "Olmsted's 'Journey in the Back Country' . . .": *Letters of Charles Eliot Norton*, ed. Sara Norton and M. A. DeWolfe Howe (Boston: Houghton Mifflin, 1913), 211.

191 "rebuke and allay . . .": Review of *A Journey in the Back Country, North American Review*, October 20, 1860: 571.

191 "a new edition . . .": Review of *A Journey in the Back Country*, London *Times*, December 8, 1860.

192 "Though the lameness . . .": Katharine Prescott Wormeley, *The Other Side of War; with the Army of the Potomac. Letters from the Headquarters of the United States Sanitary*

Commission during the Peninsular Campaign in Virginia in 1862 (Boston: Ticknor & Company, 1889), 62–63.

192 "tranquillity and seclusion— . . .": Frederick Law Olmsted to Henry H. Elliott, August 27, 1860, FLOP.

193 "I hope I shall have been . . .": Frederick Law Olmsted to John Olmsted, October 21, 1860, FLOP.

193 "I know your time . . .": Frederick Law Olmsted to Andrew Haswell Green, December 28, 1860, FLOP.

193 "Have the bridges . . .": Frederick Law Olmsted to the Board of Commissioners of the Central Park, January 22, 1861, FLOP.

193 "Instead of $100 . . .": Ibid.

194 "If either of those gentlemen . . .": Ibid..

194 "Have you heard . . .": Ibid.

194 "With such an arrangement . . .": Ibid.

195 "the able superintendent . . .": "Central Park in Spring," *New York World,* March 11, 1861: 7.

195 "He is precisely the man . . .": Henry Whitney Bellows, "Cities and Parks," *The Atlantic Monthly,* April 1861, 422.

196 "No! you dare not make . . .": Frederick Law Olmsted, *The Cotton Kingdom: A Traveler's Observations on Cotton and Slavery in the American Slave States* (New York: Alfred A. Knopf, 1953), 7.

196 "an indispensable work . . .": Ibid., Arthur M. Schlesinger, "Editor's Introduction," ix.

197 "Events multiply . . .": quoted by Geoffrey C. Ward, *The Civil War: An Illustrated History* (New York: Alfred A. Knopf, 1990), 42.

197 "I have, I suppose, . . .": Frederick Law Olmsted to Henry Whitney Bellows, June 1, 1861, FLOP.

197 "I do ask . . .": Frederick Law Olmsted to Board of Commissioners of the Central Park, March 28, 1861, FLOP.

198 "I have made no definite . . .": Frederick Law Olmsted to John Olmsted, June 26, 1861, FLOP.

198 "The appointment is a great honor . . .": Mary Cleveland Olmsted to John Olmsted, June 22, 1861, FLOP.

Chapter Twenty-Eight: A good big work

199 "Mr. F. L. Olmsted . . .": Henry Whitney Bellows to James Miller McKim, August 18, 1865, FLOP.

199 "Our plans have a breadth . . .": William Quentin Maxwell, *Lincoln's Fifth Wheel: The Political History of the United States Sanitary Commission* (New York: Longmans, Green & Company, 1956), 8.

200 "I do not get on . . .": Frederick Law Olmsted to Mary Cleveland Olmsted, July 2, 1861, FLOP.

201 "They start and turn pale . . .": Frederick Law Olmsted to Mary Cleveland Olmsted, July 29, 1861, FLOP.

201 "Our army, previous to . . .": Frederick Law Olmsted, "Report on the Demoralization of the Volunteers," September 5, 1861, FLOP.

202 "an able paper, . . .": George Templeton Strong, *Diary of the Civil War, 1860–1865* (New York: Macmillan, 1962), 180.

202 "It is no longer right...": Frederick Law Olmsted, "Report on the Demoralization of the Volunteers," September 5, 1861, FLOP.

202 "It is a good big work...": Frederick Law Olmsted to Bertha Olmsted, January 28, 1862, FLOP.

203 "1st The visitation of regimental camps, ...": Frederick Law Olmsted to Lewis Henry Steiner, August 12, 1861, FLOP.

204 "I want that as soon as practicable...": Frederick Law Olmsted to Henry Whitney Bellows, December 21, 1861, FLOP.

204 "humanity ministering to wants...": William Quentin Maxwell, *Lincoln's Fifth Wheel: The Political History of the United States Sanitary Commission* (New York: Longmans, Green & Company, 1956), 115.

205 "We have a girl, ...": Frederick Law Olmsted to Charles Loring Brace, November 8, 1861, FLOP.

205 "They used to call it spunk...": Frederick Law Olmsted to Mary Cleveland Olmsted, November 6, 1861, FLOP.

206 "Mr. Fred. Law Olmsted...": *New York World,* February 15, 1862.

206 "I shall go to Port Royal, ...": Frederick Law Olmsted to John Olmsted, February 24, 1862, FLOP.

207 "Our success is suddenly wonderfully complete,": Frederick Law Olmsted to John Olmsted, April 19, 1862, FLOP.

207 "Yet it may all slip...": Ibid.

207 "The alternative is going...": Ibid.

Chapter Twenty-Nine: Yeoman's war

209 "As far as I can judge, ...": Katharine Prescott Wormeley, *The Other Side of War; with the Army of the Potomac. Letters from the Headquarters of the United States Sanitary Commission during the Peninsular Campaign in Virginia in 1862* (Boston: Ticknor & Company, 1889), 17.

209 "They beat the doctors...": Frederick Law Olmsted to Henry Whitney Bellows, May 25, 1862, FLOP.

209 "In little things...": Katharine Prescott Wormeley, *The Other Side of War; with the Army of the Potomac. Letters from the Headquarters of the United States Sanitary Commission during the Peninsular Campaign in Virginia in 1862* (Boston: Ticknor & Company, 1889), 187.

210 "At the time of which I am now writing, ...": Frederick Law Olmsted to Henry Whitney Bellows, June 3, 1862, FLOP.

211 "You *can't conceive*...": Katharine Prescott Wormeley, *The Other Side of War; with the Army of the Potomac. Letters from the Headquarters of the United States Sanitary Commission during the Peninsular Campaign in Virginia in 1862* (Boston: Ticknor & Company, 1889), 102.

211 "The horror of war...": Frederick Law Olmsted to Mary Cleveland Olmsted, June 11, 1862, FLOP.

212 "Defeat! No; we have retreated...": Katharine Prescott Wormeley, *The Other Side of War; with the Army of the Potomac. Letters from the Headquarters of the United States Sanitary Commission during the Peninsular Campaign in Virginia in 1862* (Boston: Ticknor & Company, 1889), 177.

212 "I like him at first sight...": Ibid., n. 9, 387.

213 "Did I say somewhere that Mr. Olmsted...": Ibid., 205.

Chapter Thirty: "Six months more pretty certainly"

214 "I grew daily more yellow, . . .": Frederick Law Olmsted to Mary Cleveland Olmsted, August 30, 1862, FLOP.

215 "We will be as frugal . . .": Frederick Law Olmsted to Mary Cleveland Olmsted, October 11, 1862, FLOP.

216 "If Jenkins or Knapp ask . . .": Frederick Law Olmsted to Henry Whitney Bellows, December 27, 1862, FLOP.

216 "I believe that Olmsted's sense, . . .": George Templeton Strong, *Diary of the Civil War, 1860–1865* (New York: Macmillan, 1962), 276.

217 "He works like a dog . . .": Ibid., 291.

217 "I go west . . .": Frederick Law Olmsted to Henry Whitney Bellows, February 4, 1863, FLOP.

217 "There will be a battle . . .": George Templeton Strong, *Diary of the Civil War, 1860–1865* (New York: Macmillan, 1962), 304–5.

217 "He is one of the most . . .": Frederick Law Olmsted to John Olmsted, April 1, 1863, FLOP.

218 "Reminiscences of Cranch . . .": Ibid.

219 "If I should leave . . .": Frederick Law Olmsted to John Olmsted, April 18, 1863, FLOP.

219 "You have no right . . .": Frederick Law Olmsted to John Olmsted, April 25, 1863, FLOP.

219 "However wanting in sagacity . . .": Frederick Law Olmsted to John Olmsted, May 2, 1863, FLOP.

219 "I would limp . . .": Frederick Law Olmsted to Charles Loring Brace, October 4, 1862, FLOP.

220 "I have been thinking . . .": Robert Fridlington, "Two Nation Portraits," *The Nation*, January 3, 1966: 10.

220 "secure a more careful, . . .": "Prospectus for a Weekly Journal," June 25, 1863, FLOP.

220 "at some time . . .": Ibid.

220 "The thing starts . . .": Frederick Law Olmsted to Mary Cleveland Olmsted, June 26, 1863, FLOP.

221 "I think we can hold . . .": Frederick Law Olmsted to Mary Cleveland Olmsted, July 7, 1863, FLOP.

221 "I am really oppressed . . .": Frederick Law Olmsted to Henry Whitney Bellows, July 28, 1863, FLOP.

221 "I don't believe . . .": Frederick Law Olmsted to Edwin Lawrence Godkin, August 1, 1863, FLOP.

Chapter Thirty-One: A letter from Dana

223 "I am rather disposed . . .": Frederick Law Olmsted to John Olmsted, August 10, 1863, FLOP.

223 "one of the most gigantic. . .": J. C. Frémont and Frederick Billings, *The Mariposas Estate* (London: Whittingham & Wilkins, 1861), 27.

223 "I think that I shall make up my mind . . .": Frederick Law Olmsted to Mary Cleveland Olmsted, August 12, 1863, FLOP.

224 "I don't know . . .": Henry Whitney Bellows to Frederick Law Olmsted, August 13, 1863, FLOP.

224 "If the Sanitary Commission . . .": Frederick Law Olmsted to Henry Whitney Bellows, August 16, 1863, FLOP.

225 "I think the faith . . .": Henry Whitney Bellows to Frederick Law Olmsted, August 13, 1863, FLOP.

225 "Olmsted has not a mercenary nerve . . .": George Templeton Strong Manuscript Diary, August 11, 1863, New-York Historical Society.

225 "If I should die, . . .": Frederick Law Olmsted to Henry Whitney Bellows, August 15, 1863, FLOP.

225 "A poor man . . .": Frederick Law Olmsted to Henry Whitney Bellows, August 16, 1863, FLOP.

225 "If they will really put the management . . .": Ibid.

225 "My ambition for you, . . .": Henry Whitney Bellows to Frederick Law Olmsted, August 18, 1863, FLOP.

226 "Olmsted has completed his arrangement . . .": George Templeton Strong, *Diary of the Civil War, 1860–1865* (New York: Macmillan, 1962), 350.

226 "We can only console ourselves . . .": *New-York Daily Times,* September 14, 1863.

Chapter Thirty-Two: Never happier

228 "Ever since you left . . .": Frederick Newman Knapp to Frederick Law Olmsted, October 14, 1863, FLOP.

231 "Things are worse here . . .": Frederick Law Olmsted to Mary Cleveland Olmsted, October 31, 1863, FLOP.

231 "It is my conviction . . .": J. C. Frémont and Frederick Billings, *The Mariposas Estate* (London: Whittingham & Wilkins, 1861), 27 & 3.

231 "The Board do not feel . . .": *The Mariposa Company, 34 Wall Street, New York, Organized 25th June, 1863* (New York: W. C. Bryant & Company, 1863), 24.

232 "I don't want the men . . .": Frederick Law Olmsted to James Hoy, March 2, 1864, FLOP.

232 "The mob got the worst . . .": Frederick Law Olmsted to James Hoy, March 5, 1864, FLOP.

233 "I am sadly damaged . . .": Frederick Law Olmsted to Henry Whitney Bellows, April 28, 1864, FLOP.

233 "accommodate my own work . . .": Frederick Law Olmsted to Calvert Vaux, March 25, 1864, FLOP.

233 "I have had my full share . . .": Frederick Law Olmsted to John Olmsted, March 11, 1864, FLOP.

233 "There is a great dearth . . .": Mary Cleveland Olmsted, undated fragment, FLOP.

233 "We went in a carriage . . .": Frederick Law Olmsted to John Olmsted, June 25, 1864, FLOP.

234 "He is a kind of little . . .": *The Papers of Frederick Law Olmsted, Vol. V, The California Frontier 1863–1865,* ed. Victoria Post Ranney (Baltimore: Johns Hopkins University Press, 1986), 18–19.

234 "I am sitting in Olmsted's office . . .": Ibid., 50.

235 "I never was happier, . . .": Frederick Law Olmsted to Edwin Lawrence Godkin, April 4, 1864, FLOP.

235 "I know of no simile . . .": Mary Cleveland Olmsted to Calvert Vaux, 1864, JCOC.

236 "We are camped . . .": Frederick Law Olmsted to John Olmsted, August 17, 1864, FLOP.

237 "a country still waiting . . .": quoted by John Lukacs, "Neither the Wilderness Nor the Shopping Mall," *New Oxford Review,* April 1995: 8.

237 "I find the old symptoms . . .": Frederick Law Olmsted to John Olmsted, September 14, 1864, FLOP.

237 "I am very well . . .": Frederick Law Olmsted to Frederick Newman Knapp, September 28, 1864, FLOP.

238 "I am going to lay out . . .": Ibid.

239 "I am for the present making money . . .": Frederick Law Olmsted to John Olmsted, March 11, 1864, FLOP.

239 "I look therefore . . .": Frederick Law Olmsted to Edwin Lawrence Godkin, April 4, 1864, FLOP.

239 "The mining stocks here . . .": Frederick Law Olmsted to Edwin Lawrence Godkin, July 24, 1864, FLOP.

Chapter Thirty-Three: Olmsted shortens sail

240 "My impression is that Mariposa . . .": Frederick Law Olmsted to Mary Cleveland Olmsted, January 8, 1865, FLOP.

241 "there is a tremendous libel suit . . .": Edwin Lawrence Godkin to Frederick Law Olmsted, December 25, 1864, FLOP.

241 "a sort of bunkum message . . .": Frederick Law Olmsted to Edwin Lawrence Godkin, January 22, 1865, FLOP.

242 "We have lived so very happily . . .": Frederick Law Olmsted to Mary Cleveland Olmsted, January 18, 1865, FLOP.

243 "I have another landscape gardening nibble . . .": Frederick Law Olmsted to Mary Cleveland Olmsted, January 25, 1865, FLOP.

243 "You must then look . . .": Frederick Law Olmsted, "Preface to the Plan for Mountain View Cemetery, Oakland, California," May 1865, FLOP.

245 "The brooding forms . . .": Ibid.

245 "to give an appearance . . .": Ibid.

245 "No place of burial . . .": Ibid.

245 "It is an accursed country . . .": Frederick Law Olmsted to Calvert Vaux, March 12, 1865, FLOP.

246 "I want you to prepare . . .": Frederick Law Olmsted to Mary Cleveland Olmsted, March 1, 1865, FLOP.

246 "Take an interest in the Howard plan . . .": Frederick Law Olmsted to Mary Cleveland Olmsted, undated, FLOP.

246 "I was called upon to advise . . .": Frederick Law Olmsted to Edwin Lawrence Godkin, April 4, 1865, FLOP.

247 "I don't think that you are sufficiently conscientious . . .": Edwin Lawrence Godkin to Frederick Law Olmsted, April 2, 1865, FLOP.

247 ". . . singing Glory! Hallelujah! . . .": Frederick Law Olmsted to Frederick Newman Knapp, April 9, 1865, FLOP.

247 "When Olmsted is blue, . . .": George Templeton Strong, *Diary of the Civil War, 1860–1865* (New York: Macmillan, 1962), 243.

248 "I can hardly contain myself . . .": Frederick Law Olmsted to Frederick Newman Knapp, April 12, 1865, FLOP.

248 "At any rate . . .": Frederick Law Olmsted to Frederick Newman Knapp, April 16, 1865, FLOP.

248 "stupendous folly . . .": "Letter from Mr. Raymond, United States Commissioner,"

The Mariposa Estate: Its Past, Present and Future (New York: Russells American Steam Printing House, 1868), 28.

248 "the fundamental mistake . . .": Ibid., 27.

Chapter Thirty-Four: A heavy sort of book

251 "I wish you could find . . .": Frederick Law Olmsted to Edwin Lawrence Godkin, May 14, 1865, FLOP.

251 "There are men of high position . . .": Ibid.

251 "He has a cigar in his mouth, . . .": Frederick Law Olmsted, "Notes on the Pioneer Condition," FLOP.

252 "I was not prepared to find . . .": Frederick Law Olmsted, "Section 1, A Pioneer Community of the Present Day," FLOP.

253 "I have been for some time . . .": Frederick Law Olmsted to John Olmsted, April 18, 1863, FLOP.

253 "I am cogitating a heavy sort of book . . .": Frederick Law Olmsted to Edwin Lawrence Godkin, November 29, 1864, FLOP.

253 "Civilization is, in fact, the best . . .": Frederick Law Olmsted, *A Journey in the Back Country* (New York: Mason Brothers, 1860), 288.

253 "Nothing is more certain, . . .": Horace Bushnell, *Work and Play* (New York: Charles Scribner's Sons, 1903), 229.

254 "You stand by me . . .": Frederick Law Olmsted to John Wheeler Harding, October 20, 1864, FLOP.

255 "added more new . . .": *Johnson's New Universal Cyclopaedia* (New York: A. J. Johnson & Son, 1877), Vol. IV, Pt.I, 79.

255 "What are the habits, . . .": Frederick Law Olmsted to Frederick Newman Knapp, December 13, 1867, FLOP.

Chapter Thirty-Five: Calvert Vaux doesn't take no for an answer

256 "Your paper needs . . .": Frederick Law Olmsted to Edwin Lawrence Godkin, June 10, 1865, FLOP.

257 "I do know that . . .": Frederick Law Olmsted to Samuel Bowles, September 26, 1865, FLOP.

257 "The union of the deepest sublimity . . .": Frederick Law Olmsted, "Preliminary Report upon the Yosemite and Big Tree Grove," FLOP.

257 "It is necessary . . .": Ibid.

258 "It is but sixteen years, . . .": Ibid.

258 "The enjoyment of scenery . . .": Ibid.

259 "Your plans . . .": Frederick Law Olmsted to Calvert Vaux, March 12, 1865, FLOP.

260 "Never say die, . . .": Calvert Vaux to Frederick Law Olmsted, May 10, 1865, FLOP.

260 "I shall tell . . .": Calvert Vaux to Frederick Law Olmsted, May 12, 1865, FLOP.

260 "There is no other place . . .": Frederick Law Olmsted to Calvert Vaux, June 8, 1865, FLOP.

260 "Mr. Vaux has made . . .": Frederick Law Olmsted to Edward C. Miller, June 26, 1865, FLOP.

261 "I feel it no less . . .": Calvert Vaux to Frederick Law Olmsted, June 3, 1865, FLOP.

261 "If I don't wholly adopt...": Frederick Law Olmsted to Calvert Vaux, August 1, 1865, FLOP.

261 "The art is not gardening...": Ibid.

Chapter Thirty-Six: Loose Ends

263 "drive the San Franciscans...": Frederick Law Olmsted to Calvert Vaux, August 1, 1865, FLOP.

263 "YOU ARE CHOSEN": Frederick Law Olmsted to James Miller McKim, September 7, 1865, FLOP.

263 "I have no intention of accepting...": Frederick Law Olmsted to John Olmsted, August 28, 1865, FLOP.

264 "I should be satisfied...": Calvert Vaux to Frederick Law Olmsted, July 21, 1865, FLOP.

264 "I decline.": Ibid.

264 "as if I had just come out from a cold bath...": Frederick Law Olmsted to John Olmsted, August 28, 1865, FLOP.

264 "No funds here yet...": Howard Potter to Frederick Law Olmsted, September 22, 1865, FLOP.

A MAGNIFICENT OPENING
Chapter Thirty-Seven: Olmsted and Vaux plan a perfect park

269 "an easy affair...": Calvert Vaux to Frederick Law Olmsted, July 8, 1865, FLOP.

271 "the feeling of relief...": Olmsted, Vaux & Co., "Preliminary Report to the Commissioners for Laying Out a Park in Brooklyn, New York: Being a Consideration of Circumstances of Site and Other Conditions Affecting the Design of Public Pleasure Grounds," *Landscape into Cityscape: Frederick Law Olmsted's Plans for a Greater New York City,* ed. Albert Fein (Ithaca, N.Y.: Cornell University Press, 1967), 98.

271 "for people to come together...": Ibid., 101.

271 "These trees are in two principal divisions...": Ibid., 107.

271 "Although we cannot have...": Ibid., 106-7.

271 "taking a very irregular course,...": Ibid., 115.

272 "...in a park,...": Ibid., 101.

273 "principal natural entrance,": Calvert Vaux to Frederick Law Olmsted, January 9, 1865, FLOP.

273 "the three grand elements...": Olmsted, Vaux & Co., "Preliminary Report to the Commissioners for Laying Out a Park in Brooklyn, New York: Being a Consideration of Circumstances of Site and Other Conditions Affecting the Design of Public Pleasure Grounds," *Landscape into Cityscape: Frederick Law Olmsted's Plans for a Greater New York City,* ed. Albert Fein (Ithaca, N.Y.: Cornell University Press, 1967), 111.

273 "a meditation on post–Civil War...": Laurie Olin, "Form, Meaning, and Expression in Landscape Architecture," *Landscape Journal,* Fall 1988: 163.

274 "A scene in nature...": Olmsted, Vaux & Co., "Preliminary Report to the Commissioners for Laying Out a Park in Brooklyn, New York: Being a Consideration of Circumstances of Site and Other Conditions Affecting the Design of Public Pleasure Grounds," *Landscape into Cityscape: Frederick Law Olmsted's Plans for a Greater New York City,* ed. Albert Fein (Ithaca, N.Y.: Cornell University Press, 1967), 104-5.

274 "should be a pleasure-ground . . .": Frederick Law Olmsted, "Preliminary Report in Regard to a Plan of Public Pleasure Grounds for the City of San Francisco," March 31, 1866, FLOP.

275 "I like the plan myself, . . .": H. P. Coon to Frederick Law Olmsted, June 29, 1866, FLOP.

276 "We have put four hundred men . . .": Frederick Law Olmsted to Charles Eliot Norton, July 15, 1866, FLOP.

277 "We felt a little cheated . . .": Frederick Law Olmsted to Charles Eliot Norton, September 12, 1866, FLOP.

277 "enlarge the scale . . .": Olmsted, Vaux & Co., "Report of the Landscape Architects & Superintendents," January 1, 1867, FLOP.

Chapter Thirty-Eight: Metropolitan

278 "[Olmsted's] reputation is such . . .": *The Papers of Frederick Law Olmsted, Vol. VI, The Years of Olmsted, Vaux & Company, 1865–1874,* ed. David Schuyler and Jane Turner Censer (Baltimore: Johns Hopkins University Press, 1992), n. 4, 79.

278 "We go over all . . .": *The Papers of Frederick Law Olmsted, Vol. V, The California Frontier, 1863–1865,* ed. Victoria Post Ranney (Baltimore: Johns Hopkins University Press, 1992), 55.

279 " 'The Nation' is a weekly comfort . . .": *Letters of Charles Eliot Norton,* ed. Sara Norton and M. A. DeWolfe Howe (Boston: Houghton Mifflin, 1913), 297.

280 "Olmsted, Vaux & Co., . . .": *The Nation,* May 1, 1866: 560.

280 "We regard Brooklyn . . .": Olmsted, Vaux & Co., "Preliminary Report to the Commissioners for Laying Out a Park in Brooklyn, New York: Being a Consideration of Circumstances of Site and Other Conditions Affecting the Design of Public Pleasure Grounds," *Landscape into Cityscape: Frederick Law Olmsted's Plans for a Greater New York City,* ed. Albert Fein (Ithaca, N.Y.: Cornell University Press, 1967), 99.

281 "the ground might be . . .": Olmsted, Vaux & Co., "Report of the Landscape Architects & Superintendents," January 1, 1867, FLOP.

281 "The city of New York is, . . .": Olmsted, Vaux & Co., "Report of the Landscape Architects and Superintendents to the President of the Board of Commissioners of Prospect Park, Brooklyn," *Landscape into Cityscape: Frederick Law Olmsted's Plans for a Greater New York City,* ed. Albert Fein (Ithaca, N.Y.: Cornell University Press, 1967), 153.

281 "the present street system, . . .": Ibid., 133.0

281 "On a level plain, . . .": Frederick Law Olmsted, "Preliminary Report in Regard to a Plan of Public Pleasure Grounds for the City of San Francisco," March 31, 1866, FLOP.

282 "the house lots of these streets . . .": Olmsted, Vaux & Co., "Report of the Landscape Architects and Superintendents to the President of the Board of Commissioners of Prospect Park, Brooklyn," *Landscape into Cityscape: Frederick Law Olmsted's Plans for a Greater New York City,* ed. Albert Fein (Ithaca, N.Y.: Cornell University Press, 1967), 161.

282 ". . . connection may thus be had . . .": Ibid., 126–27.

Chapter Thirty-Nine: A stopover in Buffalo

287 "The business opened at once . . .": Frederick Law Olmsted to Mary Cleveland Olmsted, August 23, 1868, FLOP.

287 "to hear an address . . .": Frederick Law Olmsted to Mary Cleveland Olmsted, August 25, 1868, FLOP.

287 "with tolerable smoothness . . .": Frederick Law Olmsted to Mary Cleveland Olmsted, August 26, 1868, FLOP.

288 "I did a deal of talking . . .": Frederick Law Olmsted to Calvert Vaux, August 29, 1868, FLOP.

288 "We should recommend . . .": Olmsted, Vaux & Co., "Mr. Olmsted's Report," *Preliminary Report Respecting a Public Park in Buffalo and a Copy of the Legislature Authorizing Its Establishment* (Buffalo: Matthews & Warren, 1869), 18.

Chapter Forty: Thirty-nine thousand trees

290 "The motive is like this . . .": Frederick Law Olmsted to Mary Cleveland Olmsted, August 23, 1868, FLOP.

291 "a big speculation": Frederick Law Olmsted to Calvert Vaux, August 29, 1868, FLOP.

291 "to be selected by Olmsted, . . .": Frederick Law Olmsted, "Draft of Proposed Agreement Between the Development Company and the Landscape Architects," *Landscape Architecture* 22, no. 4, July 1931: 278–79.

291 "at best affords . . .": Frederick Law Olmsted, "Preliminary Report Upon the Proposed Suburban Village at Riverside Near Chicago, by Olmsted, Vaux & Co., Landscape Architects," *Landscape Architecture* 21, no. 4, July 1931: 263.

291 He recommended acquiring . . .: "Prospectus of the Riverside Improvement Enterprise," *Landscape Architecture* 21, no. 4, July 1931: 280.

291 "Having a means of communication . . .": Frederick Law Olmsted, "Preliminary Report Upon the Proposed Suburban Village at Riverside Near Chicago, by Olmsted, Vaux & Co., Landscape Architects," *Landscape Architecture* 21, no. 4, July 1931: 266.

292 "I propose to lay . . .": Frederick Law Olmsted to Calvert Vaux, March 12, 1865, FLOP.

292 "The essential qualification . . .": Frederick Law Olmsted, "Preliminary Report Upon the Proposed Suburban Village at Riverside Near Chicago, by Olmsted, Vaux & Co., Landscape Architects," *Landscape Architecture* 21, no. 4, July 1931: 275.

293 "We should recommend . . .": Ibid., 268–69.

293 "ruralistic beauty . . .": Frederick Law Olmsted to Mariana Griswold Van Rensselaer, June 11, 1893, FLOP.

293 If a stranger were blindfolded, . . .": Howard K. Menhinick, "Riverside Sixty Years Later," *Landscape Architecture* 22, no. 2, January 1932: 109.

Chapter Forty-One: Best-laid plans

296 "It should be well thought . . .": Olmsted, Vaux & Co., "Mr. Olmsted's Report," *Preliminary Report Respecting a Public Park in Buffalo and a Copy of the Legislature Authorizing Its Establishment* (Buffalo: Matthews & Warren, 1869), 12.

296 "Let your buildings be . . .": Frederick Law Olmsted, "Public Parks and the Enlargement of Towns," Frederick Law Olmsted, *Civilizing American Cities: Writings on City Landscapes,* ed. S. B. Sutton, (Cambridge, Mass.: MIT Press, 1971), 81.

296 "We cannot judiciously attempt . . .": Frederick Law Olmsted, "Preliminary Report Upon the Proposed Suburban Village at Riverside Near Chicago, by Olmsted, Vaux & Co., Landscape Architects," *Landscape Architecture* 21, no. 4 (July 1931): 274.

297 "Nothing is decided as yet, . . .": *The Papers of Frederick Law Olmsted, Vol. V, The California Frontier, 1863–1865,* ed. Victoria Post Ranney (Baltimore: Johns Hopkins University Press, 1986), 723.

297 "Rich men and poor men, . . .": Ibid., 763.

297 "The recent rapid enlargement . . .": Frederick Law Olmsted, "Public Parks and the Enlargement of Towns," Frederick Law Olmsted, *Civilizing American Cities: Writings on City Landscapes*, S. B. Sutton, ed. (Cambridge, Mass.: MIT Press, 1971), 64.

297 "Compare advantages in respect . . .": Ibid., 58.

298 "to realize familiar . . .": see Richard Hofstadter, *The Age of Reform: From Bryan to F.D.R.* (New York: Random House, 1955), 215.

298 "the best planned city, . . .": Frederick Law Olmsted to George E. Waring Jr., April 13, 1876, FLOP.

298 "which will be completed . . .": "Riverside (Progress Prospectus)," *Landscape Architecture* 21, no. 4 (July 1931): 286.

299 "We have had to commence . . .": Frederick Law Olmsted to Edward Everett Hale, October 21, 1869, FLOP.

299 "the most interesting . . .": Ibid.

299 "Both Colfax and Olmsted . . .": *Chicago Times*, February 20, 1867.

300 "I am shocked and pained . . .": Frederick Law Olmsted to Emery E. Childs, October 28, 1869, FLOP.

300 "There is but one object . . .": Olmsted, Vaux & Co., "Report Accompanying Plan for Laying Out the South Park," Frederick Law Olmsted, *Civilizing American Cities: Writings on City Landscapes*, ed. S. B. Sutton (Cambridge, Mass.: MIT Press, 1971), 156–57.

301 "I don't see, Mr. Olmsted, . . .": General Superintendent of South Park to Theodora Kimball, December 8, 1922, FLOP.

301 "After my excitement . . .": Frederick Law Olmsted to Ignaz Anton Pilat, September 26, 1863, FLOP.

301 "You certainly cannot set . . .": Olmsted, Vaux & Co., "Report Accompanying Plan for Laying Out the South Park," Frederick Law Olmsted, *Civilizing American Cities: Writings on City Landscapes*, ed. S. B. Sutton (Cambridge, Mass.: MIT Press, 1971), 164.

Chapter Forty-Two: Henry Hobson Richardson

303 "That is all I wanted, . . .": Mariana Griswold Van Rensselaer, *Henry Hobson Richardson and His Works* (Boston: Houghton Mifflin, 1888), 18.

304 "The most beguiling . . .": Ibid., 118–19.

304 he probably recommended Richardson . . .: see Jeffrey Karl Ochsner, *H. H. Richardson: Complete Architectural Works* (Cambridge, Mass.: MIT Press, 1982), 54.

304 "He was of good height, . . .": "A Great Artist's Struggle," *Boston Evening Transcript*, October 8, 1886.

305 "the district is much less healthy, . . .": Frederick Law Olmsted et al., "Report to the Staten Island Improvement Commission of a Preliminary Scheme of Improvements," *Landscape into Cityscape: Frederick Law Olmsted's Plans for a Greater New York City*, ed. Albert Fein (Ithaca, N.Y.: Cornell University Press, 1967), 190.

305 "suburban district of great beauty, . . .": Ibid., 189.

305 "If the interior land . . .": Ibid., 203.

306 "three gentlemen, residents . . .": Frederick Law Olmsted to William Butler Duncan, September 22, 1870, FLOP.

306 "a gentleman trained . . .": Ibid.

307 generally considered a breakthrough.: Henry-Russell Hitchcock, *The Architecture of H. H. Richardson and His Times* (Cambridge, Mass.: MIT Press, 1966), 111.

Chapter Forty-Three: Olmsted's dilemma

309 "I am poorly qualified . . .": Frederick Law Olmsted to Frederick J. Kingsbury, April 20, 1871, FLOP.
309 "I am longer at breakfast . . .": Ibid.
310 "I feel myself so nearly desperate . . .": Frederick Law Olmsted to Samuel Bowles, June 2, 1871, FLOP.
310 "not tied to any architectural firm. . . .": Samuel Bowles to Frederick Law Olmsted, May 3, 1871, FLOP.
310 "You write in view . . .": Frederick Law Olmsted to Samuel Bowles, June 2, 1871, FLOP.
310 "I am looking in earnest . . .": Frederick Law Olmsted to Frederick J. Kingsbury, October 8, 1871, FLOP.
311 "important papers, contracts, . . .": Frederick Law Olmsted, "Chicago in Distress," *The Nation*, November 9, 1871: 305.
311 "The appointment of Stebbins . . .": Frederick Law Olmsted to Charles Loring Brace, November 24, 1871, FLOP.
312 "The Park has suffered . . .": Frederick Law Olmsted to Columbus Ryan, February 27, 1872, FLOP.
312 "At the Dairy . . .": Frederick Law Olmsted, "To Those Having the Care of Young Children," *Frederick Law Olmsted: Landscape Architect, 1822–1903*, ed. Frederick Law Olmsted Jr. and Theodora Kimball (New York: G. P. Putnam's Sons, 1928), 418.
312 "It appeared to me . . .": Frederick Law Olmsted to James Miller McKim, June 28, 1872, FLOP.
312 "It is hereby mutually agreed . . .": *Frederick Law Olmsted: Landscape Architect, 1822–1903*, ed. Frederick Law Olmsted Jr. and Theodora Kimball (New York: G. P. Putnam's Sons, 1928), n. 1, 94.

Chapter Forty-Four: Alone

314 "Why! Who's this? . . .": Frederick Law Olmsted to Frederick J. Kingsbury, January 28, 1873, FLOP.
315 "He was a very good man . . .": Ibid.
316 "May my last end . . .": Frederick Law Olmsted to Charles Loring Brace, December 21, 1873, FLOP.
317 "Mr. Olmsted and Mr. Weidenmann . . .": *Frederick Law Olmsted: Landscape Architect, 1822–1903*, ed. Frederick Law Olmsted Jr. and Theodora Kimball (New York: G. P. Putnam's Sons, 1928), 18.
317 "The barriers and hedges of society . . .": *New-York Times*, October 9, 1860.

Chapter Forty-Five: "More interesting than nature"

321 "what has been considered . . .": Frederick Law Olmsted to Edward Clark, October 1, 1881, *Annual Report of the Architect of the United States Capitol* (Washington, 1882), 14–15.
321 "diffidence in my ability . . .": Frederick Law Olmsted, *Mount Royal* (New York: G. P. Putnam, 1881), 8.
323 "I would observe . . .": Frederick Law Olmsted to the Commissioners of Mount-Royal Park, November 21, 1874, Canadian Institute for Historical Microproductions.

323 "It would be wasteful . . .": Frederick Law Olmsted, *Mount Royal* (New York: G. P. Putnam, 1881), 42.

323 "so that a good horse, . . .": John Nolen, "Mount Royal, Montreal: A Mountain Park," *House & Garden,* February 1906: 83.

324 "Regard the work . . .": Frederick Law Olmsted, *Civilizing American Cities: Writings on City Landscapes,* ed. S. B. Sutton (Cambridge, Mass.: MIT Press, 1971), 203.

324 "You can shape . . .": Ibid., 207.

324 "They address the other members . . .": Frederick Law Olmsted, *Mount Royal* (New York: G. P. Putnam, 1881), 14.

324 "the term park, . . .": Ibid., 9.

325 "one of the most successful designs . . .": John Nolen, "Mount Royal, Montreal: A Mountain Park," *House & Garden,* February 1906: 83.

325 "prophylactic and therapeutic . . .": Frederick Law Olmsted, *Mount Royal* (New York: G. P. Putnam, 1881), 22.

Chapter Forty-Six: Olmsted in demand

326 "wedding journey, . . .": Mariana Griswold Van Rensselaer, *Henry Hobson Richardson and His Works* (Boston: Houghton Mifflin, 1888), 27.

327 "Mr. Olmsted . . . was . . .": Ibid., 74.

328 "If a proposed cathedral, . . .": Frederick Law Olmsted and J. James R. Croes, "Preliminary Report of the Landscape Architect and the Civil and Topographical Engineer, upon the Laying Out of the Twenty-third and Twenty-fourth Wards," *Landscape into Cityscape: Frederick Law Olmsted's Plans for a Greater New York City,* ed. Albert Fein (Ithaca, N.Y.: Cornell University Press, 1967), 352–53.

328 "There are many houses . . .": Ibid., 355.

328 "Even on a flat alluvial site, . . .": Ibid., 356–57.

328 "What is meant . . .": Ibid., 365.

329 "A judicious laying out . . .": Ibid., 357.

329 "The most fantastic plat . . .": Glenn Chesney Quiett, *They Built the West; an Epic of Rails and Cities* (New York: D. Appleton-Century Company, 1934), 414.

330 "the plan of a Metropolis; . . .": Frederick Law Olmsted and J. James R. Croes, "Preliminary Report of the Landscape Architect and the Civil and Topographical Engineer, upon the Laying Out of the Twenty-third and Twenty-fourth Wards," *Landscape into Cityscape: Frederick Law Olmsted's Plans for a Greater New York City,* ed. Albert Fein (Ithaca, N.Y.: Cornell University Press, 1967), 352.

Chapter Forty-Seven: "I shall be free from it on the 1st of January"

332 "The Park is still a prize . . .": *New-York Times,* April 28, 1875.

332 "There were symptoms . . .": Frederick Law Olmsted, "The Spoils of the Park: With a Few Leaves from the Deep-Laden Note-Books of A Wholly Unpractical Man," *Frederick Law Olmsted: Landscape Architect, 1822–1903,* ed. Frederick Law Olmsted Jr. and Theodora Kimball (New York: G. P. Putnam's Sons, 1928), 136–37.

333 "to be read over and committed substantively . . .": Frederick Law Olmsted, "Instructions," undated, JCOC.

333 "I know that it is feasible . . .": Frederick Law Olmsted to John Charles Olmsted, September 14, 1877, JCOC.

333 "[Your letters] are . . .": Frederick Law Olmsted to John Charles Olmsted, October 7, 1877, JCOC.

334 "drifting with the currents . . .": Frederick Law Olmsted to John Charles Olmsted, December 1, 1877, JCOC.

334 "You are not a man of genius . . .": Ibid.

334 "Don't be so cowardly . . .": Ibid.

334 "It is evident that there was little occasion . . .": Frederick Law Olmsted to John Charles Olmsted, December 18, 1877, JCOC.

335 "I agree to what you say . . .": John Charles Olmsted to Frederick Law Olmsted, December 27, 1877, JCOC.

335 "with the understanding . . .": John Charles Olmsted to Frederick Law Olmsted, December 3, 1877, JCOC.

335 "Mr. F. L. Olmsted, . . .": *Frederick Law Olmsted: Landscape Architect, 1822–1903*, ed. Frederick Law Olmsted Jr. and Theodora Kimball (New York: G. P. Putnam's Sons, 1928), 110.

335 "It will not be thought . . .": Ibid., 137.

336 "I shall go at once . . .": Frederick Law Olmsted to John Charles Olmsted, December 15, 1877, JCOC.

336 "after 10 days at sea . . .": Frederick Law Olmsted to John Charles Olmsted, December 16, 1877, JCOC.

336 "I shall be free from it . . .": Frederick Law Olmsted to John Charles Olmsted, December 25, 1877. JCOC.

336 "Think it well out . . .": Ibid.

336 "*It is therefore Resolved, . . .*": *Frederick Law Olmsted: Landscape Architect, 1822–1903*, ed. Frederick Law Olmsted Jr. and Theodora Kimball (New York: G. P. Putnam's Sons, 1928), 110–11.

337 "I am glad you are going abroad . . .": Charles Eliot Norton to Frederick Law Olmsted, January 5, 1878, FLOP.

337 "He seems to have enjoyed . . .": John Charles Olmsted to Mary Cleveland Olmsted, February 7, 1878, JCOC.

337 "If ever an artist . . .": Edouard André, *Traité général de la composition des parcs et jardins* (Paris: Masson, 1879), 188. Author's translation.

337 "the disease, whatever it is, . . .": John Charles Olmsted to Mary Cleveland Olmsted, March 16, 1878, JCOC.

338 "He has formed no idea . . .": Ibid.

338 "chivying English disposition": Mary Cleveland Olmsted to John Charles Olmsted, February 24, 1878, FLOP.

338 "Father thinks Mr. Vaux's letter . . .": Ibid.

STANDING FIRST
Chapter Forty-Eight: An arduous convalescence

341 "I am doing but little professionally . . .": *Frederick Law Olmsted: Landscape Architect, 1822–1903*, ed. Frederick Law Olmsted Jr. and Theodora Kimball (New York: G. P. Putnam's Sons, 1928), 23.

342 "No aid I could give . . .": Frederick Law Olmsted to Charles Henry Dalton, May 13, 1878, FLOP.

342 "The central purpose of this work . . .": Frederick Law Olmsted, "Paper on the Problem and Its Solution Read Before the Boston Society of Architects," April 2, 1886, FLOP.

342 "The object of this crookedness, . . .": Ibid.
343 "What are your plans . . .": Ibid.

Chapter Forty-Nine: Fairstead

347 "You can have no idea . . .": Frederick Law Olmsted to Charles Loring Brace, March 7, 1882, FLOP.
347 "The president once notified me . . .": Frederick Law Olmsted, "The Spoils of the Park," *Frederick Law Olmsted: Landscape Architect, 1822–1903,* ed. Frederick Law Olmsted Jr. and Theodora Kimball (New York: G. P. Putnam's Sons, 1928), 135.
348 "Consideration of the responsibility . . .": Ibid., 155.
348 "borderland": see John R. Stilgoe, *Borderland: Origins of the American Suburb, 1820–1939* (New Haven: Yale University Press, 1988).
348 "I enjoy this suburban . . .": Frederick Law Olmsted to Charles Loring Brace, March 7, 1882, FLOP.
349 "having the general appearance . . .": Frederick Law Olmsted to S. H. Wiley, June 29, 1866, FLOP.
349 "Mr. Richardson . . . was constantly . . .": *American Architect and Building News,* January 7, 1888: 4.
351 "In what may be termed . . .": Frederick Law Olmsted to John Charles Olmsted, December 25, 1877, FLOP.
351 "beautiful thing in shingles": Henry Hobson Richardson to Frederick Law Olmsted, February 6, 1883, FLOP.
353 "to mix shrubs . . .": [Charles W. Eliot], *Charles Eliot: Landscape Architect* (Boston: Houghton Mifflin, 1902), 36.
353 "Less wildness and disorder . . .": Frederick Law Olmsted to John Charles Olmsted, September 12, 1884, FLOP.
354 "I am to go about . . .": [Charles W. Eliot], *Charles Eliot: Landscape Architect* (Boston: Houghton Mifflin, 1902), 35.
354 "influencing men of means . . .": Frederick Law Olmsted to John Charles Olmsted, December 25, 1877, FLOP.
354 "We put them to such work . . .": Frederick Law Olmsted to George W. Curtis, August 22, 1891, FLOP.

Chapter Fifty: The character of his business

355 "You decidedly have the best . . .": Frederick Law Olmsted to Charles Loring Brace, November 1, 1884, FLOP.
356 "Instead of being shocked . . .": Ibid.
356 "I enjoyed Fred O's letter, . . .": Frederick J. Kingsbury to Charles Loring Brace, January 10, 1885, FLOP.
356 "I think it comes harder . . .": Frederick Law Olmsted to Charles Loring Brace, November 1, 1884, FLOP.
356 "You are preaching truths . . .": Charles Eliot Norton to Frederick Law Olmsted, October 23, 1881, FLOP.
356 "You are compelled to throw . . .": Ibid.
357 "I keep working as close . . .": Frederick Law Olmsted to Charles Loring Brace, November 1, 1884, FLOP.

357 no fewer than sixteen private estates . . .: Charles E. Beveridge and Carolyn F. Hoffman, *The Master List of Design Projects of the Olmsted Firm 1857–1950* (Boston: National Association for Olmsted Parks, 1987).

357 One of the few magazine articles . . .: Frederick Law Olmsted, "Plan for a Small Homestead," *Garden and Forest*, May 2, 1888.

357 "If what I advise . . .": Frederick Law Olmsted to Charles Follen McKim, December 24, 1883, FLOP.

358 "where building seemed . . .": Frederick Law Olmsted to John Charles Olmsted, May 30, 1884, FLOP.

358 "I was ill treated . . .": Ibid.

358 "Temple [a nurseryman] will . . .": Frederick Law Olmsted to John Charles Olmsted, May 24, 1884, FLOP.

358 "As the house was not . . .": Frederick Law Olmsted to John C. Phillips, September 27, 1881, FLOP.

359 "proper summer lodge, . . .": Ibid.

Chapter Fifty-One: The sixth park

360 "should receive orders . . .": Frederick Law Olmsted to the Park Commissioners of Boston, September 8, 1884, FLOP.

361 "Eccentric and quaint": Frederick Law Olmsted to John Charles Olmsted, May 15, 1892, FLOP.

361 "the usual characteristics . . .": Frederick Law Olmsted, "Notes on the Plan of Franklin Park and Related Matters," *The Papers of Frederick Law Olmsted, Supplementary Series, Vol. I, Writings on Public Parks, Parkways, and Park Systems*, ed. Charles E. Beveridge and Carolyn F. Hoffman (Baltimore: Johns Hopkins University Press, 1997), 473.

362 "To sustain the designed character . . .": Ibid., 483–84.

362 "without underwood, . . .": Ibid., 488.

362 "cannot, therefore, be prepared . . .": Ibid., 484.

363 "To provide opportunity . . .": Frederick Law Olmsted, "General Plan of Franklin Park," Boston Parks and Recreation, *Franklin Plan Master Plan 1991: Volume I, Master Plan Overview and Recommendations* (Boston: Boston Parks and Recreation, 1991), 149.

363 "there are some . . .": Frederick Law Olmsted, "Notes on the Plan of Franklin Park and Related Matters," *The Papers of Frederick Law Olmsted, Supplementary Series, Vol. I, Writings on Public Parks, Parkways, and Park Systems*, ed. Charles E. Beveridge and Carolyn F. Hoffman (Baltimore: Johns Hopkins University Press, 1997), 478.

364 "The highest value of a park . . .": Frederick Law Olmsted, "Trees in Streets and in Parks," *The Sanitarian* 10, September 1882: 517.

364 "Let it not be . . .": Frederick Law Olmsted, "Notes on the Plan of Franklin Park and Related Matters," *The Papers of Frederick Law Olmsted, Supplementary Series, Vol. I, Writings on Public Parks, Parkways, and Park Systems*, ed. Charles E. Beveridge and Carolyn F. Hoffman (Baltimore: Johns Hopkins University Press, 1997), 524.

Chapter Fifty-Two: Olmsted meets the Governor

367 "His eyes were bloodshot, . . .": Mariana Griswold Van Rensselaer, *Henry Hobson Richardson and His Works* (Boston: Houghton Mifflin, 1888), 118.

367 "Eidlitz asked me . . .": Ibid., 119.

368 "He passed away . . .": Frederick Law Olmsted to Mariana Griswold Van Rensselaer, May 2, 1886, FLOP.

368 He never had as much to do; . . .": Ibid.

368 "The daylight part of the journey . . .": Frederick Law Olmsted to John Charles Olmsted, September 23, 1886, FLOP.

369 "There is not any word . . .": Frederick Law Olmsted to Charles W. Eliot, June 8, 1886, FLOP.

369 "The site is settled . . .": Frederick Law Olmsted to John Charles Olmsted, September 29, 1886, FLOP.

369 "It was a high interest speculation, . . .": Frederick Law Olmsted to John Charles Olmsted, October 9, 1886, FLOP.

369 "our responsibility for the design . . .": Frederick Law Olmsted to David Bennett Hill, July 21, 1886, FLOP.

370 "I am sorry I don't see . . .": Frederick Law Olmsted to John Charles Olmsted, October 14, 1886, FLOP.

370 "You write easily, . . .": Frederick Law Olmsted to Charles Eliot, October 28, 1886, FLOP.

370 "If we are to look . . .": quoted in Paul V. Turner et al., *The Founders and the Architects: The Design of Stamford University* (Stamford, Calif.: Stamford University, 1976).

371 "Mr. Olmsted and myself . . .": Ibid.

371 "The very quietness and reserve . . .": Charles A. Coolidge to Frederick Law Olmsted, May 3, 1886, FLOP.

371 "The Gov. replied . . .": Ibid.

372 "There is a story . . .": Frederick Law Olmsted to Mariana Griswold Van Rensselaer, May 17, 1887, FLOP.

Chapter Fifty-Three: Olmsted and Vaux, together again

373 "Mr. Vaux is a very good landscape architect . . .": *Art Amateur* 8, February 1883: 68.

374 "He helped me . . .": Frederick Law Olmsted to Mariana Griswold Van Rensselaer, May 17, 1887, FLOP.

374 "He can't take writing . . .": John Charles Olmsted to Calvert Vaux, February 22, 1887, FLOP.

374 "the most difficult problem . . .": Frederick Law Olmsted to James Terry Gardner, October 3, 1879, Gardner papers, New York State Library, Albany, N.Y.

374 "incomparable greater beauty . . .": Frederick Law Olmsted and Calvert Vaux, "General Plan for the Improvement of the Niagara Reservation," *The Papers of Frederick Law Olmsted, Supplementary Series, Vol. I, Writings on Public Parks, Parkways, and Park Systems*, ed. Charles E. Beveridge and Carolyn F. Hoffman (Baltimore: Johns Hopkins University Press, 1997), 551.

375 "We are far from thinking . . .": Ibid., 542.

375 Vaux's biographer, . . .: Francis R. Kowsky, *Country, Park, & City: The Architecture and Life of Calvert Vaux* (New York: Oxford University Press, 1998), 306.

377 "I am too old a man . . .": Frederick Law Olmsted to Leland Stanford, August 7, 1890, FLOP.

377 "We are gradually improving . . .": Leland Stanford to Frederick Law Olmsted, November 9, 1891, FLOP.

Chapter Fifty-Four: "Make a small pleasure ground and gardens"

379   "I am at this time . . .": Frederick Law Olmsted to Ariel Lathrop, July 7, 1890, FLOP.

379   "I came to Asheville . . .": Frederick Law Olmsted to Frederick J. Kingsbury, January 20, 1891, FLOP.

379   "But the soil seems . . .": Ibid.

380   "a delicate, refined and bookish man, . . .": Ibid.

381   "I very much like your new plan . . .": Frederick Law Olmsted to Richard Morris Hunt, March 2, 1889, FLOP.

381   Hunt had not yet visited . . .: John M. Bryan, *Biltmore Estate: The Most Distinguished Private Place* (New York: Rizzoli, 1994), 40.

381   "natural and comparatively wild . . .": Frederick Law Olmsted to George W. Vanderbilt, July 12, 1889, FLOP.

381   "There are one or two points . . .": Frederick Law Olmsted to William A. Stiles, March 10, 1895, FLOP.

381   "He has accepted every . . .": Ibid.

383   "A place out-of-doors is wanted . . .": Frederick Law Olmsted to Richard Morris Hunt, March 2, 1889, FLOP.

384   "We have a good deal of work . . .": Frederick Law Olmsted to John Murray Forbes, July 2, 1891, FLOP.

384   "a private work . . .": Frederick Law Olmsted to W. A. Thompson, November 6, 1889, FLOP.

Chapter Fifty-Five: Olmsted drives hard

385   "It strikes me as your best work . . .": Frederick Law Olmsted to Charles Loring Brace, January 18, 1890, FLOP.

385   "His death was a shock . . .": Frederick Law Olmsted to Frederick J. Kingsbury, January 20, 1891, FLOP.

385   "What a good ancient philosopher . . .": Charles Eliot Norton to Frederick Law Olmsted, September 26, 1890, FLOP.

385   "I enjoy my children. . . .": Frederick Law Olmsted to Frederick J. Kingsbury, September 6, 1893, FLOP.

385   "much better equipped . . .": Frederick Law Olmsted to Charles Loring Brace, January 18, 1890, FLOP.

385   "I have all my life . . .": Frederick Law Olmsted to Frederick Law Olmsted Jr., September 5, 1890, FLOP.

386   "swampy, the surface of a large part . . .": *A History of the World's Columbian Exposition*, ed. Rossiter Johnson (New York: D. Appleton & Company, 1897), 35.

386   "it was one of the greatest advantages . . .": John Charles Olmsted to Charles Eliot, March 25, 1896, FLOP.

386   "We have carried our first point . . .": Frederick Law Olmsted to John Charles Olmsted, November 24, 1890, FLOP.

386   "inspired confidence in all . . .": Charles Moore, *Daniel H. Burnham: Architect Planner of Cities* (Boston: Houghton Mifflin, 1921), vol. I, 29.

387   "Harry Codman's knowledge . . .": Ibid., 45.

389   "cordial and unqualified approval . . .": Frederick Law Olmsted, "The Landscape

Architecture of the World's Columbian Exposition," *Inland Architect and News Record,* September 1893: 20.

389 "We had a breakfast . . .": Charles Moore, *Daniel H. Burnham: Architect Planner of Cities* (Boston: Houghton Mifflin, 1921), vol. I, 46.

389 "the general comradeship . . .": Frederick Law Olmsted to Mariana Griswold Van Rensselaer, November 7, 1892, FLOP.

389 "Look here, old fellow, . . .": Charles Moore, *Daniel H. Burnham: Architect Planner of Cities* (Boston: Houghton Mifflin, 1921), vol. I, 47.

390 "one hundred thousand small willows; . . .": Frederick Law Olmsted, "The Landscape Architecture of the World's Columbian Exposition," *Inland Architect and News Record,* September 1893: 21.

390 "I never had more before me . . .": Frederick Law Olmsted to Charles Loring Brace, January 18, 1890, FLOP.

391 "They show, I think, . . .": Frederick Law Olmsted, "Report by F.L.O.," April 1892, FLOP.

391 "All these châteaux . . .": Philip Codman to Henry Sargent Codman, May 1, 1892, FLOP.

391 "I am having a great deal of enjoyment . . .": Frederick Law Olmsted to Mary Cleveland Olmsted, May 3, 1892, FLOP.

391 "More than a failure. . . .": Frederick Law Olmsted to Frederick J. Kingsbury, September 6, 1893, FLOP.

391 "I fear that against the clear blue sky . . .": Frederick Law Olmsted to Rudolph Ulrich, March 11, 1893, FLOP.

392 "having an educative effect . . .": Frederick Law Olmsted to Elizabeth Baldwin, December 16, 1890, FLOP.

392 "I am as one standing on a wreck . . .": Frederick Law Olmsted to Gifford Pinchot, January 19, 1893, FLOP.

392 "It looks as if the time . . .": Frederick Law Olmsted to John Charles Olmsted, October 17, 1893, FLOP.

Chapter Fifty-Six: The fourth muse

393 "A director of faith . . .": Charles Moore, *Daniel H. Burnham: Architect Planner of Cities* (Boston: Houghton Mifflin, 1921), vol. I, 75.

394 "You know who these men are . . .": Ibid., 74.

395 reported both Olmsteds . . .: *New-York Times,* March 26, 1893.

395 "Mr. O. ailing": Charles Eliot's pocket diary, March 26, 1898, JCOC.

396 "The general design of the grounds . . .": Charles Moore, *Daniel H. Burnham: Architect Planner of Cities* (Boston: Houghton Mifflin, 1921), vol. I, 79.

396 "roses as roses, . . .": Frederick Law Olmsted, "The Landscape Architecture of the World's Columbian Exposition," *Inland Architect and News Record,* September 1893: 18.

396 "I design with a view . . .": Frederick Law Olmsted to Mariana Griswold Van Rensselaer, May 17, 1887, FLOP

397 "the queerest thing . . .": Frederick Law Olmsted to Mariana Griswold Van Rensselaer, June 17, 1893, FLOP.

397 "If people generally get to understand . . .": Frederick Law Olmsted to Mariana Griswold Van Rensselaer, November 7, 1892, FLOP.

397 "Everywhere there is a *growing* interest . . .": Frederick Law Olmsted to Daniel H. Burnham, June 20, 1893, FLOP.

397 "The landscape-plan is the key . . .": Montgomery Schuyler, "Last Words about the World's Fair," *Architectural Record,* January-March 1894: 294.

397 "We should try to make . . .": Frederick Law Olmsted to Daniel H. Burnham, January 26, 1891, FLOP.

398 "to supply a means of appropriate decoration . . .": Frederick Law Olmsted to Charles McClave, November 7, 1892, FLOP.

398 "The effects of the boats . . .": Frederick Law Olmsted, "The Landscape Architecture of the World's Columbian Exposition," *Inland Architect and News Record,* September 1893: 21.

398 "The canoes would add a feature . . .": Frederick Law Olmsted to Daniel H. Burnham, January 26, 1891, FLOP.

398 "Why not skipping . . .": Ibid.

398 "The influence of the Exposition . . .": Montgomery Schuyler, "Last Words about the World's Fair," *Architectural Record,* January-March 1894: 292.

399 "You know that these men of the enemy . . .": Frederick Law Olmsted to William A. Stiles, March 10, 1895, FLOP.

399 "formal stateliness that our architectural . . .": Ibid.

Chapter Fifty-Seven: Dear Rick

400 "I am doubting some . . .": Frederick Law Olmsted to John Charles Olmsted, October 27, 1893, FLOP.

400 "With reference to your future business . . .": Frederick Law Olmsted to John Charles Olmsted, March 13, 1894, FLOP.

400 "convenient, rapid, agreeable . . .": Frederick Law Olmsted to Joel Hurt, December 5, 1890, FLOP.

401 "It is far and away . . .": Frederick Law Olmsted to partners, November 1, 1893, FLOP.

401 "I like him very much, . . .": Frederick Law Olmsted to Charles Eliot Norton, September 24, 1890, FLOP.

401 "I want you to be prepared . . .": Frederick Law Olmsted to Frederick Law Olmsted Jr., September 5, 1890, FLOP.

401 "The more you see . . .": Frederick Law Olmsted to Frederick Law Olmsted Jr., August 1, 1894, FLOP.

402 "Are you gaining any . . .": Frederick Law Olmsted to Frederick Law Olmsted Jr., December 23, 1894, FLOP.

402 "I am as ready to give . . .": Ibid.

403 "I shall not take you . . .": Frederick Law Olmsted to Frederick Law Olmsted Jr., undated, FLOP.

403 "then I am compelled . . .": Frederick Law Olmsted Jr. to Frederick Law Olmsted, January 1, 1895, Olmsted Associate Records.

403 "You seem to me to have . . .": Frederick Law Olmsted to Frederick Law Olmsted Jr., January 1, undated, FLOP.

403 "Stick to it. . . .": Frederick Law Olmsted to Frederick Law Olmsted Jr., January 7, 1895, FLOP.

403 "It is too late . . .": Frederick Law Olmsted to Frederick Law Olmsted Jr., undated, FLOP.

403 "I should be disposed to keep . . .": Frederick Law Olmsted to Frederick Law Olmsted Jr., February 3, 1895, FLOP.

404 "If man is not to live . . .": Frederick Law Olmsted, "Trees in Streets and in Parks," *The Sanitarian*, September 1882: 514.

404 "a finer, more beautiful, . . .": Frederick Law Olmsted to George W. Vanderbilt, December 30, 1893, FLOP.

404 "Water-side trees by the lake; . . .": Frederick Law Olmsted to George W. Vanderbilt, July 12, 1889, FLOP.

404 "I must yet for a time . . .": Frederick Law Olmsted to George W. Vanderbilt, December 30, 1893, FLOP.

404 "Father does not keep track . . .": Frederick Law Olmsted Jr. to John Charles Olmsted, December 20, 1894, FLOP.

405 "If Rick had not been with me . . .": Frederick Law Olmsted to John Charles Olmsted, May 10, 1895, FLOP.

Chapter Fifty-Eight: Sunset

406 "each without slightest memory . . .": "J. G. Langton reminisces," January 31, 1921, FLOP.

406 "I am still here because . . .": Frederick Law Olmsted to Frederick Law Olmsted Jr., August 13, 1895, FLOP.

406 "before you write . . .": John Charles Olmsted to Frederick Law Olmsted, September 2, 1895, FLOP.

406 "A queer situation . . .": Frederick Law Olmsted to Charles Eliot, undated, stamped "Rec'd August 19, 1895," JCOC.

407 "Nothing goes as far . . .": Frederick Law Olmsted to Frederick Law Olmsted Jr., October 14, 1895, FLOP.

407 "Keep me here . . .": Mary Cleveland Olmsted to John Charles Olmsted, September 29, 1895, JCOC.

407 "I am grateful for your letter . . .": Frederick Law Olmsted to Charles Eliot, September 26, 1895, JCOC.

407 "He makes us very nervous . . .": Mary Cleveland Olmsted to John Charles Olmsted, September 27, 1895, JCOC.

408 "My doctors wish me to think . . .": Frederick Law Olmsted to Frederick Law Olmsted Jr., November 7, 1895, FLOP.

408 "I am going down hill rapidly. . . .": Frederick Law Olmsted to John Charles Olmsted, December 12, 1895, JCOC.

408 "He gives up all hope . . .": Mary Cleveland Olmsted to Frederick Law Olmsted Jr., undated, FLOP.

409 "If she had some good-natured . . .": John Charles Olmsted to Frederick Law Olmsted Jr., April 24, 1896, FLOP.

410 "John is John & must be taken . . .": Mary Cleveland Olmsted to Frederick Law Olmsted Jr., May 29, 1896, FLOP.

410 "make L.A. respected . . .": Frederick Law Olmsted to Frederick Law Olmsted Jr., September 5, 1890, FLOP.

411 "F. L. OLMSTED IS DEAD . . .": *New-York Times*, August 29, 1903.

411 "I have felt much for you . . .": Charles Eliot Norton to Frederick Law Olmsted Jr., September 3, 1903, FLOP.

411 "It was a meager unsatisfactory service . . .": John Charles Olmsted to Sophia White Olmsted, September 8, 1903, JCOC.

INDEX

Page numbers in *italics* refer to illustrations.

Mariposa Weekly Gazette, 237
Marshall, William, 83
Martin, Howard, 227, 231, 242, 336
Maryland, 214, 215*n*, 326
Mason Brothers, 190, 228
Massachusetts, 106
Massachusetts Agricultural College, 280
Massachusetts Horticultural Society, 45
Massachusetts Institute of Technology,
    354, 368
Mead, William Rutherford, 357
Meade, George G., 221
medicine, nineteenth-century, 37
Meigs, Montgomery, 21–22, 204, 210, 308
Melville, Herman, 91, 136, 137, 149
Methodism, 66, 67
Metropolitan Museum of Art, 313, 373,
    380
Mexicans, in California, 251, 252
Mexican War, 106
Mexico, 126, 131, 132
Michelangelo, 57
Michigan, Lake, 300, 301, 302, 386, 387, 390
middle names, as genteel fashion, 23
Mill, John Stuart, 196, 316
Miller, Edward, 243, 245, 246, 250, 262, 263,
    276
Miller, J. W., 149
Miller & Curtis, 149, 150, 151, 161, 163, 192
Millet, Francis D., 393
Mills, Darius, 240, 241, 245–46
Mississippi, 123, 196
Mississippi River, 218
Missouri, 106, 139, 215, 217
Missouri Compromise (1820), 105–6, 125,
    148
Miss Rockwell's school, 27, 29
Modern Painters (Ruskin), 82
Monds, Maria, 56
Montana, 348, 369
Montmorency Falls, 277, 326
Montreal, Mount Royal (Mont Réal) in,
    13–14, 321–25, *322,* 326, 350, 355
Moraine Farm, 359, 380
Morning Courier & New-York Enquirer, 174
Morrisania, 328, 329–30
Morris Cove, Conn., 149–52
Morton, Peter, 49
Mould, Jacob Wrey, 169, 175–76, 184, 199,
    313, 318, 373
Mountain View Cemetery, 238, 243, *244,*
    245, 262, 263, 269
Mount Auburn Cemetery, 45

Mount Royal (Mont Réal), 13–14, 321–25,
    322, 350, 355
Mount Saint Vincent, Central Park,
    187–89
Mozart, Wolfgang Amadeus, 57
Mr. Perkins's academy, 26
Muddy River Improvement, 342–45, 360
mulattoes, 115, 122
Mumford, Lewis, 91
Murfreesboro, Tenn., 217
mutiny, of seamen, 55

Napoleon III, Emperor of France, 180
Narrows, the, 282, 283–84
Nashville, Tenn., 125, 146
Natchitoches, La., 124–25, 128
Nation, 20, 278–80, 307, 311
National Era, 141
National Park System, 238
Navy, U.S., 55, 197, 205
Nebraska, 125, 133
Needham, Mass., 308
Neill, Letitia, 98, 104
Neu Braunfels, Tex., 129, 130
Nevada Territory, 231, 232
Newberry, John S., 200, 202, 215–16, 217,
    221, 306
New Britain, Conn., 308
Newburgh, N.Y., 65–66, 71, 74
New England Emigrant Aid Company,
    138–39, 148
New Hampshire, 40, 106, 277
New Haven, Conn., 69
    FLO's visits to, 47, 61–64, 71
New Jersey, 280, 285, 349, *350,* 357–58
New Orleans, La., 111–12, 118–19, 122–23,
    303, 330
New Rochelle, N.Y., 192
New York, N.Y., 32, 104, 208, 321, 386, 393–96
    Commissioners' Plan for, 43, 192, 328
    described, 43–44, 65
    FLO in, 21–22, 37, 42–46, 49–50, 54, 65,
        74, 134–42, 145–49, 155–79, 183–98,
        205, 214, 220, 223, 269–84
    FLO offered street commissioner post
        in, 207
    FLO's house in, 314, 347
    Greater, 281
    Great Fire of 1835 in, 44, 78
    literary world of, 108, 134, 137, 199
    museums in, 313, 373, 380
    parks in, 44, 94; *see also* Central Park;
        Prospect Park

ILLUSTRATION

AND PHOTOGRAPH CREDITS

ILLUSTRATIONS

All plans drawn by Shawn D. Seaman

TEXT PHOTOGRAPHS

Pages 339 (bottom): Brown Brothers; 267: Collection of the New-York Historical Society; 89, 153 (right), 339 (top right): Courtesy of National Park Service, Frederick Law Olmsted National Historic Site, Brookline, Massachusetts; 415: Frederick Law Olmsted Association; 339 (top left): Massachusetts Historical Society; 4, 17, 153 (left): Society for the Preservation of New England Antiquities

INSERT PHOTOGRAPHS

Pages 14: Alexander Alland Sr./Corbis-Bettmann; 6: Chicago Historical Society (ICHi-02525, Photographer: C. D. Arnold); 9 (top and bottom), 10 (top and bottom), 12 (top and bottom), 13 (top and bottom): Collection of the New-York Historical Society; 1 (middle), 3 (top): Corbis-Bettmann; 4: Courtesy of the Frances Loeb Library, Graduate School of Design, Harvard University; 8 (top and bottom): Courtesy of National Park Service, Frederick Law Olmsted National Historic Site, Brookline, Massachusetts; 1 (bottom): Culver Pictures; 7 (top and bottom): Frederick Law Olmsted Association; 2 (bottom): Frederick Law Olmsted Papers, Department of History, American University, Washington, D.C.; 3 (bottom): Historic American Buildings Survey, Library of Congress; 15, 16 (top and bottom): Lawrenceville School; 2 (top): Manuscript Division, Library of Congress; 1 (top), 5 (top and bottom): Society for the Preservation of New England Antiquities; 11: Underwood & Underwood/Corbis-Bettmann